NORAGAMI
STRAY GOD

ADACHITOKA

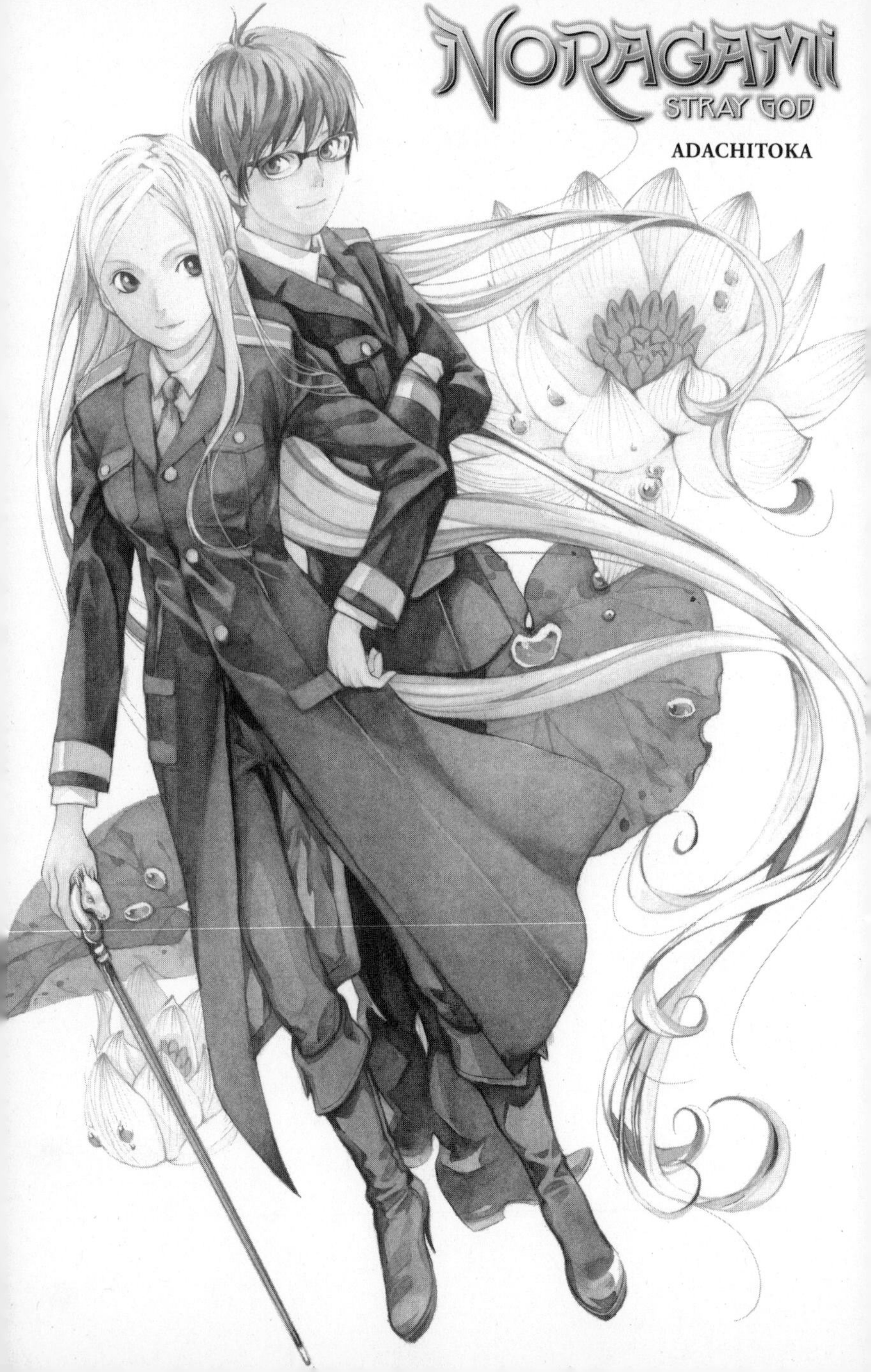

Characters

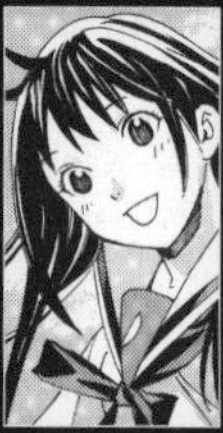

HIYORI IKI

A middle school student who has become half ayakashi.

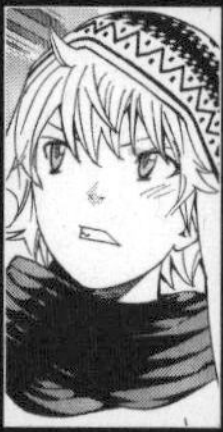

YUKINÉ

Yato's shinki who turns into a sword.

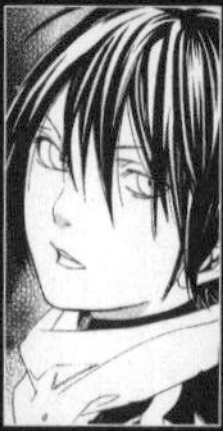

YATO

A minor deity who always wears a sweatsuit.

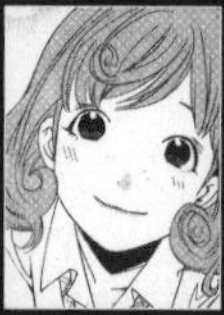

KOFUKU

A goddess of poverty who calls herself Ebisu after the god of fortune.

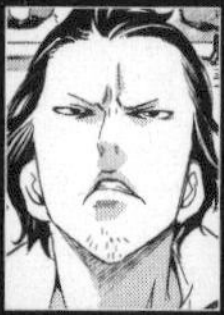

DAIKOKU

Kofuku's shinki who summons storms.

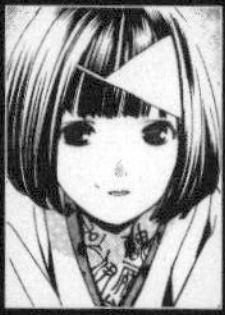

STRAY

A girl who wears a ghostly crown, and has writing all over her body.

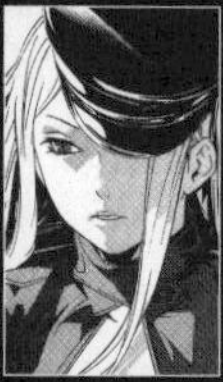

BISHAMONTEN

A powerful warrior god who seeks vengeance on Yato.

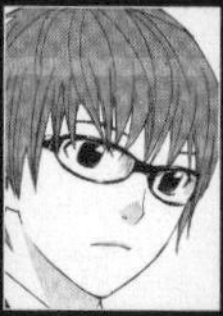

KAZUMA

A navigational shinki who serves as guide to Bishamon.

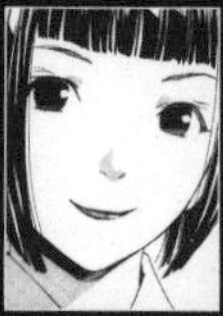

MAYU

Formerly Yato's shinki, now Tenjin's shinki.

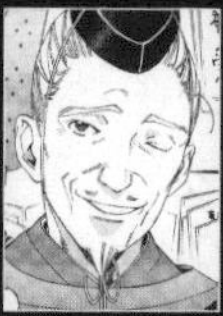

TENJIN

The God of Learning, Sugawara no Michizane.

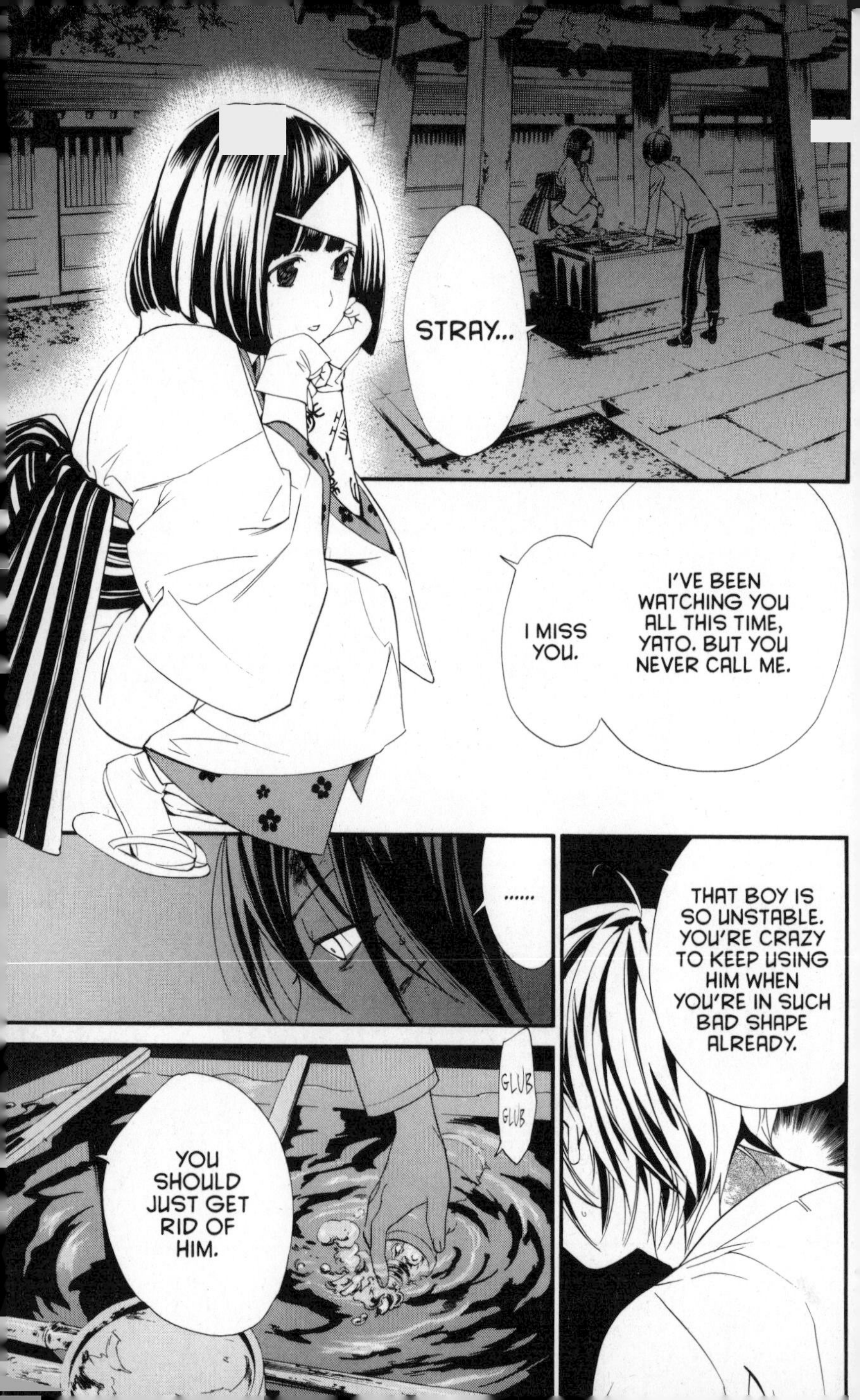
STRAY...
I'VE BEEN WATCHING YOU ALL THIS TIME, YATO. BUT YOU NEVER CALL ME.
I MISS YOU.
THAT BOY IS SO UNSTABLE. YOU'RE CRAZY TO KEEP USING HIM WHEN YOU'RE IN SUCH BAD SHAPE ALREADY.
......
GLUB GLUB
YOU SHOULD JUST GET RID OF HIM.

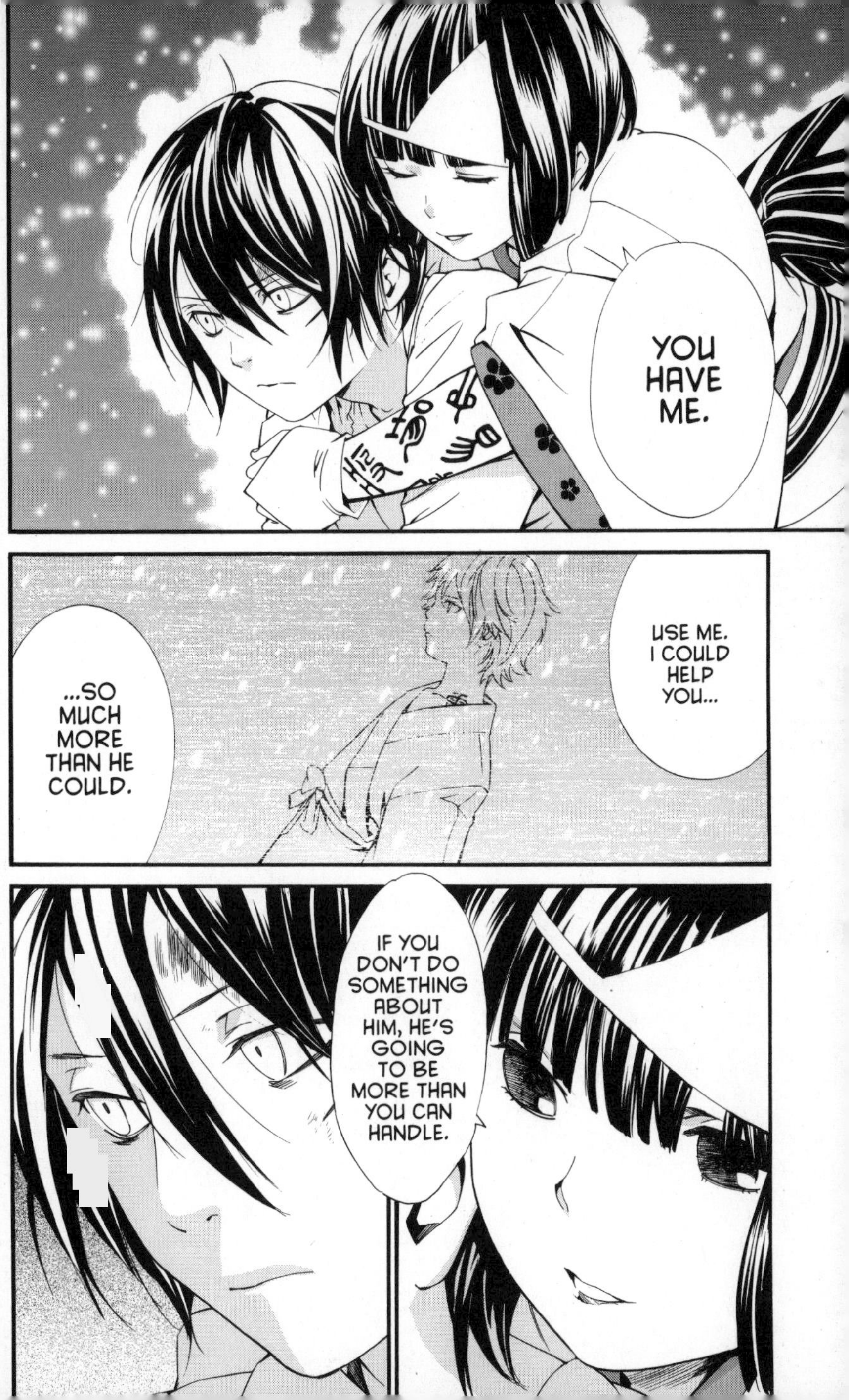
YOU HAVE ME.
USE ME. I COULD HELP YOU...
...SO MUCH MORE THAN HE COULD.
IF YOU DON'T DO SOMETHING ABOUT HIM, HE'S GOING TO BE MORE THAN YOU CAN HANDLE.

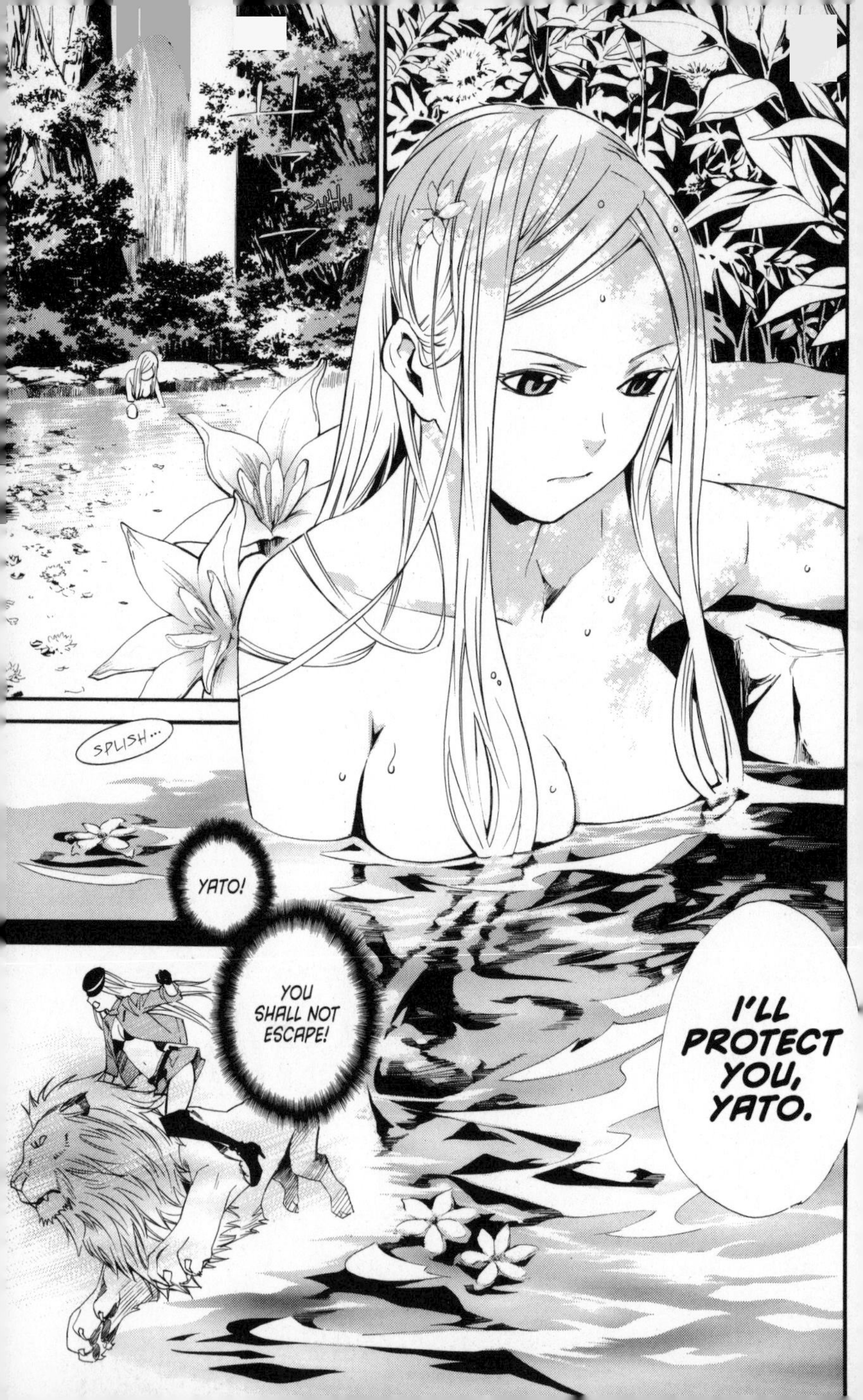
I'LL PROTECT YOU, YATO.
SHHHH
SPLISH...
YATO!
YOU SHALL NOT ESCAPE!

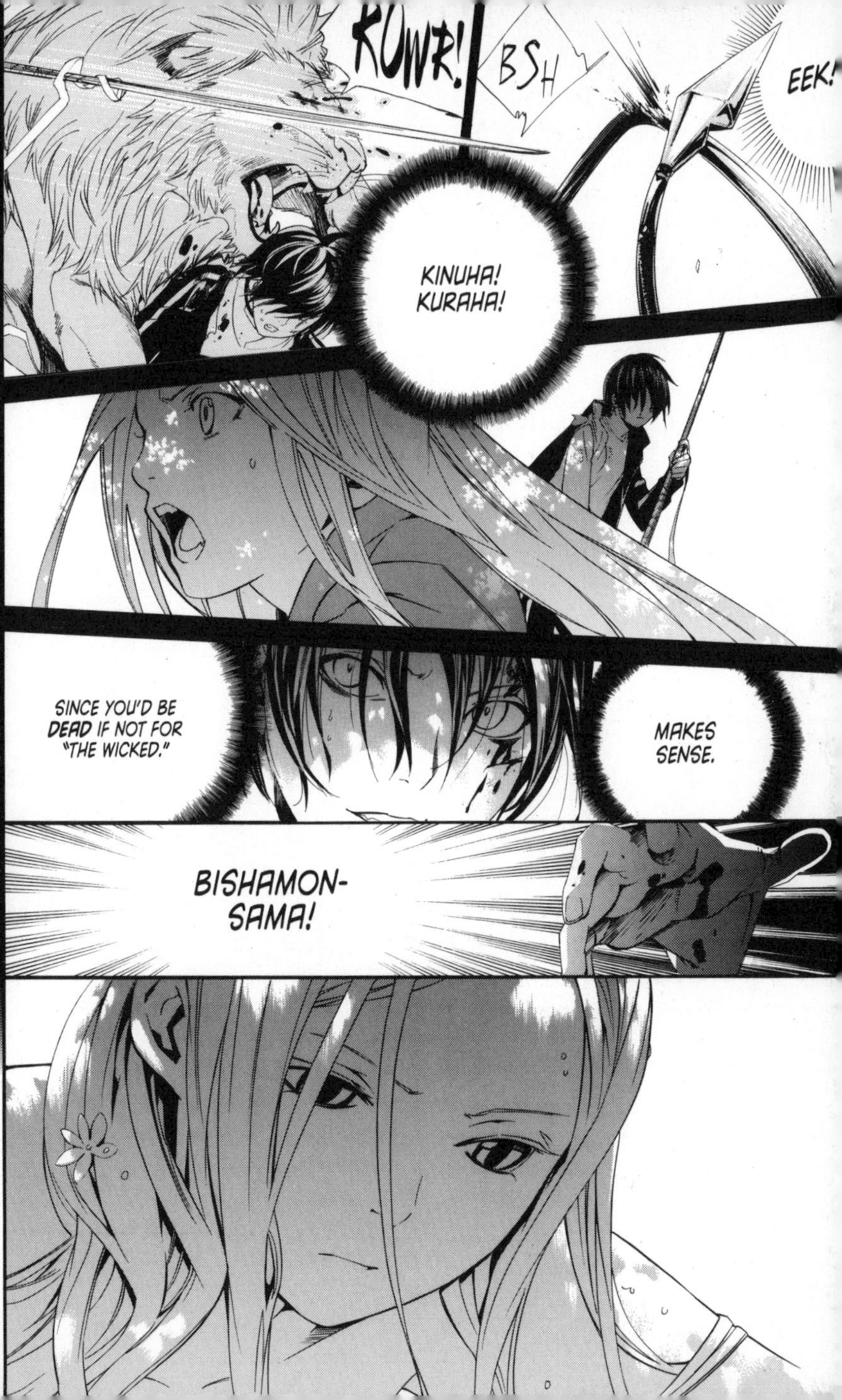
EEK!
BSH
KUWR!
KINUHA! KURAHA!
MAKES SENSE.
SINCE YOU'D BE DEAD IF NOT FOR "THE WICKED."
BISHAMON-SAMA!

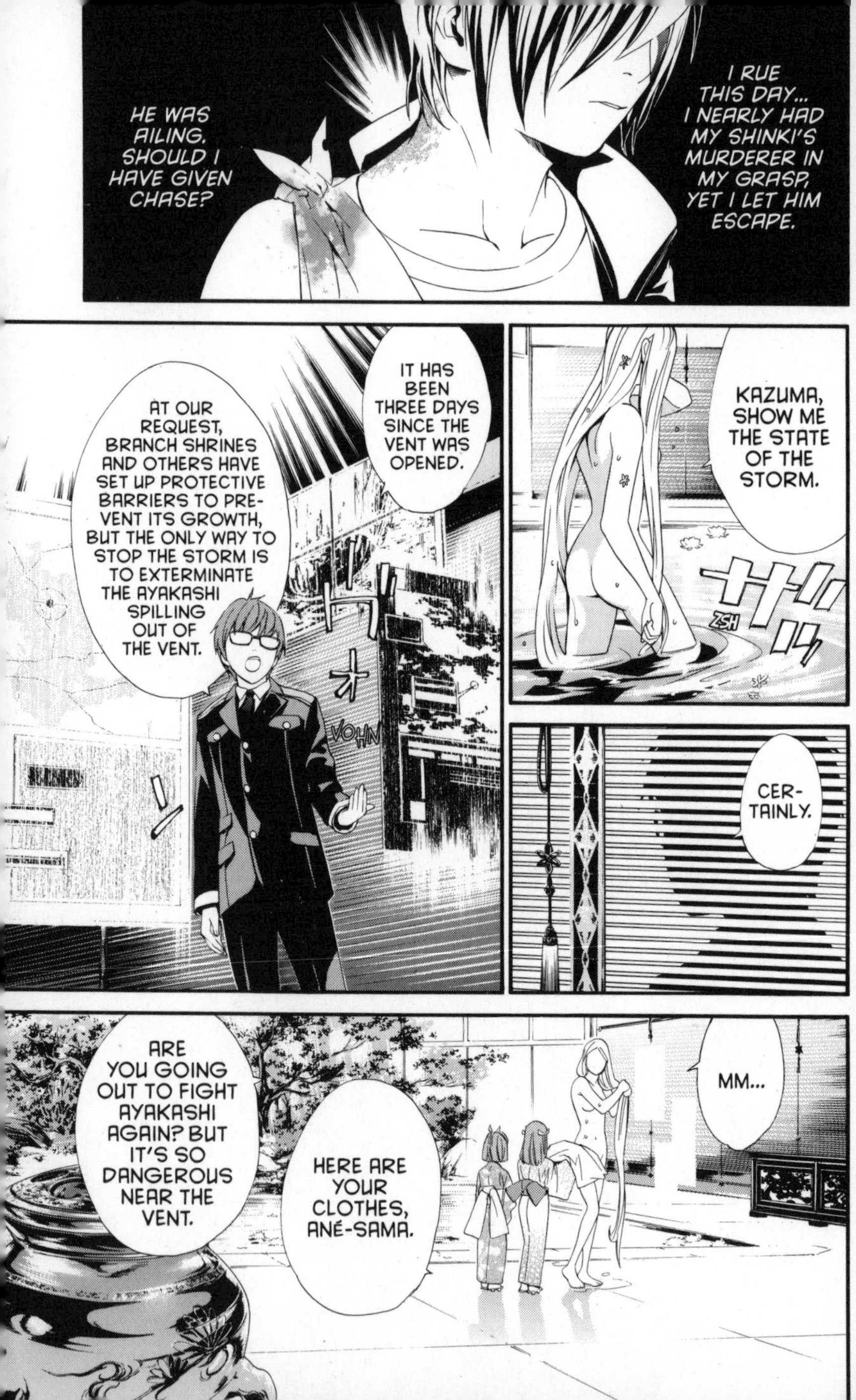
I RUE THIS DAY... I NEARLY HAD MY SHINKI'S MURDERER IN MY GRASP, YET I LET HIM ESCAPE.
HE WAS AILING. SHOULD I HAVE GIVEN CHASE?
KAZUMA, SHOW ME THE STATE OF THE STORM.
ZSH
CERTAINLY.
IT HAS BEEN THREE DAYS SINCE THE VENT WAS OPENED.
AT OUR REQUEST, BRANCH SHRINES AND OTHERS HAVE SET UP PROTECTIVE BARRIERS TO PREVENT ITS GROWTH, BUT THE ONLY WAY TO STOP THE STORM IS TO EXTERMINATE THE AYAKASHI SPILLING OUT OF THE VENT.
VOHN
MM...
HERE ARE YOUR CLOTHES, ANÉ-SAMA.
ARE YOU GOING OUT TO FIGHT AYAKASHI AGAIN? BUT IT'S SO DANGEROUS NEAR THE VENT.

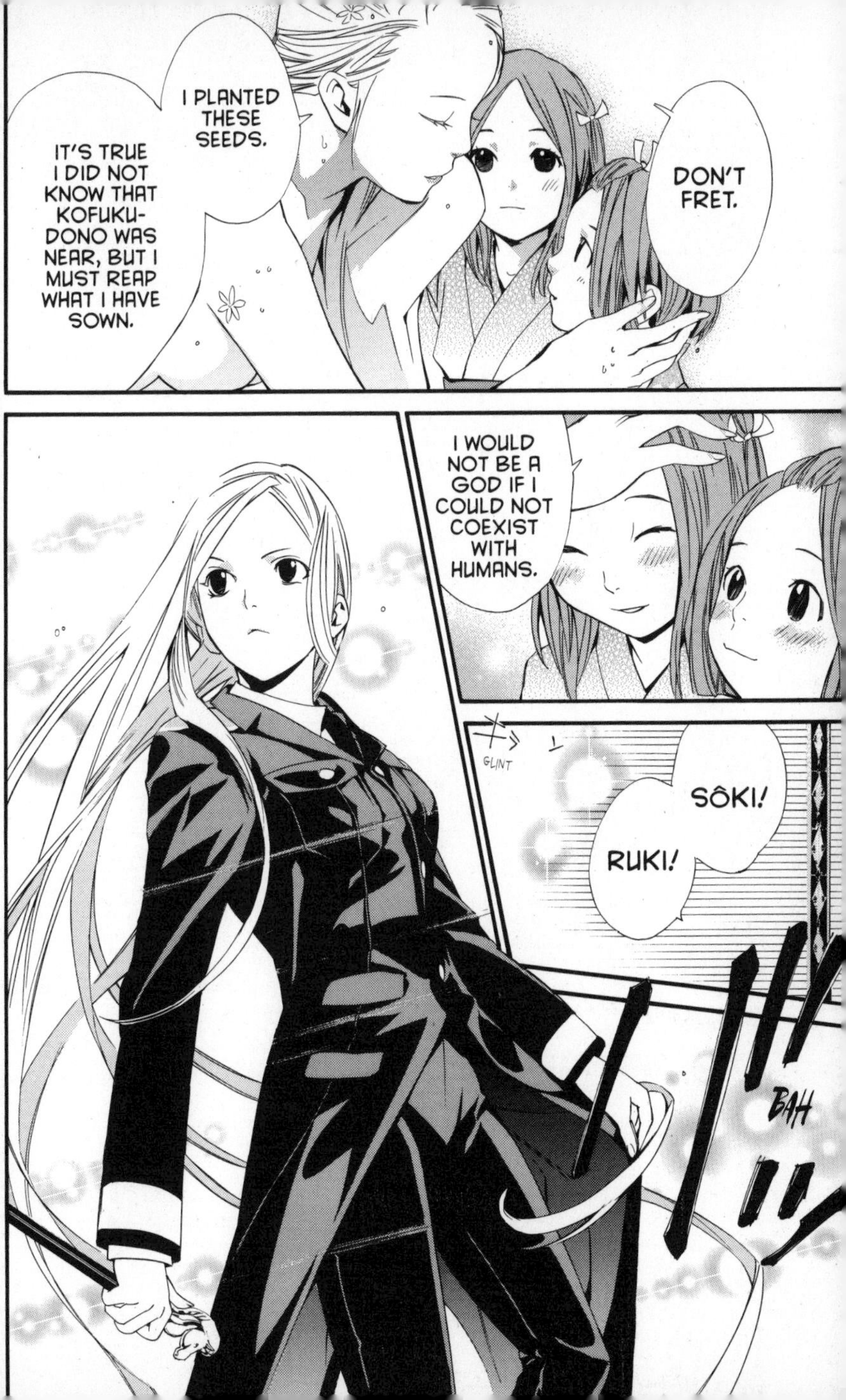
DON'T FRET.
I PLANTED THESE SEEDS.
IT'S TRUE I DID NOT KNOW THAT KOFUKU-DONO WAS NEAR, BUT I MUST REAP WHAT I HAVE SOWN.
I WOULD NOT BE A GOD IF I COULD NOT COEXIST WITH HUMANS.
SÔKI!
RUKI!
GLINT
BAH

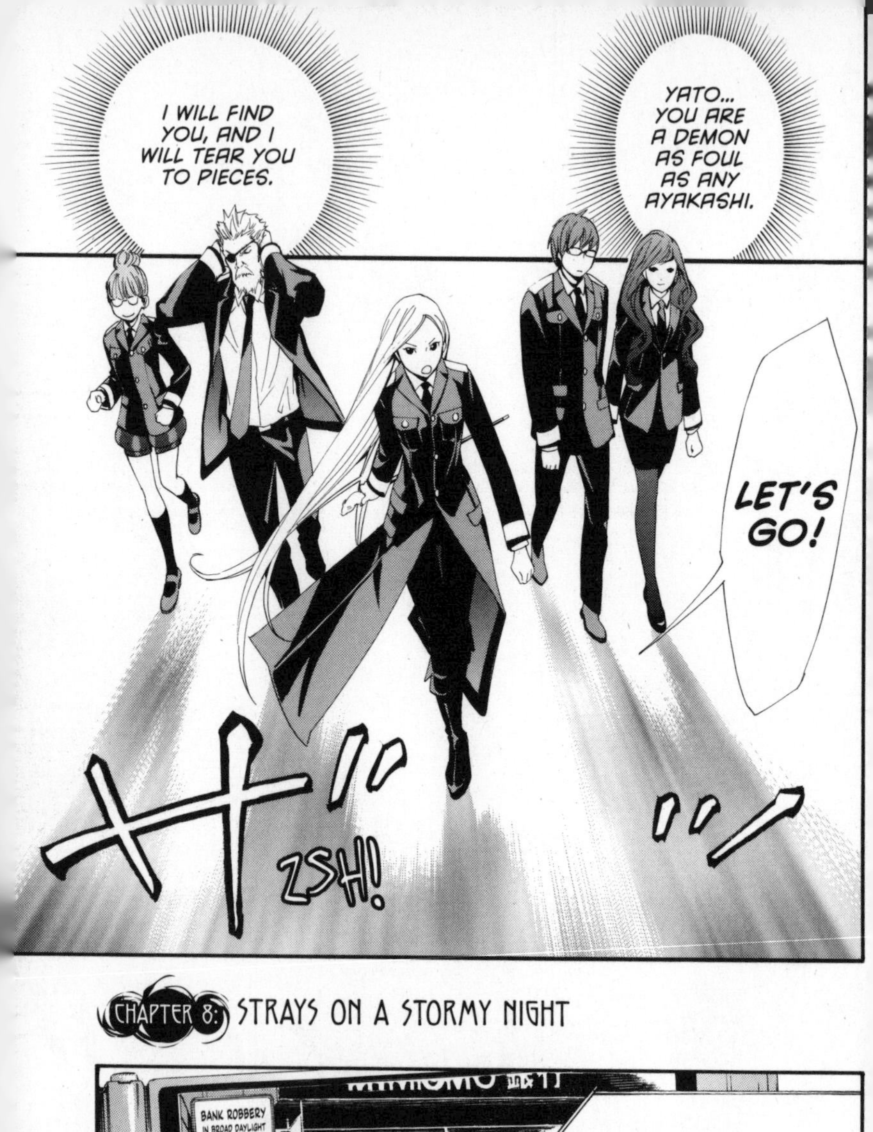
YATO... YOU ARE A DEMON AS FOUL AS ANY AYAKASHI.
I WILL FIND YOU, AND I WILL TEAR YOU TO PIECES.
LET'S GO!
ZSH!

CHAPTER 8: STRAYS ON A STORMY NIGHT

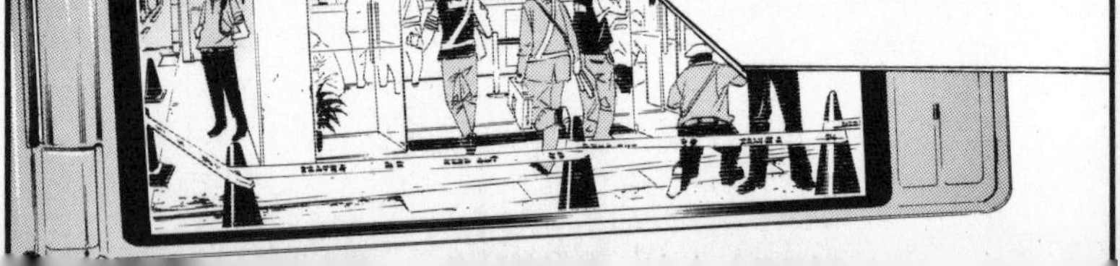
BANK ROBBERY IN BROAD DAYLIGHT
AT 11 A.M. THIS MORNING, A ROBBER BROKE INTO A BANK IN THE CITY...

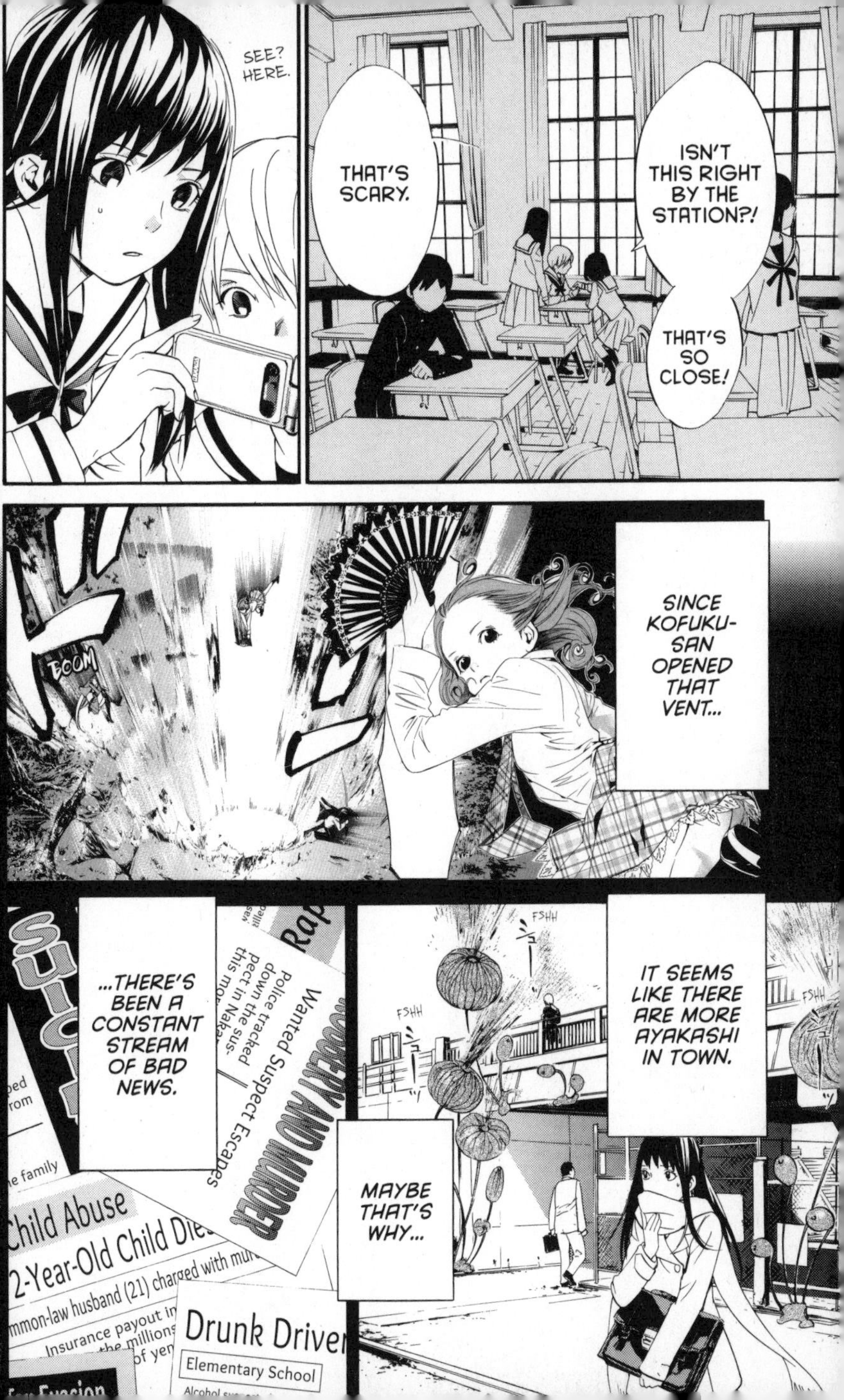
ISN'T THIS RIGHT BY THE STATION?!
THAT'S SO CLOSE!
THAT'S SCARY.
SEE? HERE.
SINCE KOFUKU-SAN OPENED THAT VENT...
BOOM
IT SEEMS LIKE THERE ARE MORE AYAKASHI IN TOWN.
FSHH
FSHH
FSHH
MAYBE THAT'S WHY...
...THERE'S BEEN A CONSTANT STREAM OF BAD NEWS.
Wanted Suspect Escapes
Child Abuse
Drunk Driver
Elementary School

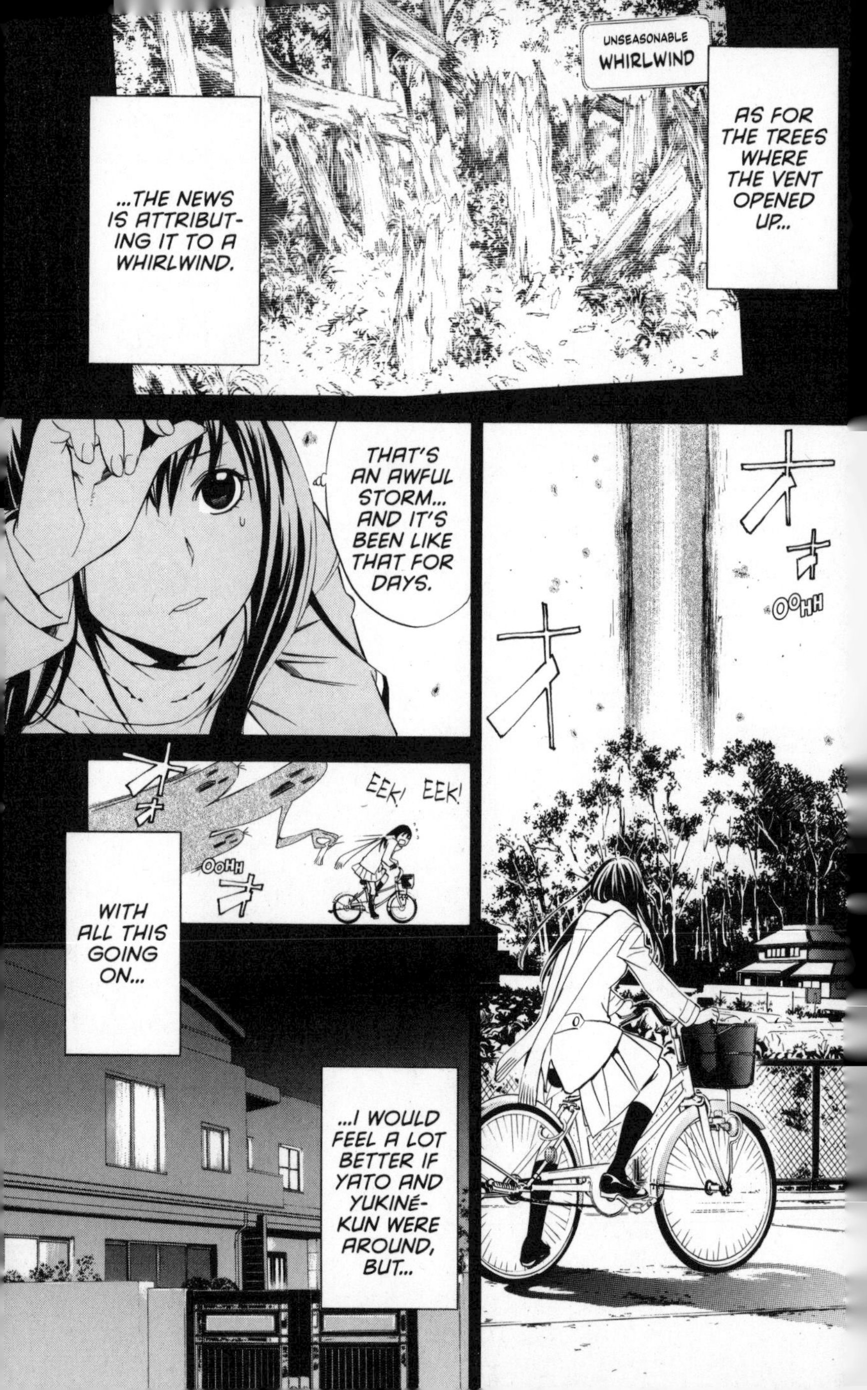
AS FOR THE TREES WHERE THE VENT OPENED UP...
UNSEASONABLE WHIRLWIND
...THE NEWS IS ATTRIBUTING IT TO A WHIRLWIND.
OOHH
THAT'S AN AWFUL STORM... AND IT'S BEEN LIKE THAT FOR DAYS.
EEK! EEK!
OOHH
WITH ALL THIS GOING ON...
...I WOULD FEEL A LOT BETTER IF YATO AND YUKINÉ-KUN WERE AROUND, BUT...

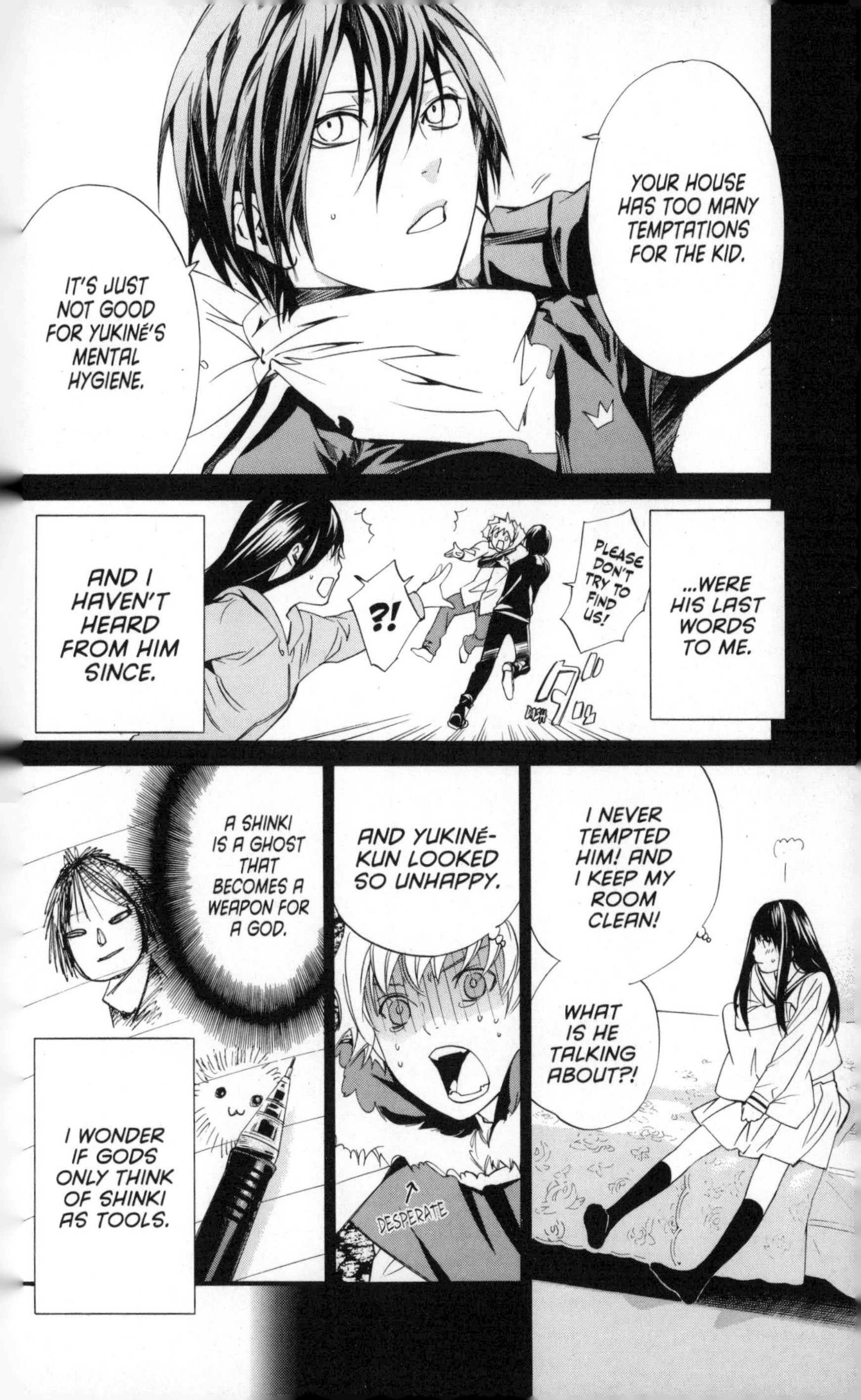
YOUR HOUSE HAS TOO MANY TEMPTATIONS FOR THE KID.
IT'S JUST NOT GOOD FOR YUKINÉ'S MENTAL HYGIENE.
...WERE HIS LAST WORDS TO ME.
PLEASE DON'T TRY TO FIND US!
?!
DASH
AND I HAVEN'T HEARD FROM HIM SINCE.
I NEVER TEMPTED HIM! AND I KEEP MY ROOM CLEAN!
WHAT IS HE TALKING ABOUT?!
AND YUKINÉ-KUN LOOKED SO UNHAPPY.
DESPERATE
A SHINKI IS A GHOST THAT BECOMES A WEAPON FOR A GOD.
I WONDER IF GODS ONLY THINK OF SHINKI AS TOOLS.

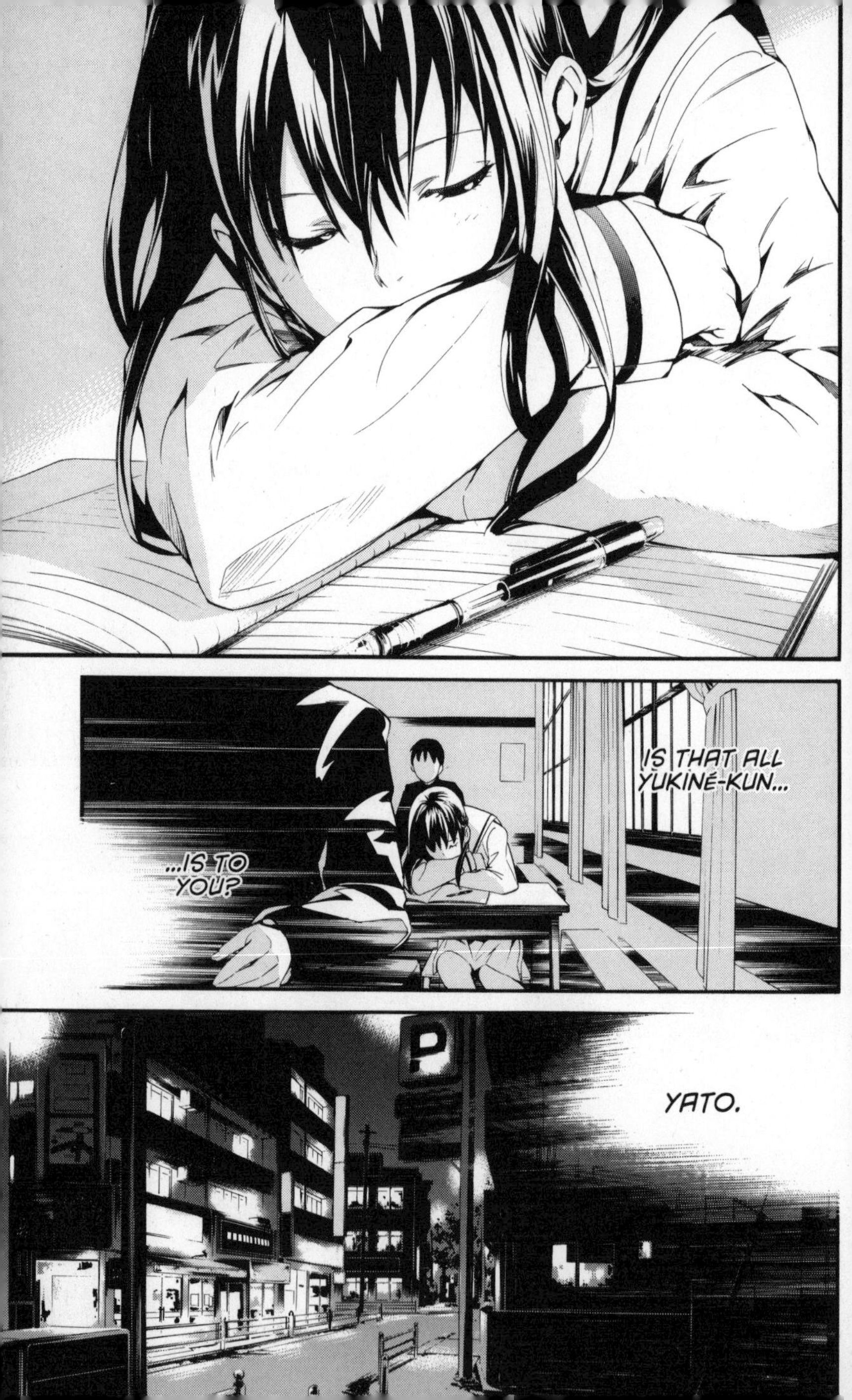
IS THAT ALL YUKINÉ-KUN...
...IS TO YOU?
YATO.

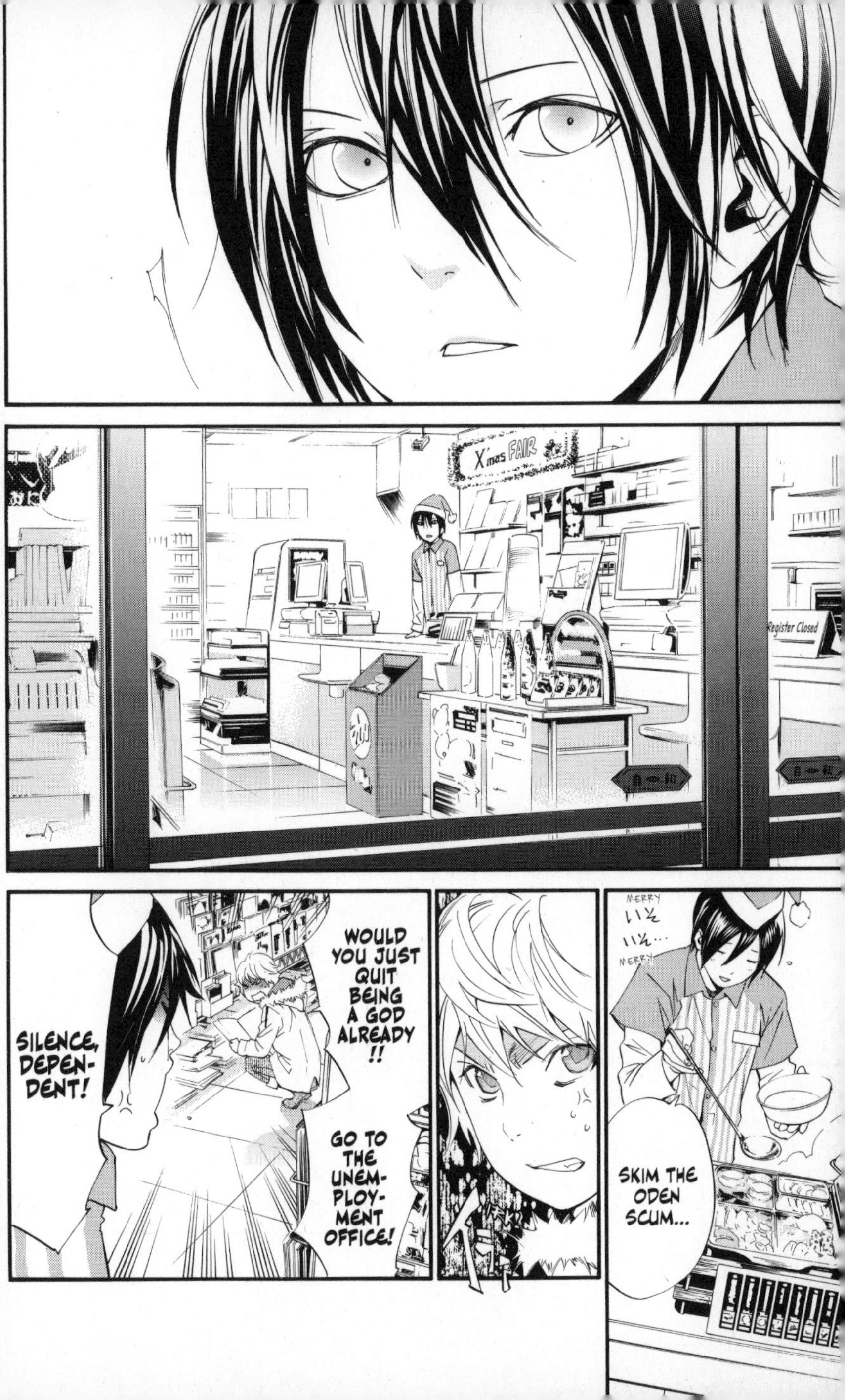
X'mas FAIR
Register Closed
MERRY
いえ
いえ…
MERRY!
SKIM THE ODEN SCUM...
WOULD YOU JUST QUIT BEING A GOD ALREADY!!
SILENCE, DEPENDENT!
GO TO THE UNEMPLOYMENT OFFICE!

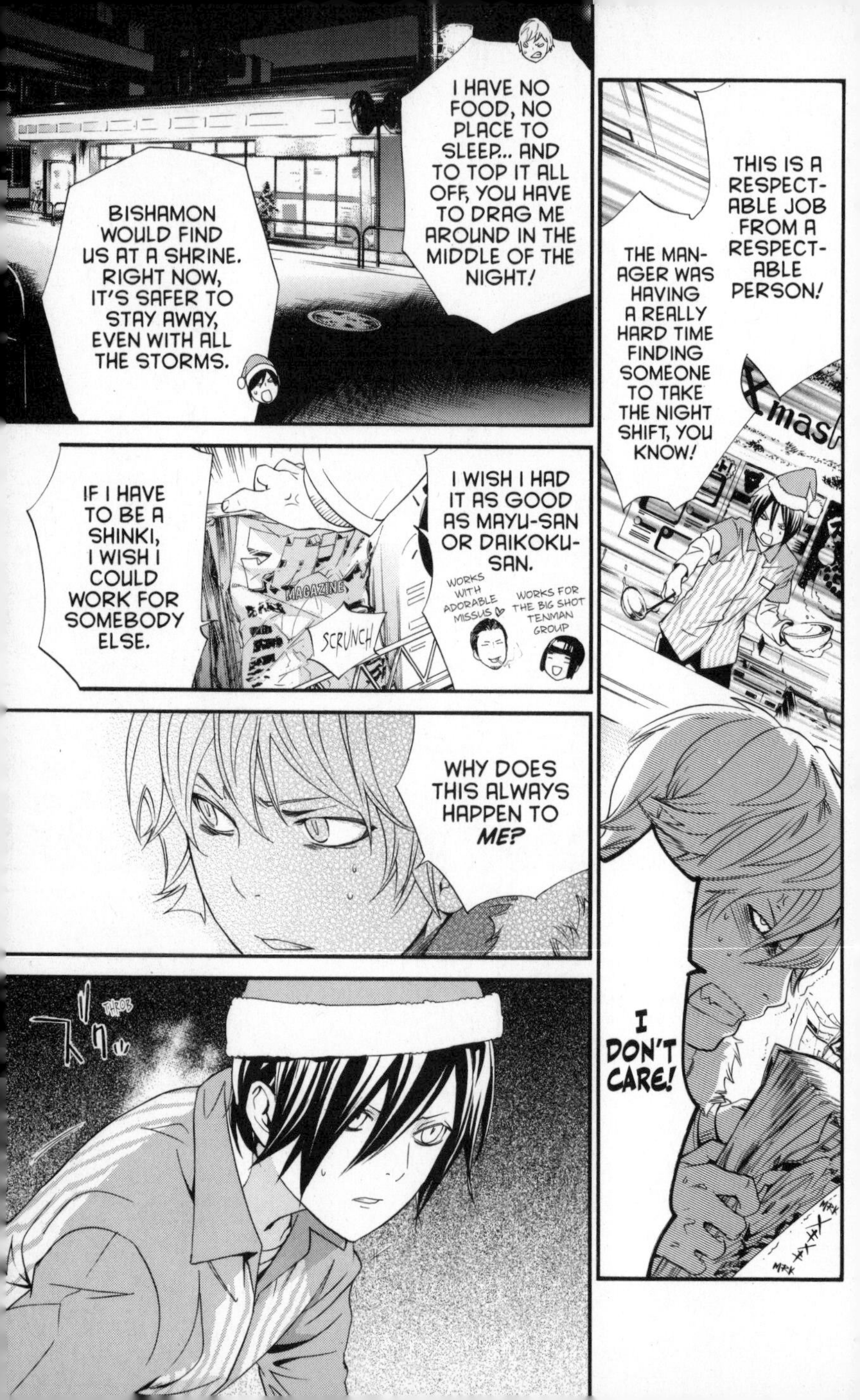
THIS IS A RESPECTABLE JOB FROM A RESPECTABLE PERSON!
THE MANAGER WAS HAVING A REALLY HARD TIME FINDING SOMEONE TO TAKE THE NIGHT SHIFT, YOU KNOW!
Xmas
I DON'T CARE!
MRK MRK
I HAVE NO FOOD, NO PLACE TO SLEEP... AND TO TOP IT ALL OFF, YOU HAVE TO DRAG ME AROUND IN THE MIDDLE OF THE NIGHT!
BISHAMON WOULD FIND US AT A SHRINE. RIGHT NOW, IT'S SAFER TO STAY AWAY, EVEN WITH ALL THE STORMS.
I WISH I HAD IT AS GOOD AS MAYU-SAN OR DAIKOKU-SAN.
WORKS FOR THE BIG SHOT TENMAN GROUP
WORKS WITH ADORABLE MISSUS ♡
IF I HAVE TO BE A SHINKI, I WISH I COULD WORK FOR SOMEBODY ELSE.
MAGAZINE
SCRUNCH
WHY DOES THIS ALWAYS HAPPEN TO *ME?*
THROB

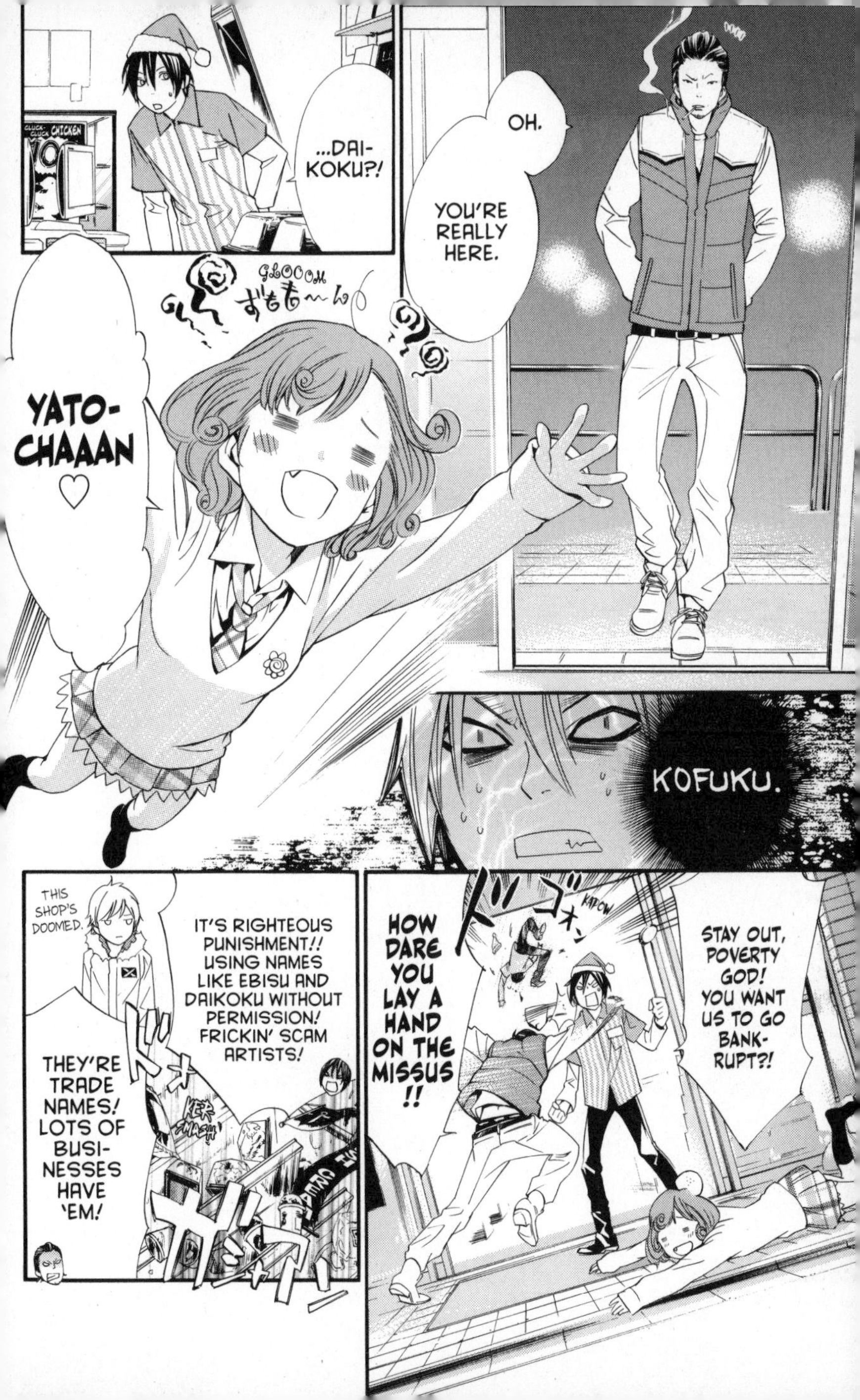

OH.
YOU'RE REALLY HERE.
...DAI-KOKU?!
CLUCK-CLUCK CHICKEN
GLOOOM ずももも〜ん
YATO-CHAAAN ♡
KOFUKU.
STAY OUT, POVERTY GOD! YOU WANT US TO GO BANK-RUPT?!
KAPOW
HOW DARE YOU LAY A HAND ON THE MISSUS!!
IT'S RIGHTEOUS PUNISHMENT!! USING NAMES LIKE EBISU AND DAIKOKU WITHOUT PERMISSION! FRICKIN' SCAM ARTISTS!
THIS SHOP'S DOOMED.
KER-SMASH
THEY'RE TRADE NAMES! LOTS OF BUSI-NESSES HAVE 'EM!

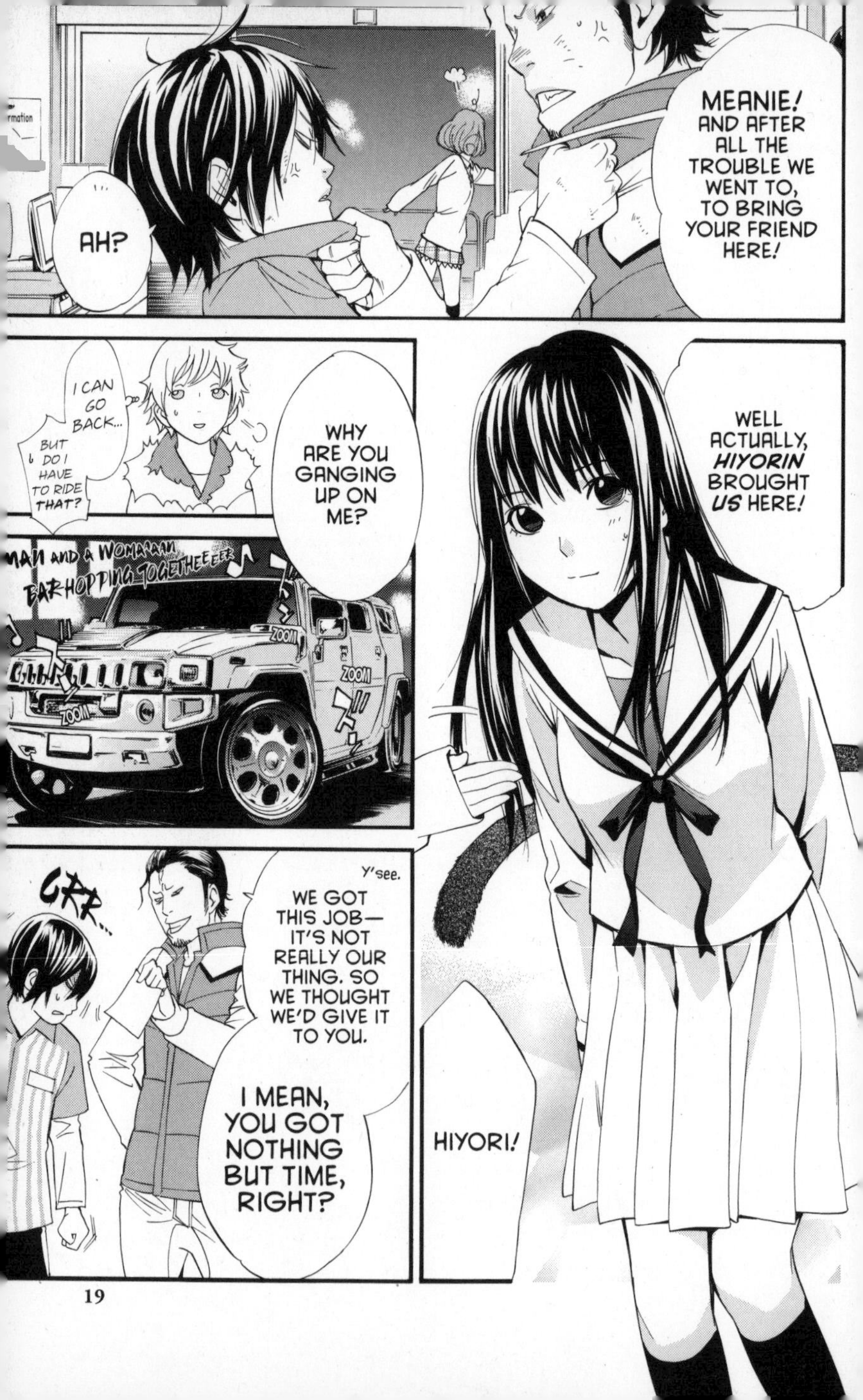

MEANIE! AND AFTER ALL THE TROUBLE WE WENT TO, TO BRING YOUR FRIEND HERE!
AH?
WELL ACTUALLY, HIYORIN BROUGHT US HERE!
HIYORI!
WHY ARE YOU GANGING UP ON ME?
I CAN GO BACK...
BUT DO I HAVE TO RIDE THAT?
MAN AND A WOMAAAN BAR-HOPPING TOGETHEEEER
ZOOM
ZOOM
ZOOM
Y'see.
WE GOT THIS JOB— IT'S NOT REALLY OUR THING. SO WE THOUGHT WE'D GIVE IT TO YOU.
I MEAN, YOU GOT NOTHING BUT TIME, RIGHT?
GRR...

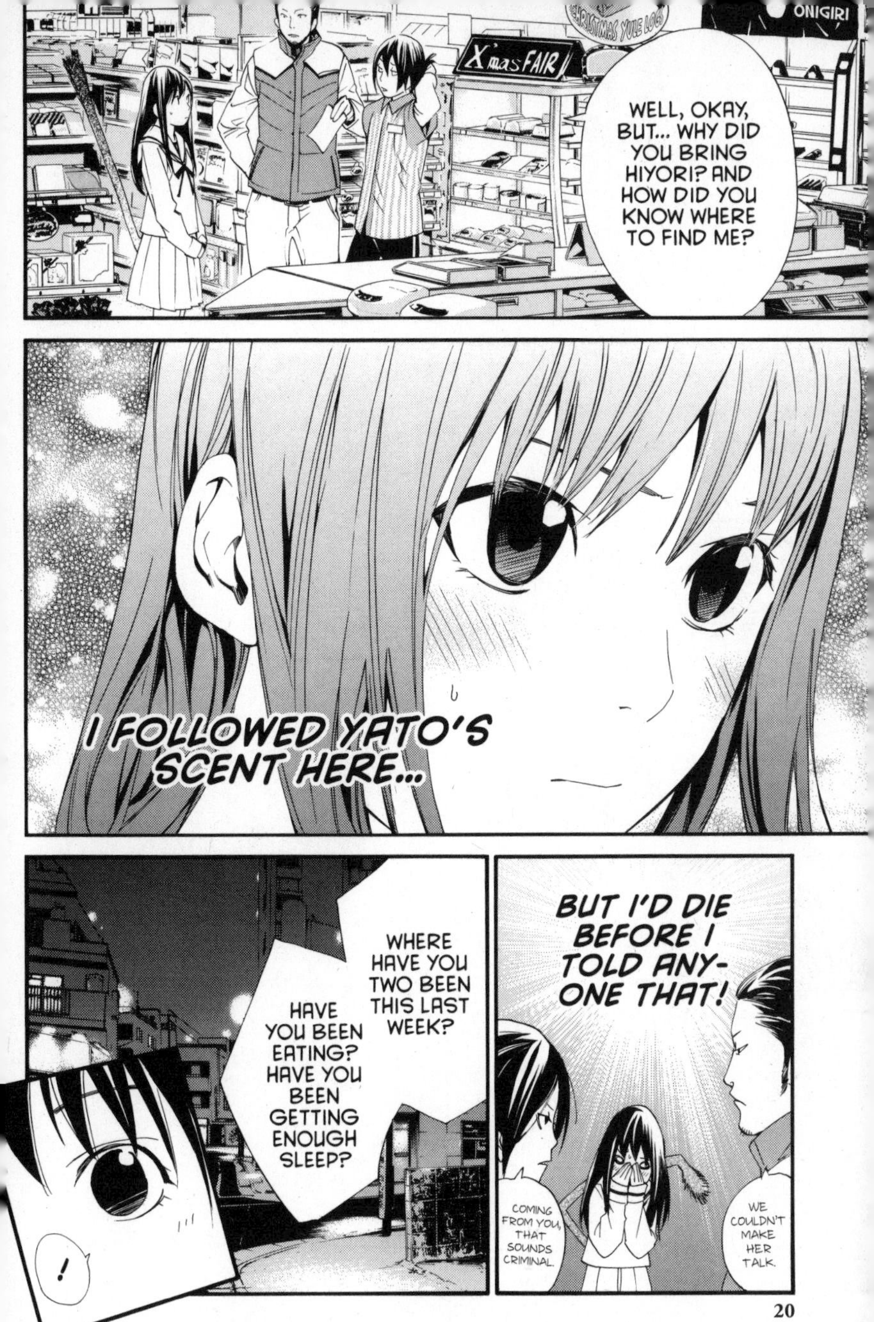
ONIGIRI
CHRISTMAS YULE LOGS
X'mas FAIR
WELL, OKAY, BUT... WHY DID YOU BRING HIYORI? AND HOW DID YOU KNOW WHERE TO FIND ME?
I FOLLOWED YATO'S SCENT HERE...
BUT I'D DIE BEFORE I TOLD ANY-ONE THAT!
WE COULDN'T MAKE HER TALK.
COMING FROM YOU, THAT SOUNDS CRIMINAL.
WHERE HAVE YOU TWO BEEN THIS LAST WEEK?
HAVE YOU BEEN EATING? HAVE YOU BEEN GETTING ENOUGH SLEEP?
!

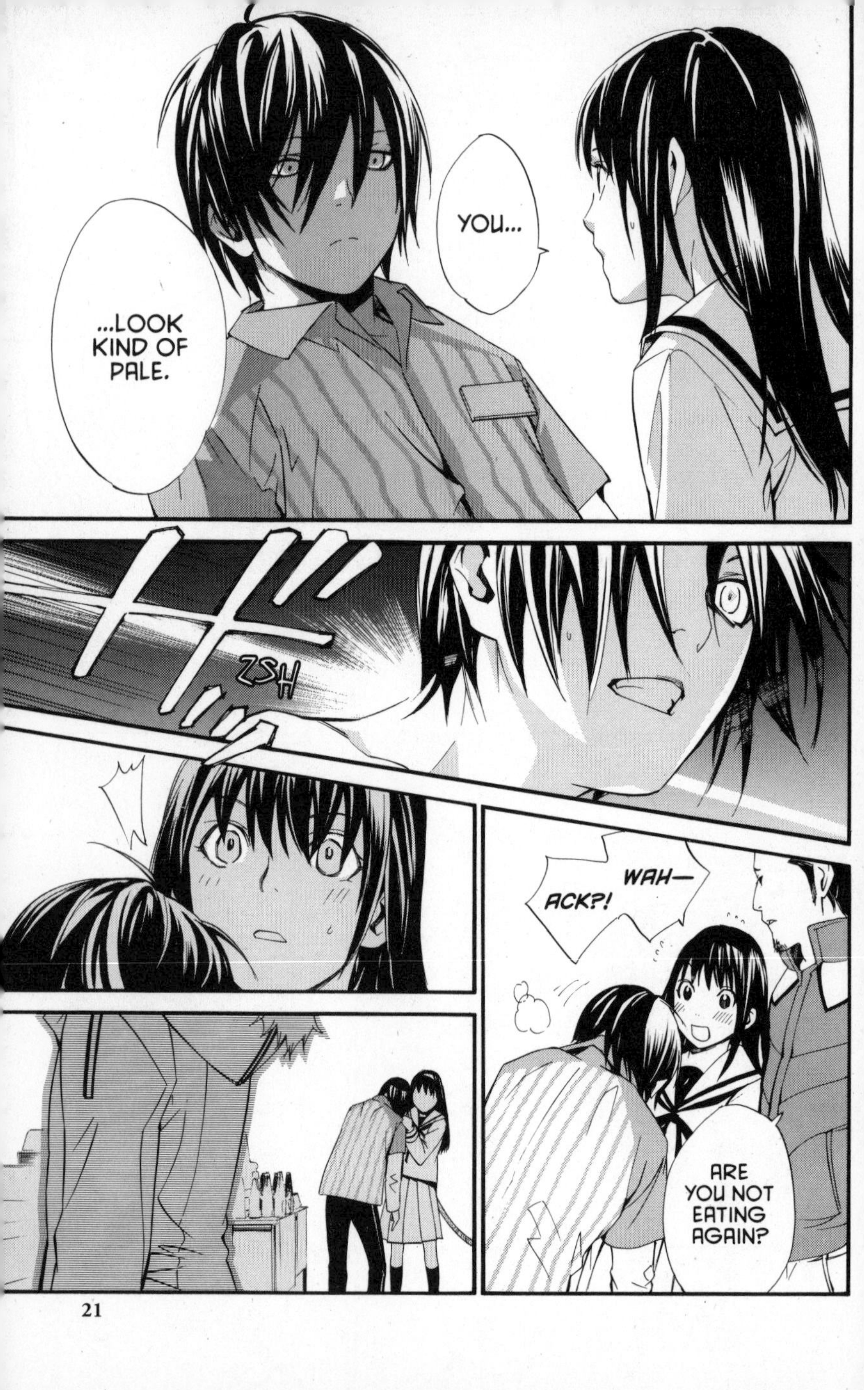
YOU...
...LOOK KIND OF PALE.
ZSH
WAH— ACK?!
ARE YOU NOT EATING AGAIN?

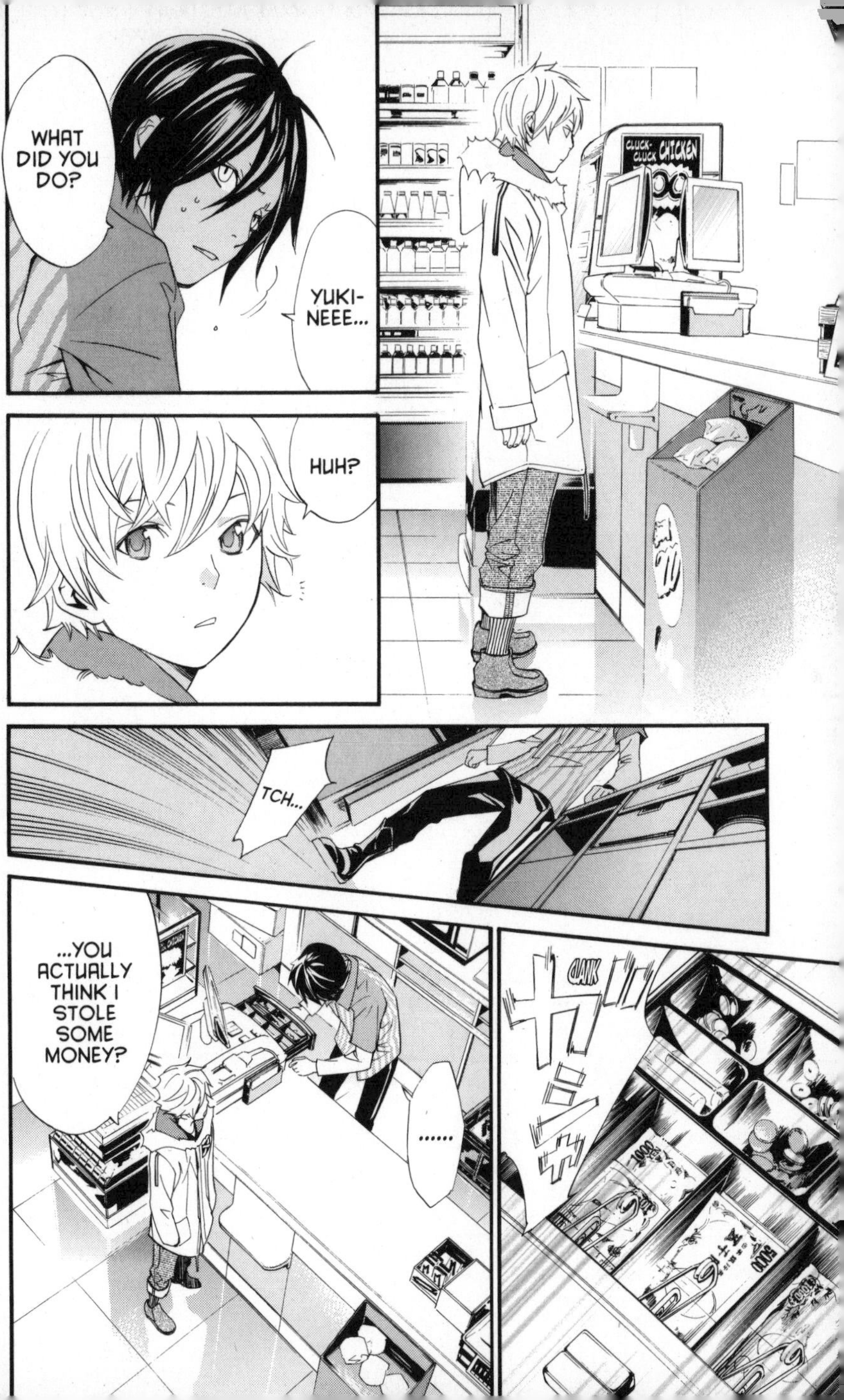
CLUCK-CLUCK CHICKEN
YUKI-NEEE...
WHAT DID YOU DO?
HUH?
TCH...
CLANK
...YOU ACTUALLY THINK I STOLE SOME MONEY?
......

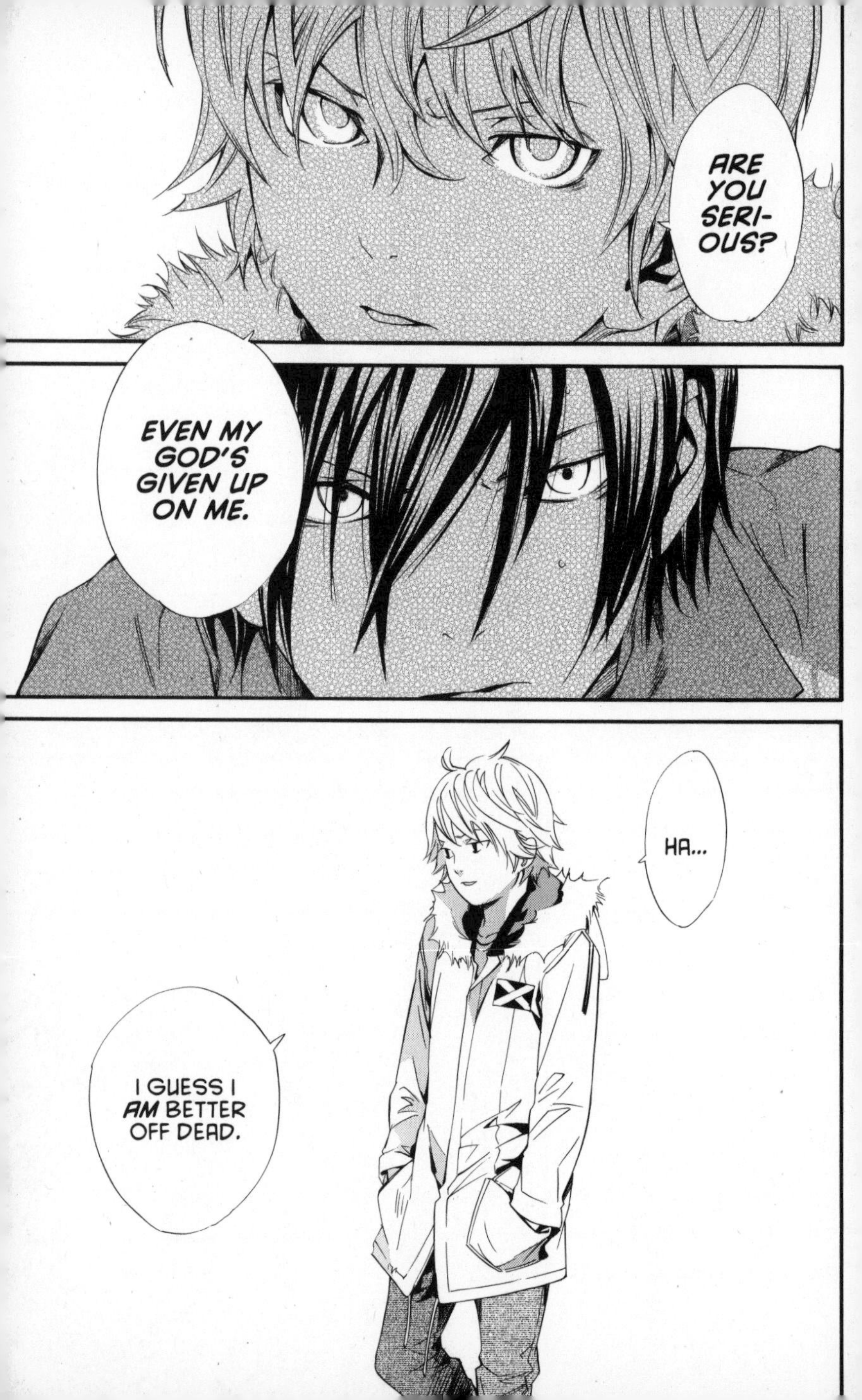
ARE YOU SERI-OUS?
EVEN MY GOD'S GIVEN UP ON ME.
HA...
I GUESS I *AM* BETTER OFF DEAD.

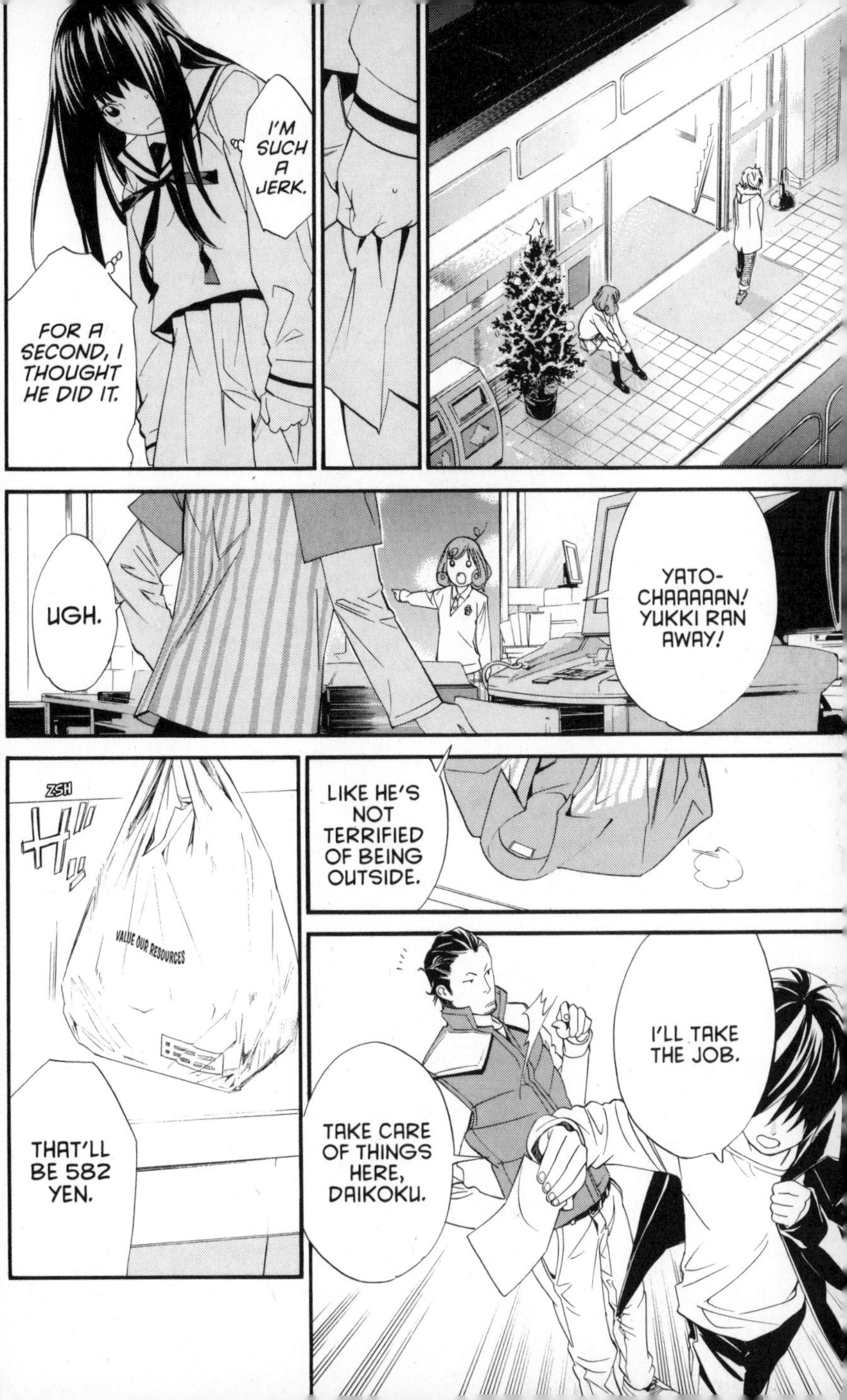
I'M SUCH A JERK.
FOR A SECOND, I THOUGHT HE DID IT.
YATO-CHAAAAAN! YUKKI RAN AWAY!
UGH.
LIKE HE'S NOT TERRIFIED OF BEING OUTSIDE.
I'LL TAKE THE JOB.
TAKE CARE OF THINGS HERE, DAIKOKU.
ZSH
VALUE OUR RESOURCES
THAT'LL BE 582 YEN.

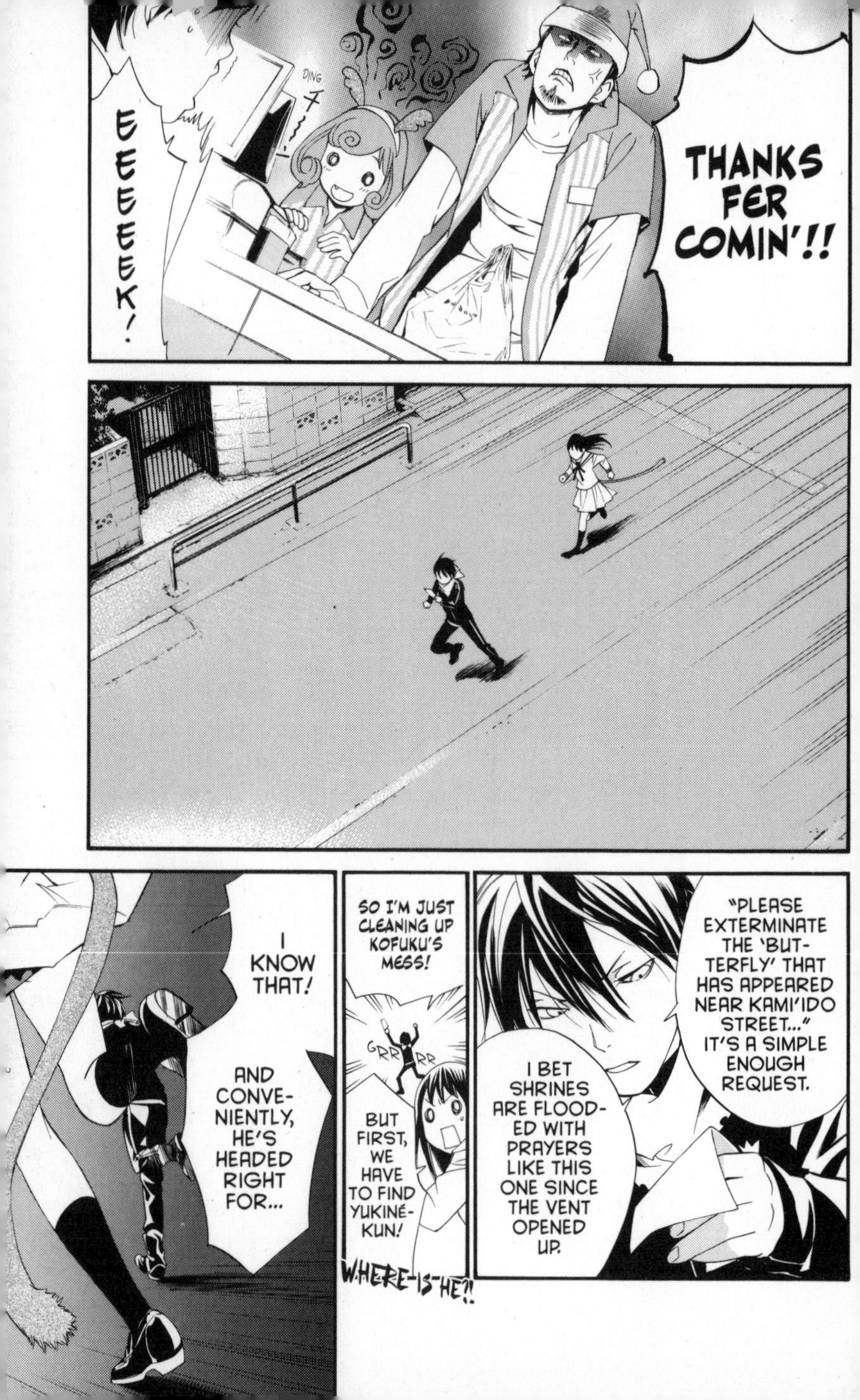
THANKS FER COMIN'!!
DING
EEEEEEK!
"PLEASE EXTERMINATE THE 'BUT-TERFLY' THAT HAS APPEARED NEAR KAMI'IDO STREET..." IT'S A SIMPLE ENOUGH REQUEST.
I BET SHRINES ARE FLOOD-ED WITH PRAYERS LIKE THIS ONE SINCE THE VENT OPENED UP.
SO I'M JUST CLEANING UP KOFUKU'S MESS!
GRRRR
BUT FIRST, WE HAVE TO FIND YUKINÉ-KUN!
WHERE-IS-HE?!
I KNOW THAT!
AND CONVE-NIENTLY, HE'S HEADED RIGHT FOR...

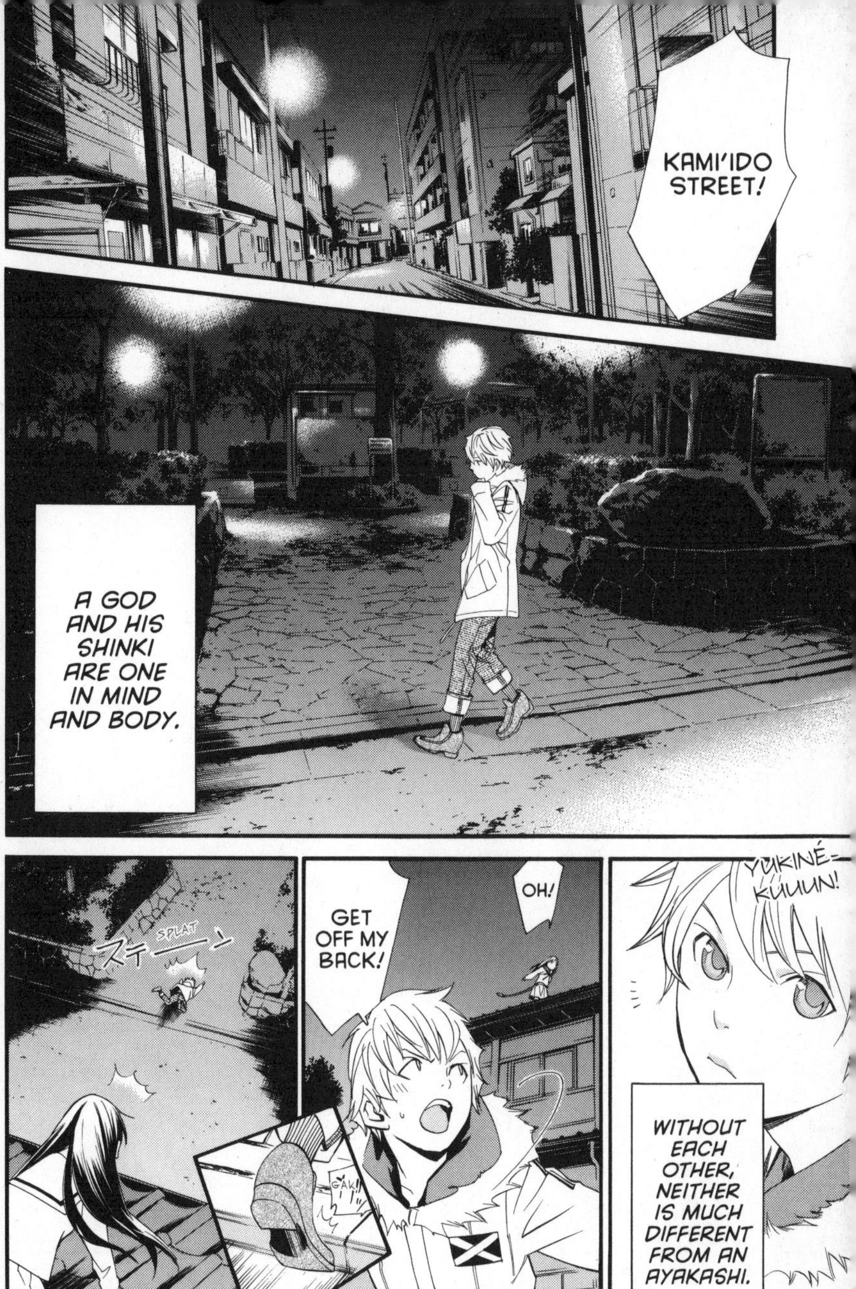
KAMI'IDO STREET!
A GOD AND HIS SHINKI ARE ONE IN MIND AND BODY.
YUKINÉ-KUUUN!
WITHOUT EACH OTHER, NEITHER IS MUCH DIFFERENT FROM AN AYAKASHI.
OH!
GET OFF MY BACK!
GAK!!
SPLAT
ステーン

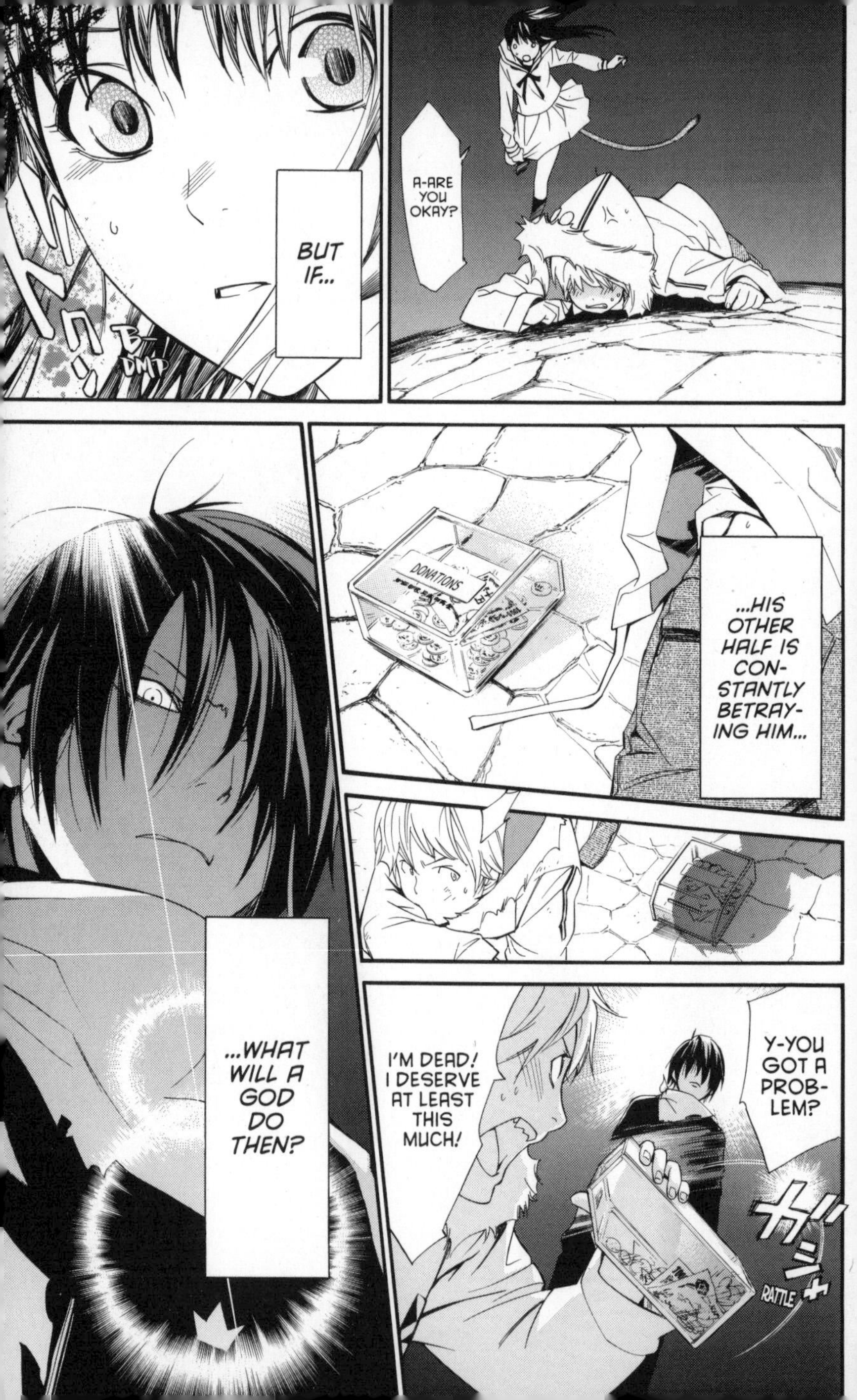
A-ARE YOU OKAY?
BUT IF...
B-DMP
DONATIONS
...HIS OTHER HALF IS CON-STANTLY BETRAY-ING HIM...
Y-YOU GOT A PROB-LEM?
I'M DEAD! I DESERVE AT LEAST THIS MUCH!
RATTLE
...WHAT WILL A GOD DO THEN?

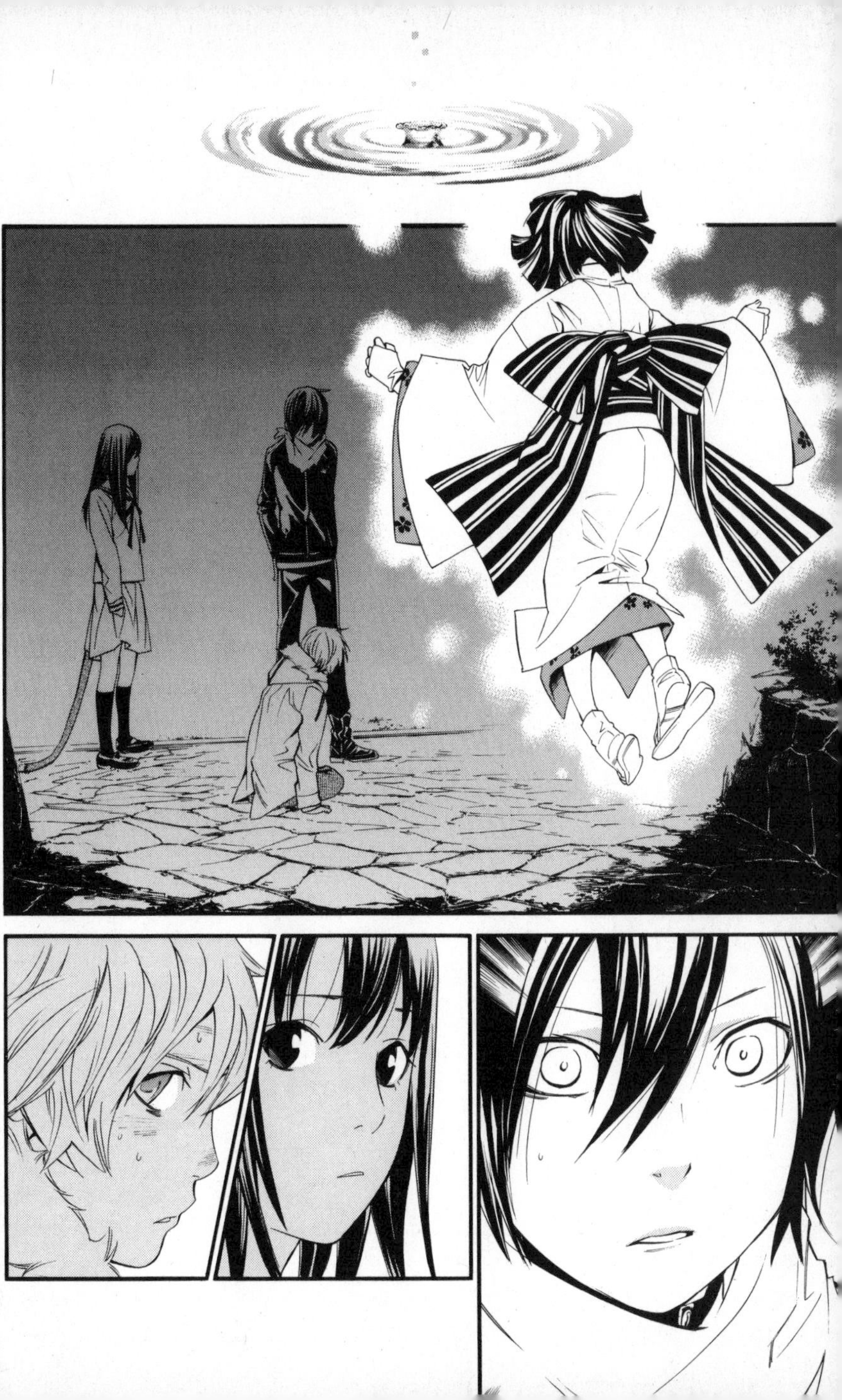

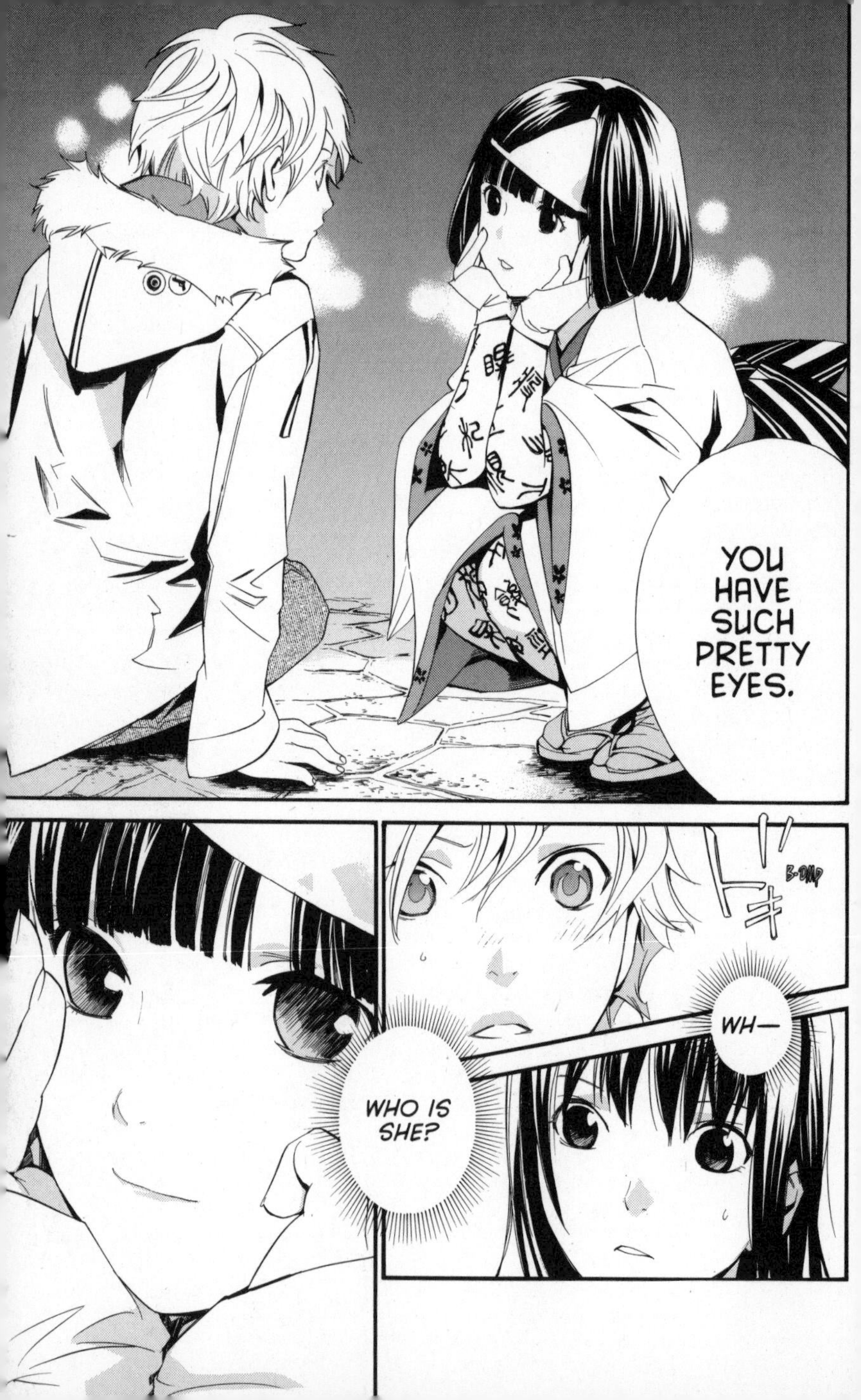
YOU HAVE SUCH PRETTY EYES.
ドキ
B-DMP
WH—
WHO IS SHE?

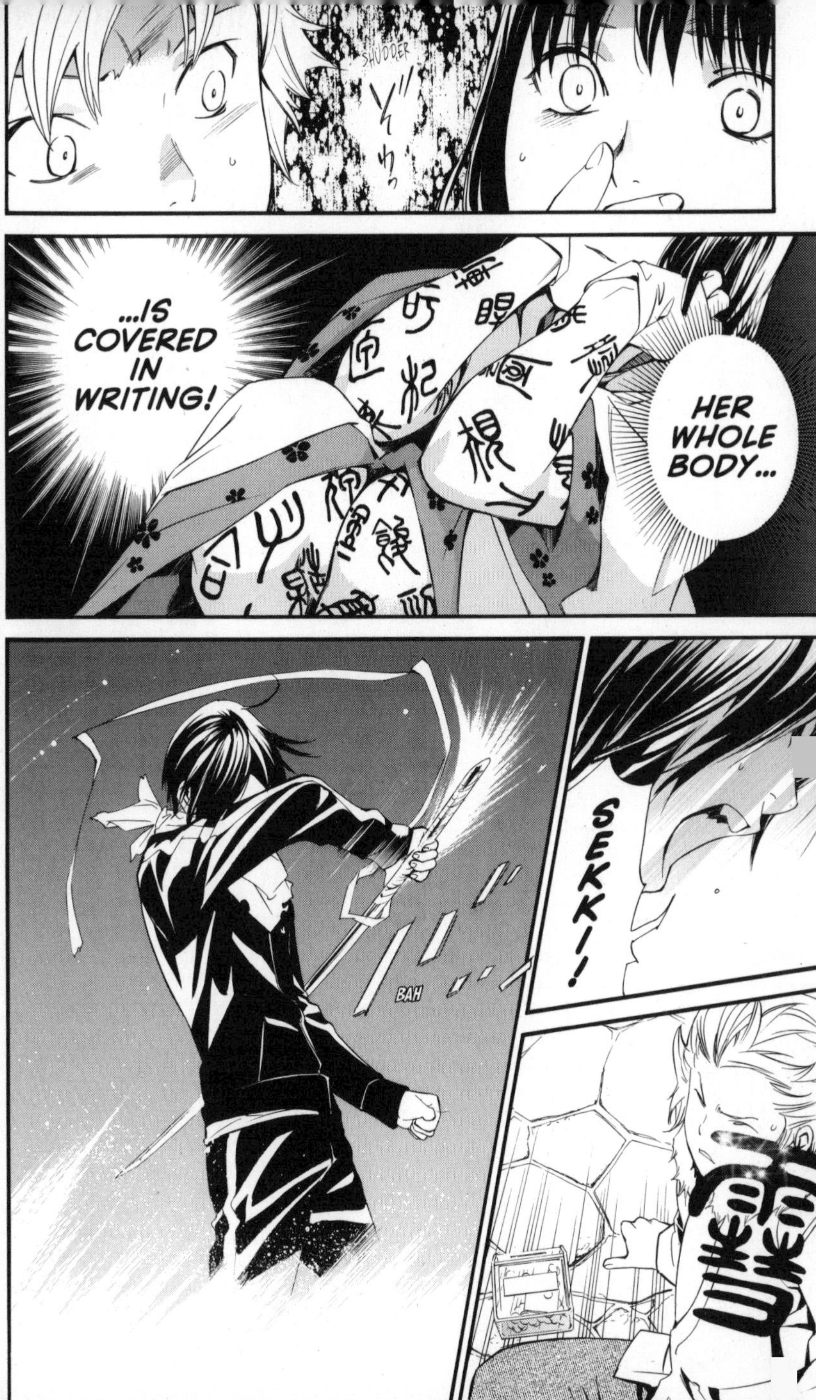
SHUDDER
ゾクッ
HER WHOLE BODY...
...IS COVERED IN WRITING!
SEKKI!!
BAH

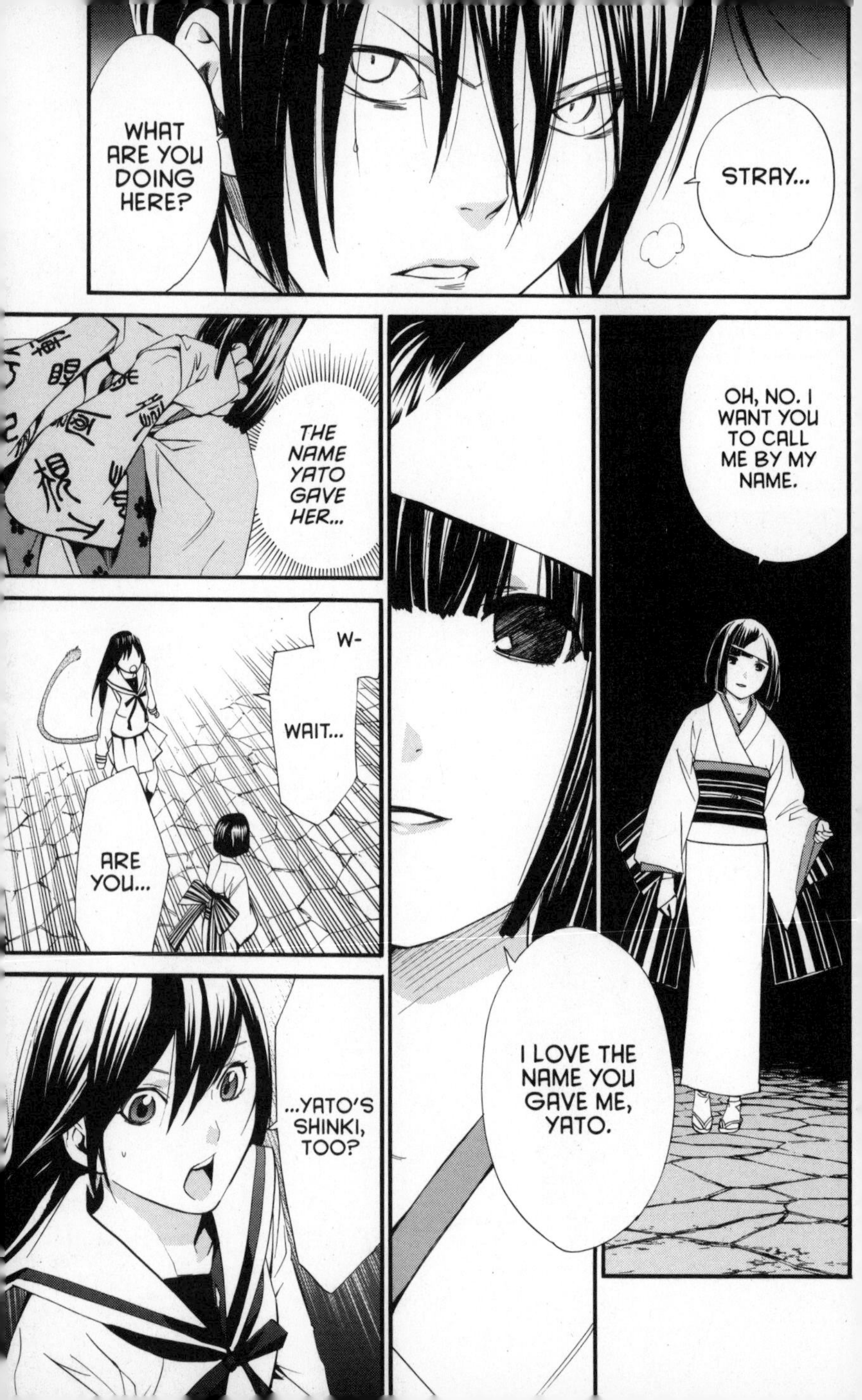
STRAY...
WHAT ARE YOU DOING HERE?
OH, NO. I WANT YOU TO CALL ME BY MY NAME.
I LOVE THE NAME YOU GAVE ME, YATO.
THE NAME YATO GAVE HER...
W-
WAIT...
ARE YOU...
...YATO'S SHINKI, TOO?

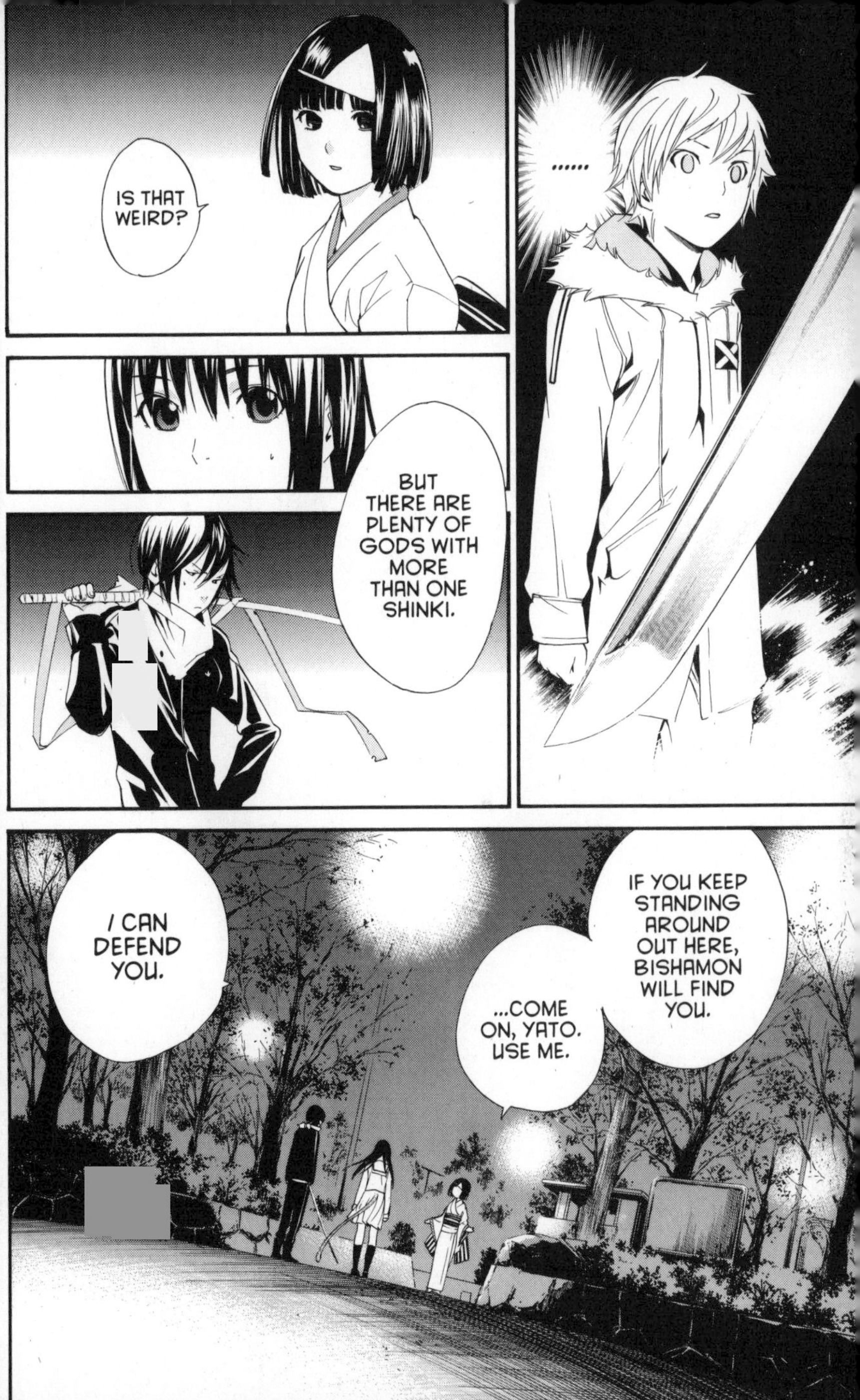
......
IS THAT WEIRD?
BUT THERE ARE PLENTY OF GODS WITH MORE THAN ONE SHINKI.
IF YOU KEEP STANDING AROUND OUT HERE, BISHAMON WILL FIND YOU.
...COME ON, YATO. USE ME.
I CAN DEFEND YOU.

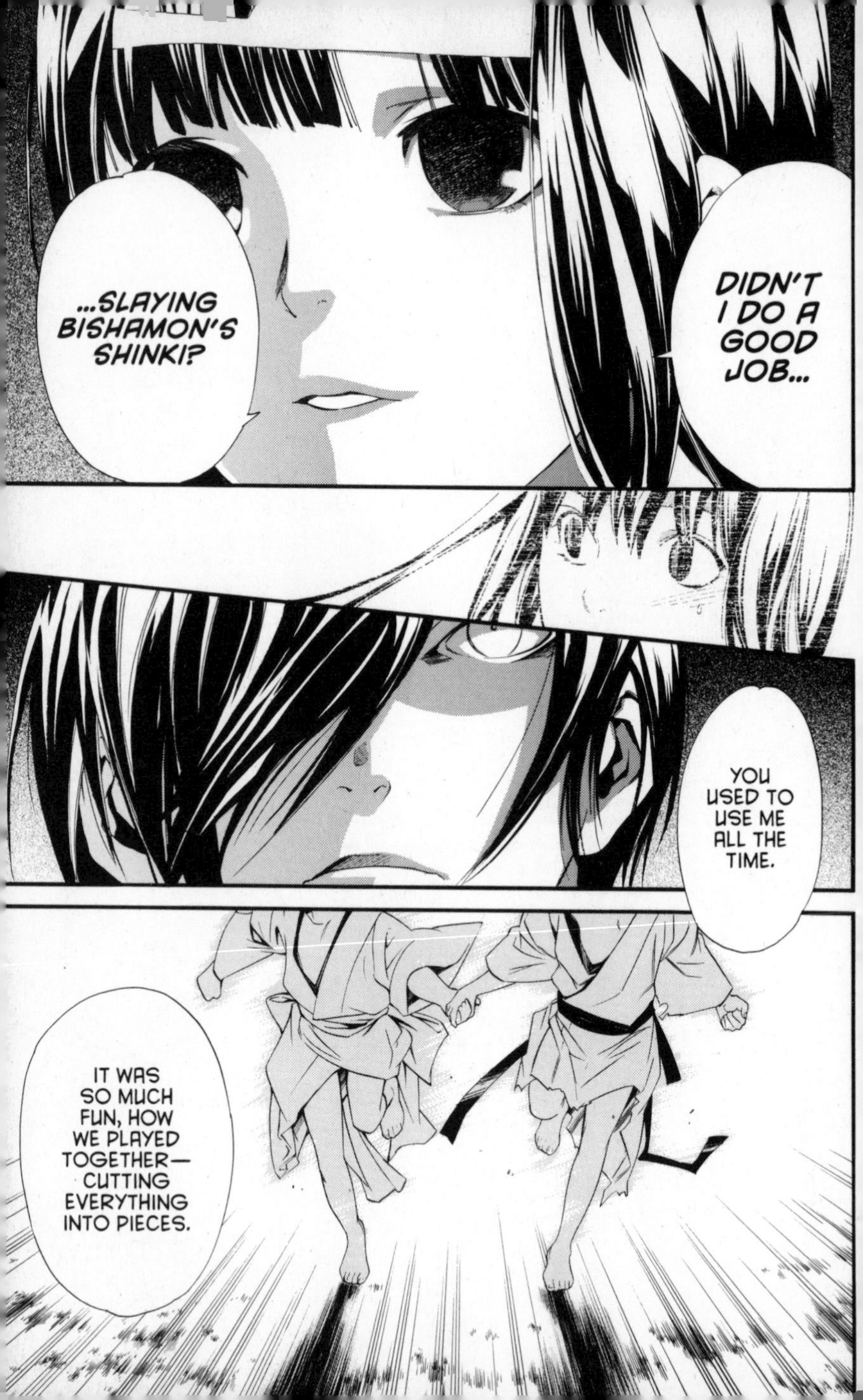
DIDN'T I DO A GOOD JOB...
...SLAYING BISHAMON'S SHINKI?
YOU USED TO USE ME ALL THE TIME.
IT WAS SO MUCH FUN, HOW WE PLAYED TOGETHER—CUTTING EVERYTHING INTO PIECES.

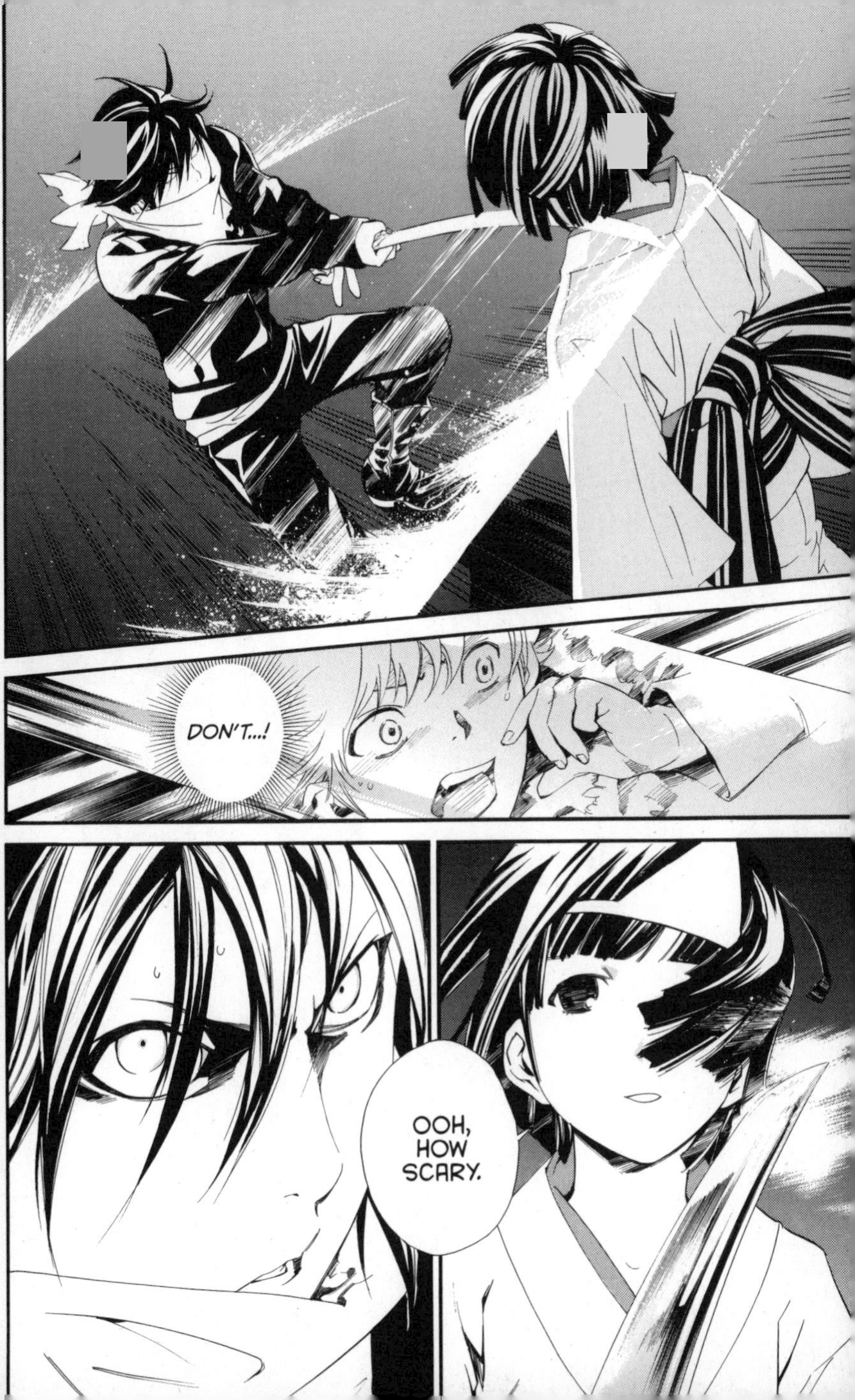
DON'T...!
OOH, HOW SCARY.

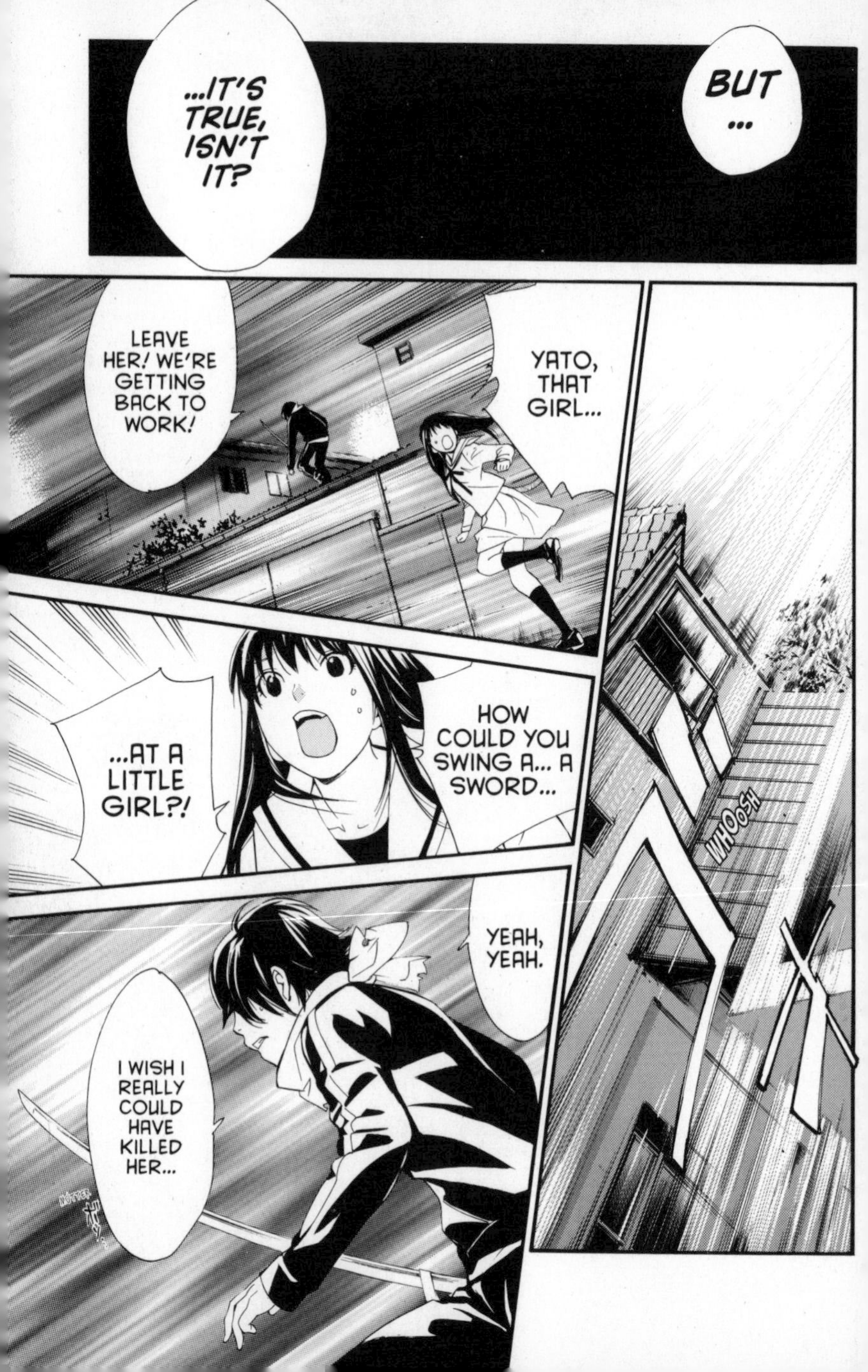
BUT ...
...IT'S TRUE, ISN'T IT?
WHOOSH
YATO, THAT GIRL...
LEAVE HER! WE'RE GETTING BACK TO WORK!
HOW COULD YOU SWING A... A SWORD...
...AT A LITTLE GIRL?!
YEAH, YEAH.
I WISH I REALLY COULD HAVE KILLED HER...

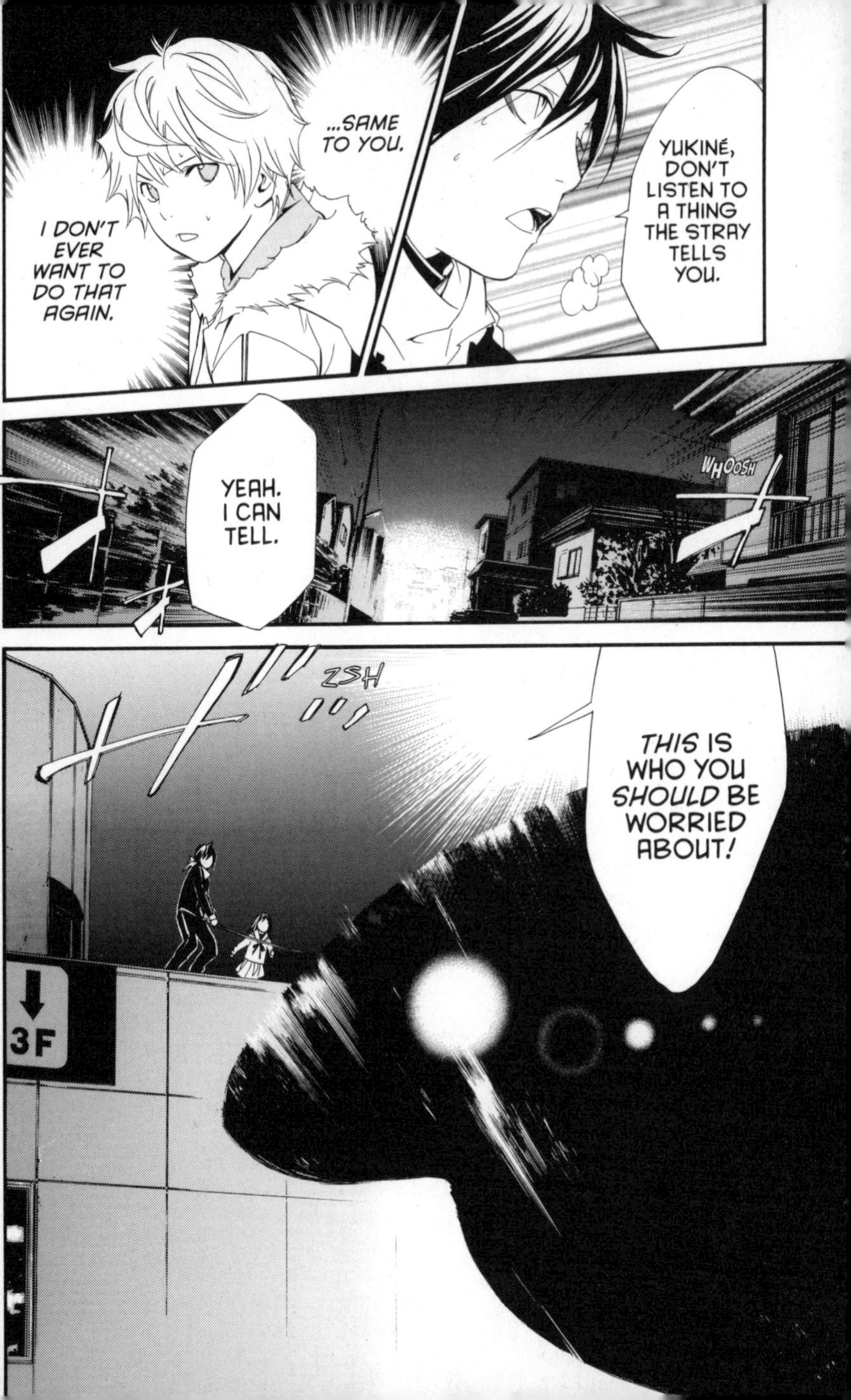
YUKINÉ, DON'T LISTEN TO A THING THE STRAY TELLS YOU.
...SAME TO YOU.
I DON'T EVER WANT TO DO THAT AGAIN.
WHOOSH
YEAH. I CAN TELL.
THIS IS WHO YOU *SHOULD* BE WORRIED ABOUT!
ZSH
3F

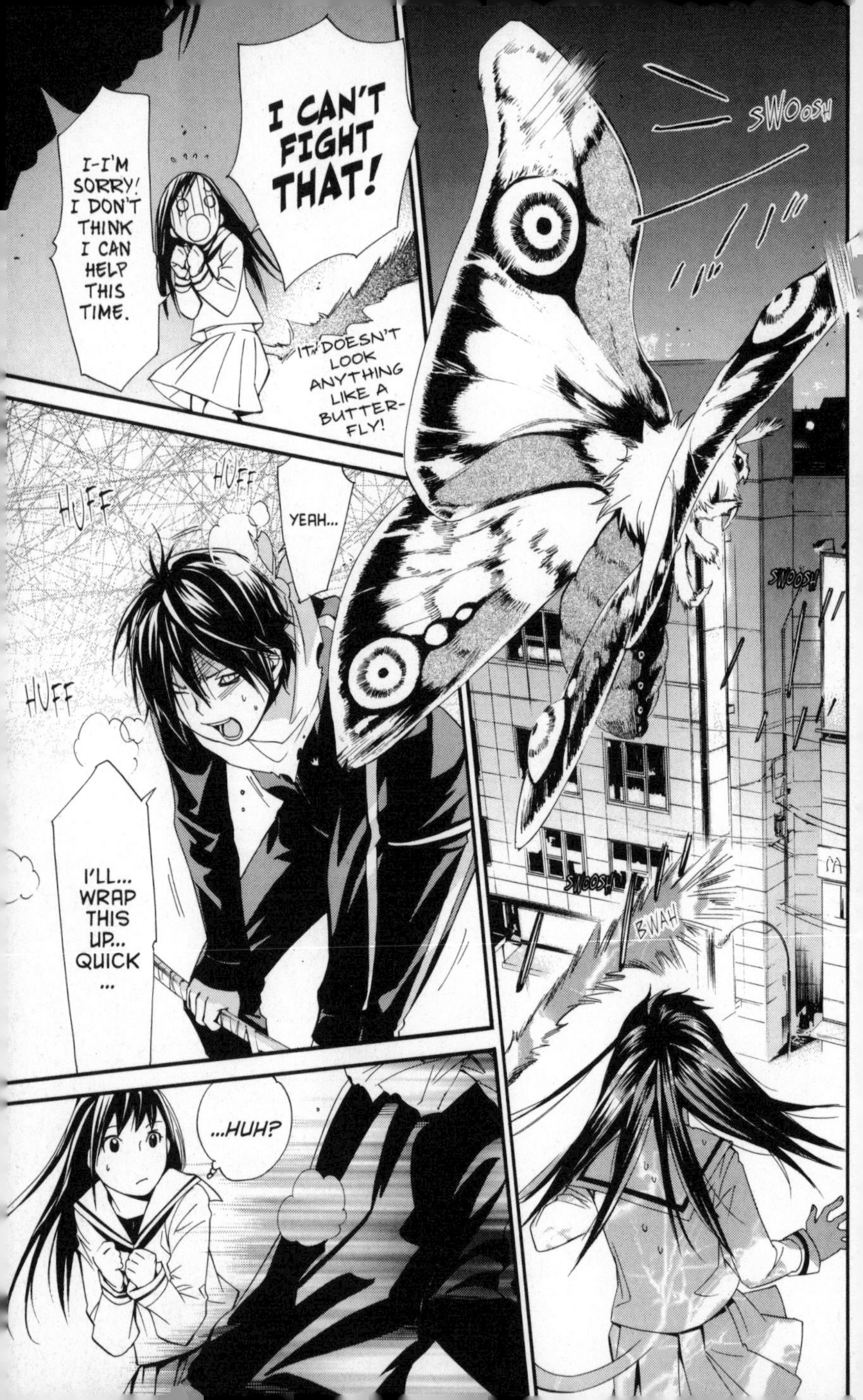

SWOOSH
SWOOSH
SWOOSH
BWAH
I CAN'T FIGHT THAT!
I-I'M SORRY! I DON'T THINK I CAN HELP THIS TIME.
IT DOESN'T LOOK ANYTHING LIKE A BUTTER-FLY!
YEAH...
HUFF
HUFF
HUFF
I'LL... WRAP THIS UP... QUICK...
...HUH?

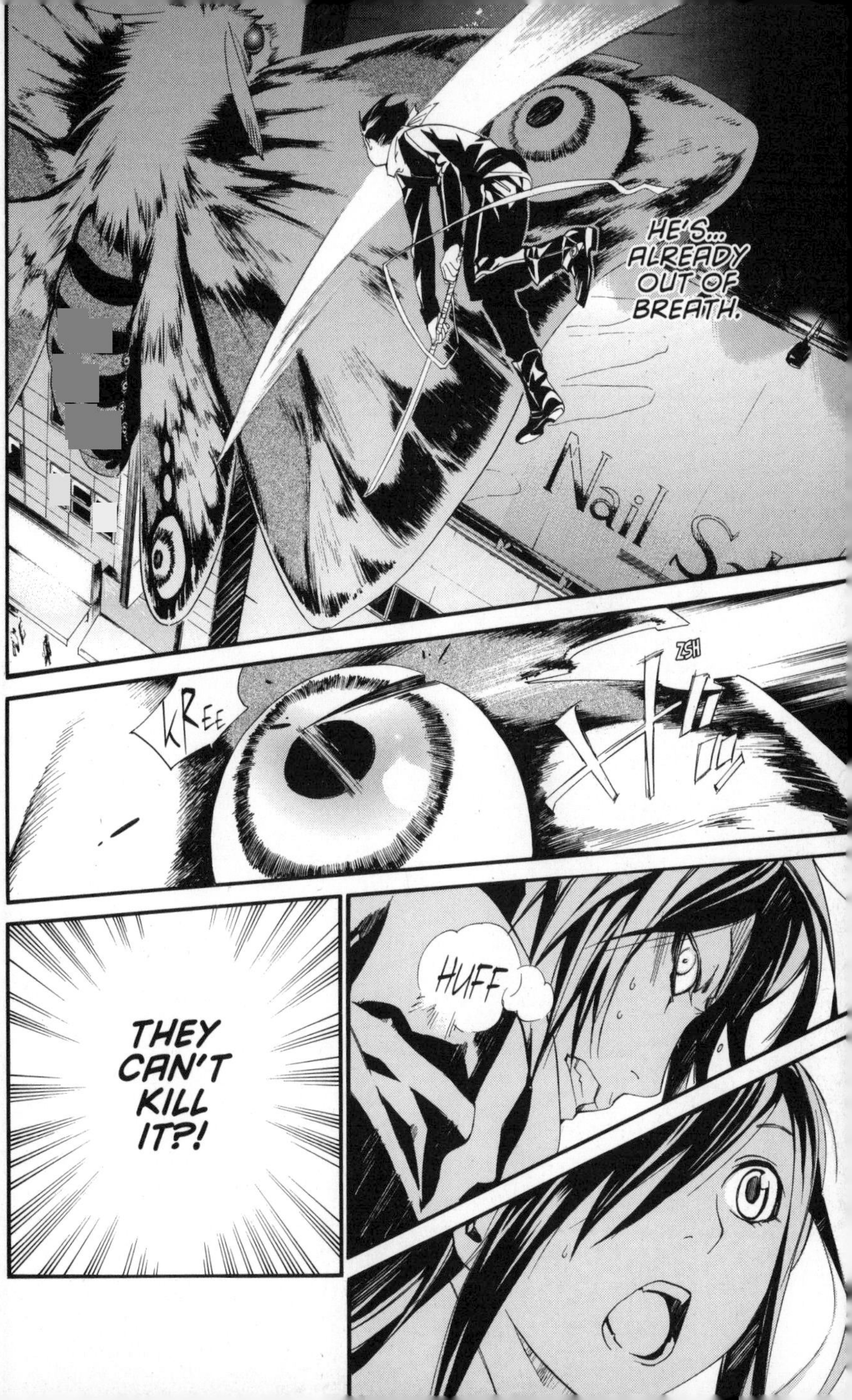
HE'S... ALREADY OUT OF BREATH.
Nail S
ZSH
KREE
HUFF
THEY CAN'T KILL IT?!

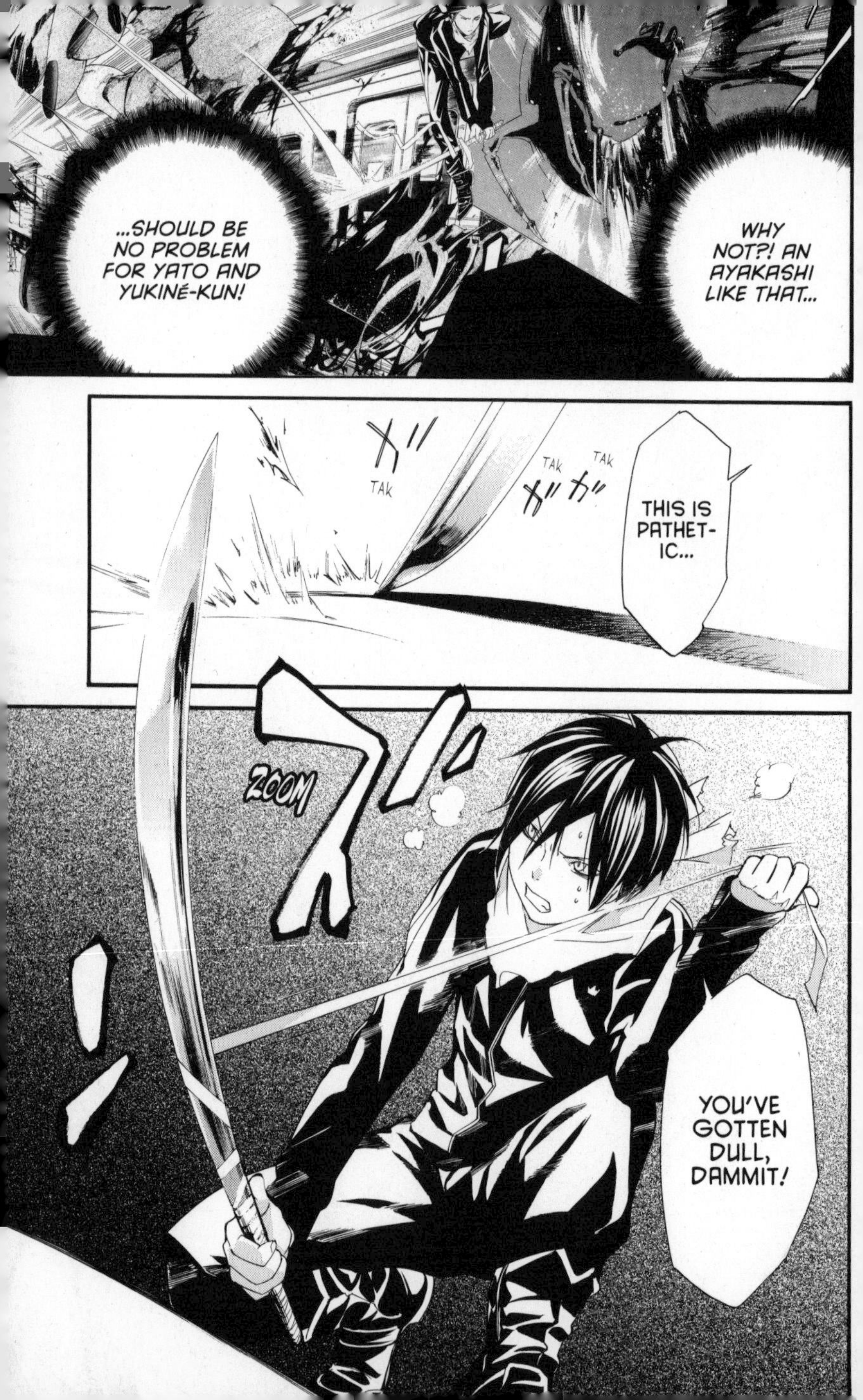
WHY NOT?! AN AYAKASHI LIKE THAT...
...SHOULD BE NO PROBLEM FOR YATO AND YUKINÉ-KUN!
TAK TAK
TAK
THIS IS PATHET-IC...
ZOOM
YOU'VE GOTTEN DULL, DAMMIT!

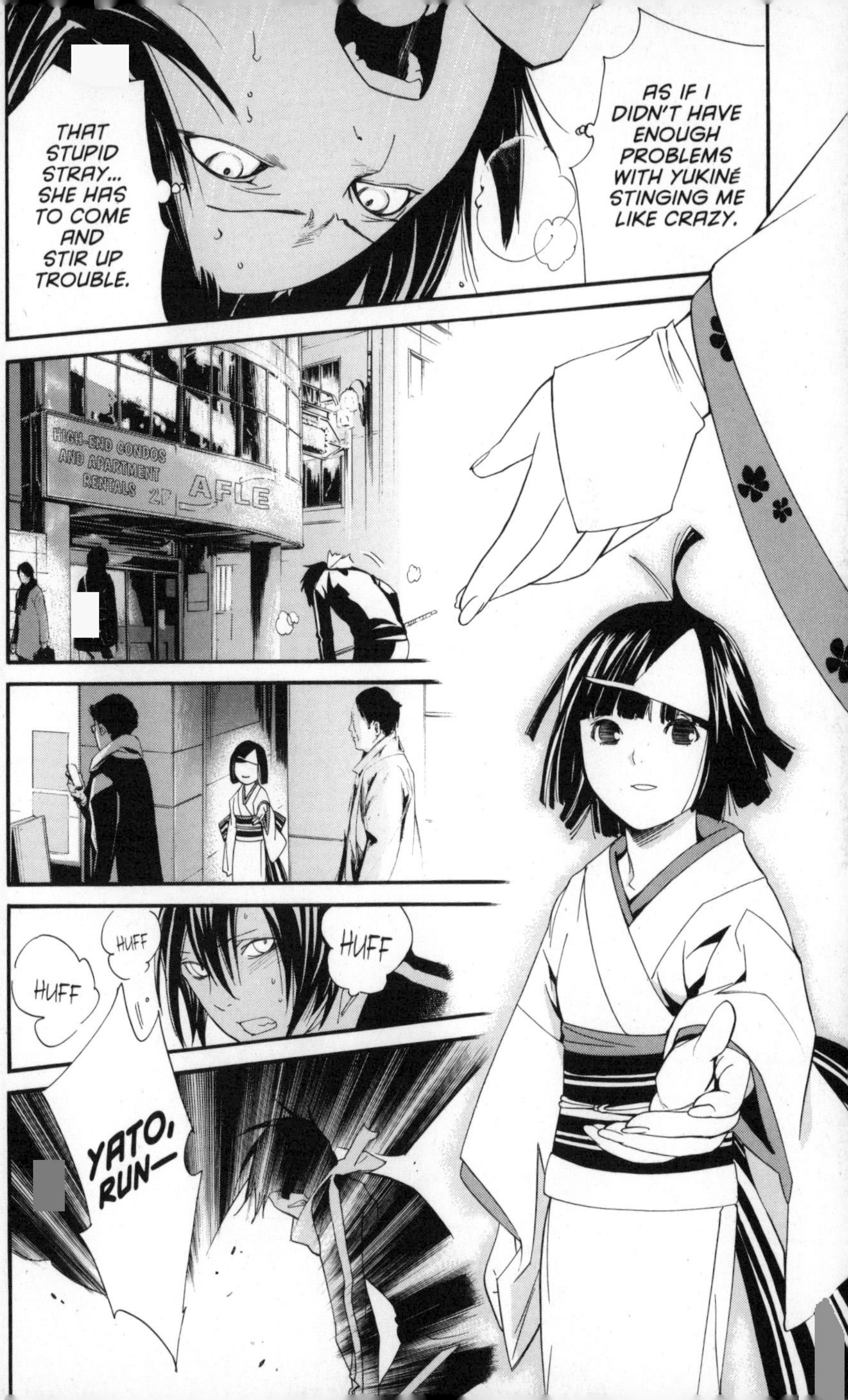
AS IF I DIDN'T HAVE ENOUGH PROBLEMS WITH YUKINÉ STINGING ME LIKE CRAZY.
THAT STUPID STRAY... SHE HAS TO COME AND STIR UP TROUBLE.
HIGH-END CONDOS AND APARTMENT RENTALS 2F
AFLE
HUFF
HUFF
HUFF
YATO, RUN—

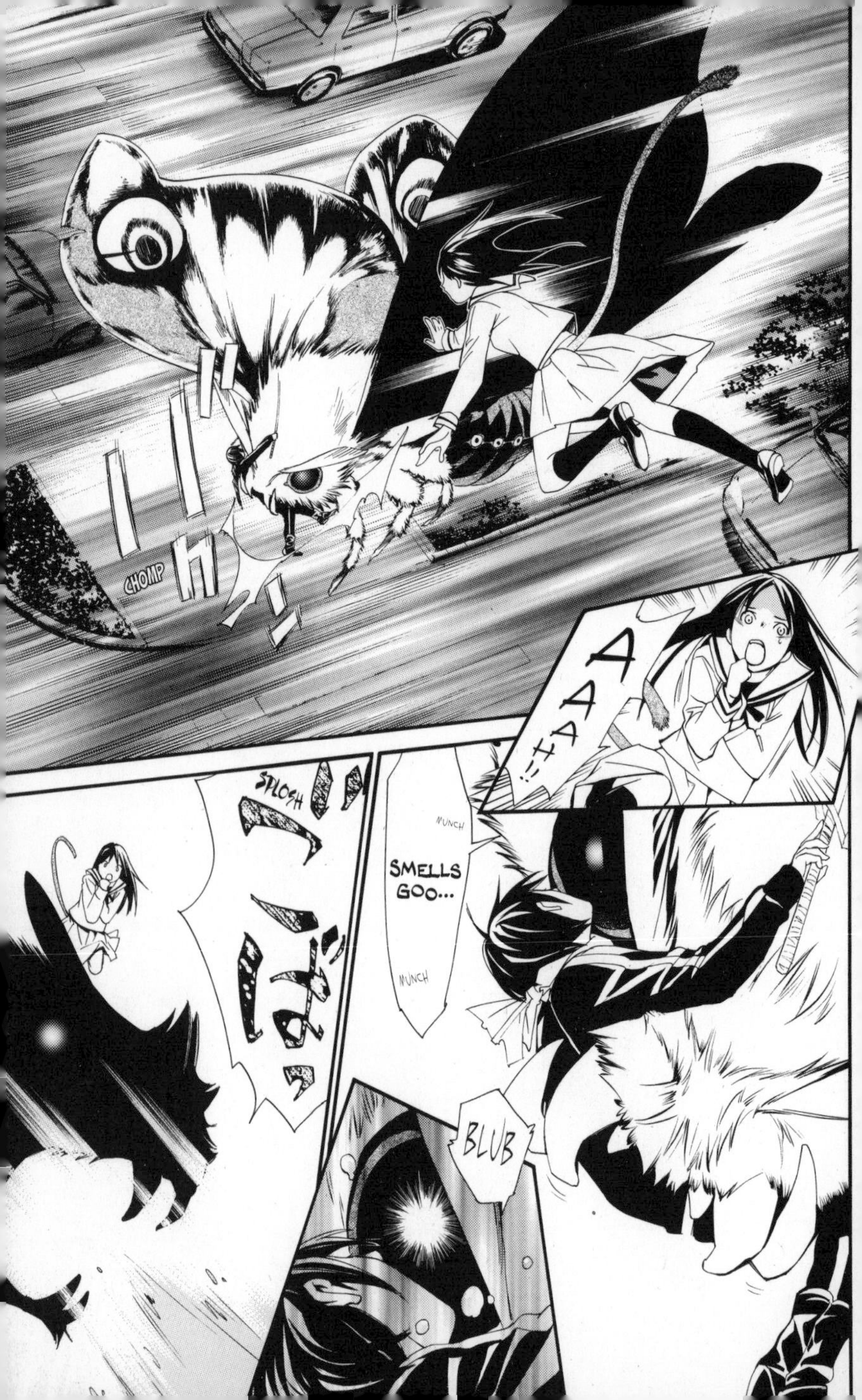
CHOMP
AAAH!!
MUNCH
SMELLS GOO...
MUNCH
SPLOSH
BLUB

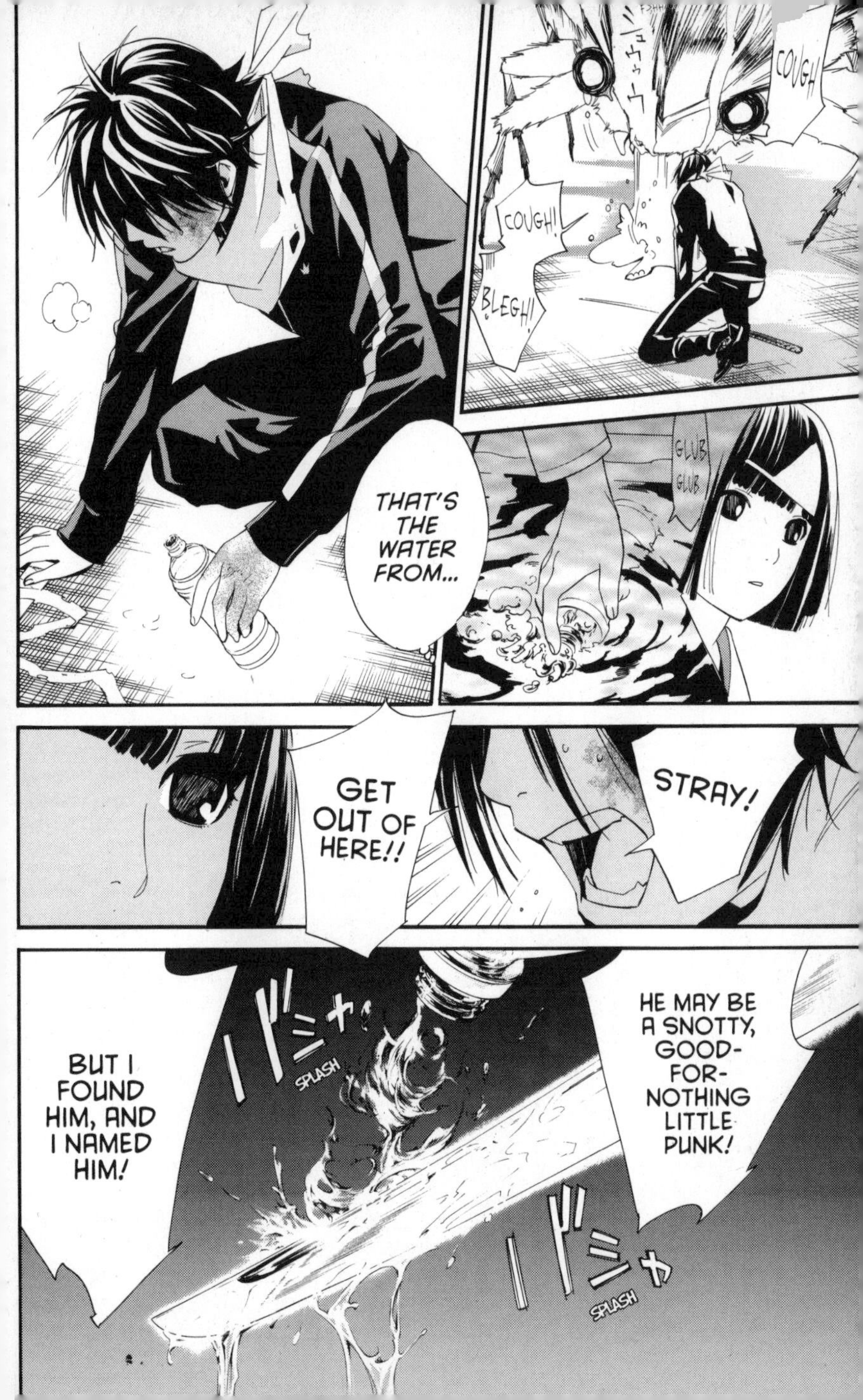
COUGH
COUGH!
BLEGH!
GLUB GLUB
THAT'S THE WATER FROM...
STRAY!
GET OUT OF HERE!!
HE MAY BE A SNOTTY, GOOD-FOR-NOTHING LITTLE PUNK!
SPLASH
SPLASH
BUT I FOUND HIM, AND I NAMED HIM!

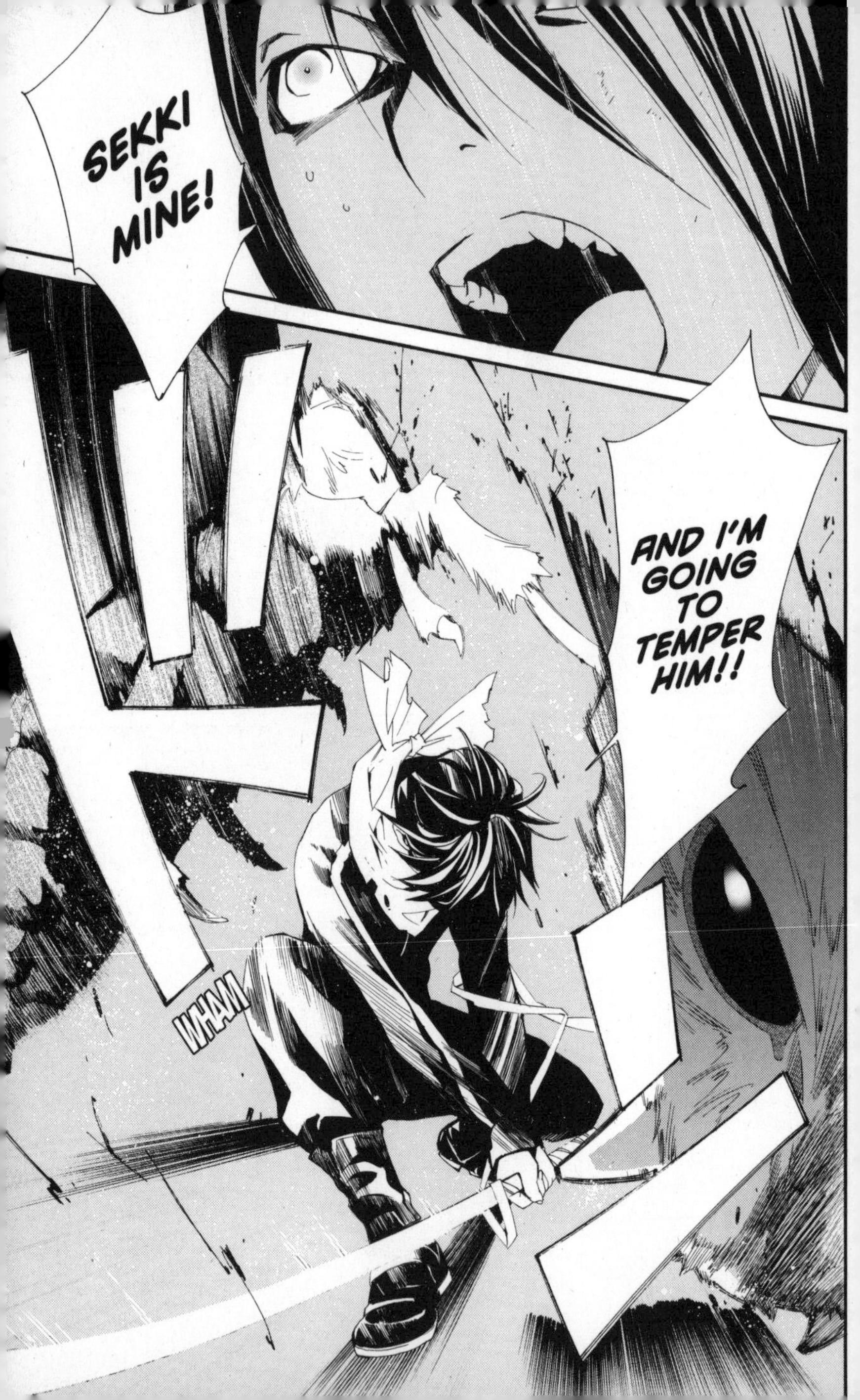
SEKKI IS MINE!
AND I'M GOING TO TEMPER HIM!!
WHAM

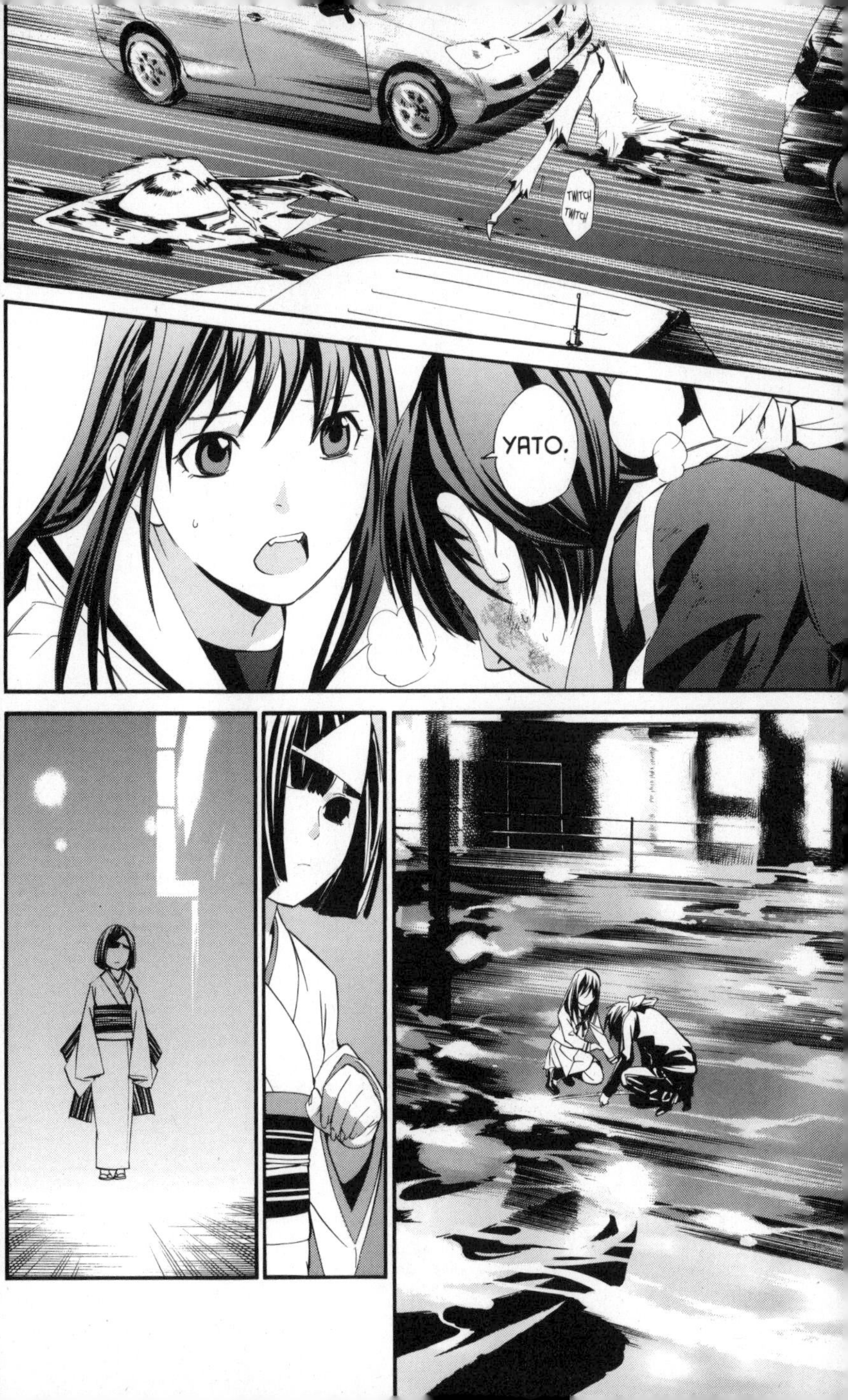
TWITCH
TWITCH
YATO.

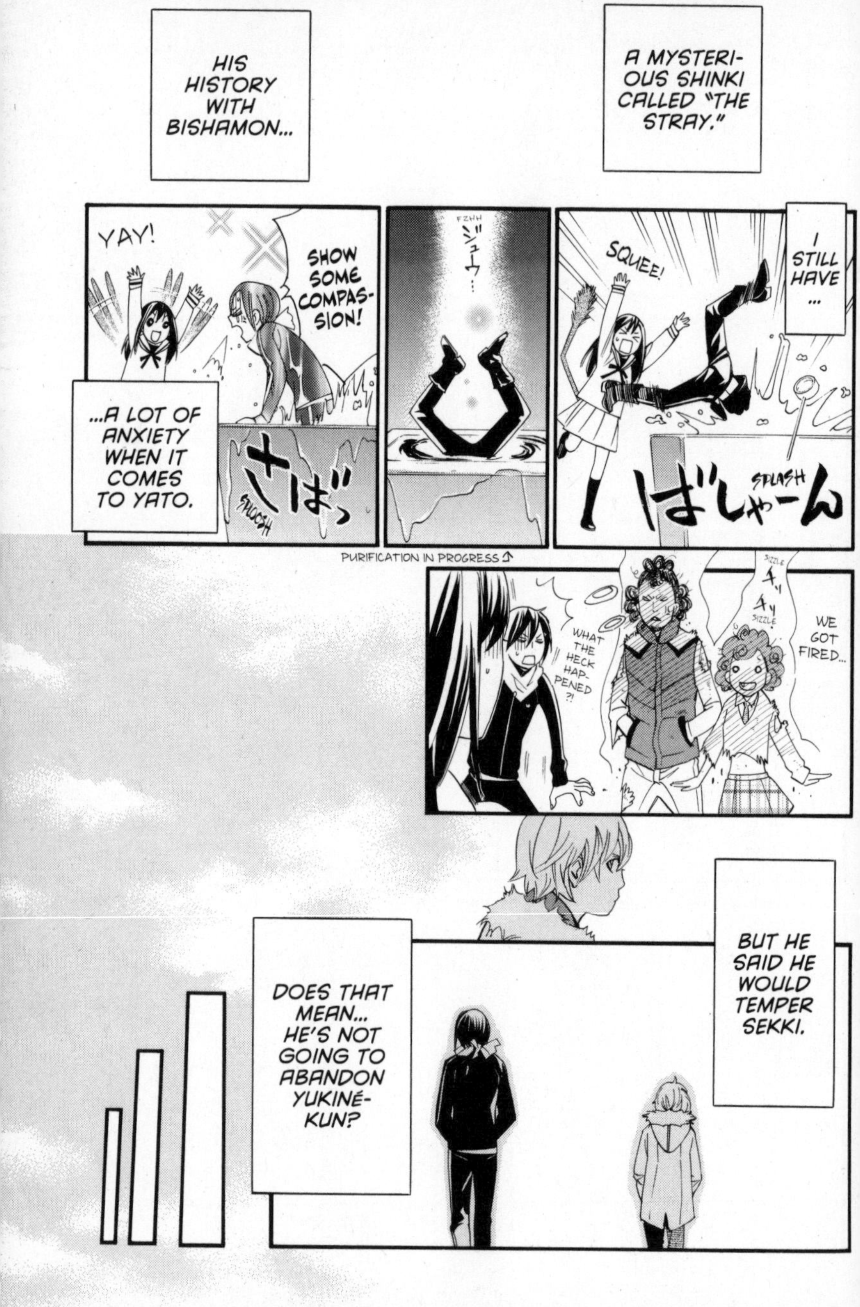
A MYSTERIOUS SHINKI CALLED "THE STRAY."
HIS HISTORY WITH BISHAMON...
I STILL HAVE ...
SQUEE!
ばしゃーん SPLASH
FZHH ジュウ…
SHOW SOME COMPASSION!
YAY!
...A LOT OF ANXIETY WHEN IT COMES TO YATO.
さばっ SPLOOSH
PURIFICATION IN PROGRESS ⇧
WE GOT FIRED...
SIZZLE
SIZZLE
WHAT THE HECK HAPPENED?!
BUT HE SAID HE WOULD TEMPER SEKKI.
DOES THAT MEAN... HE'S NOT GOING TO ABANDON YUKINÉ-KUN?

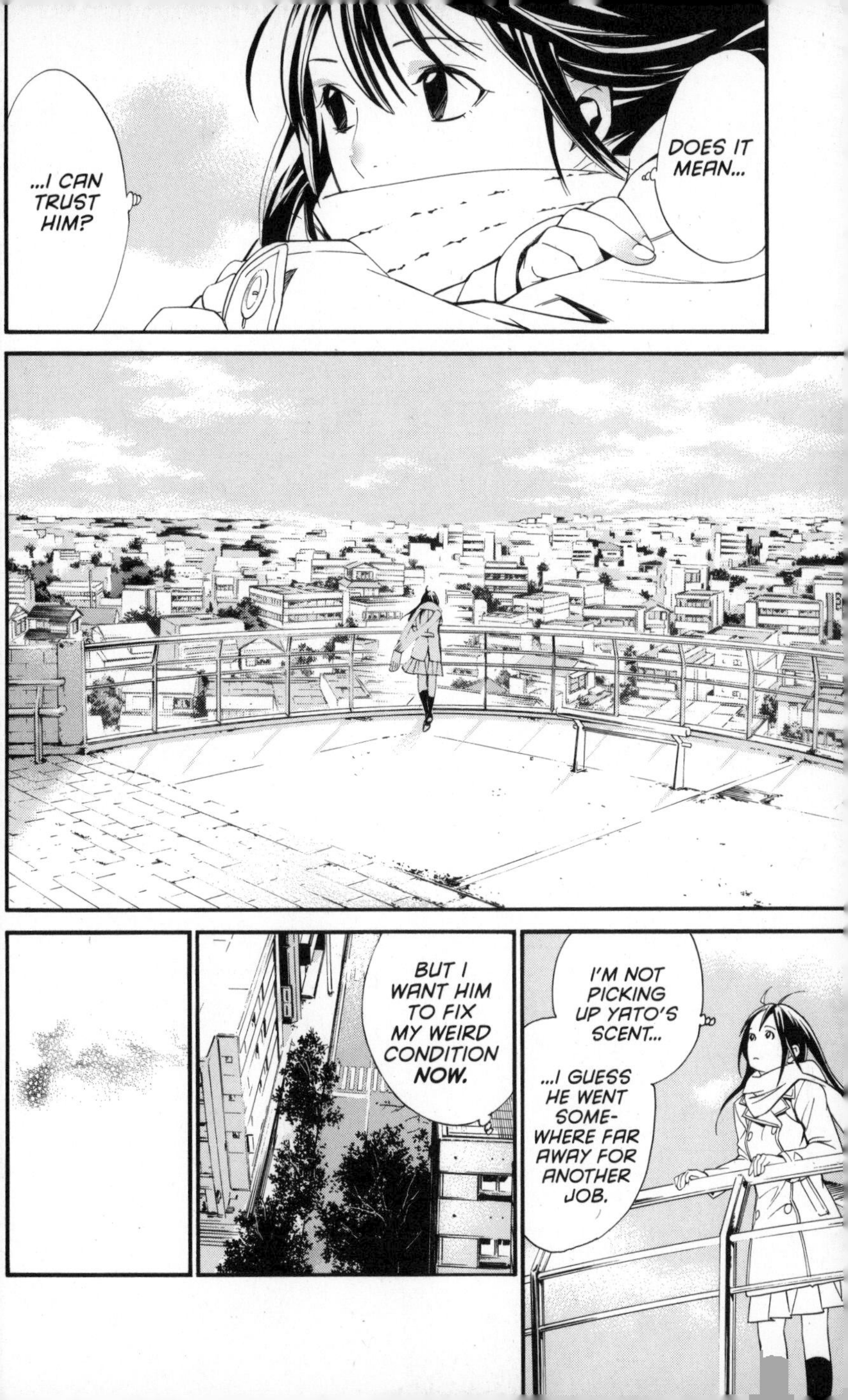
DOES IT MEAN...
...I CAN TRUST HIM?
I'M NOT PICKING UP YATO'S SCENT...
...I GUESS HE WENT SOME-WHERE FAR AWAY FOR ANOTHER JOB.
BUT I WANT HIM TO FIX MY WEIRD CONDITION NOW.

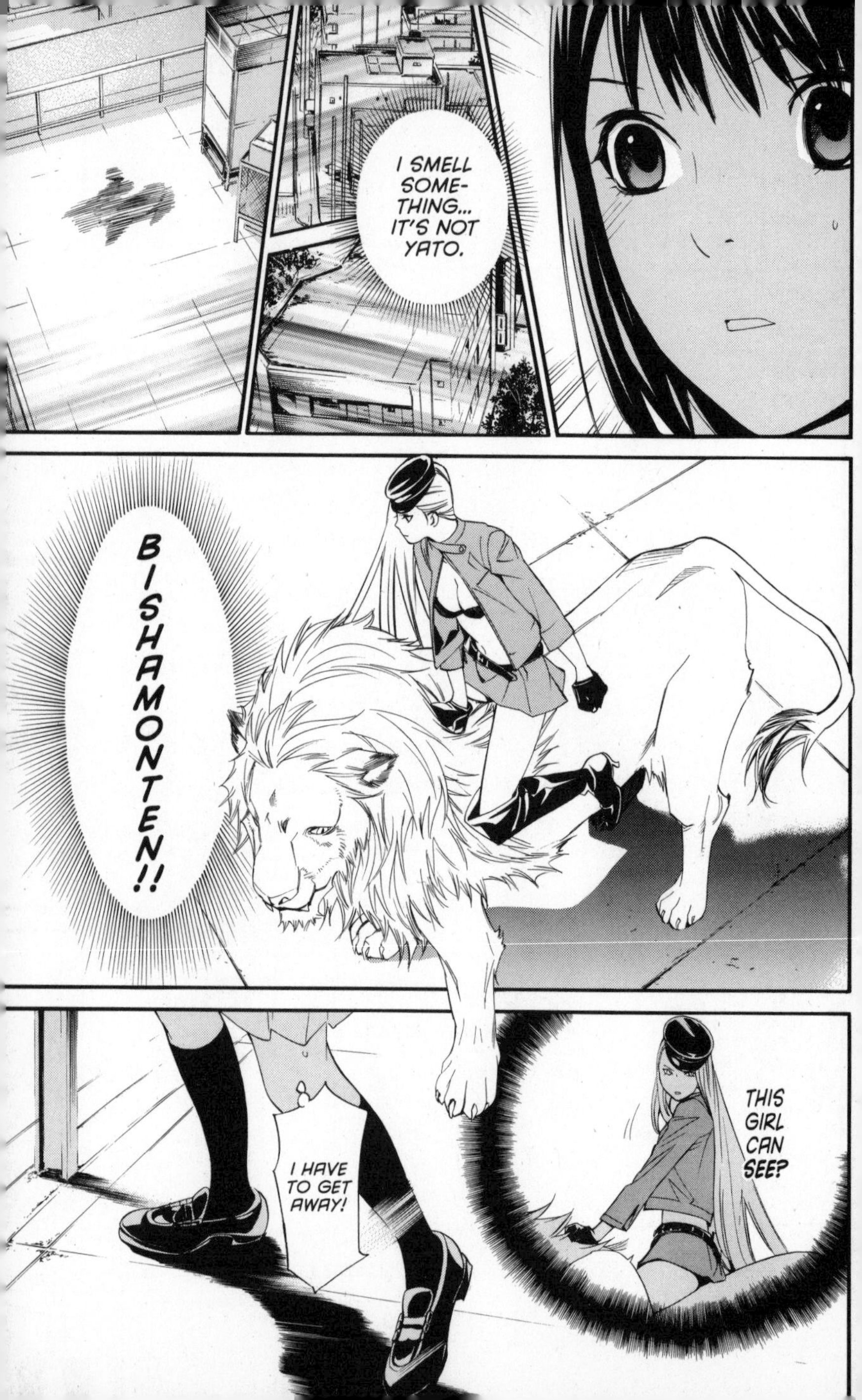
I SMELL SOME-THING... IT'S NOT YATO.
BISHAMONTEN!!
THIS GIRL CAN SEE?
I HAVE TO GET AWAY!

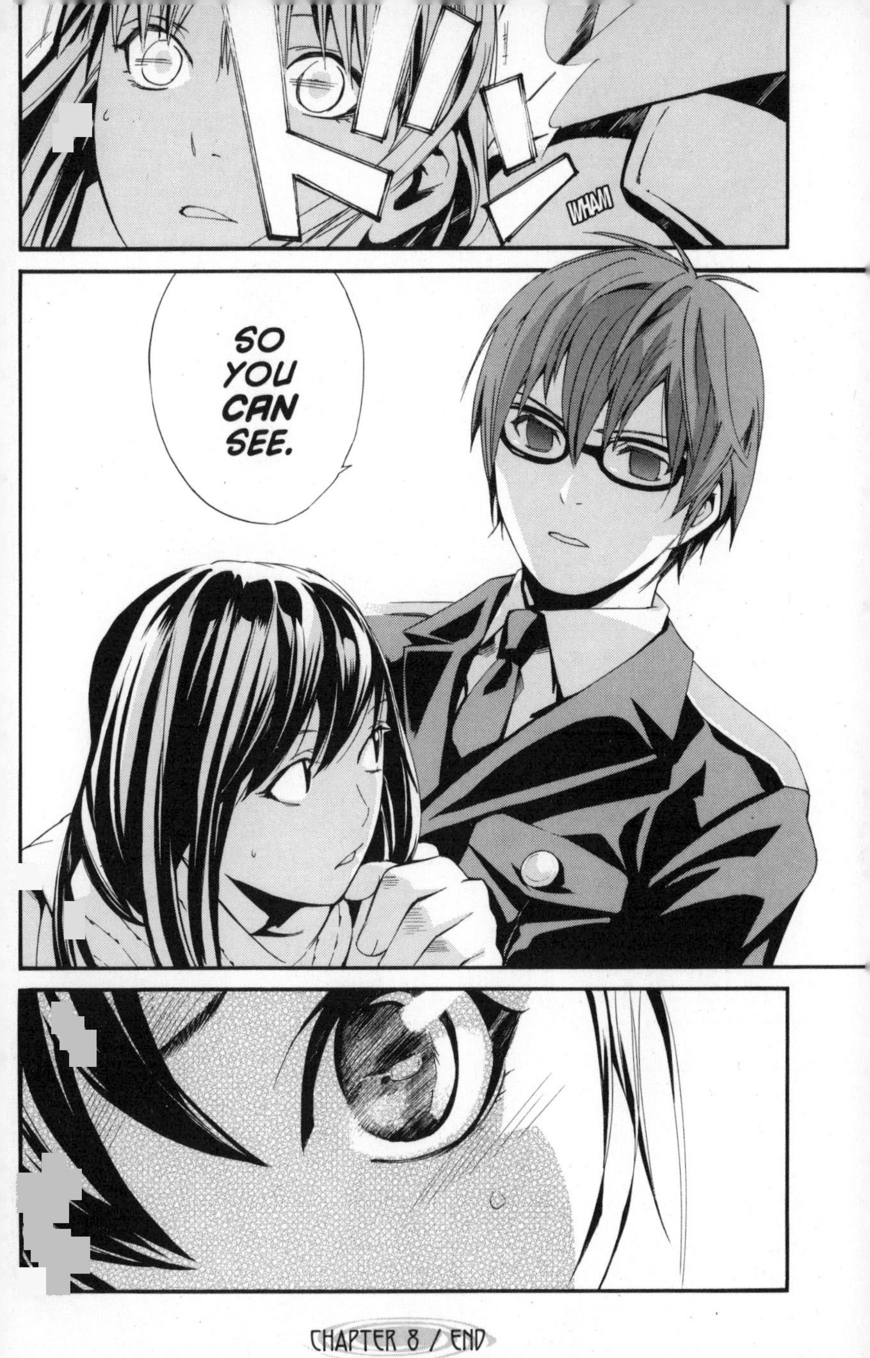
WHAM
SO YOU CAN SEE.

CHAPTER 8 / END

野

是

神

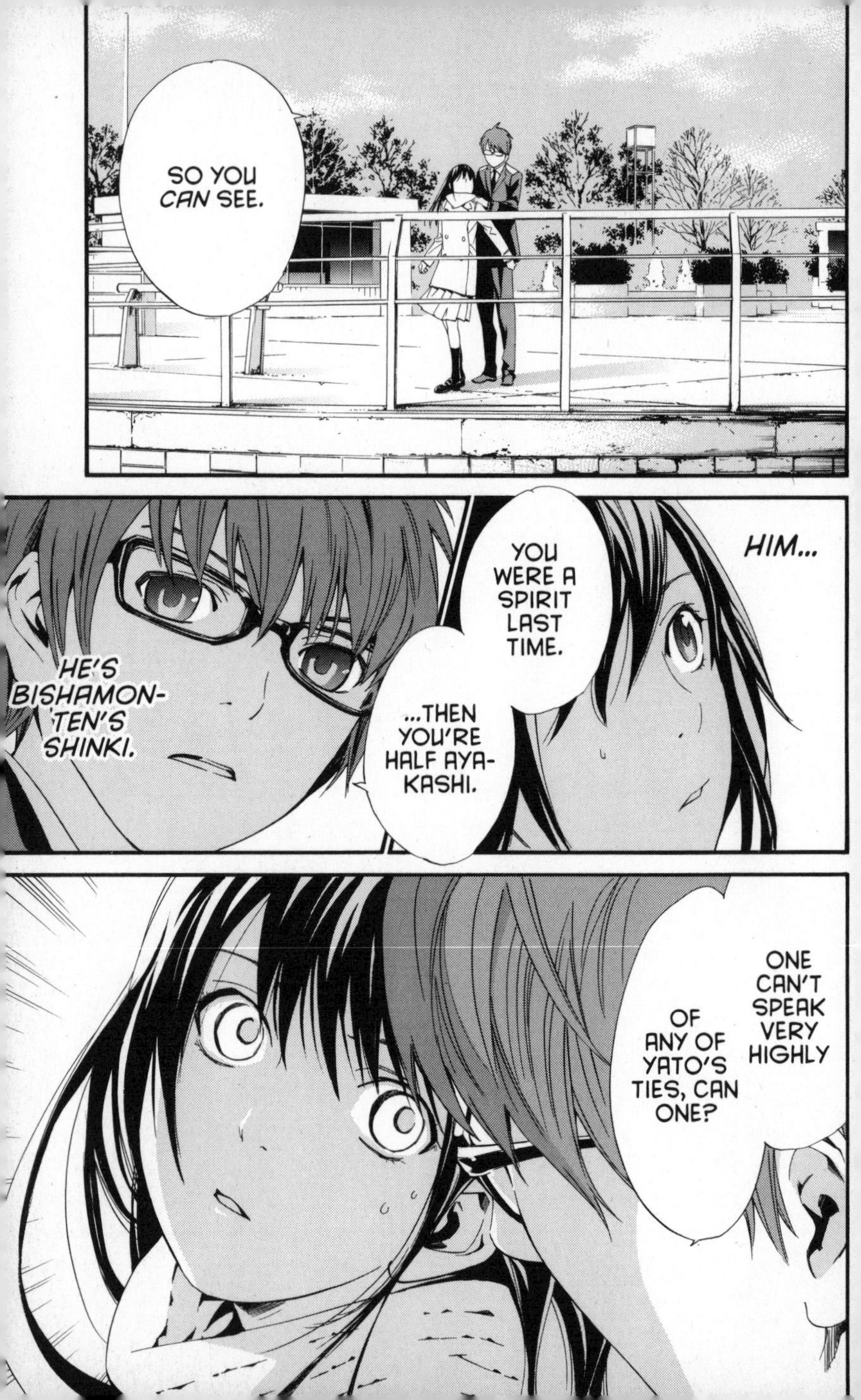
SO YOU CAN SEE.
HIM...
YOU WERE A SPIRIT LAST TIME.
...THEN YOU'RE HALF AYA-KASHI.
HE'S BISHAMON-TEN'S SHINKI.
ONE CAN'T SPEAK VERY HIGHLY
OF ANY OF YATO'S TIES, CAN ONE?

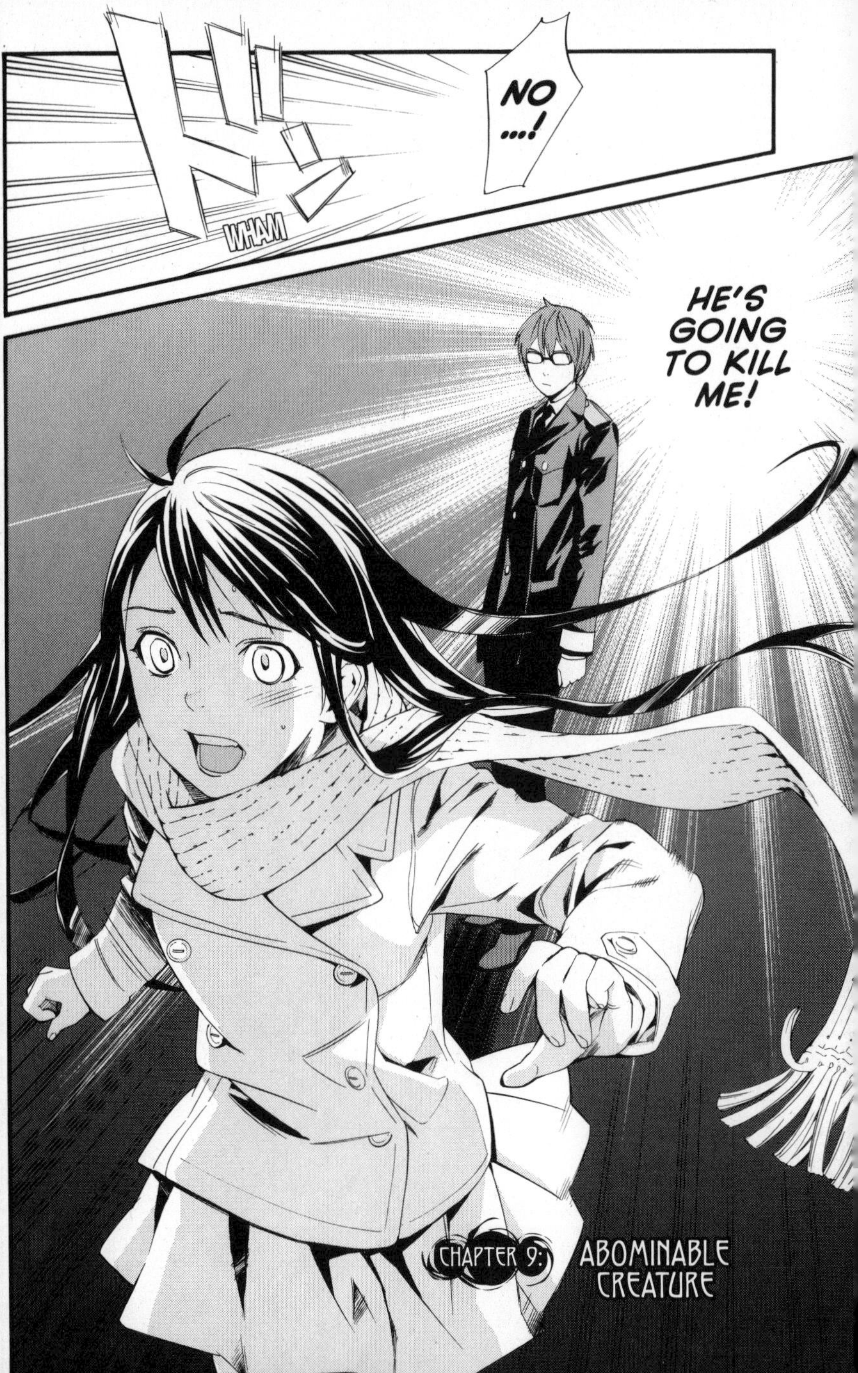

NO ...!
WHAM
HE'S GOING TO KILL ME!
CHAPTER 9: ABOMINABLE CREATURE

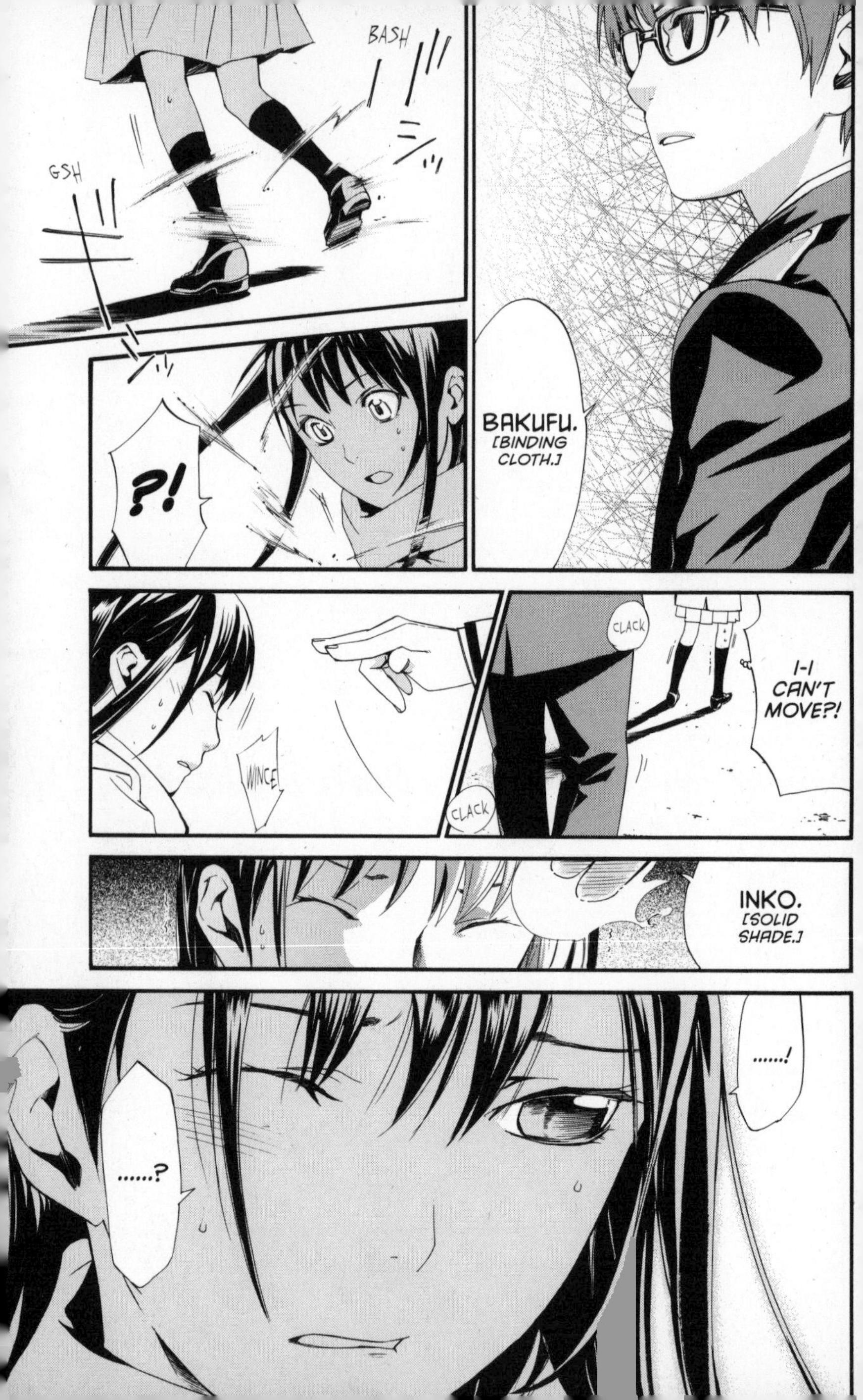
BAKUFU.
[BINDING CLOTH.]
BASH
GSH
?!
CLACK
I-I CAN'T MOVE?!
CLACK
WINCE
INKO.
[SOLID SHADE.]
......!
......?

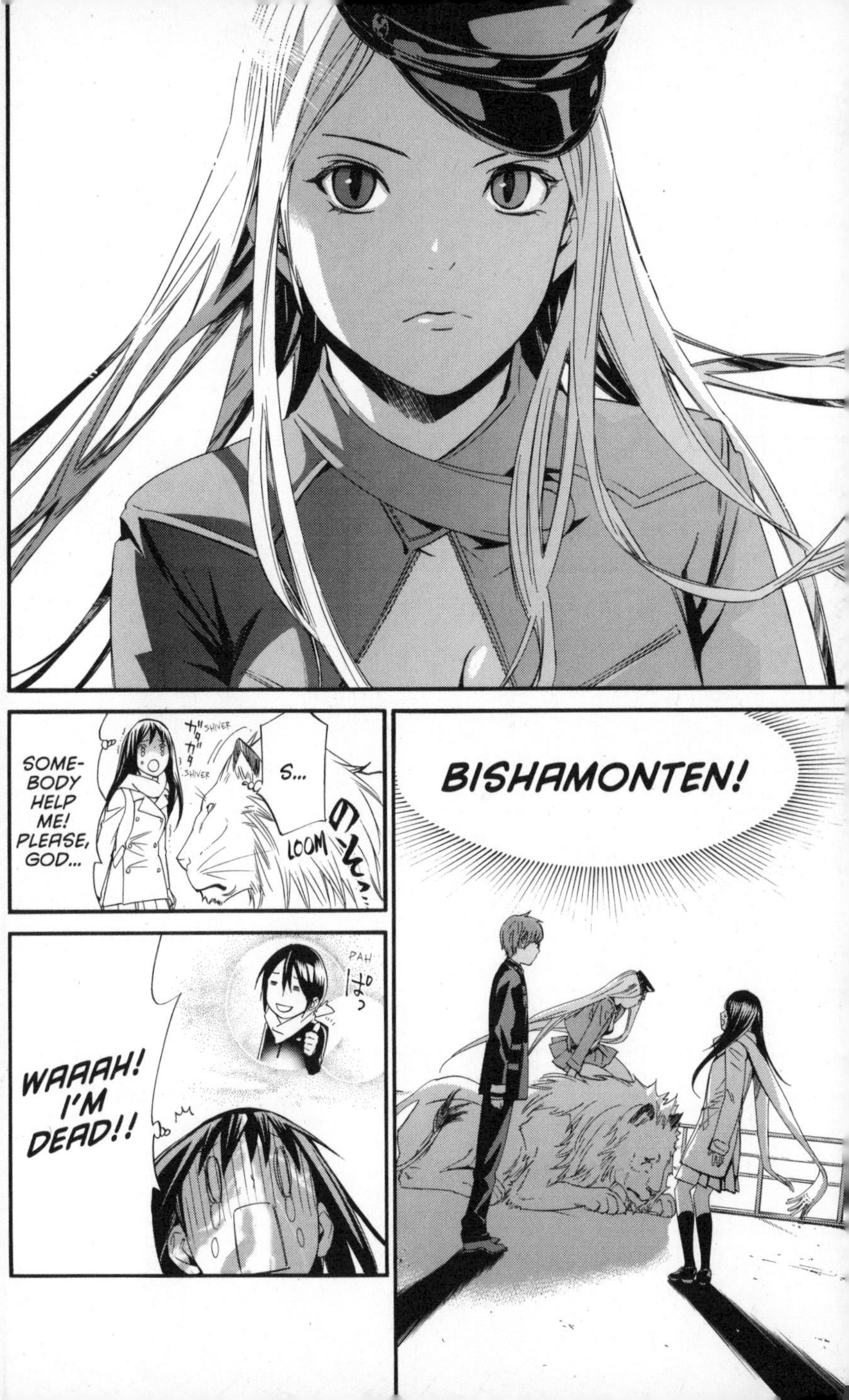
BISHAMONTEN!
S...
ガタ SHIVER
ガタ SHIVER
LOOM
SOME-BODY HELP ME! PLEASE, GOD...
PAH
ぱっ
WAAAH! I'M DEAD!!

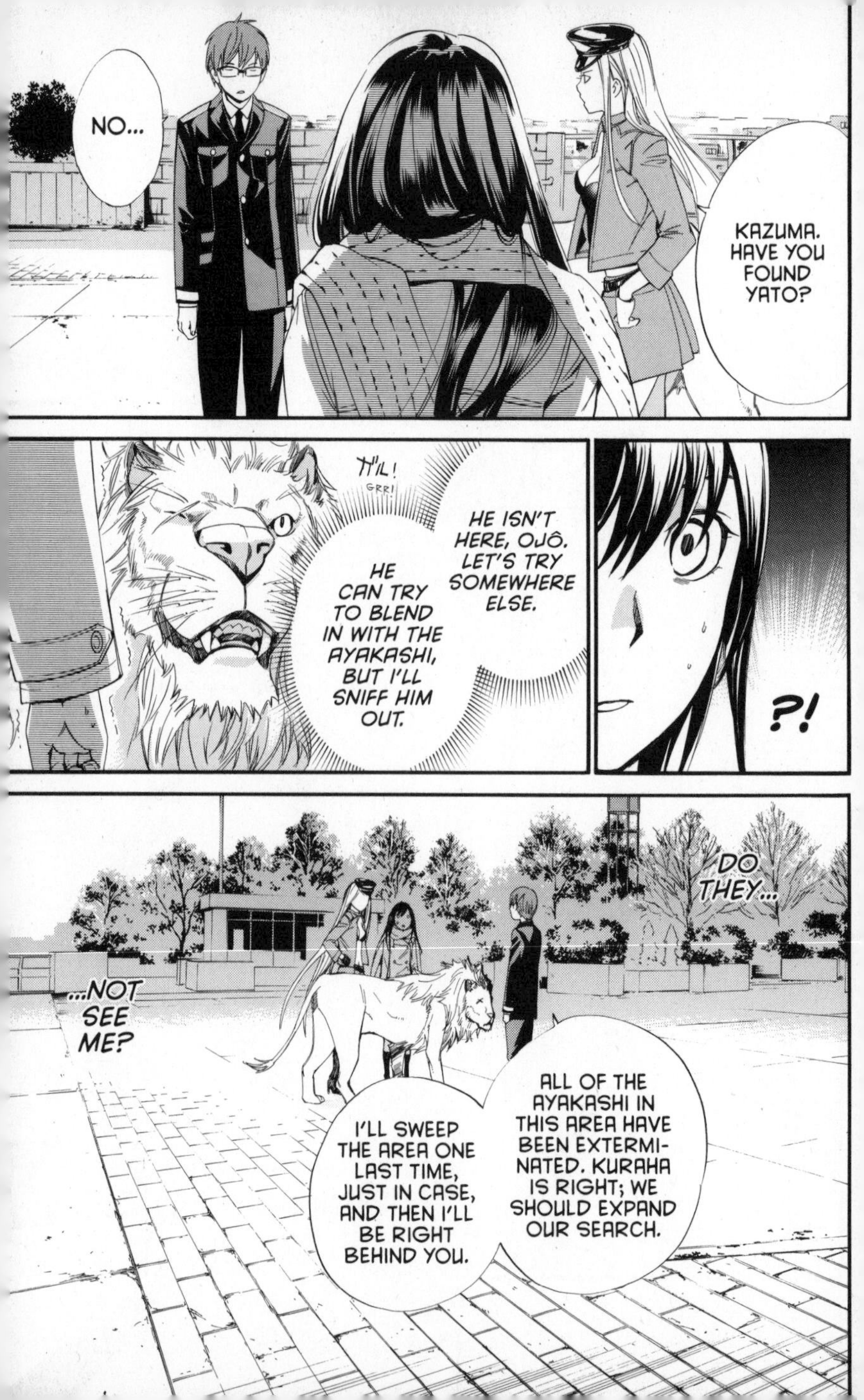
KAZUMA. HAVE YOU FOUND YATO?
NO...
?!
ガル!
GRR!
HE ISN'T HERE, OJÔ. LET'S TRY SOMEWHERE ELSE.
HE CAN TRY TO BLEND IN WITH THE AYAKASHI, BUT I'LL SNIFF HIM OUT.
DO THEY...
...NOT SEE ME?
ALL OF THE AYAKASHI IN THIS AREA HAVE BEEN EXTERMINATED. KURAHA IS RIGHT; WE SHOULD EXPAND OUR SEARCH.
I'LL SWEEP THE AREA ONE LAST TIME, JUST IN CASE, AND THEN I'LL BE RIGHT BEHIND YOU.

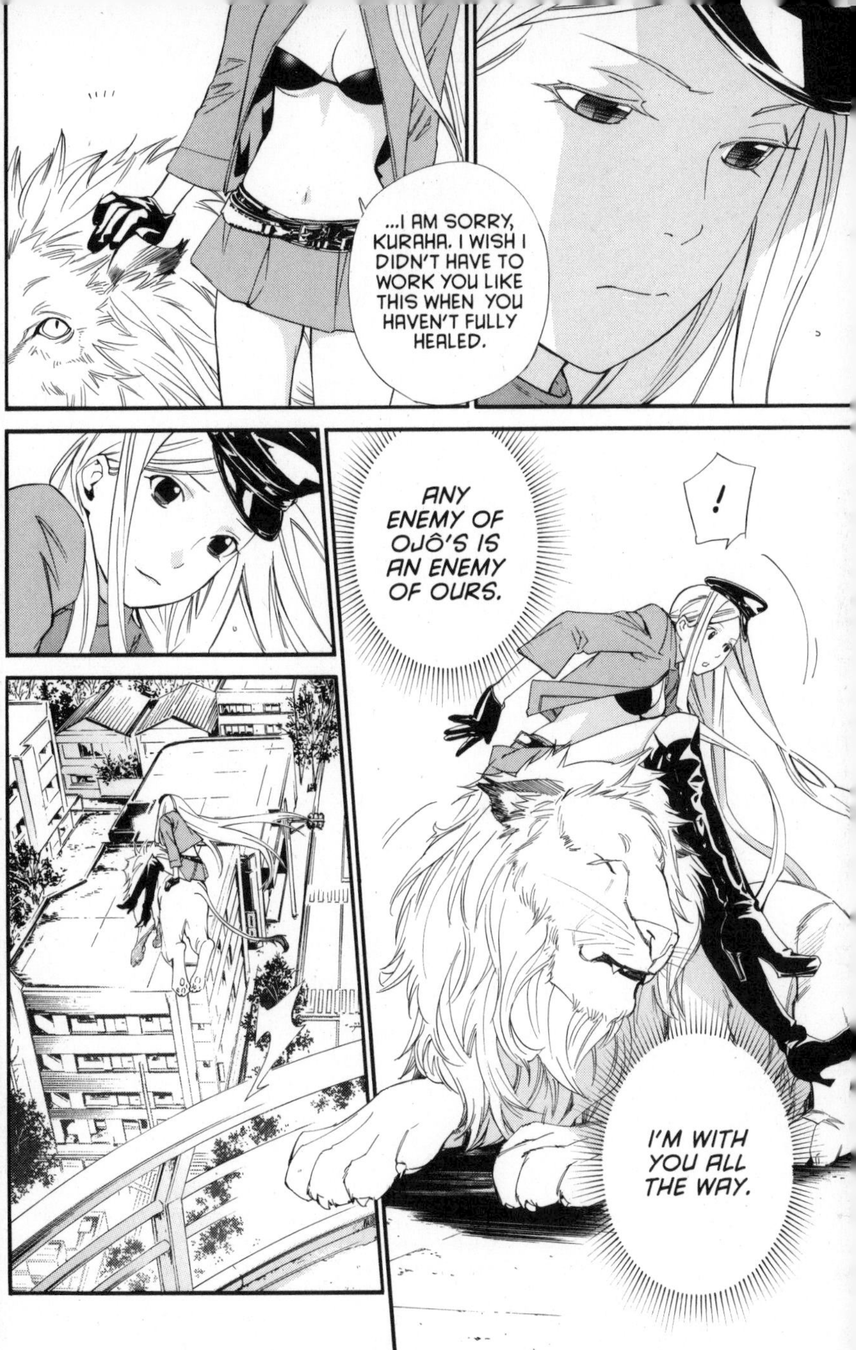
...I AM SORRY, KURAHA. I WISH I DIDN'T HAVE TO WORK YOU LIKE THIS WHEN YOU HAVEN'T FULLY HEALED.
ANY ENEMY OF OJÔ'S IS AN ENEMY OF OURS.
!
I'M WITH YOU ALL THE WAY.

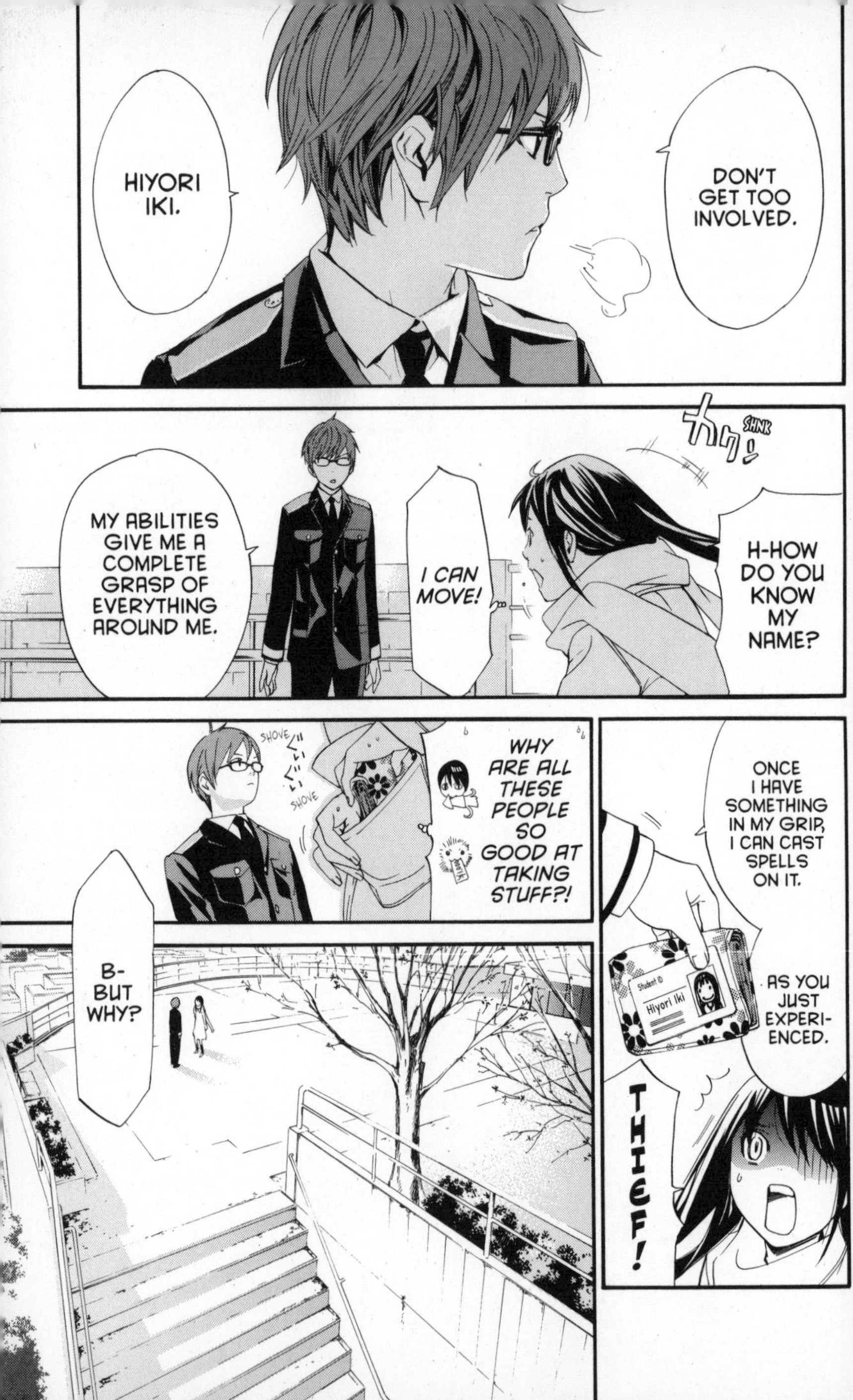
DON'T GET TOO INVOLVED.
HIYORI IKI.
カク!
SHNK
H-HOW DO YOU KNOW MY NAME?
I CAN MOVE!
MY ABILITIES GIVE ME A COMPLETE GRASP OF EVERYTHING AROUND ME.
ONCE I HAVE SOMETHING IN MY GRIP, I CAN CAST SPELLS ON IT.
Student ID
Hiyori Iki
AS YOU JUST EXPERI-ENCED.
THIEF!
WHY ARE ALL THESE PEOPLE SO GOOD AT TAKING STUFF?!
SHOVE
SHOVE
B-BUT WHY?

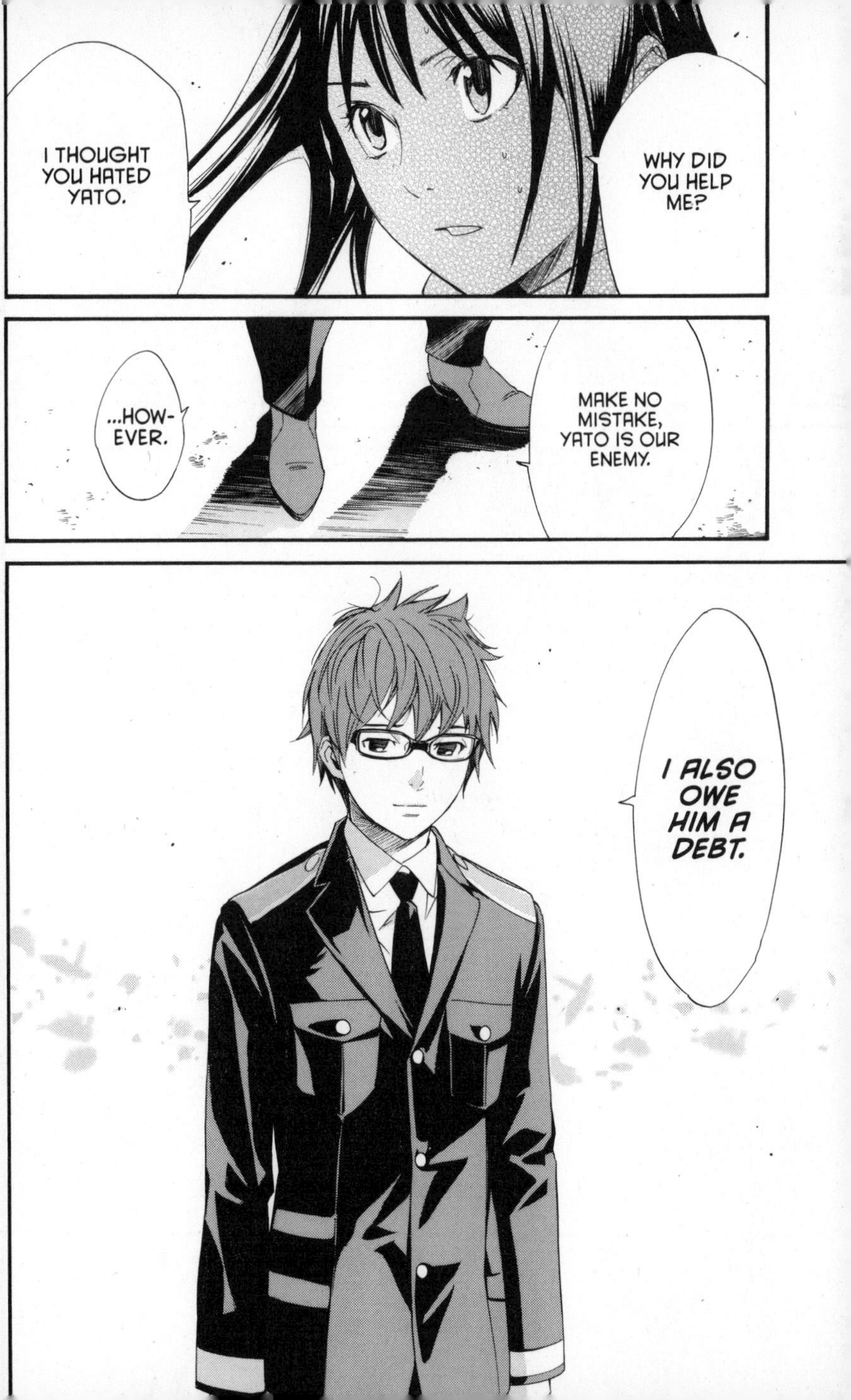
WHY DID YOU HELP ME?
I THOUGHT YOU HATED YATO.
MAKE NO MISTAKE, YATO IS OUR ENEMY.
...HOW-EVER.
I ALSO OWE HIM A DEBT.

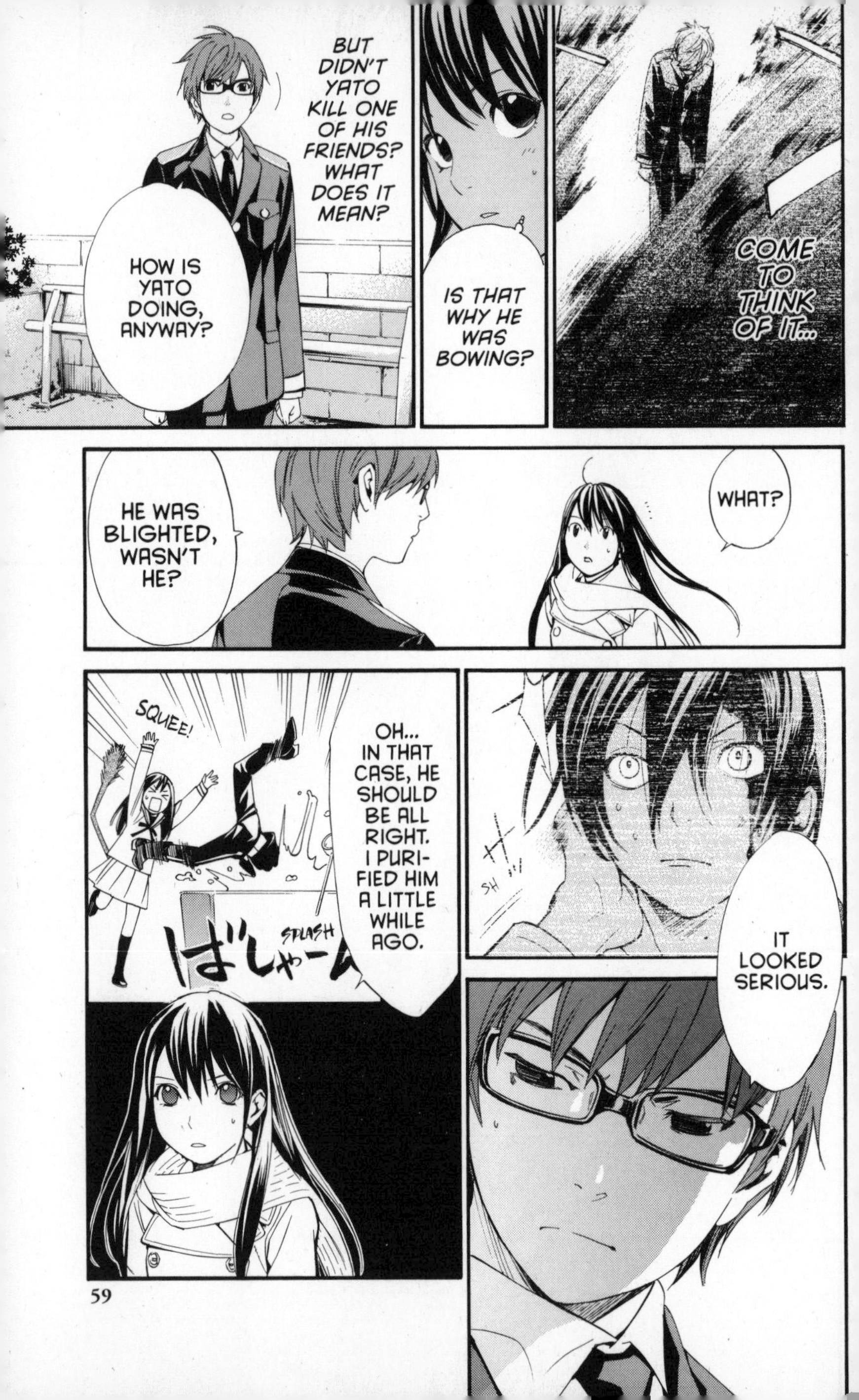
COME TO THINK OF IT...
IS THAT WHY HE WAS BOWING?
BUT DIDN'T YATO KILL ONE OF HIS FRIENDS? WHAT DOES IT MEAN?
HOW IS YATO DOING, ANYWAY?
WHAT?
HE WAS BLIGHTED, WASN'T HE?
SH
IT LOOKED SERIOUS.
OH... IN THAT CASE, HE SHOULD BE ALL RIGHT. I PURIFIED HIM A LITTLE WHILE AGO.
SQUEE!
SPLASH
ばしゃーん

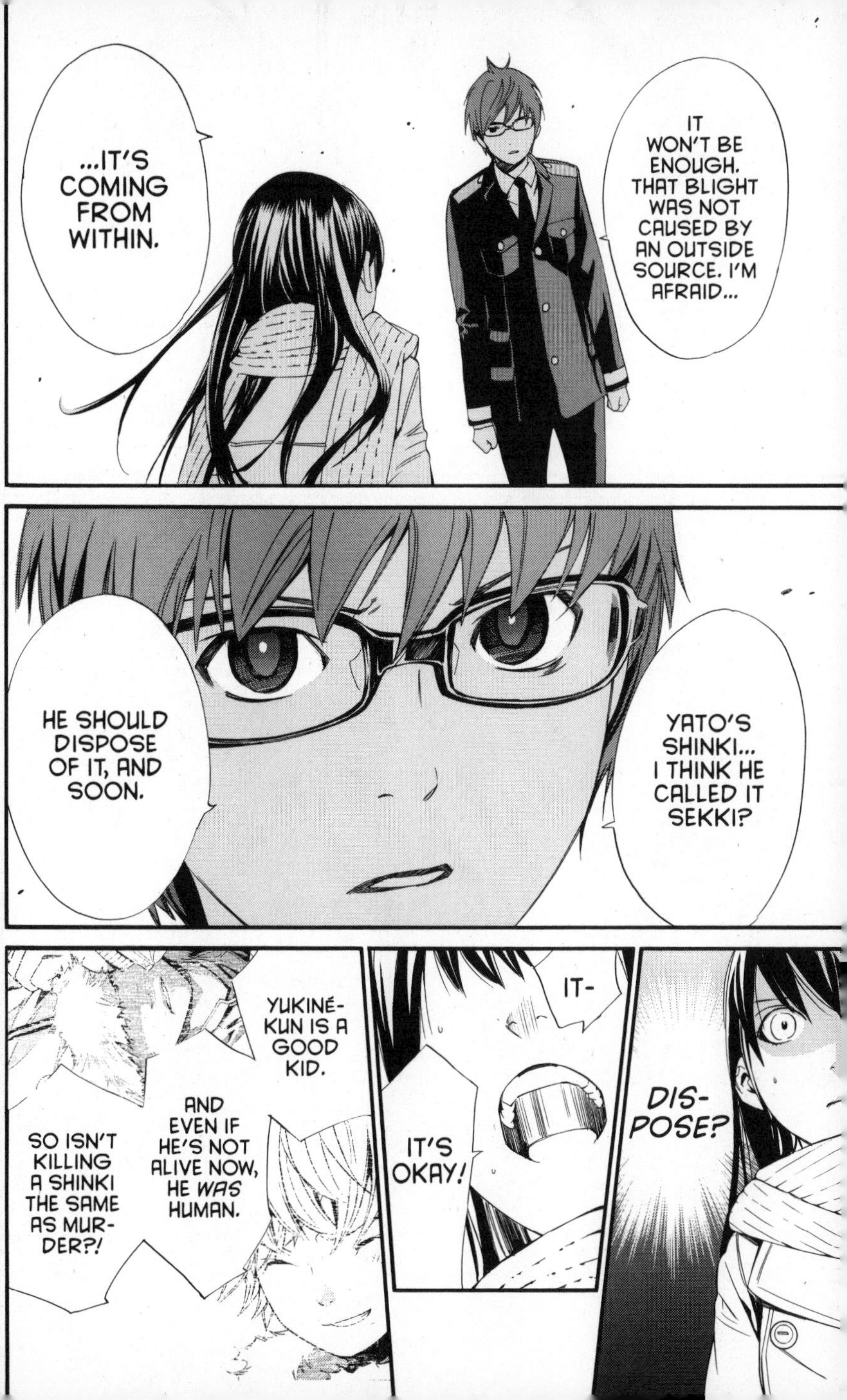
IT WON'T BE ENOUGH. THAT BLIGHT WAS NOT CAUSED BY AN OUTSIDE SOURCE. I'M AFRAID...
...IT'S COMING FROM WITHIN.
YATO'S SHINKI... I THINK HE CALLED IT SEKKI?
HE SHOULD DISPOSE OF IT, AND SOON.
DIS-POSE?
IT-
IT'S OKAY!
YUKINÉ-KUN IS A GOOD KID.
AND EVEN IF HE'S NOT ALIVE NOW, HE *WAS* HUMAN.
SO ISN'T KILLING A SHINKI THE SAME AS MURDER?!

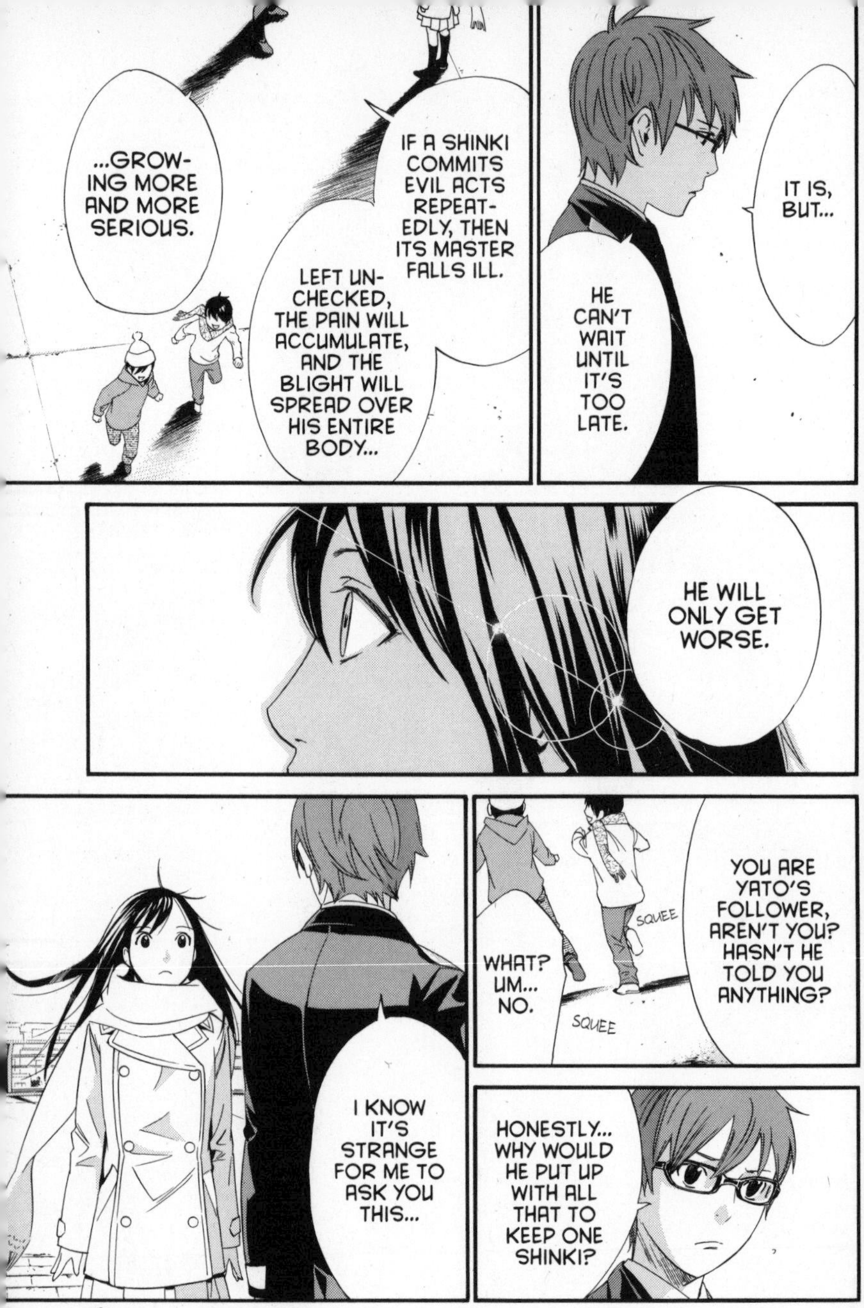
IT IS, BUT...
HE CAN'T WAIT UNTIL IT'S TOO LATE.
IF A SHINKI COMMITS EVIL ACTS REPEAT-EDLY, THEN ITS MASTER FALLS ILL.
LEFT UN-CHECKED, THE PAIN WILL ACCUMULATE, AND THE BLIGHT WILL SPREAD OVER HIS ENTIRE BODY...
...GROW-ING MORE AND MORE SERIOUS.
HE WILL ONLY GET WORSE.
YOU ARE YATO'S FOLLOWER, AREN'T YOU? HASN'T HE TOLD YOU ANYTHING?
SQUEE
WHAT? UM... NO.
SQUEE
HONESTLY... WHY WOULD HE PUT UP WITH ALL THAT TO KEEP ONE SHINKI?
I KNOW IT'S STRANGE FOR ME TO ASK YOU THIS...

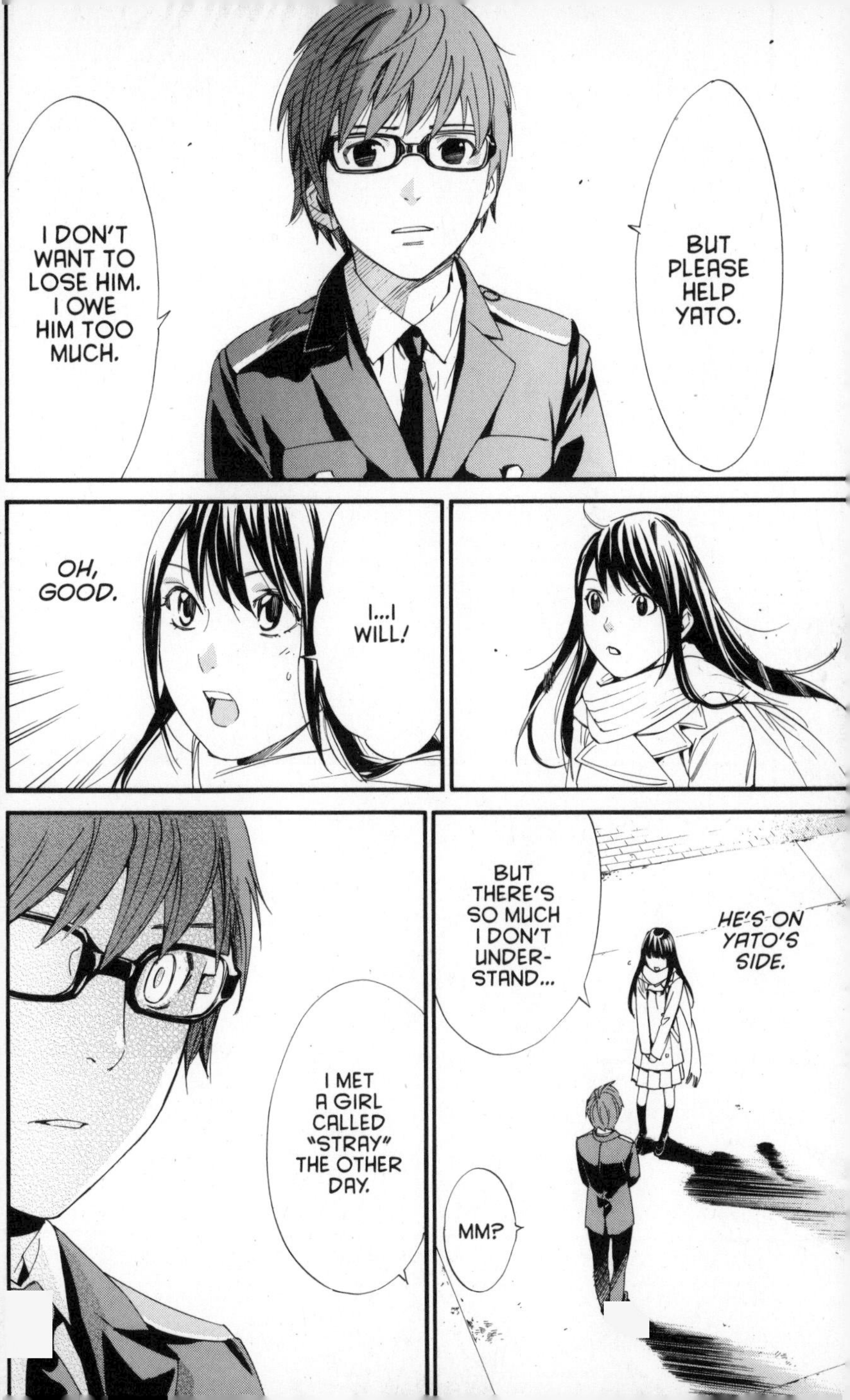
BUT PLEASE HELP YATO.
I DON'T WANT TO LOSE HIM. I OWE HIM TOO MUCH.
I...I WILL!
OH, GOOD.
HE'S ON YATO'S SIDE.
BUT THERE'S SO MUCH I DON'T UNDER-STAND...
MM?
I MET A GIRL CALLED "STRAY" THE OTHER DAY.

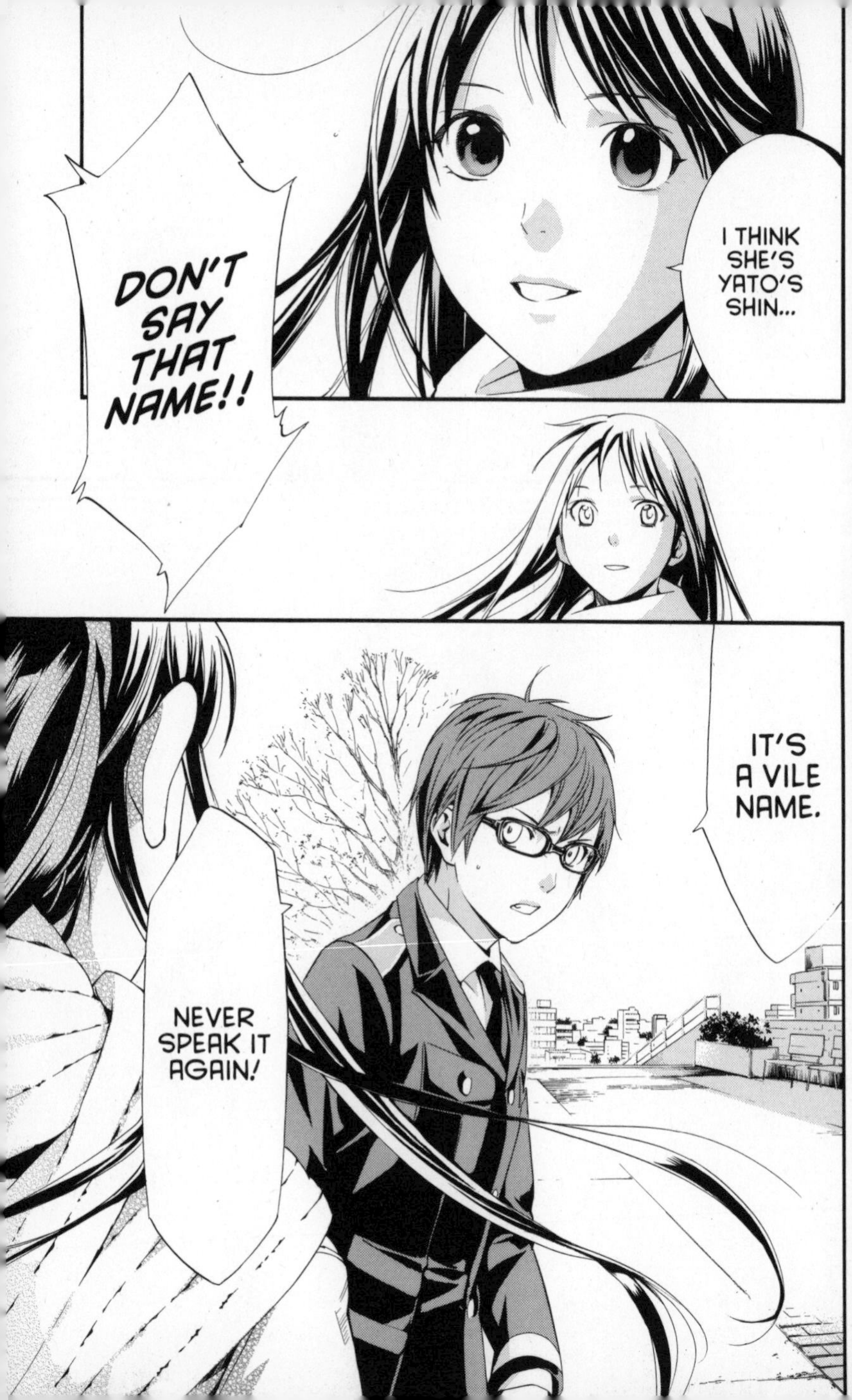
I THINK SHE'S YATO'S SHIN...
DON'T SAY THAT NAME!!
IT'S A VILE NAME.
NEVER SPEAK IT AGAIN!

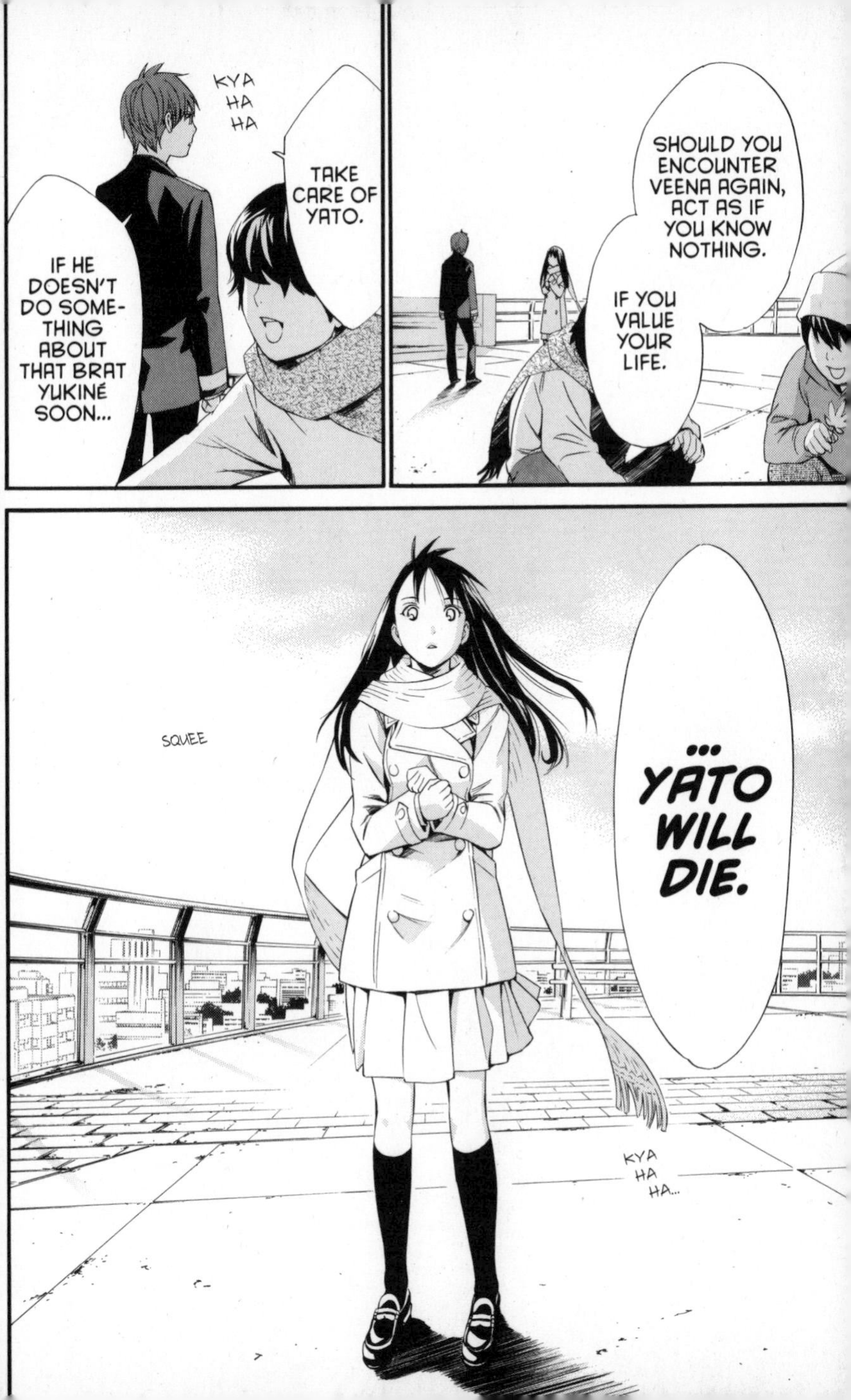
SHOULD YOU ENCOUNTER VEENA AGAIN, ACT AS IF YOU KNOW NOTHING.
IF YOU VALUE YOUR LIFE.
KYA HA HA
TAKE CARE OF YATO.
IF HE DOESN'T DO SOME-THING ABOUT THAT BRAT YUKINÉ SOON...
...YATO WILL DIE.
SQUEE
KYA HA HA...

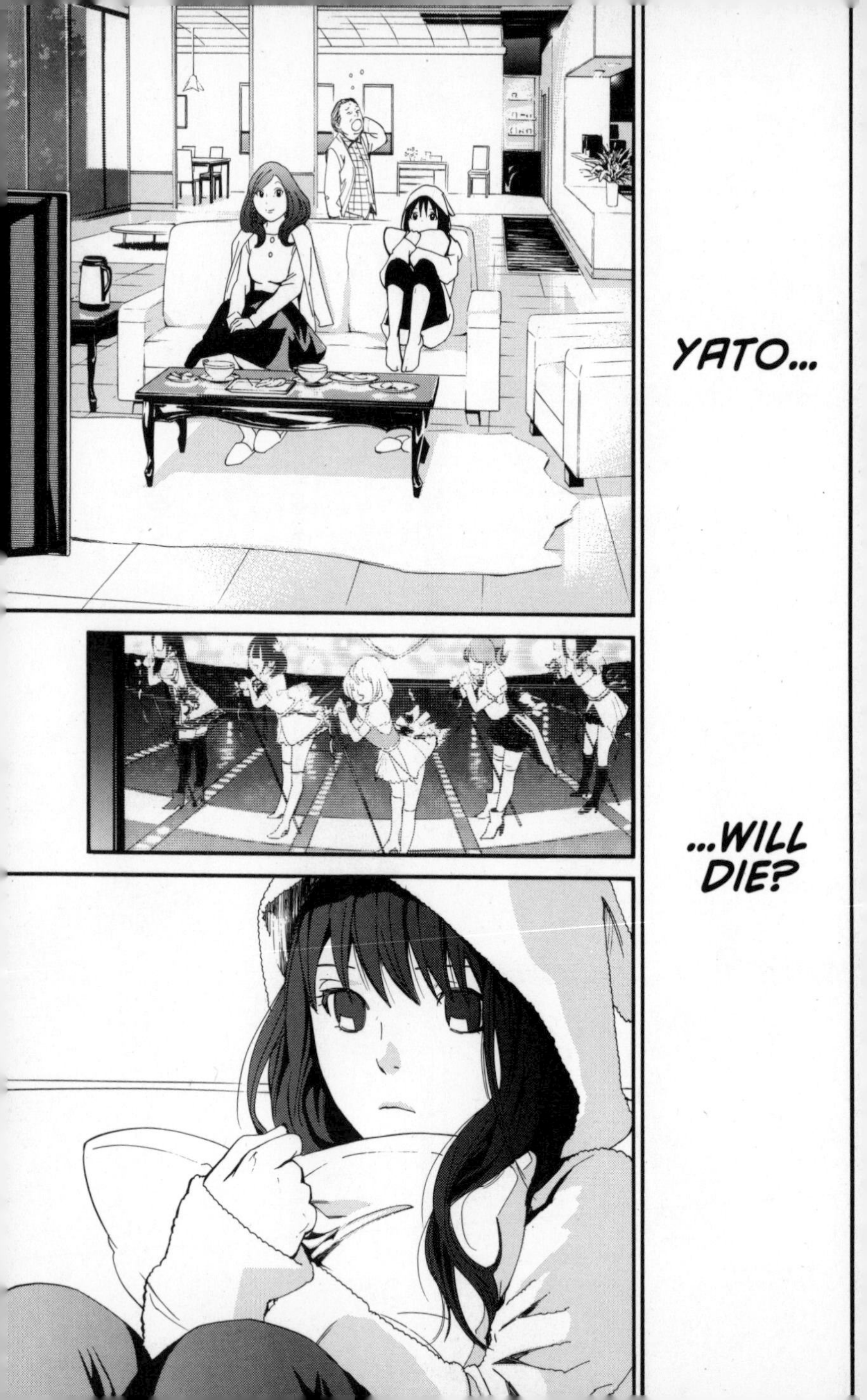
YATO...
...WILL DIE?

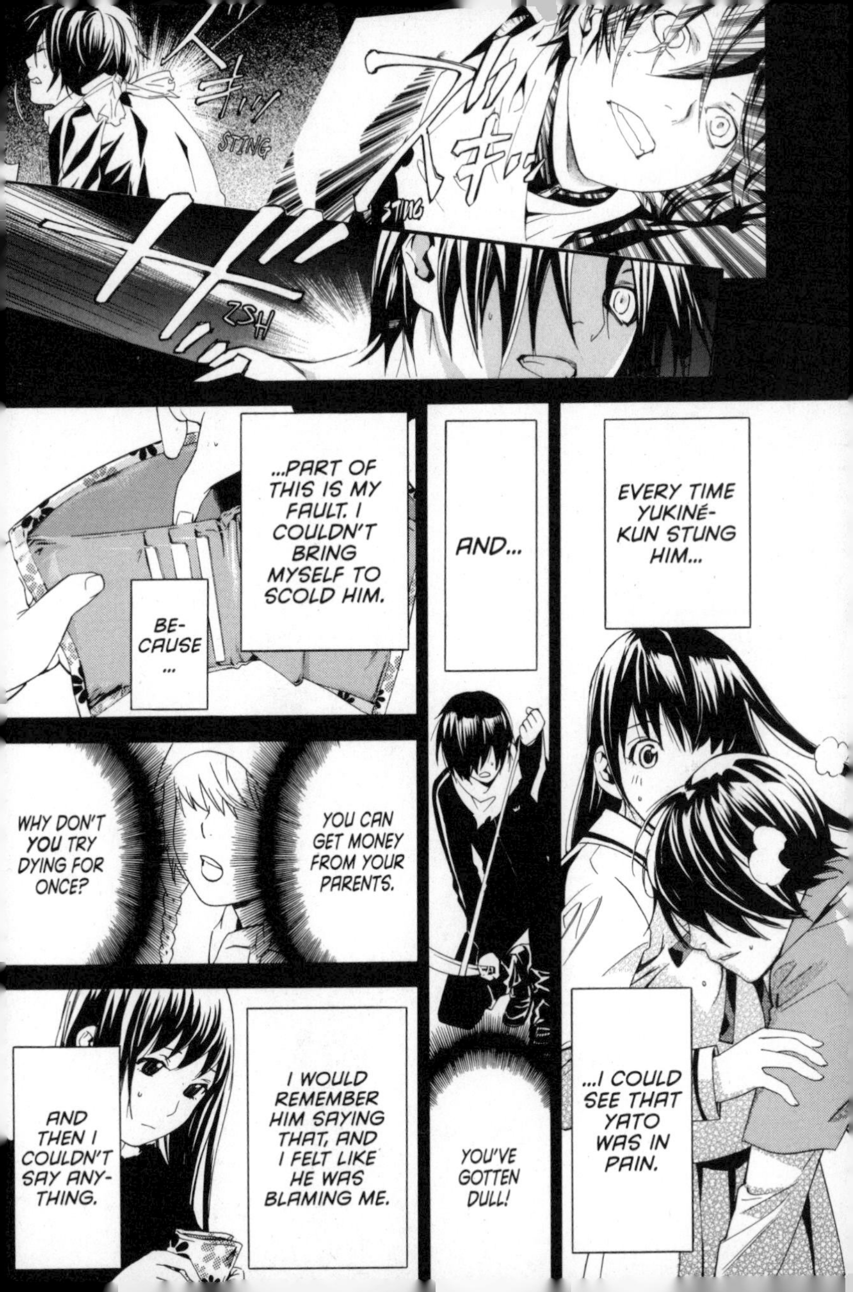
STING
STING
ZSH
EVERY TIME YUKINÉ-KUN STUNG HIM...
...I COULD SEE THAT YATO WAS IN PAIN.
AND...
YOU'VE GOTTEN DULL!
...PART OF THIS IS MY FAULT. I COULDN'T BRING MYSELF TO SCOLD HIM.
BE-CAUSE...
YOU CAN GET MONEY FROM YOUR PARENTS.
WHY DON'T YOU TRY DYING FOR ONCE?
I WOULD REMEMBER HIM SAYING THAT, AND I FELT LIKE HE WAS BLAMING ME.
AND THEN I COULDN'T SAY ANY-THING.

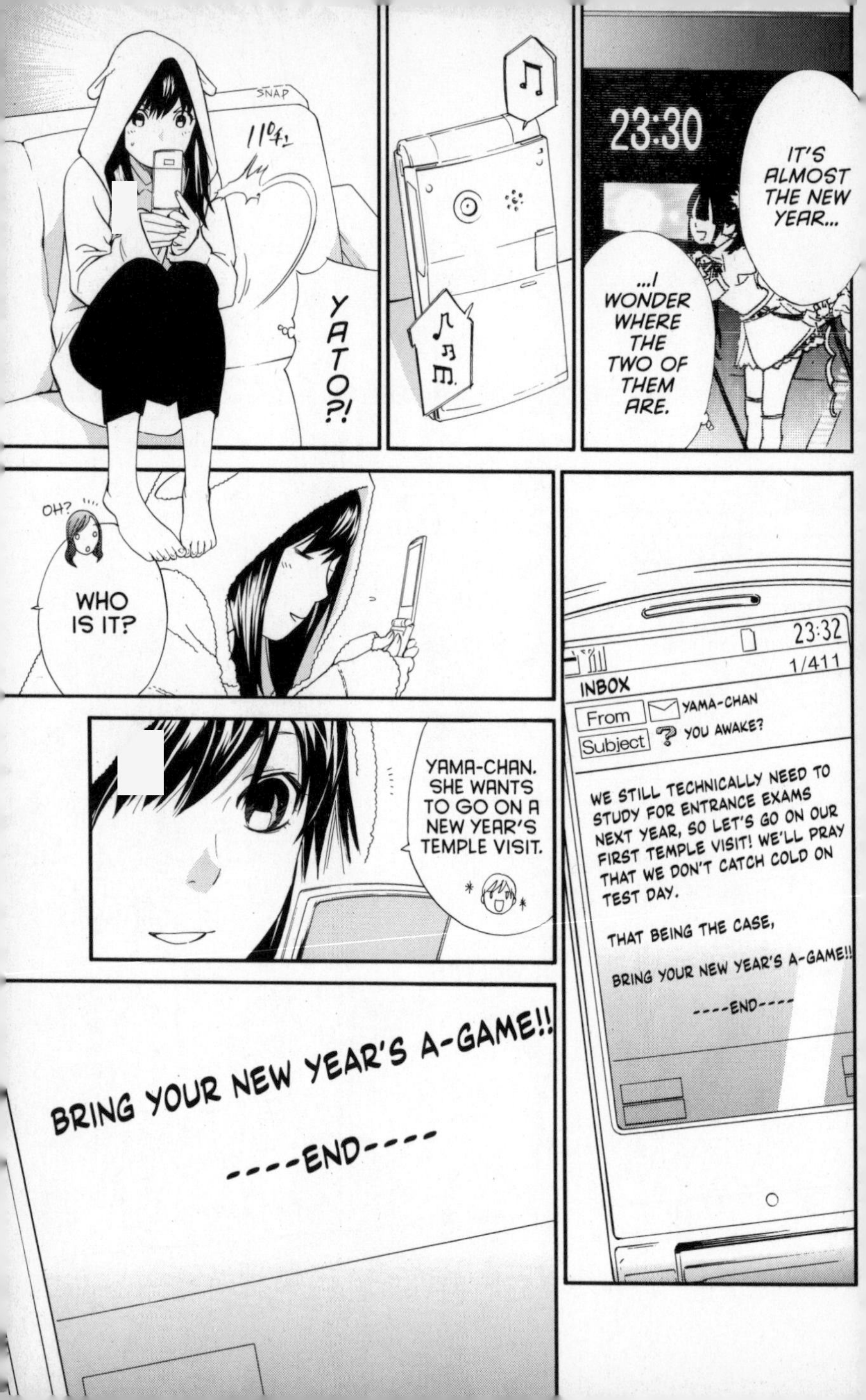
23:30
IT'S ALMOST THE NEW YEAR...
...I WONDER WHERE THE TWO OF THEM ARE.
♫
SNAP
YATO?!
OH?
WHO IS IT?
YAMA-CHAN. SHE WANTS TO GO ON A NEW YEAR'S TEMPLE VISIT.
23:32
1/411
INBOX
From YAMA-CHAN
Subject YOU AWAKE?
WE STILL TECHNICALLY NEED TO STUDY FOR ENTRANCE EXAMS NEXT YEAR, SO LET'S GO ON OUR FIRST TEMPLE VISIT! WE'LL PRAY THAT WE DON'T CATCH COLD ON TEST DAY.
THAT BEING THE CASE,
BRING YOUR NEW YEAR'S A-GAME!!
----END----
BRING YOUR NEW YEAR'S A-GAME!!
----END----

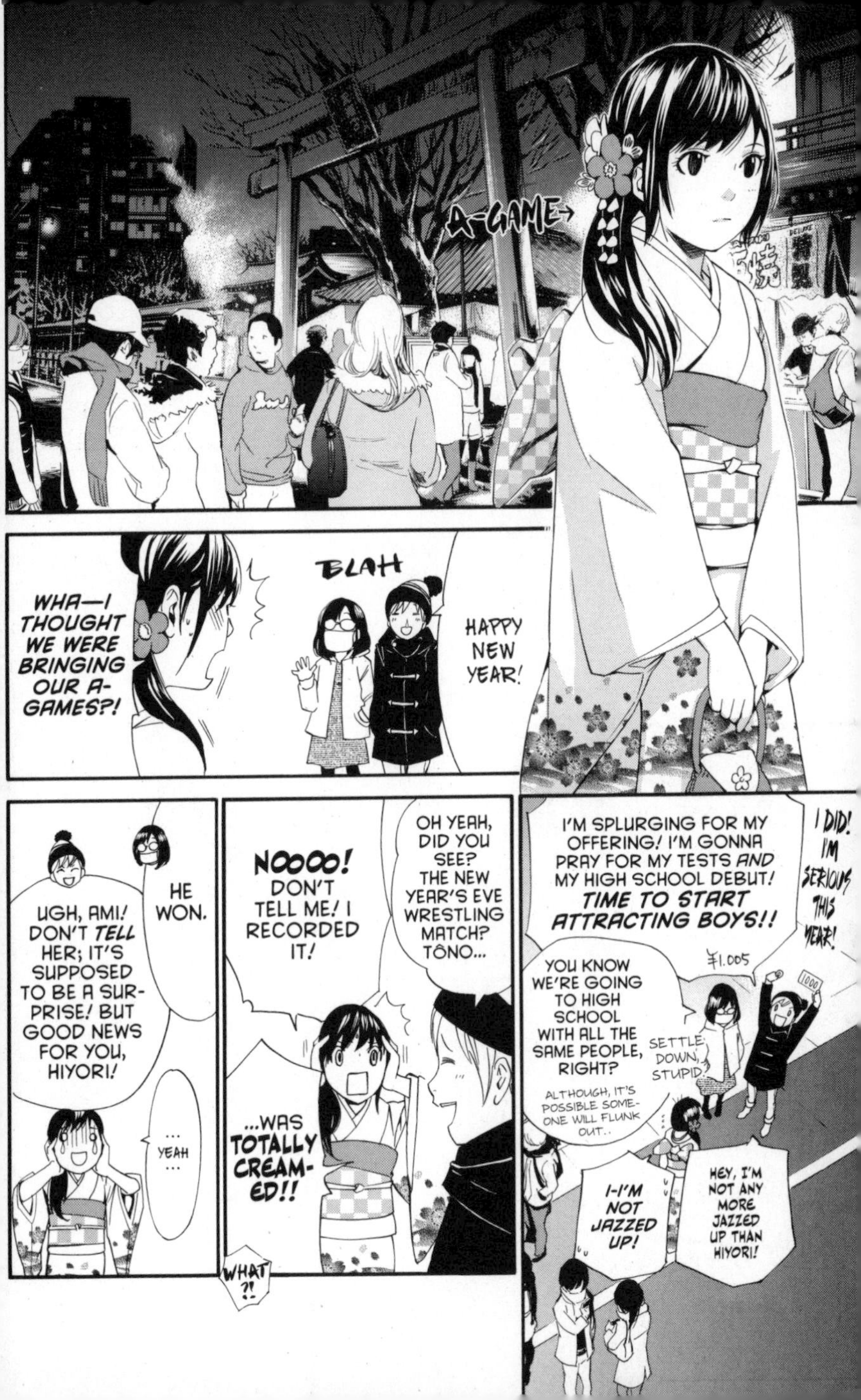
A-GAME→
HAPPY NEW YEAR!
BLAH
WHA—I THOUGHT WE WERE BRINGING OUR A-GAMES?!
I DID! I'M SERIOUS THIS YEAR!
I'M SPLURGING FOR MY OFFERING! I'M GONNA PRAY FOR MY TESTS AND MY HIGH SCHOOL DEBUT! TIME TO START ATTRACTING BOYS!!
¥1.005
1000
YOU KNOW WE'RE GOING TO HIGH SCHOOL WITH ALL THE SAME PEOPLE, RIGHT?
SETTLE DOWN, STUPID.
ALTHOUGH, IT'S POSSIBLE SOMEONE WILL FLUNK OUT..
HEY, I'M NOT ANY MORE JAZZED UP THAN HIYORI!
I-I'M NOT JAZZED UP!
OH YEAH, DID YOU SEE? THE NEW YEAR'S EVE WRESTLING MATCH? TÔNO...
NOOOO! DON'T TELL ME! I RECORDED IT!
...WAS TOTALLY CREAMED!!
WHAT?!
HE WON.
UGH, AMI! DON'T TELL HER; IT'S SUPPOSED TO BE A SURPRISE! BUT GOOD NEWS FOR YOU, HIYORI!
... YEAH ...

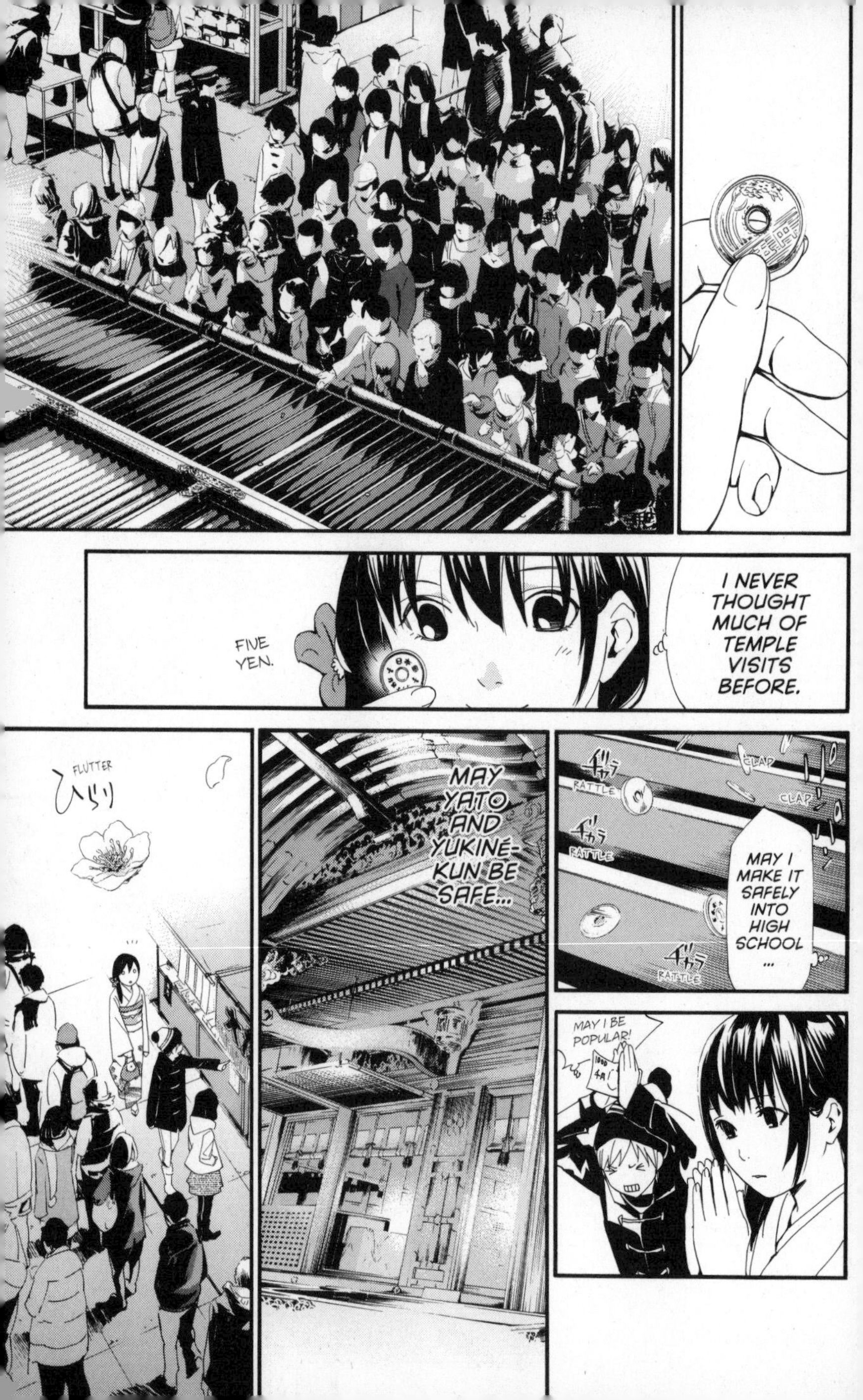
I NEVER THOUGHT MUCH OF TEMPLE VISITS BEFORE.
FIVE YEN.
CLAP
CLAP
RATTLE
RATTLE
MAY I MAKE IT SAFELY INTO HIGH SCHOOL ...
RATTLE
MAY I BE POPULAR!
MAY YATO AND YUKINÉ-KUN BE SAFE...
FLUTTER
ひらり

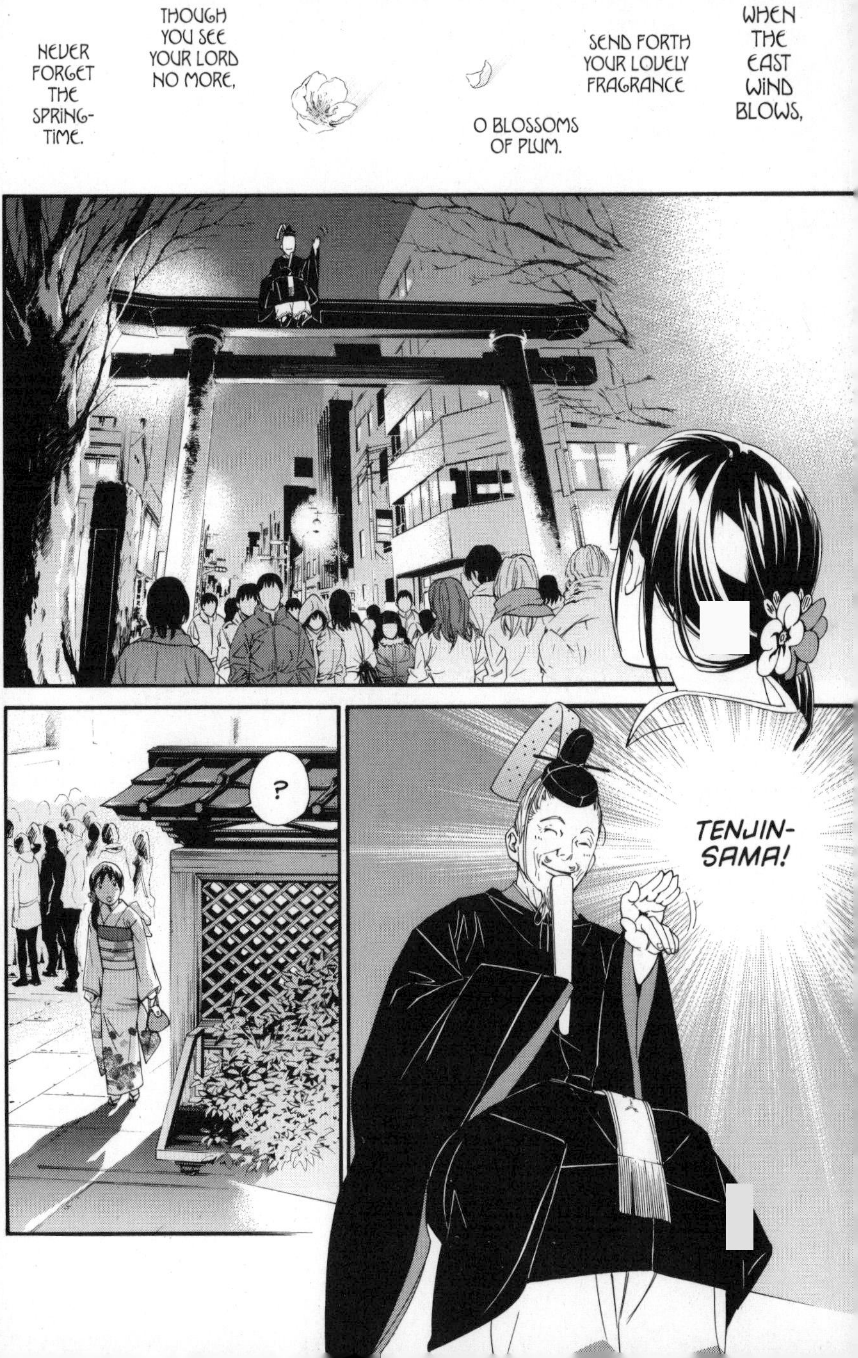
WHEN THE EAST WIND BLOWS,
SEND FORTH YOUR LOVELY FRAGRANCE
O BLOSSOMS OF PLUM.
THOUGH YOU SEE YOUR LORD NO MORE,
NEVER FORGET THE SPRING-TIME.
TENJIN-SAMA!
?

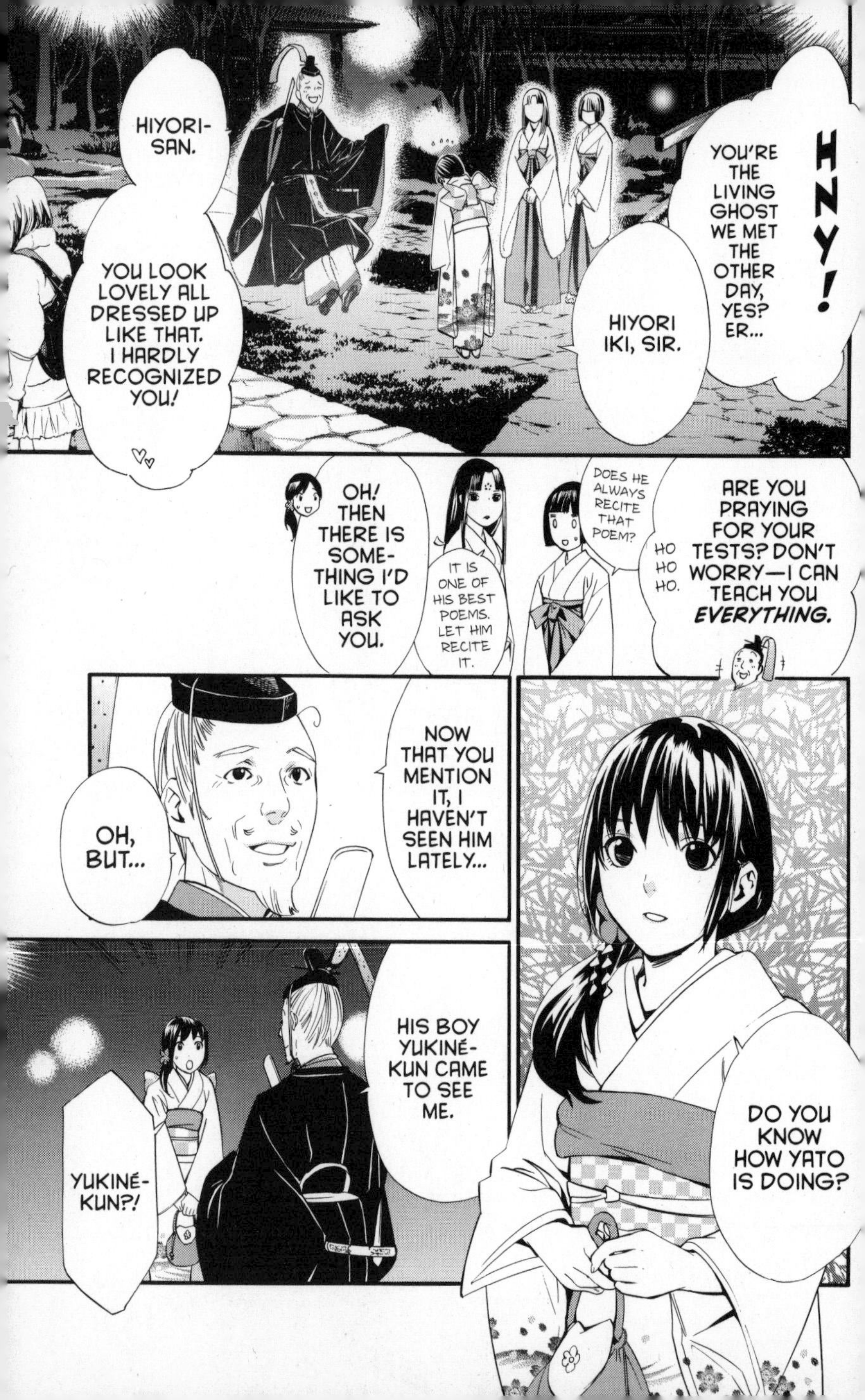
HNY!
YOU'RE THE LIVING GHOST WE MET THE OTHER DAY, YES? ER...
HIYORI IKI, SIR.
HIYORI-SAN.
YOU LOOK LOVELY ALL DRESSED UP LIKE THAT. I HARDLY RECOGNIZED YOU!
ARE YOU PRAYING FOR YOUR TESTS? DON'T WORRY—I CAN TEACH YOU *EVERYTHING.*
HO HO HO.
DOES HE ALWAYS RECITE THAT POEM?
IT IS ONE OF HIS BEST POEMS. LET HIM RECITE IT.
OH! THEN THERE IS SOMETHING I'D LIKE TO ASK YOU.
DO YOU KNOW HOW YATO IS DOING?
NOW THAT YOU MENTION IT, I HAVEN'T SEEN HIM LATELY...
OH, BUT...
HIS BOY YUKINÉ-KUN CAME TO SEE ME.
YUKINÉ-KUN?!

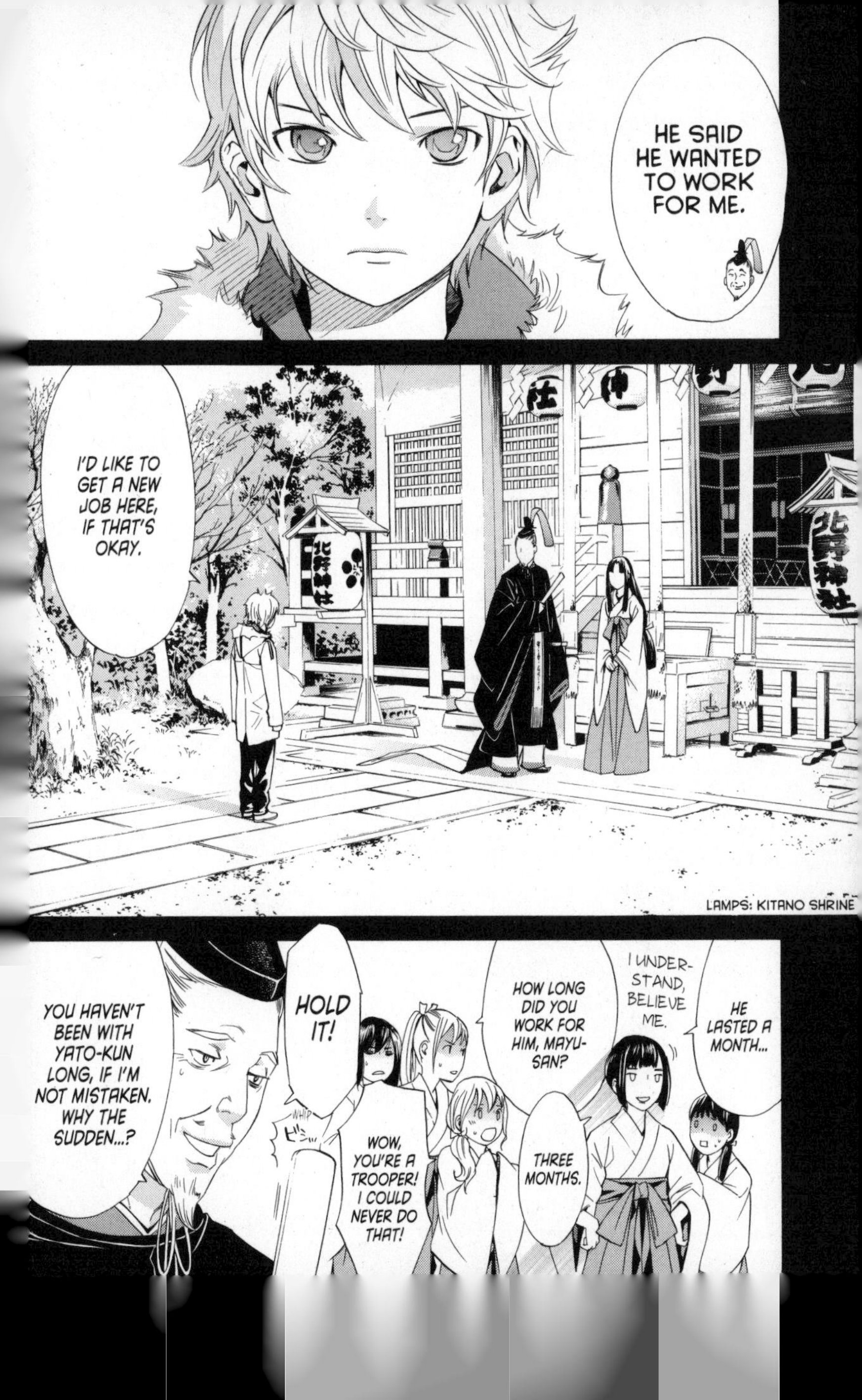
HE SAID HE WANTED TO WORK FOR ME.
I'D LIKE TO GET A NEW JOB HERE, IF THAT'S OKAY.
LAMPS: KITANO SHRINE
HE LASTED A MONTH...
I UNDER-STAND, BELIEVE ME.
HOW LONG DID YOU WORK FOR HIM, MAYU-SAN?
THREE MONTHS.
WOW, YOU'RE A TROOPER! I COULD NEVER DO THAT!
HOLD IT!
WHIP
YOU HAVEN'T BEEN WITH YATO-KUN LONG, IF I'M NOT MISTAKEN. WHY THE SUDDEN...?

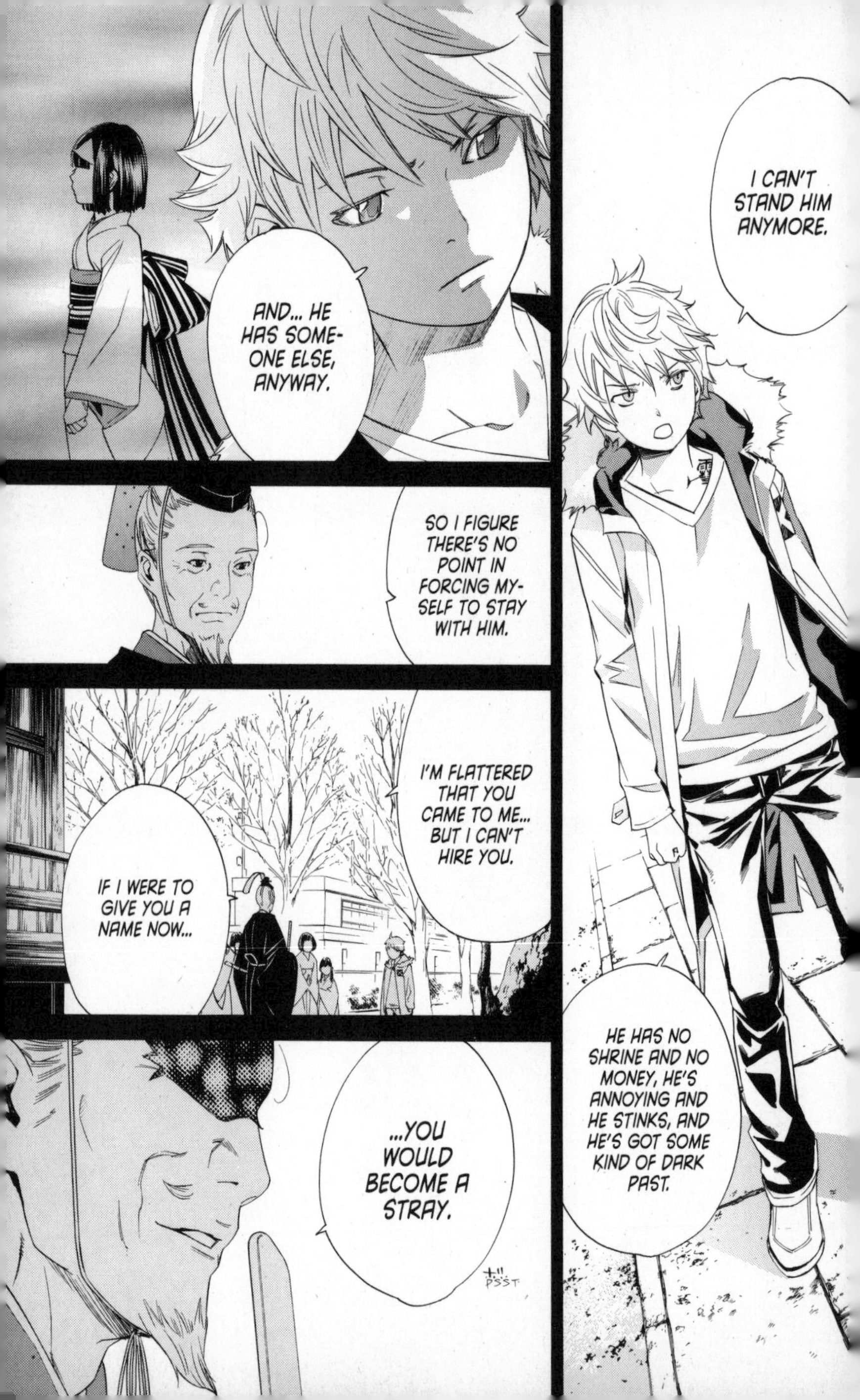
I CAN'T STAND HIM ANYMORE.
HE HAS NO SHRINE AND NO MONEY, HE'S ANNOYING AND HE STINKS, AND HE'S GOT SOME KIND OF DARK PAST.
AND... HE HAS SOME-ONE ELSE, ANYWAY.
SO I FIGURE THERE'S NO POINT IN FORCING MY-SELF TO STAY WITH HIM.
I'M FLATTERED THAT YOU CAME TO ME... BUT I CAN'T HIRE YOU.
IF I WERE TO GIVE YOU A NAME NOW...
...YOU WOULD BECOME A STRAY.
PSST

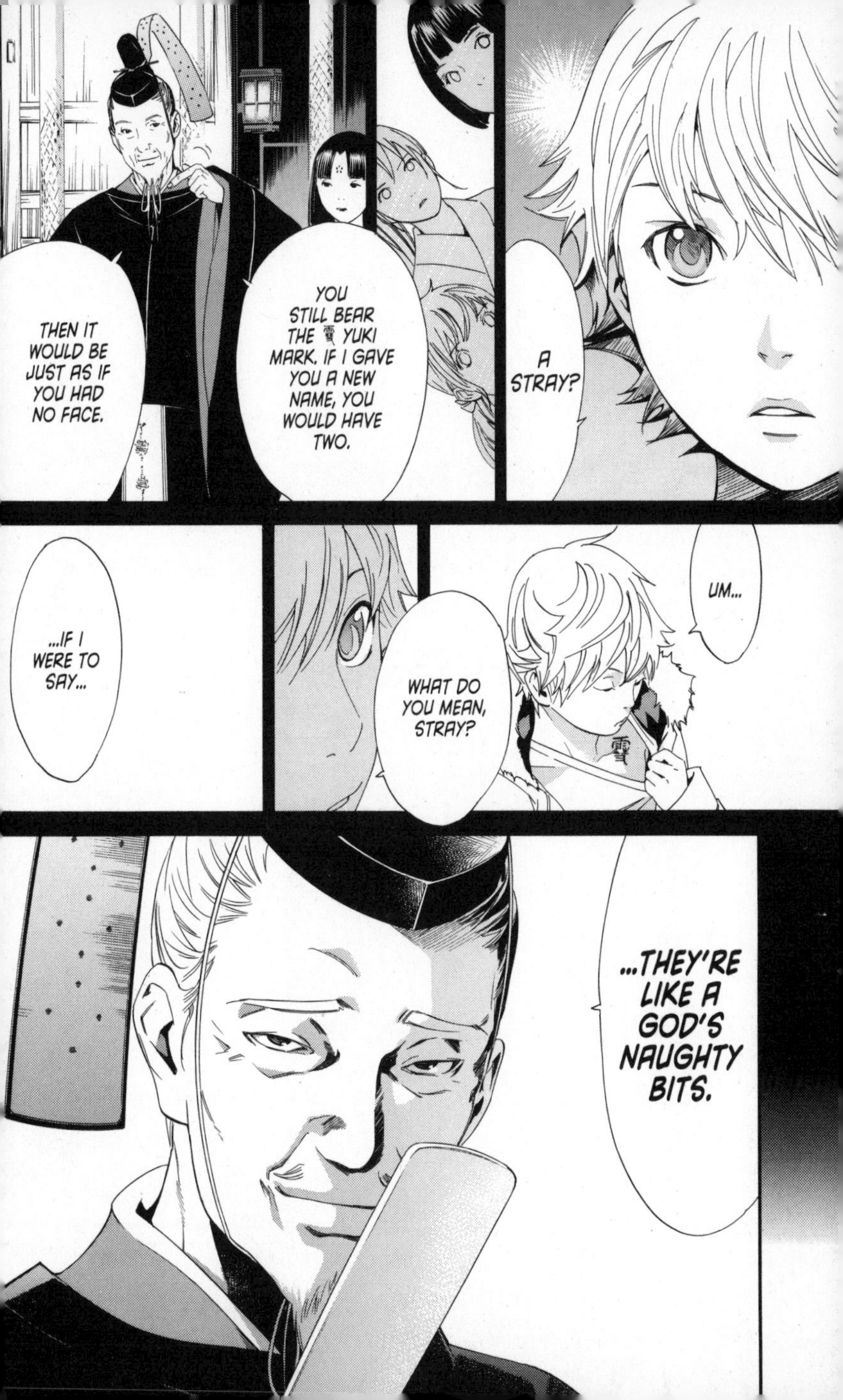
A STRAY?
YOU STILL BEAR THE 雪 YUKI MARK. IF I GAVE YOU A NEW NAME, YOU WOULD HAVE TWO.
THEN IT WOULD BE JUST AS IF YOU HAD NO FACE.
UM...
WHAT DO YOU MEAN, STRAY?
...IF I WERE TO SAY...
...THEY'RE LIKE A GOD'S NAUGHTY BITS.

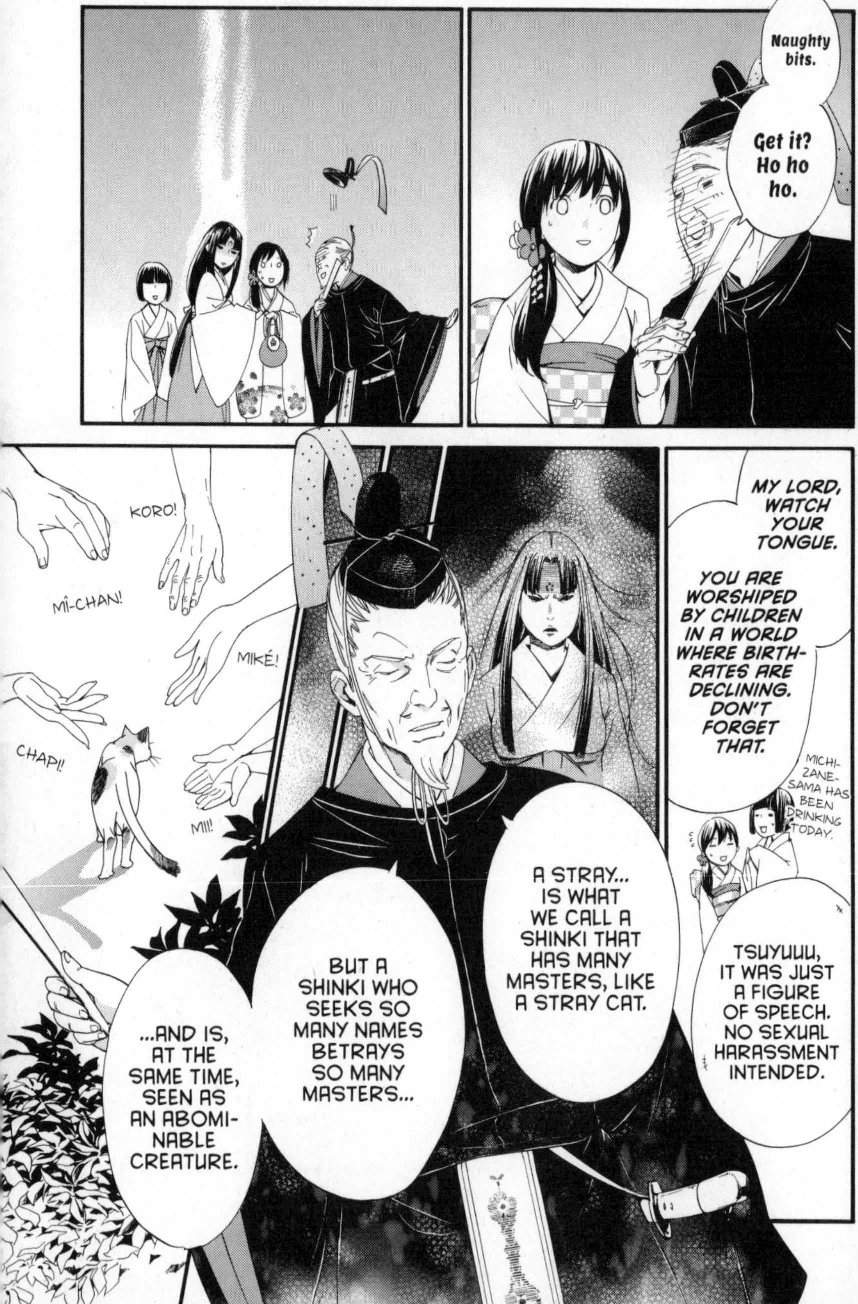
Naughty bits.
Get it? Ho ho ho.
MY LORD, WATCH YOUR TONGUE.
YOU ARE WORSHIPED BY CHILDREN IN A WORLD WHERE BIRTH-RATES ARE DECLINING. DON'T FORGET THAT.
MICHI-ZANE-SAMA HAS BEEN DRINKING TODAY.
TSUYUUU, IT WAS JUST A FIGURE OF SPEECH. NO SEXUAL HARASSMENT INTENDED.
A STRAY... IS WHAT WE CALL A SHINKI THAT HAS MANY MASTERS, LIKE A STRAY CAT.
BUT A SHINKI WHO SEEKS SO MANY NAMES BETRAYS SO MANY MASTERS...
...AND IS, AT THE SAME TIME, SEEN AS AN ABOMI-NABLE CREATURE.
KORO!
MÎ-CHAN!
MIKÉ!
CHAP!!
MII!

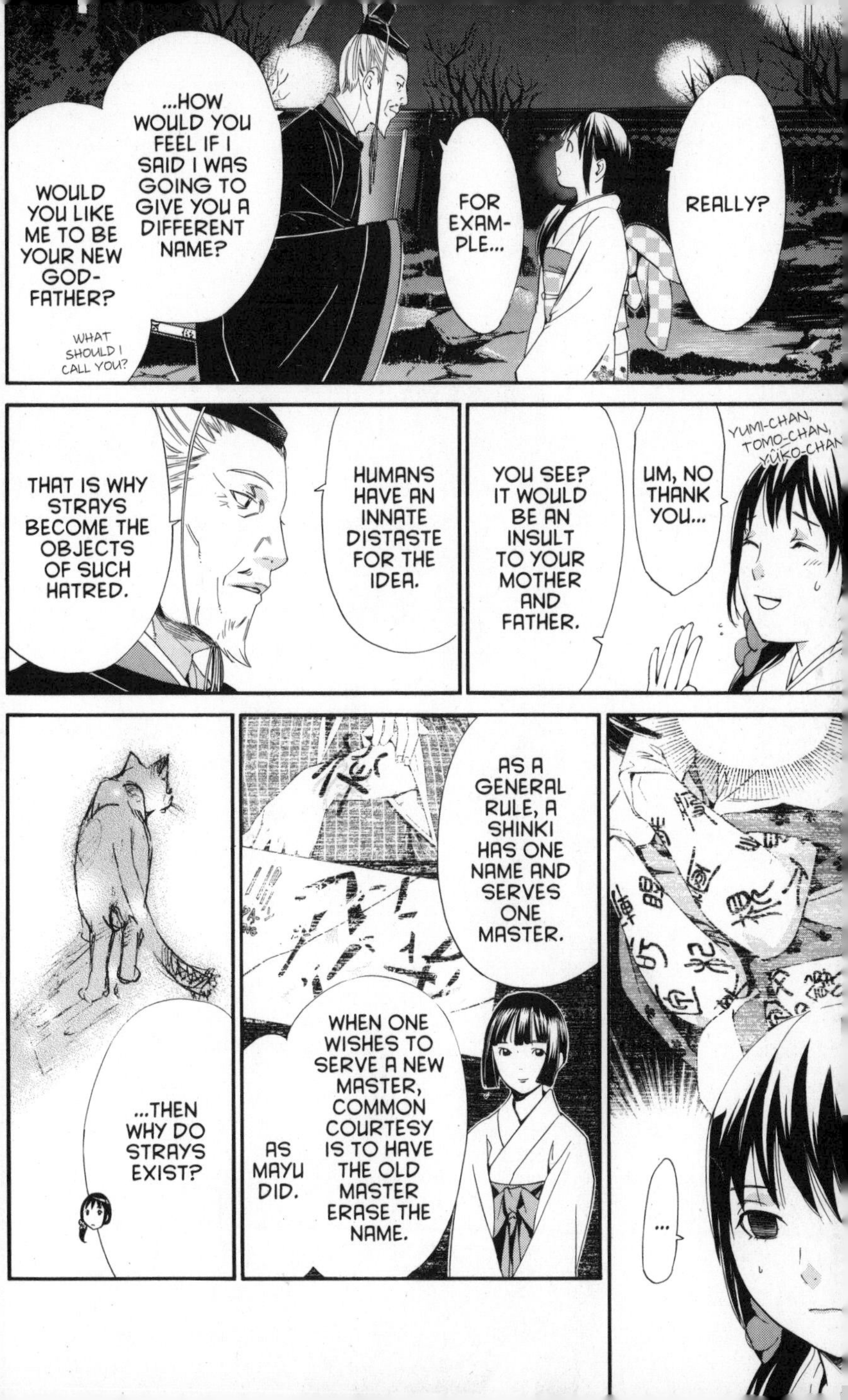
REALLY?
FOR EXAMPLE...
...HOW WOULD YOU FEEL IF I SAID I WAS GOING TO GIVE YOU A DIFFERENT NAME?
WOULD YOU LIKE ME TO BE YOUR NEW GODFATHER?
WHAT SHOULD I CALL YOU?
YUMI-CHAN, TOMO-CHAN, YÛKO-CHAN
UM, NO THANK YOU...
YOU SEE? IT WOULD BE AN INSULT TO YOUR MOTHER AND FATHER.
HUMANS HAVE AN INNATE DISTASTE FOR THE IDEA.
THAT IS WHY STRAYS BECOME THE OBJECTS OF SUCH HATRED.
...
AS A GENERAL RULE, A SHINKI HAS ONE NAME AND SERVES ONE MASTER.
WHEN ONE WISHES TO SERVE A NEW MASTER, COMMON COURTESY IS TO HAVE THE OLD MASTER ERASE THE NAME.
AS MAYU DID.
...THEN WHY DO STRAYS EXIST?

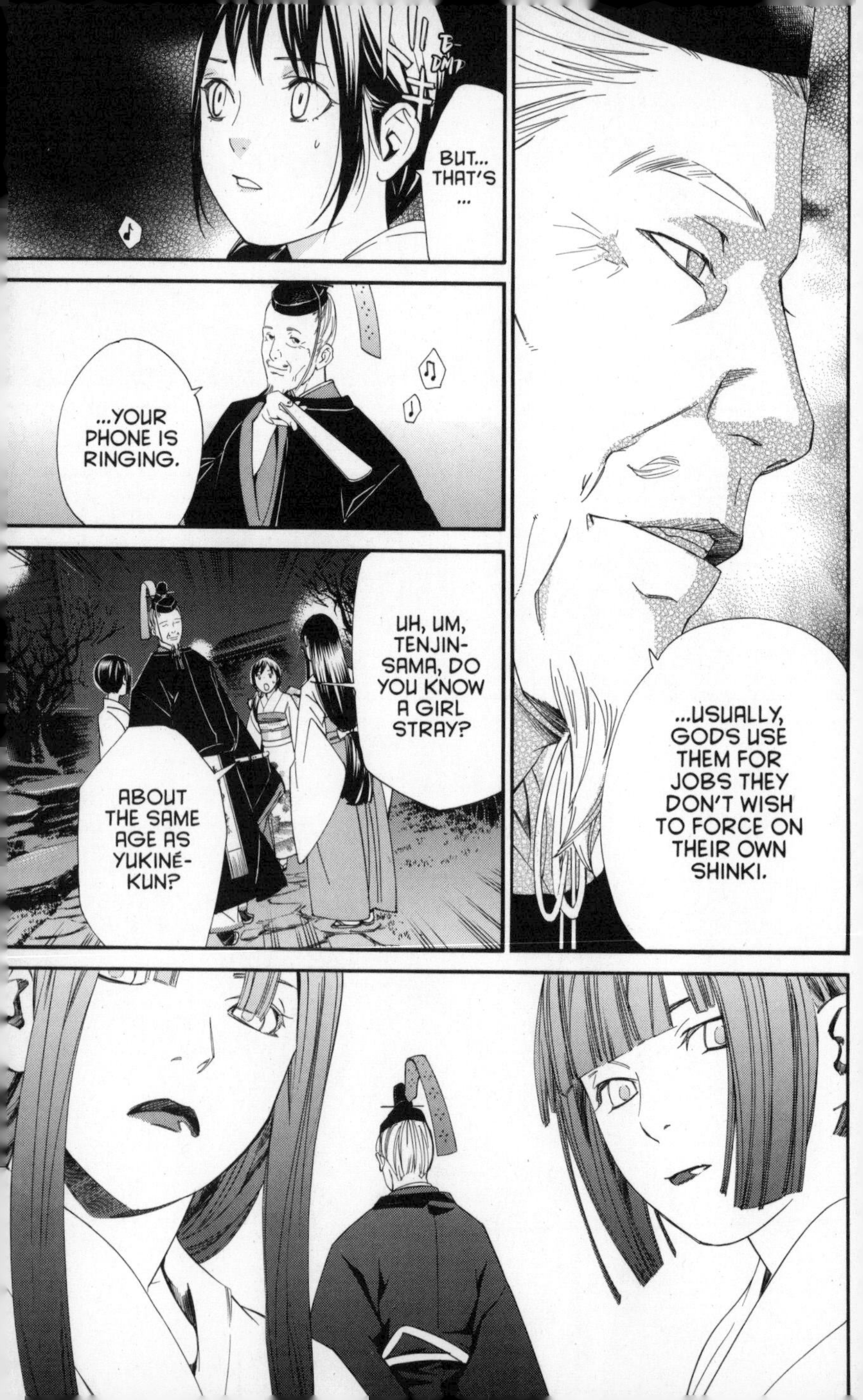
...USUALLY, GODS USE THEM FOR JOBS THEY DON'T WISH TO FORCE ON THEIR OWN SHINKI.
B-DMP
BUT... THAT'S ...
...YOUR PHONE IS RINGING.
UH, UM, TENJIN-SAMA, DO YOU KNOW A GIRL STRAY?
ABOUT THE SAME AGE AS YUKINÉ-KUN?

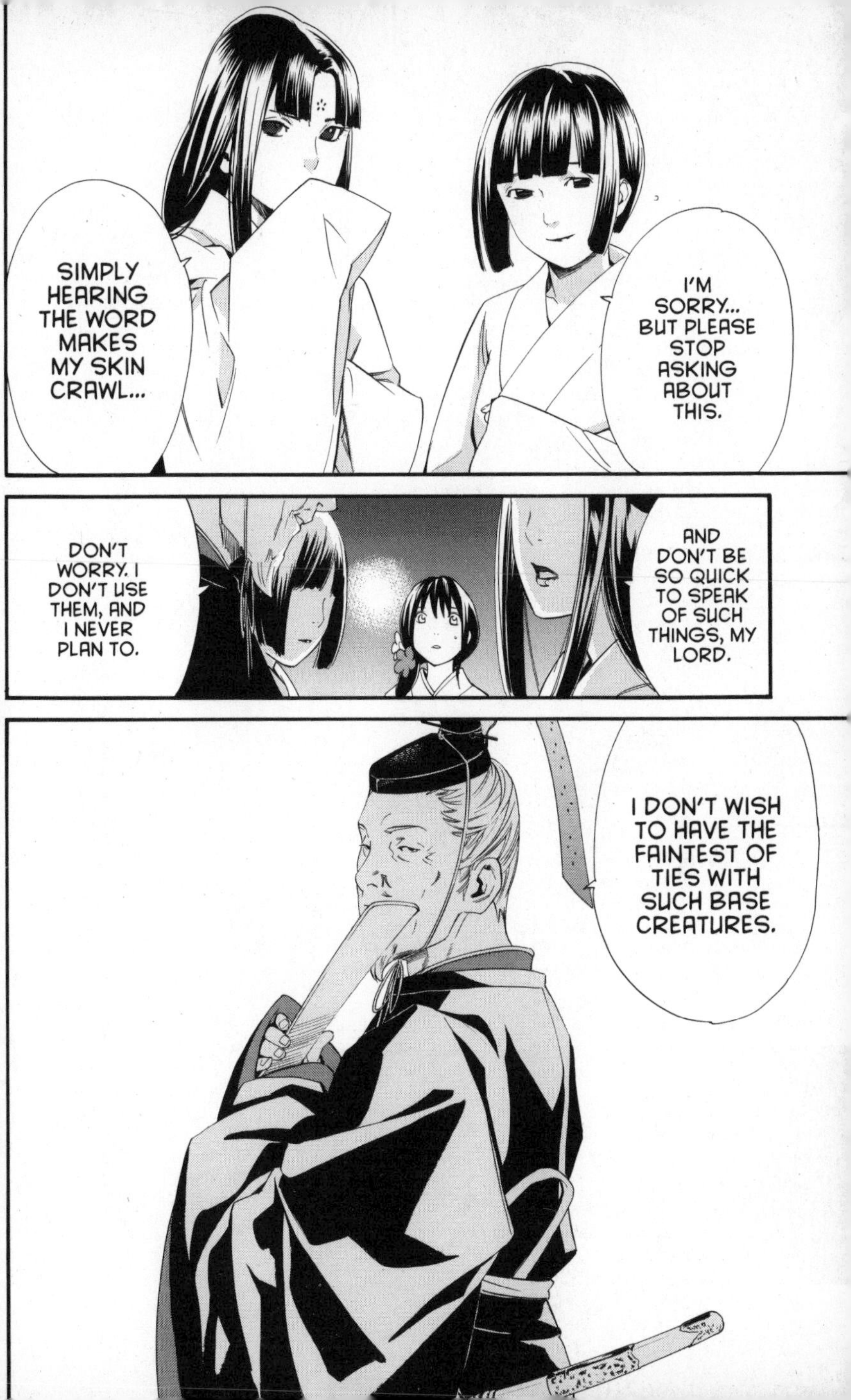
I'M SORRY... BUT PLEASE STOP ASKING ABOUT THIS.
SIMPLY HEARING THE WORD MAKES MY SKIN CRAWL...
AND DON'T BE SO QUICK TO SPEAK OF SUCH THINGS, MY LORD.
DON'T WORRY. I DON'T USE THEM, AND I NEVER PLAN TO.
I DON'T WISH TO HAVE THE FAINTEST OF TIES WITH SUCH BASE CREATURES.

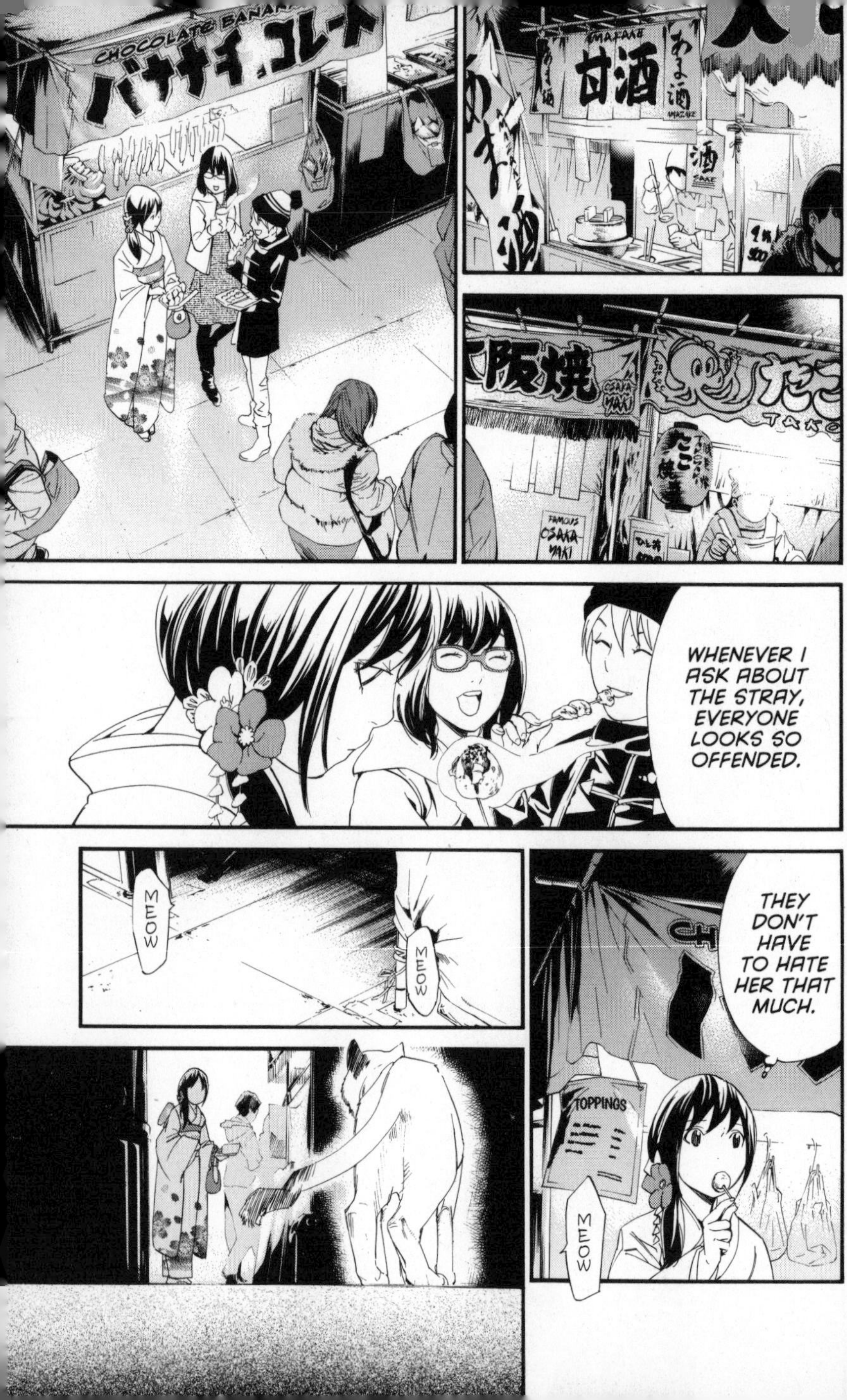

甘酒
AMAZAKE
酒
SAKE
大阪焼
OSAKA YAKI
FAMOUS OSAKA YAKI
WHENEVER I ASK ABOUT THE STRAY, EVERYONE LOOKS SO OFFENDED.
THEY DON'T HAVE TO HATE HER THAT MUCH.
TOPPINGS
MEOW
MEOW
MEOW

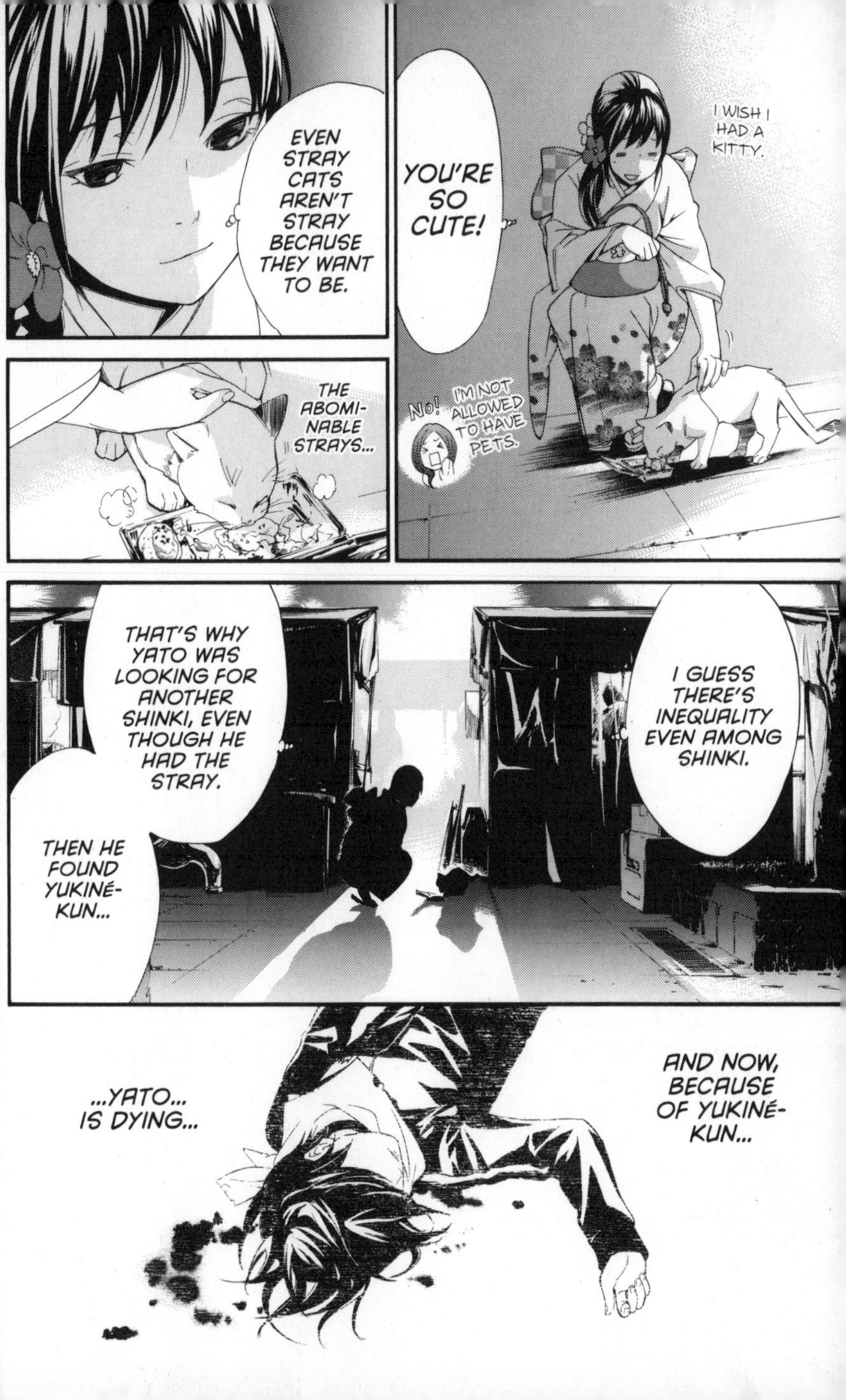
I WISH I HAD A KITTY.
YOU'RE SO CUTE!
NO! I'M NOT ALLOWED TO HAVE PETS.
EVEN STRAY CATS AREN'T STRAY BECAUSE THEY WANT TO BE.
THE ABOMINABLE STRAYS...
I GUESS THERE'S INEQUALITY EVEN AMONG SHINKI.
THAT'S WHY YATO WAS LOOKING FOR ANOTHER SHINKI, EVEN THOUGH HE HAD THE STRAY.
THEN HE FOUND YUKINÉ-KUN...
AND NOW, BECAUSE OF YUKINÉ-KUN...
...YATO... IS DYING...

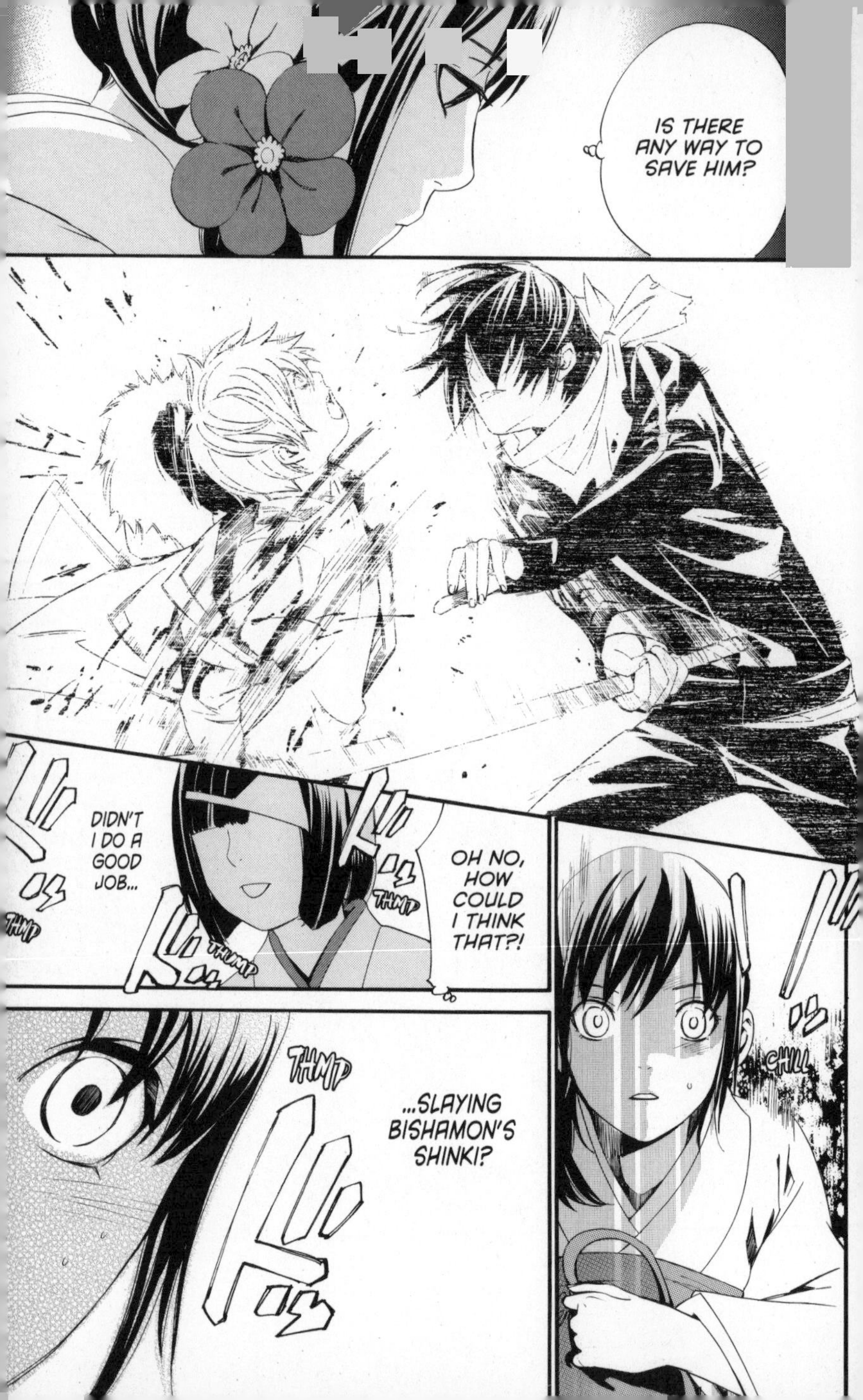
IS THERE ANY WAY TO SAVE HIM?
CHILL
OH NO, HOW COULD I THINK THAT?!
THMP
DIDN'T I DO A GOOD JOB...
THUMP
THMP
THMP
...SLAYING BISHAMON'S SHINKI?

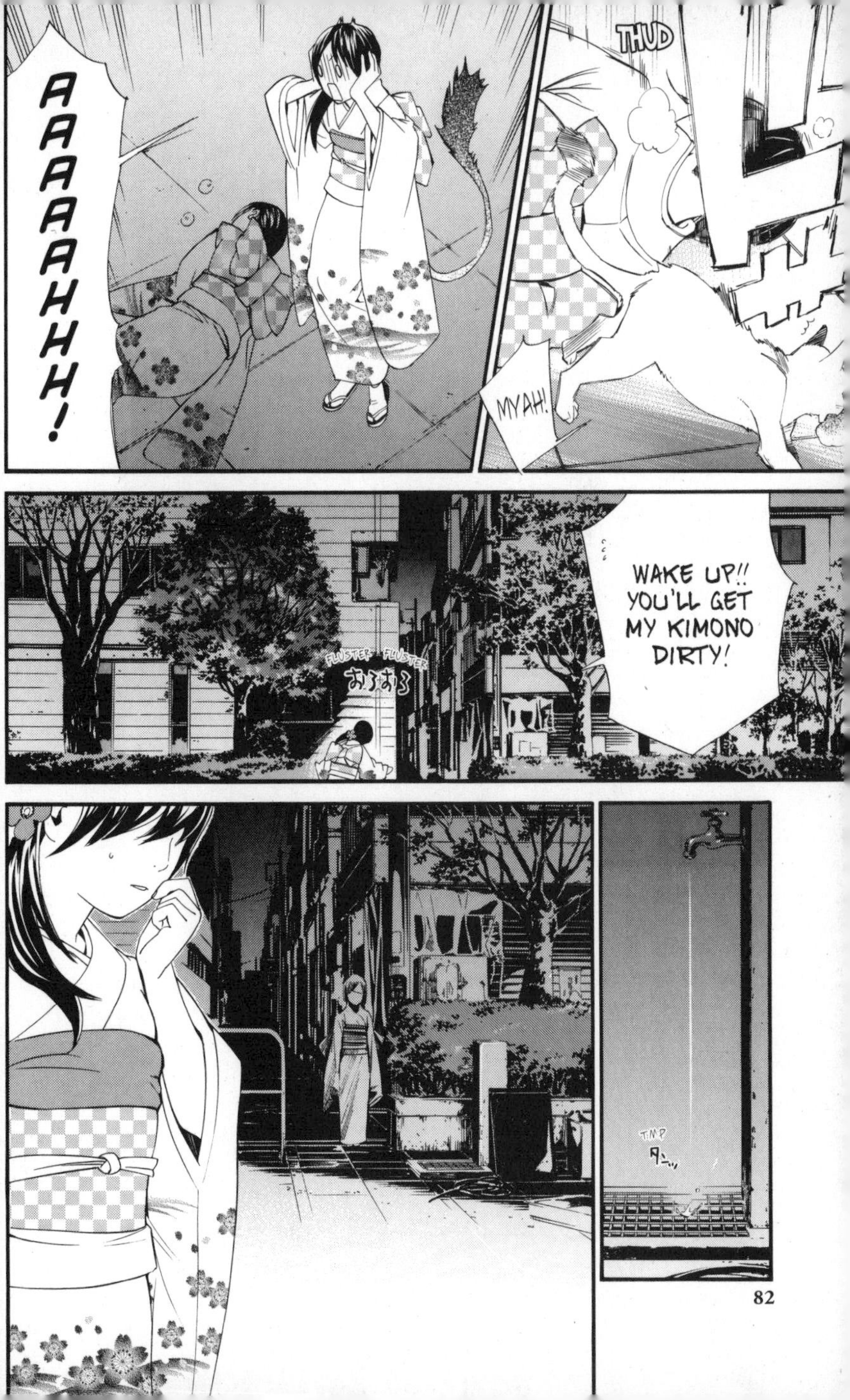
THUD
MYAH!
AAAAAHHH!
WAKE UP!! YOU'LL GET MY KIMONO DIRTY!
FLUSTER FLUSTER
おろおろ
TMP
タン…

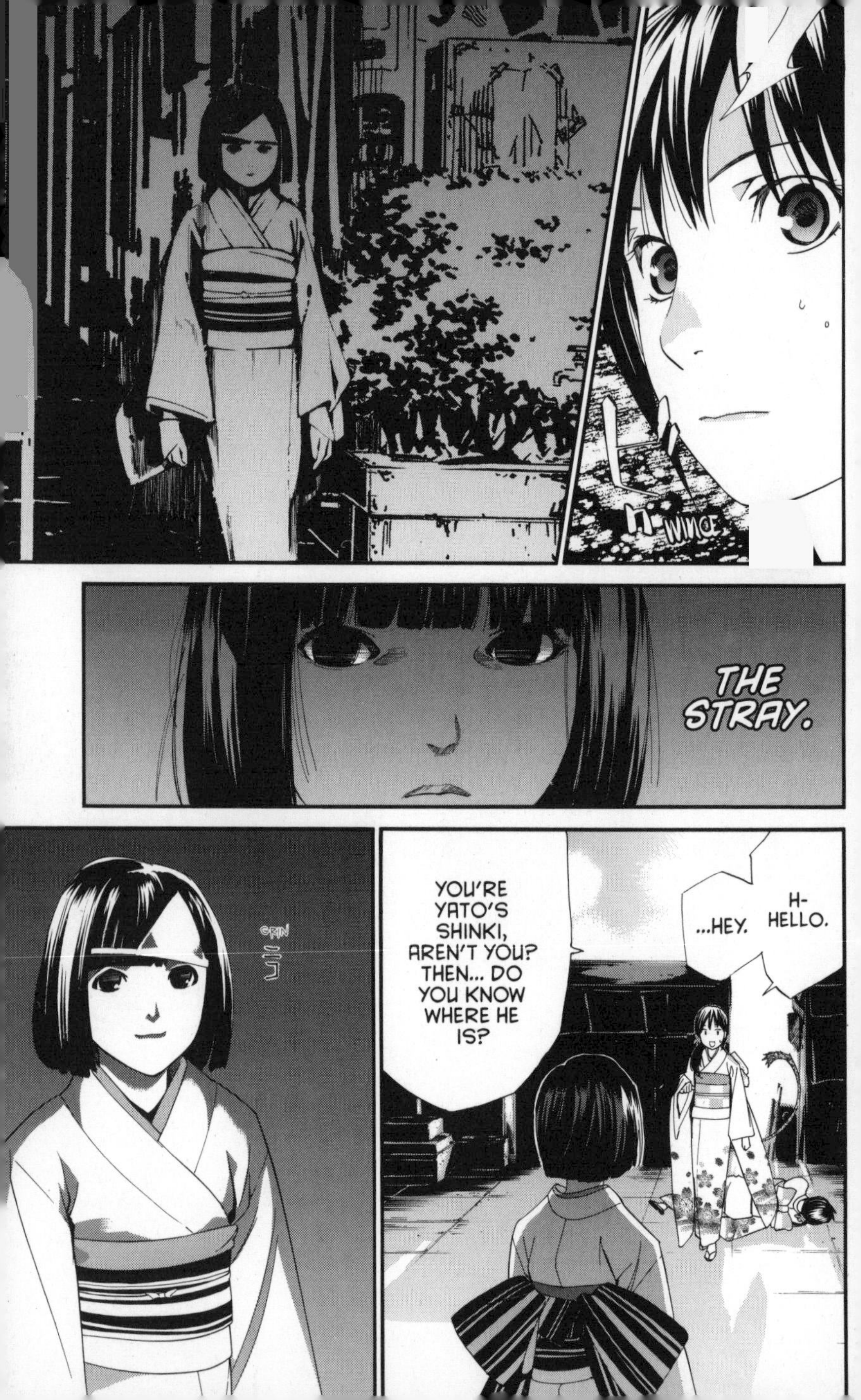
WINCE
THE STRAY.
H- HELLO.
...HEY.
YOU'RE YATO'S SHINKI, AREN'T YOU? THEN... DO YOU KNOW WHERE HE IS?
GRIN

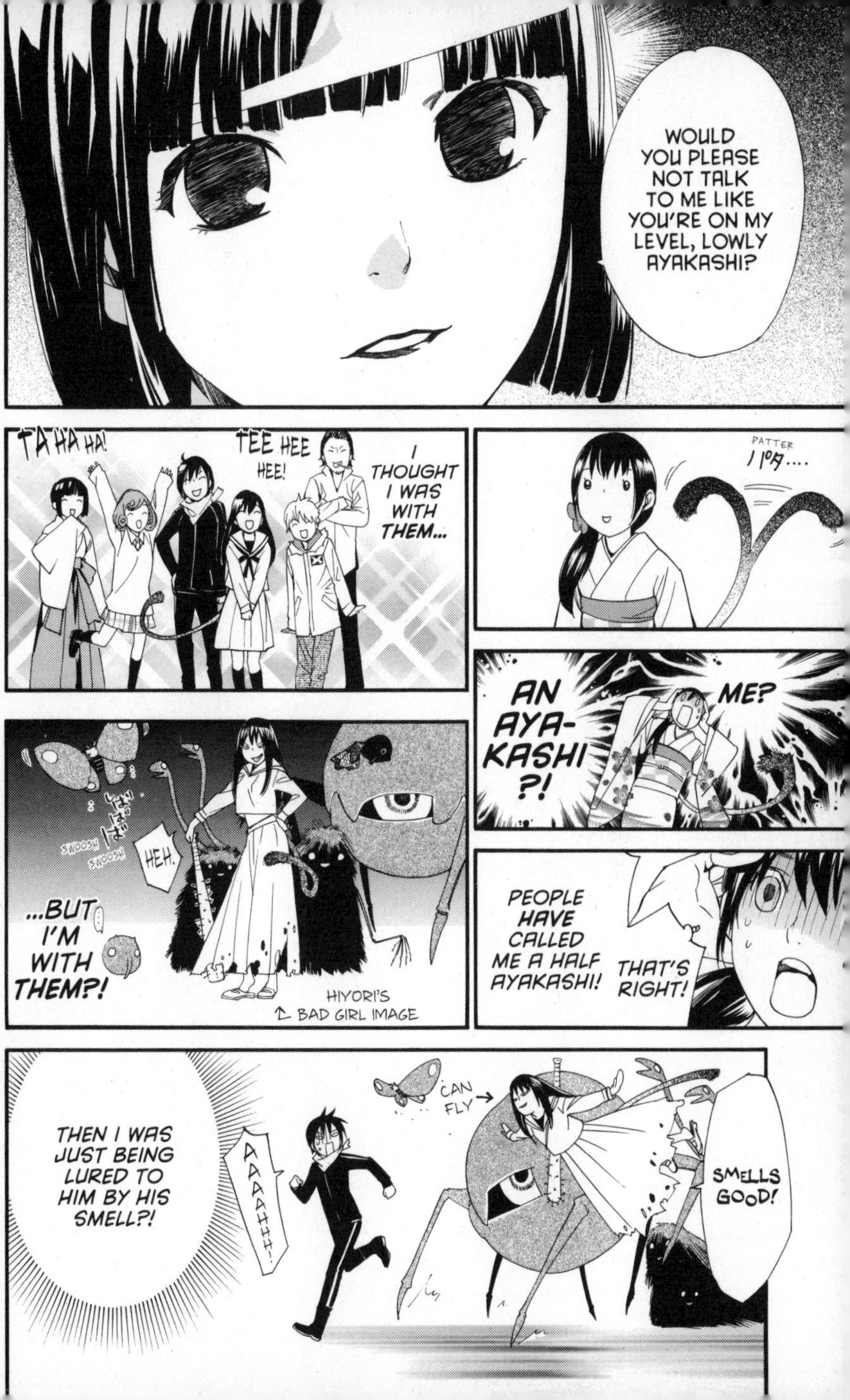
WOULD YOU PLEASE NOT TALK TO ME LIKE YOU'RE ON MY LEVEL, LOWLY AYAKASHI?
PATTER
パタ....
AN AYAKASHI?!
ME?
TA HA HA!
TEE HEE HEE!
I THOUGHT I WAS WITH THEM...
HEH.
SWOOSH SWOOSH
...BUT I'M WITH THEM?!
HIYORI'S BAD GIRL IMAGE
THAT'S RIGHT!
PEOPLE HAVE CALLED ME A HALF AYAKASHI!
SMELLS GOOD!
CAN FLY
AAAAHHH!
THEN I WAS JUST BEING LURED TO HIM BY HIS SMELL?!

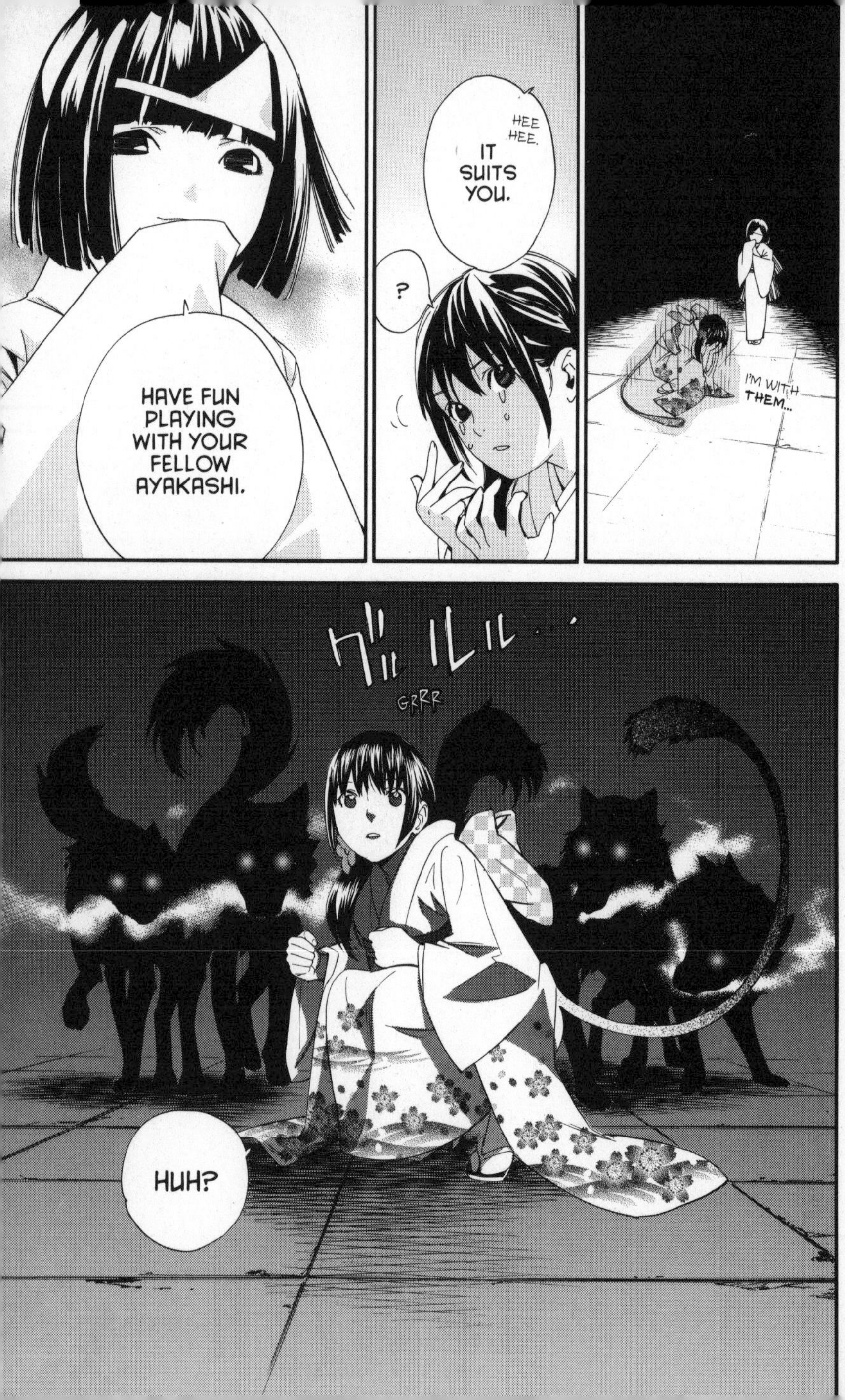
I'M WITH THEM...
HEE HEE.
IT SUITS YOU.
?
HAVE FUN PLAYING WITH YOUR FELLOW AYAKASHI.
グルルル・・
GRRR
HUH?

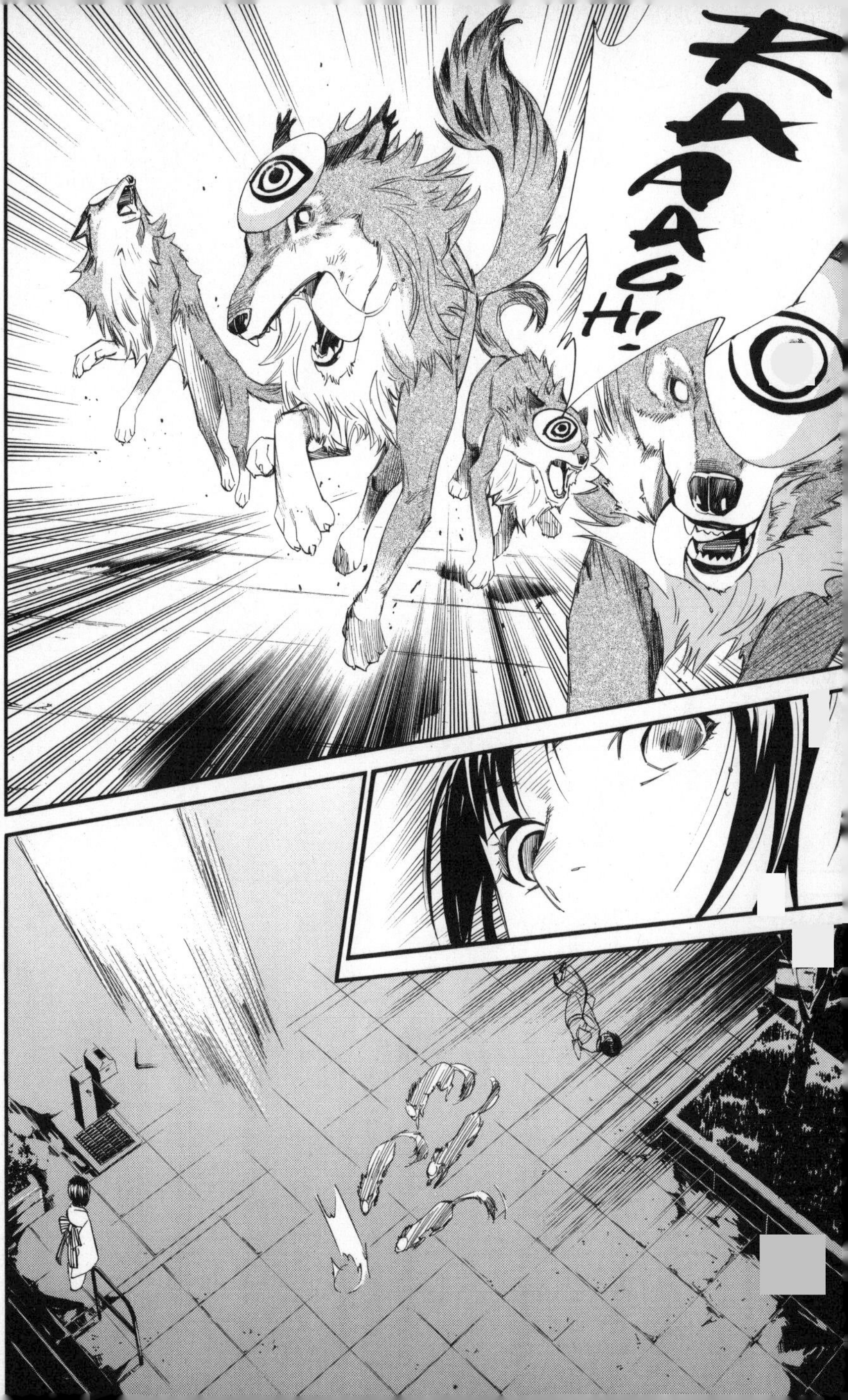
RAAAGH!

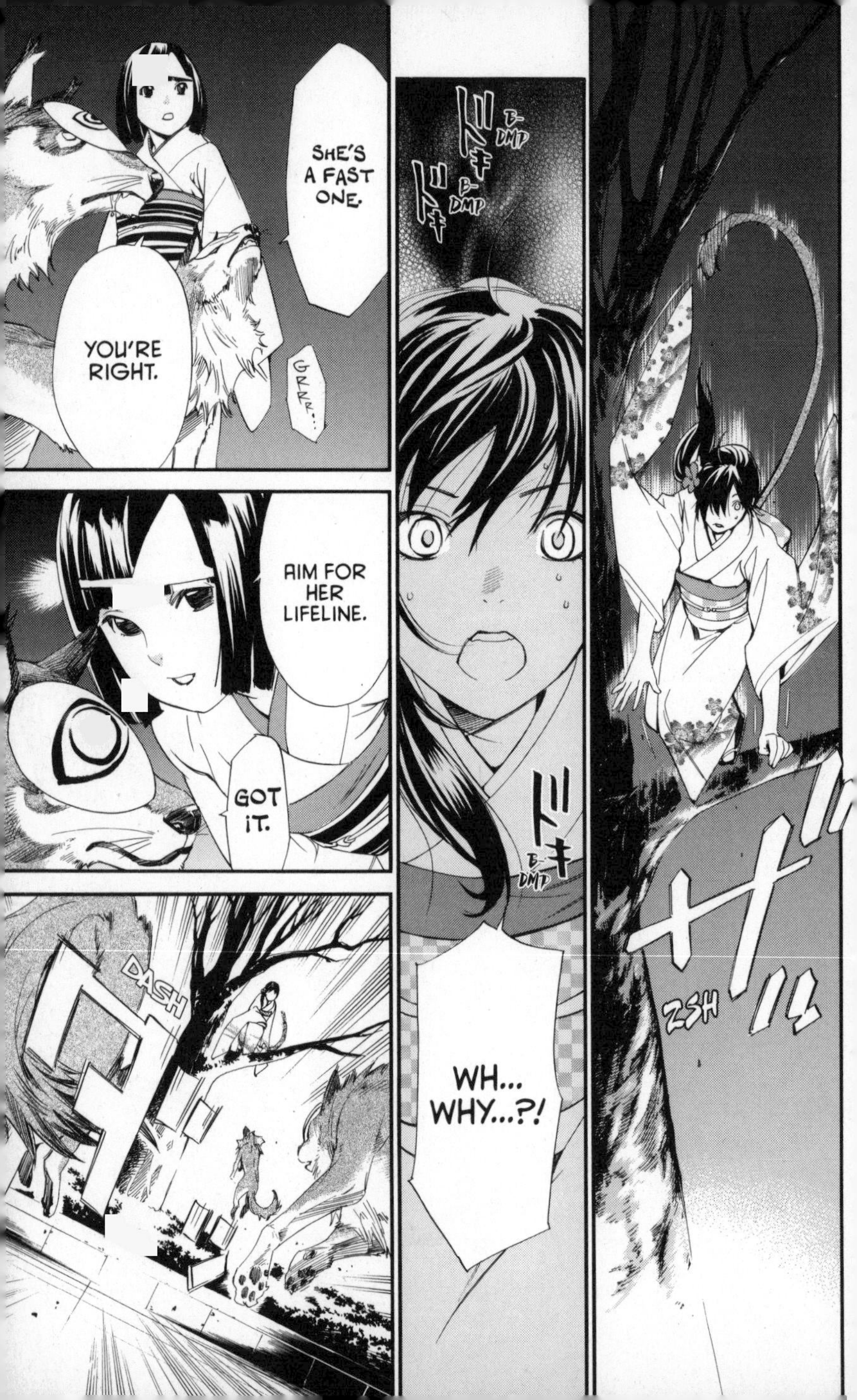
ZSH
ドキ
B-DMP
ドキ
B-DMP
ドキ
B-DMP
WH... WHY...?!
SHE'S A FAST ONE.
YOU'RE RIGHT.
GRRR...
AIM FOR HER LIFELINE.
GOT IT.
DASH

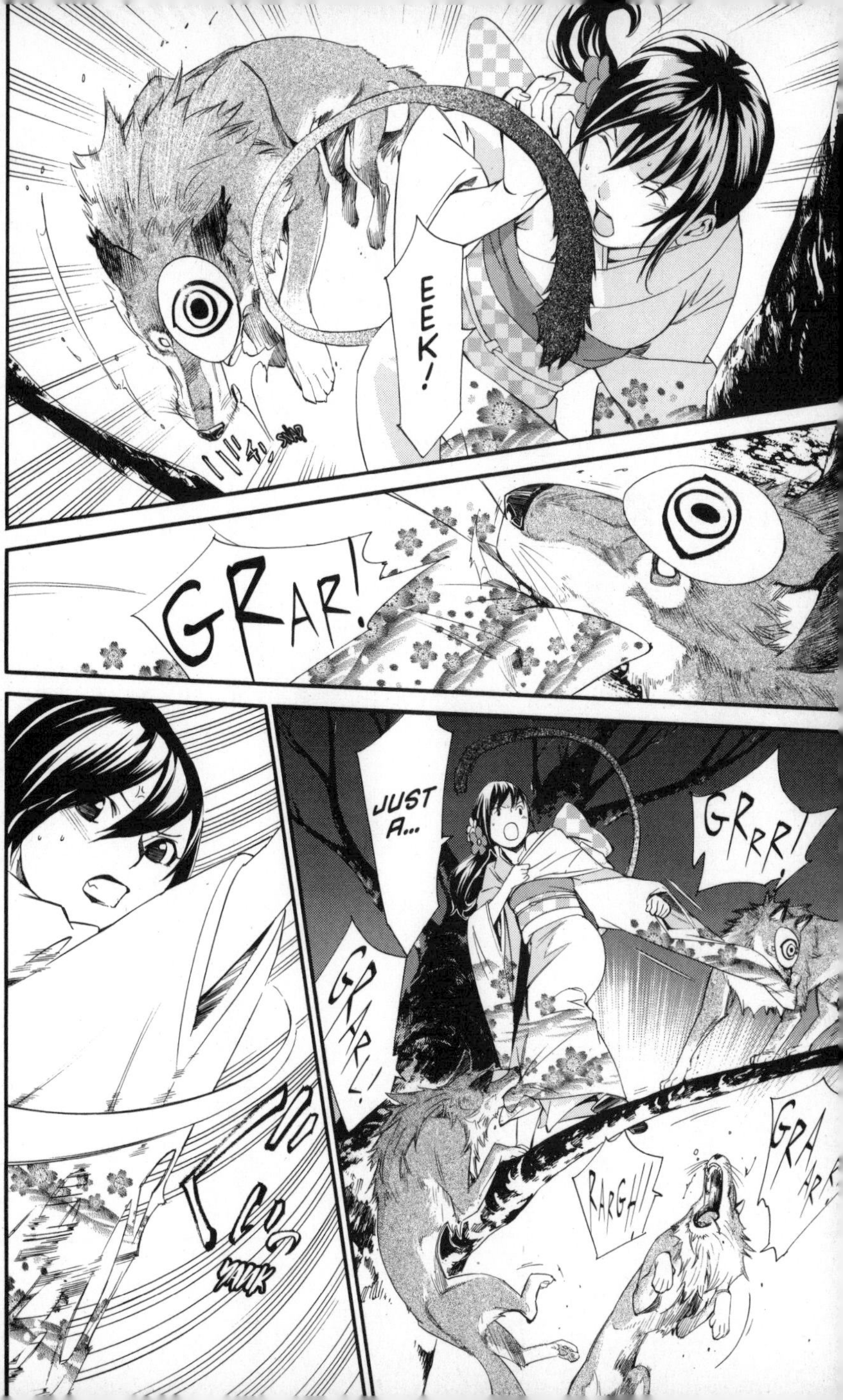
EEK!
SNAP
GRAR!
GRRR!
JUST A...
GRAHRL!
GRAAR!
RARGH!
YANK

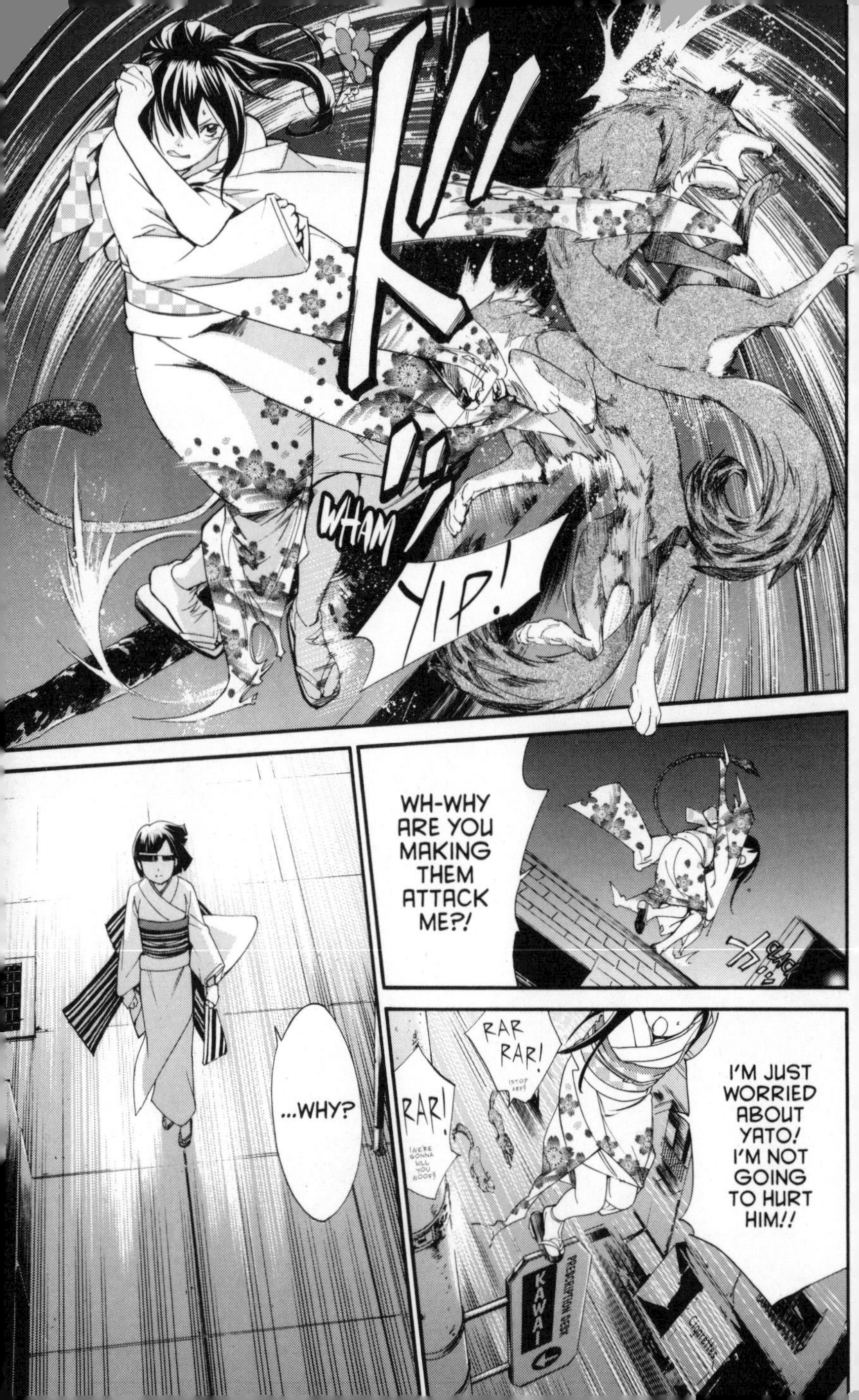

WHAM
YIP!
WH-WHY ARE YOU MAKING THEM ATTACK ME?!
I'M JUST WORRIED ABOUT YATO! I'M NOT GOING TO HURT HIM!!
RAR RAR!
(STOP ARF!)
RAR!
(WE'RE GONNA KILL YOU WOOF!)
PRESCRIPTION DESK
KAWAI
Cigarettes
...WHY?

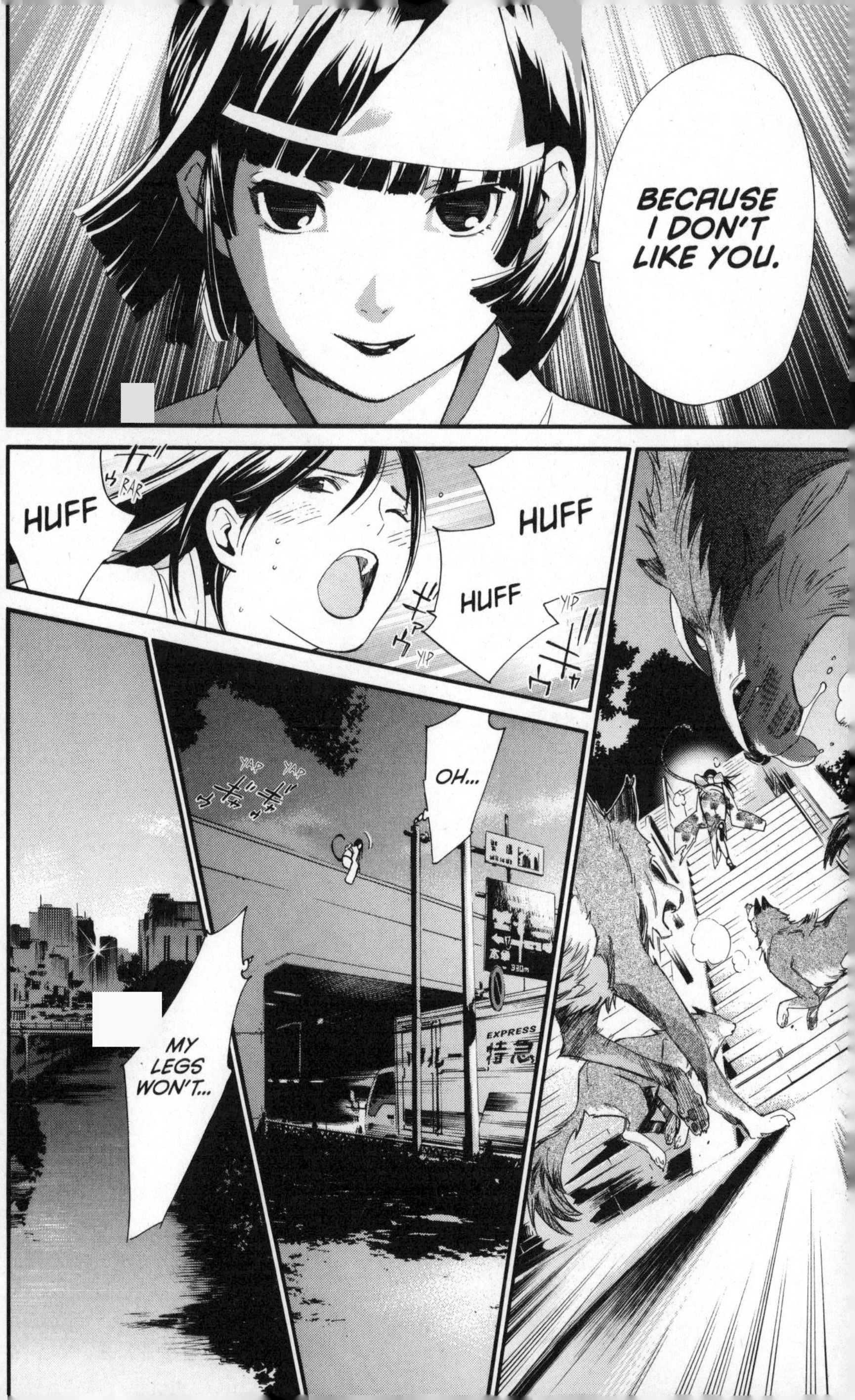
BECAUSE I DON'T LIKE YOU.
HUFF
RAR
HUFF
HUFF
YIP
YIP
OH...
YAP YAP
MY LEGS WON'T...

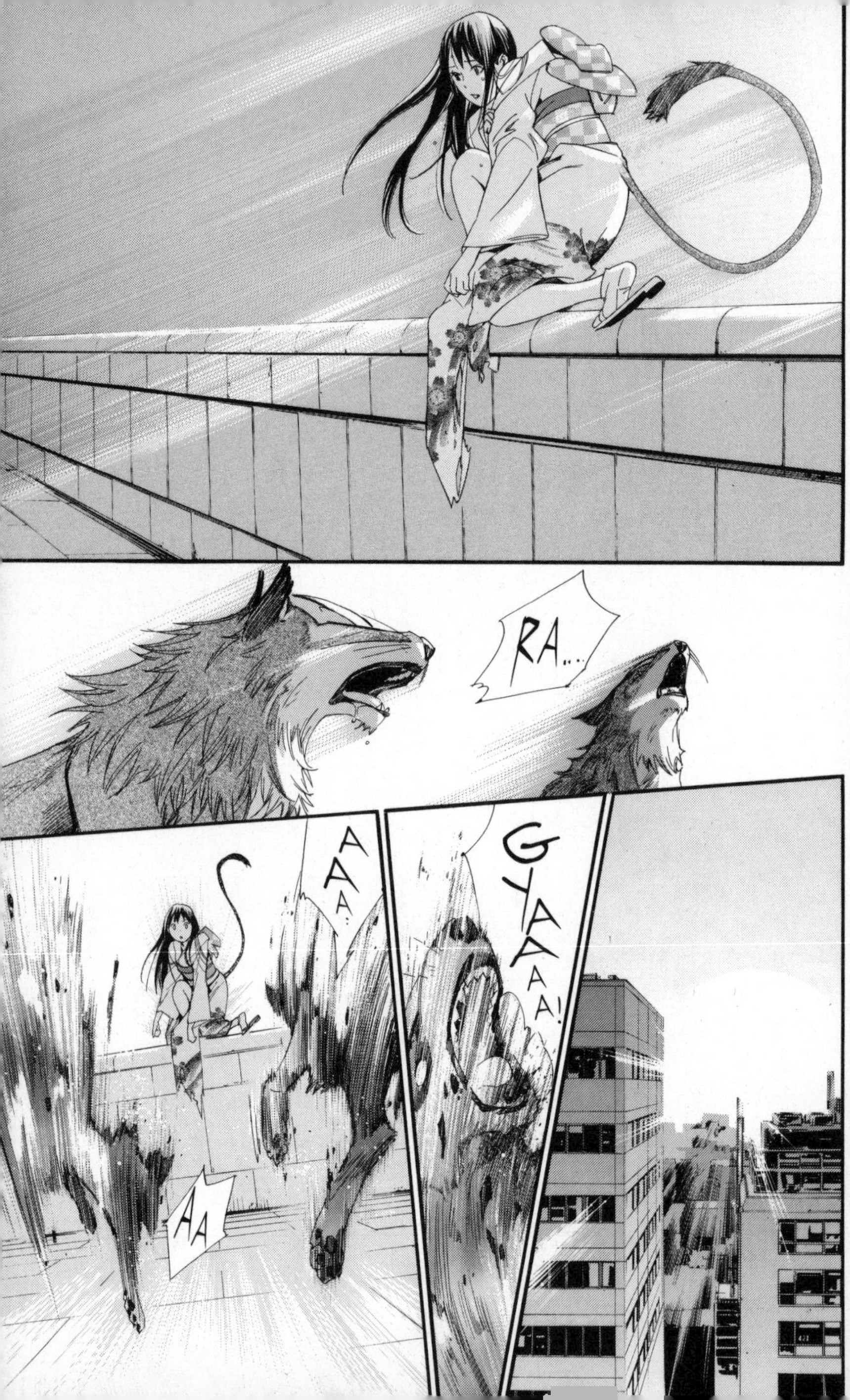
RA...
AAA...
AA
GYAAAAA!

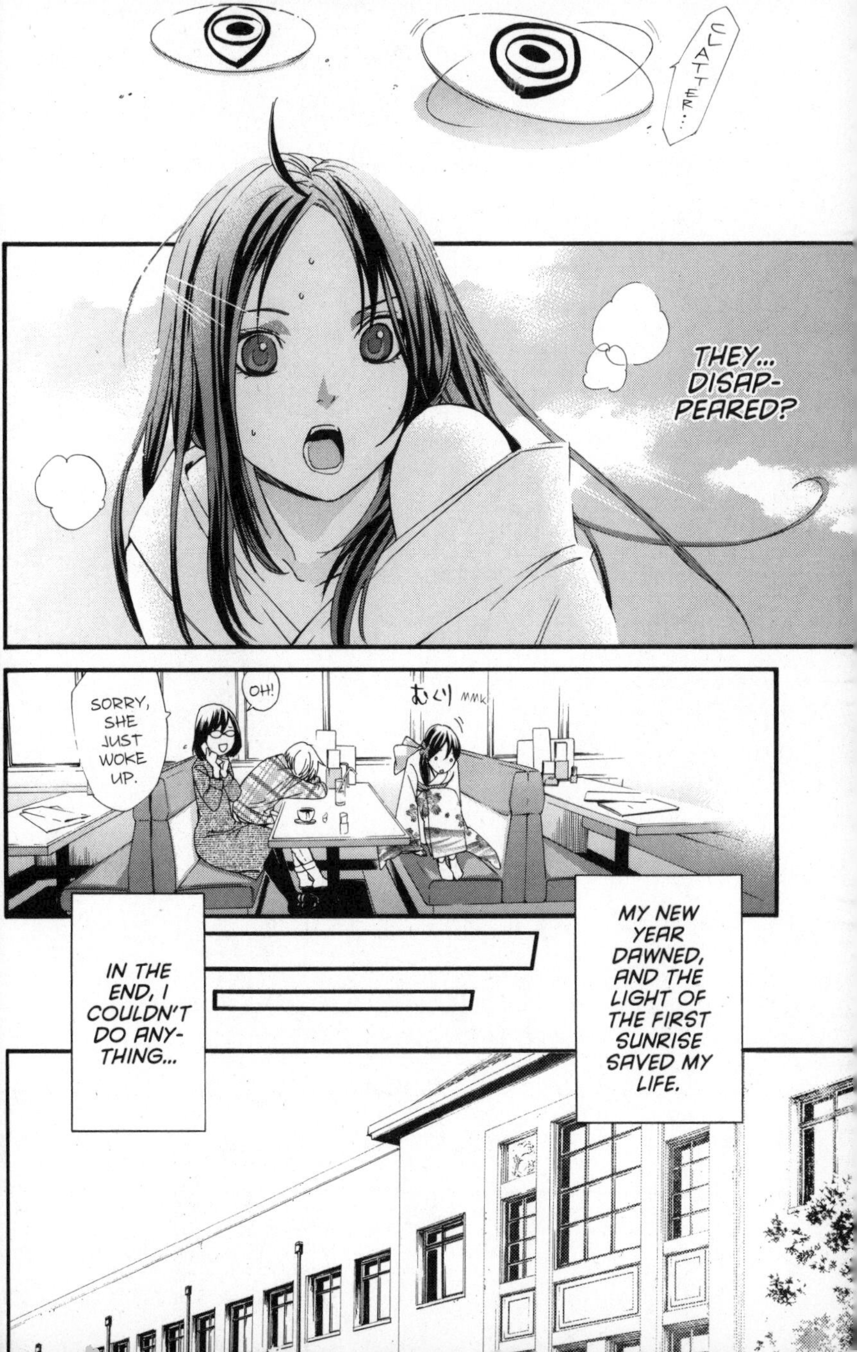
CLATTER...
THEY... DISAP-PEARED?
むくり MMK
OH!
SORRY, SHE JUST WOKE UP.
MY NEW YEAR DAWNED, AND THE LIGHT OF THE FIRST SUNRISE SAVED MY LIFE.
IN THE END, I COULDN'T DO ANY-THING...

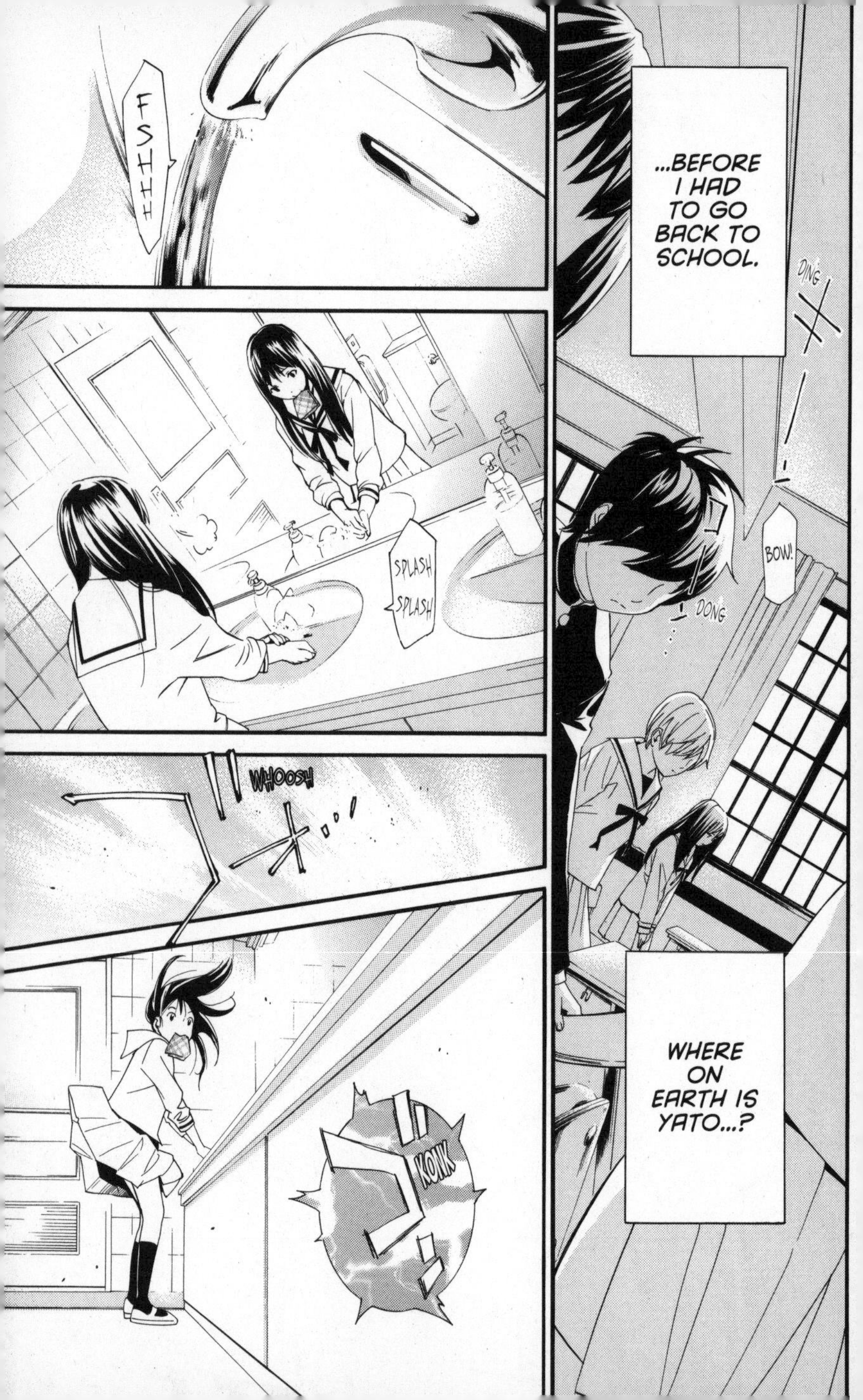
...BEFORE I HAD TO GO BACK TO SCHOOL.
DING
BOW!
DONG
WHERE ON EARTH IS YATO...?
FSHHH
SPLASH SPLASH
WHOOSH
KONK

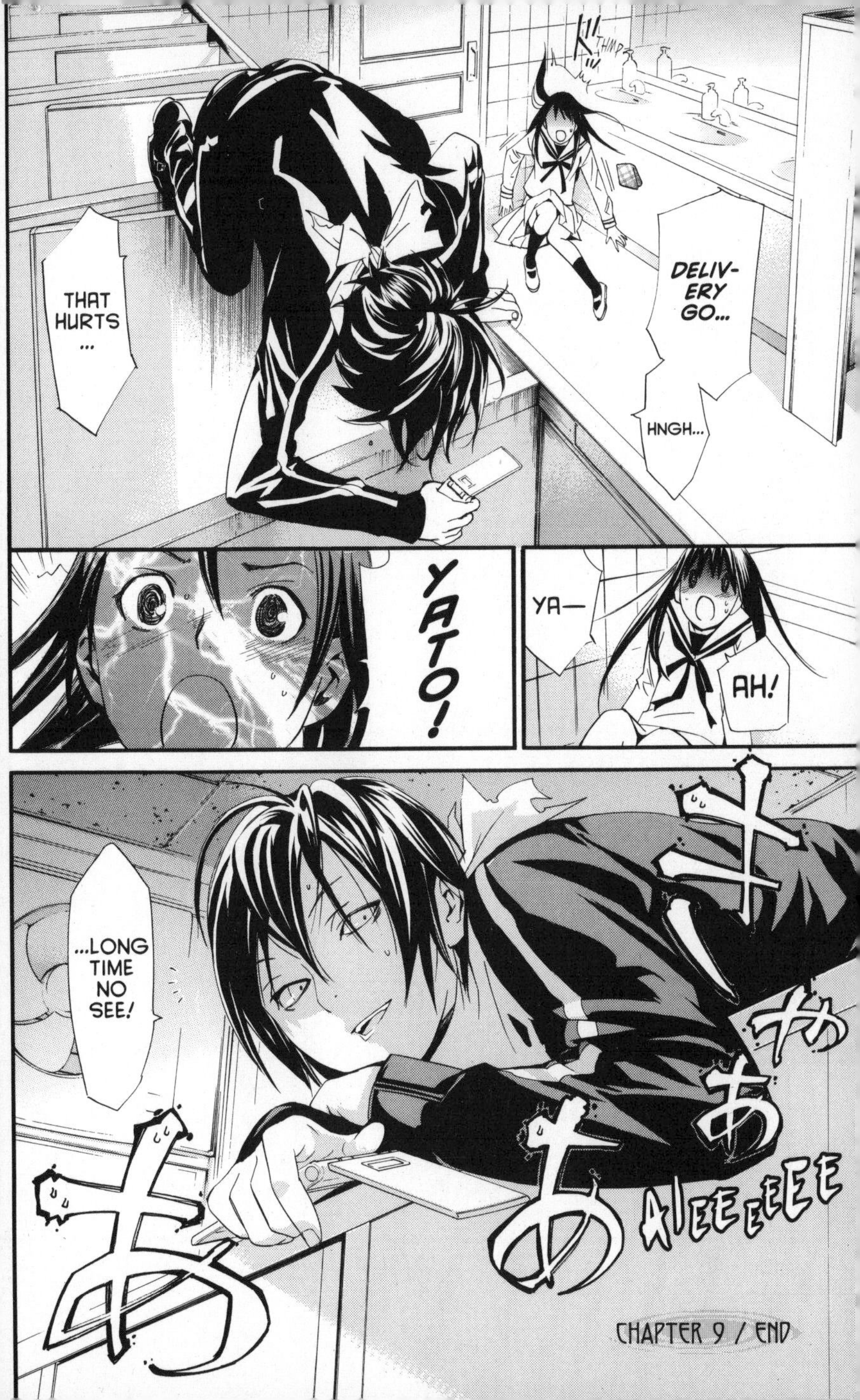
THMP
DELIV-
ERY
GO...
HNGH...
THAT
HURTS
...
YA—
AH!
YATO!
...LONG
TIME
NO
SEE!
AIEEEEEE
CHAPTER 9 / END

野

兑

神

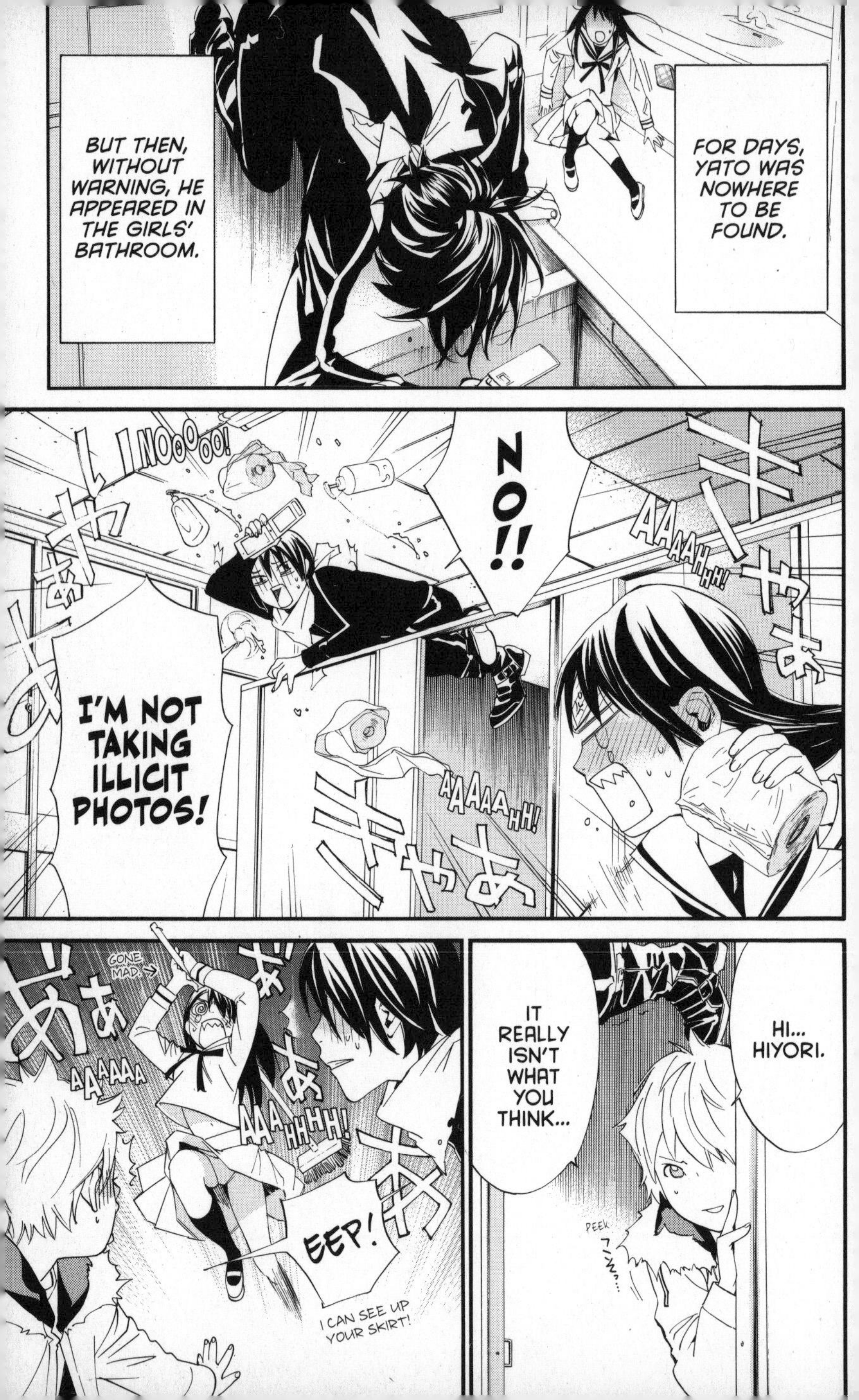
FOR DAYS, YATO WAS NOWHERE TO BE FOUND.
BUT THEN, WITHOUT WARNING, HE APPEARED IN THE GIRLS' BATHROOM.
AAAAAHHH!
NO!!
NOOOOO!
I'M NOT TAKING ILLICIT PHOTOS!
AAAAAHH!
HI... HIYORI.
IT REALLY ISN'T WHAT YOU THINK...
PEEK
AAAAHHHH!
GONE MAD.
AAAAAA
EEP!
I CAN SEE UP YOUR SKIRT!

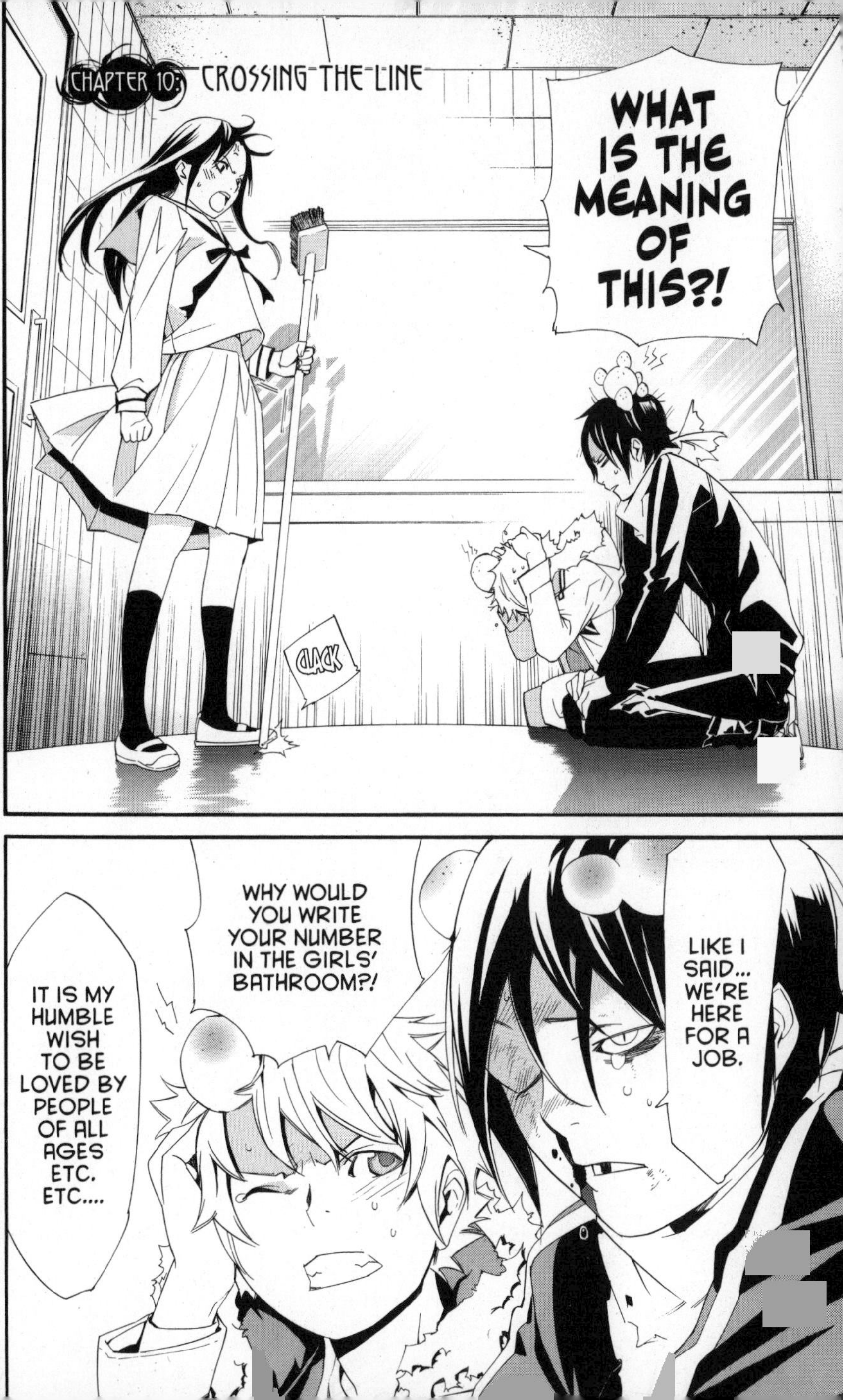
CHAPTER 10: CROSSING THE LINE
WHAT IS THE MEANING OF THIS?!
CLACK
WHY WOULD YOU WRITE YOUR NUMBER IN THE GIRLS' BATHROOM?!
LIKE I SAID... WE'RE HERE FOR A JOB.
IT IS MY HUMBLE WISH TO BE LOVED BY PEOPLE OF ALL AGES ETC. ETC....

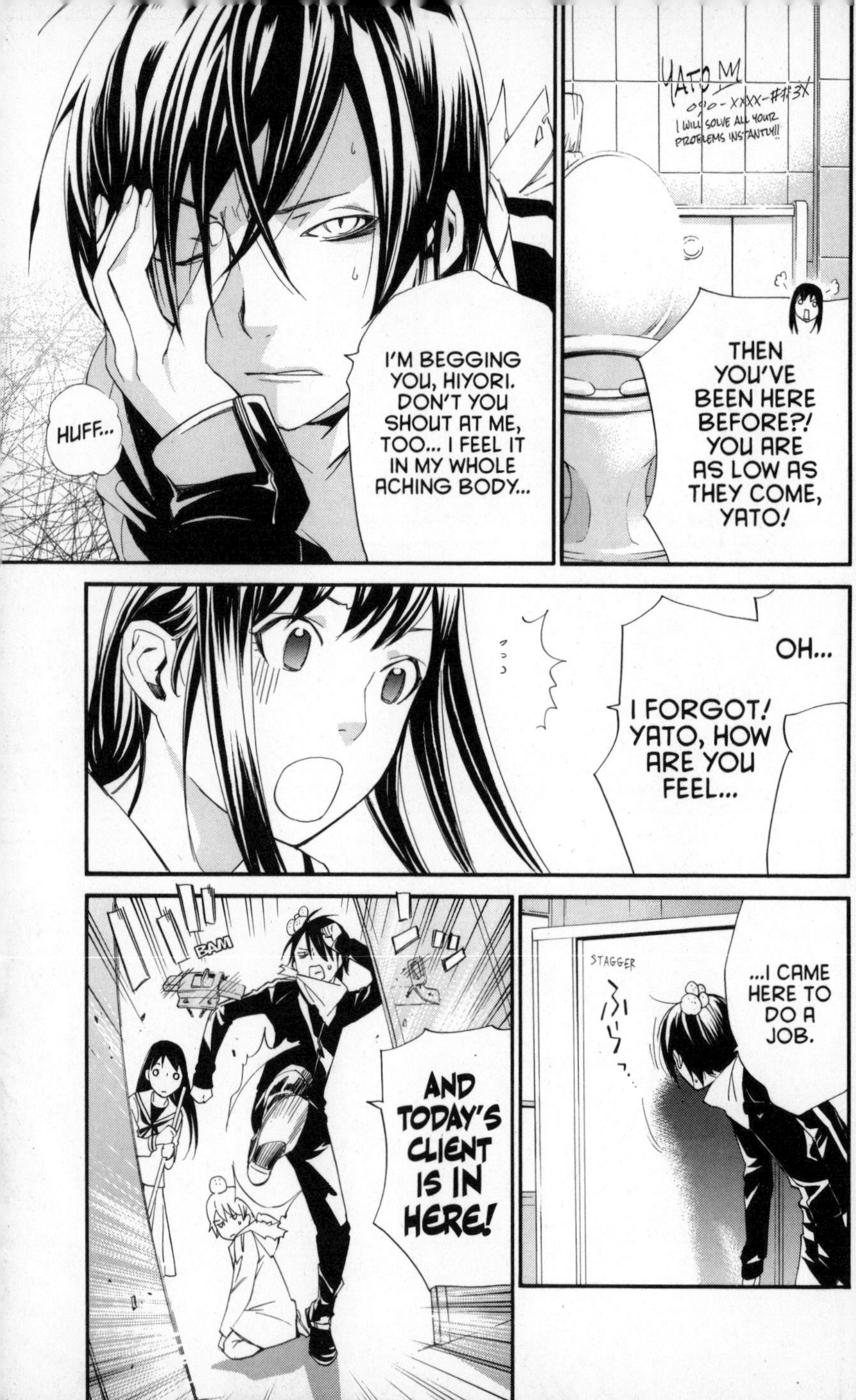
YATO
I WILL SOLVE ALL YOUR PROBLEMS INSTANTLY!!
THEN YOU'VE BEEN HERE BEFORE?! YOU ARE AS LOW AS THEY COME, YATO!
I'M BEGGING YOU, HIYORI. DON'T YOU SHOUT AT ME, TOO... I FEEL IT IN MY WHOLE ACHING BODY...
HUFF...
OH...
I FORGOT! YATO, HOW ARE YOU FEEL...
STAGGER
...I CAME HERE TO DO A JOB.
BAM
AND TODAY'S CLIENT IS IN HERE!

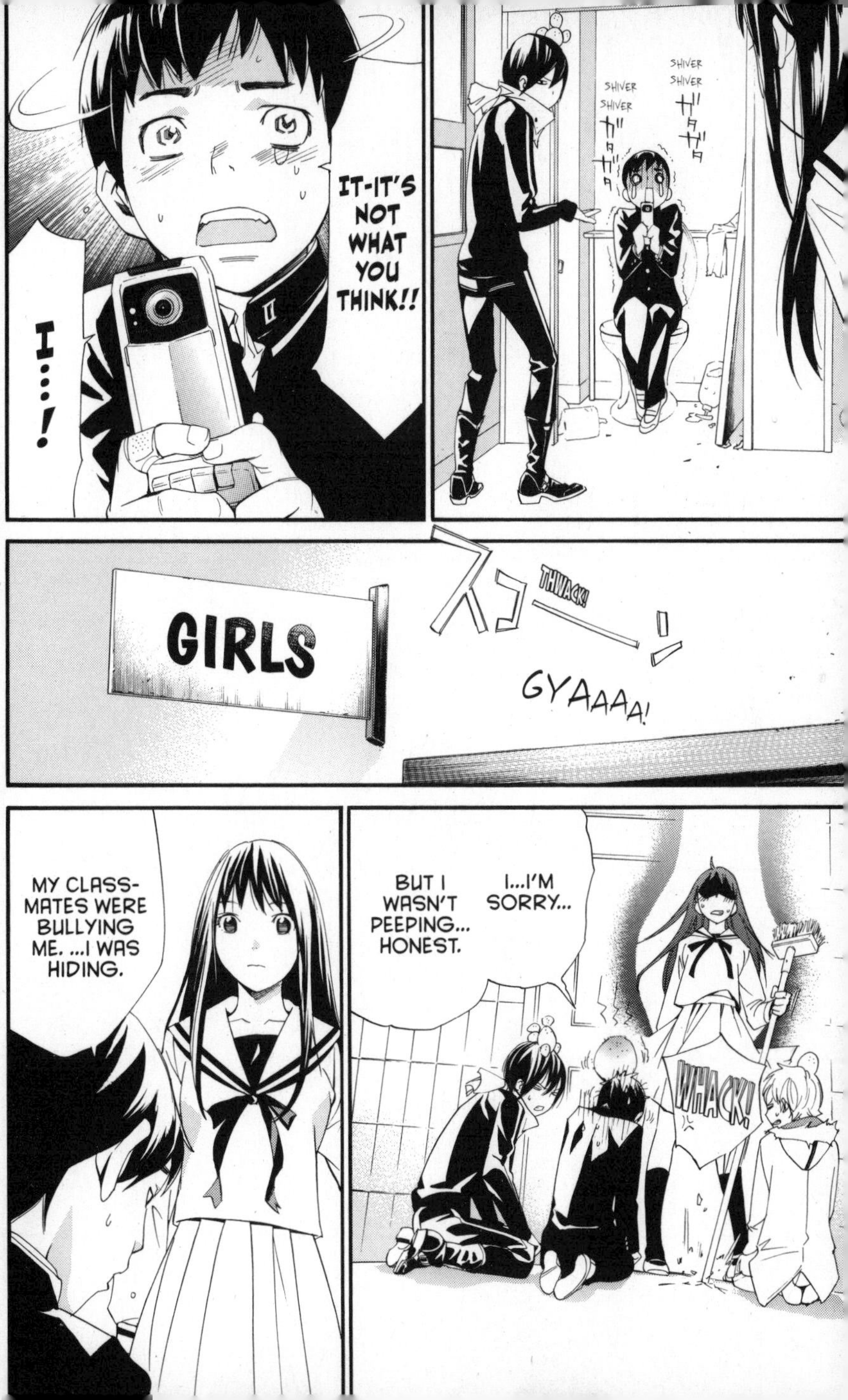
SHIVER SHIVER
ガタガタ
SHIVER SHIVER
ガタガタ
IT-IT'S NOT WHAT YOU THINK!!
I...!
THWACK!
GIRLS
GYAAAA!
I...I'M SORRY...
BUT I WASN'T PEEPING... HONEST.
WHACK!
MY CLASS-MATES WERE BULLYING ME. ...I WAS HIDING.

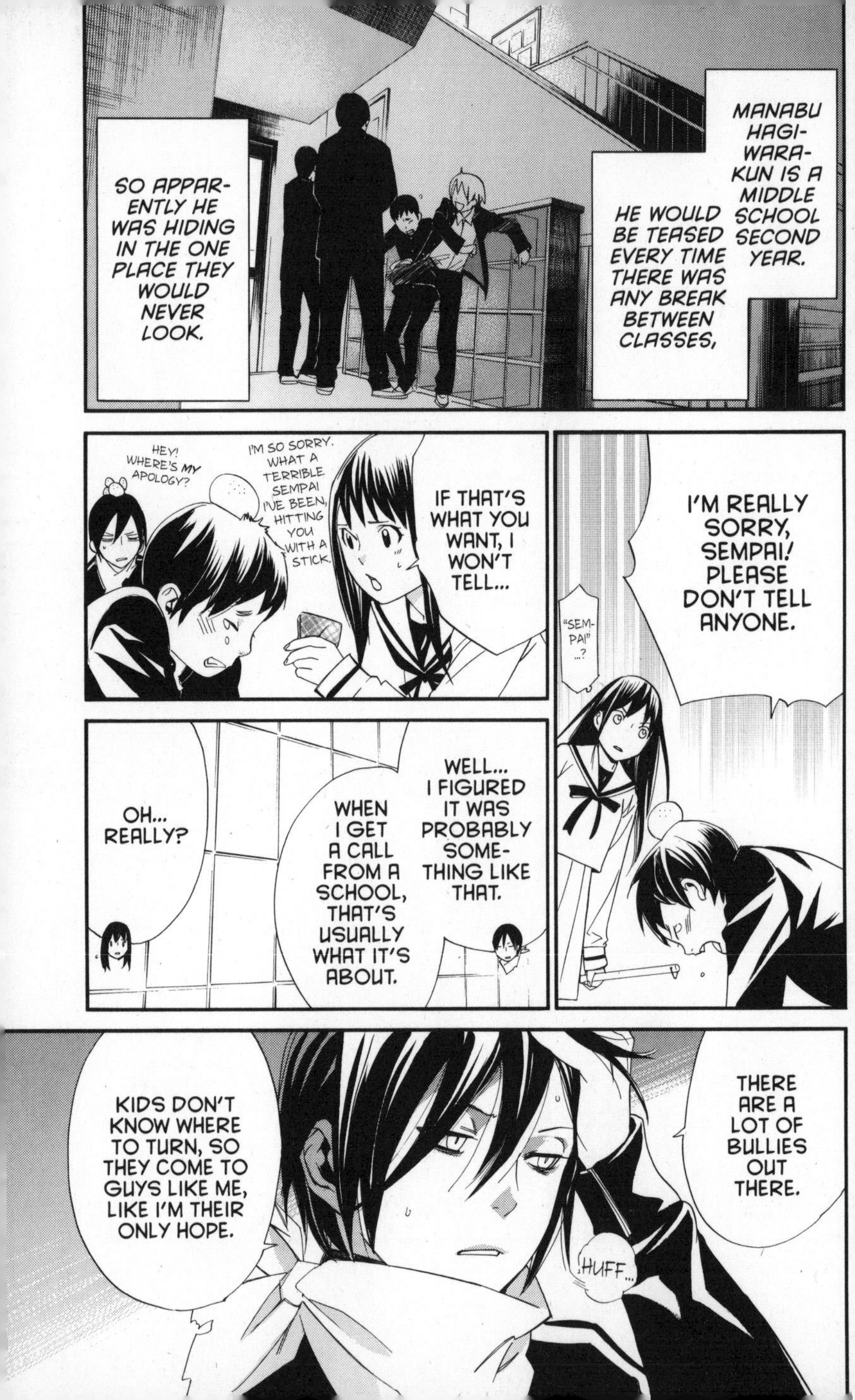
MANABU HAGIWARA-KUN IS A MIDDLE SCHOOL SECOND YEAR.
HE WOULD BE TEASED EVERY TIME THERE WAS ANY BREAK BETWEEN CLASSES,
SO APPARENTLY HE WAS HIDING IN THE ONE PLACE THEY WOULD NEVER LOOK.
I'M REALLY SORRY, SEMPAI! PLEASE DON'T TELL ANYONE.
"SEMPAI"...?
IF THAT'S WHAT YOU WANT, I WON'T TELL...
I'M SO SORRY. WHAT A TERRIBLE SEMPAI I'VE BEEN, HITTING YOU WITH A STICK.
HEY! WHERE'S MY APOLOGY?
WELL... I FIGURED IT WAS PROBABLY SOMETHING LIKE THAT.
WHEN I GET A CALL FROM A SCHOOL, THAT'S USUALLY WHAT IT'S ABOUT.
OH... REALLY?
THERE ARE A LOT OF BULLIES OUT THERE.
HUFF...
KIDS DON'T KNOW WHERE TO TURN, SO THEY COME TO GUYS LIKE ME, LIKE I'M THEIR ONLY HOPE.

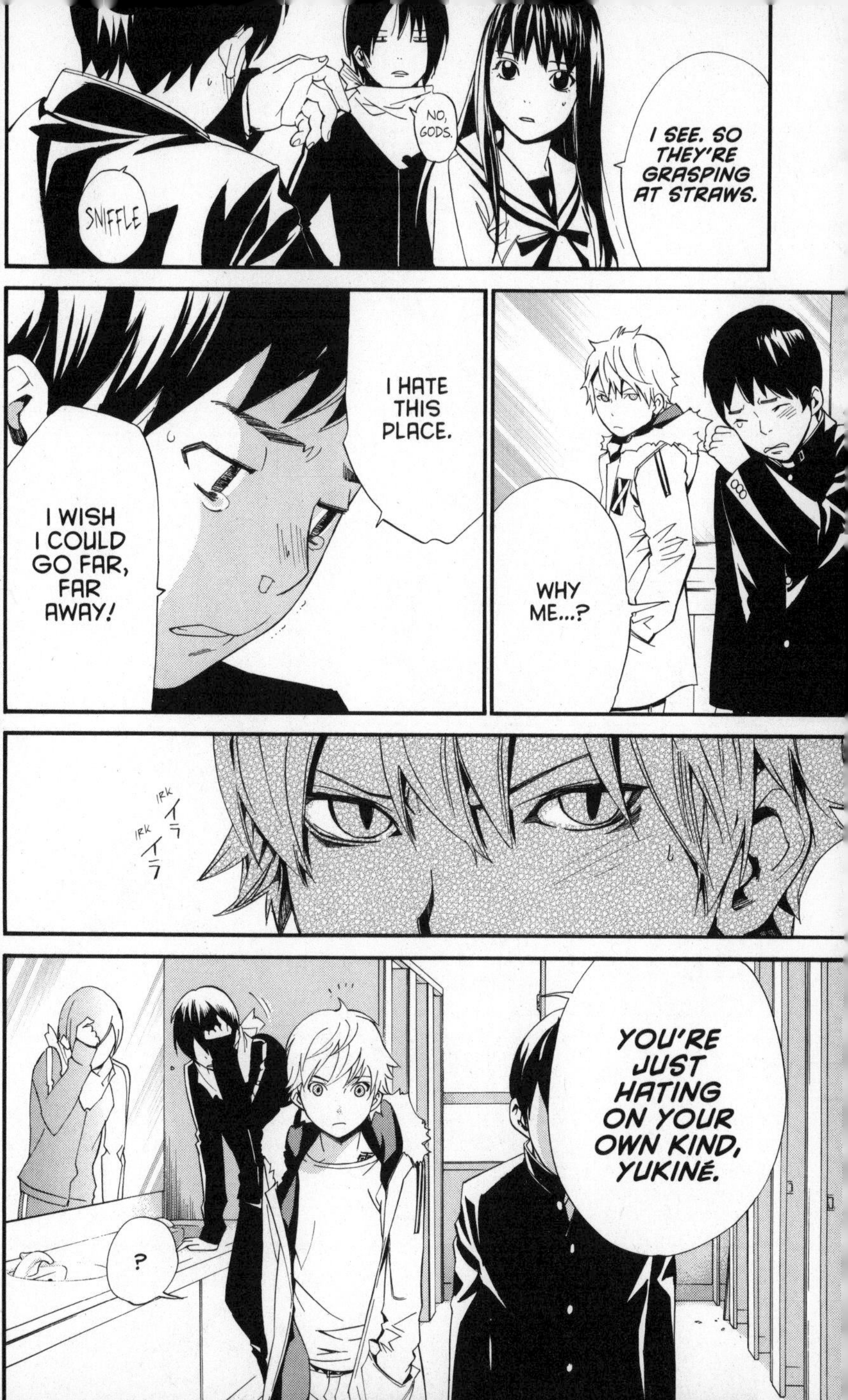
I SEE. SO THEY'RE GRASPING AT STRAWS.
NO, GODS.
SNIFFLE
WHY ME...?
I HATE THIS PLACE.
I WISH I COULD GO FAR, FAR AWAY!
IRK IRK
イラ イラ
YOU'RE JUST HATING ON YOUR OWN KIND, YUKINÉ.
?

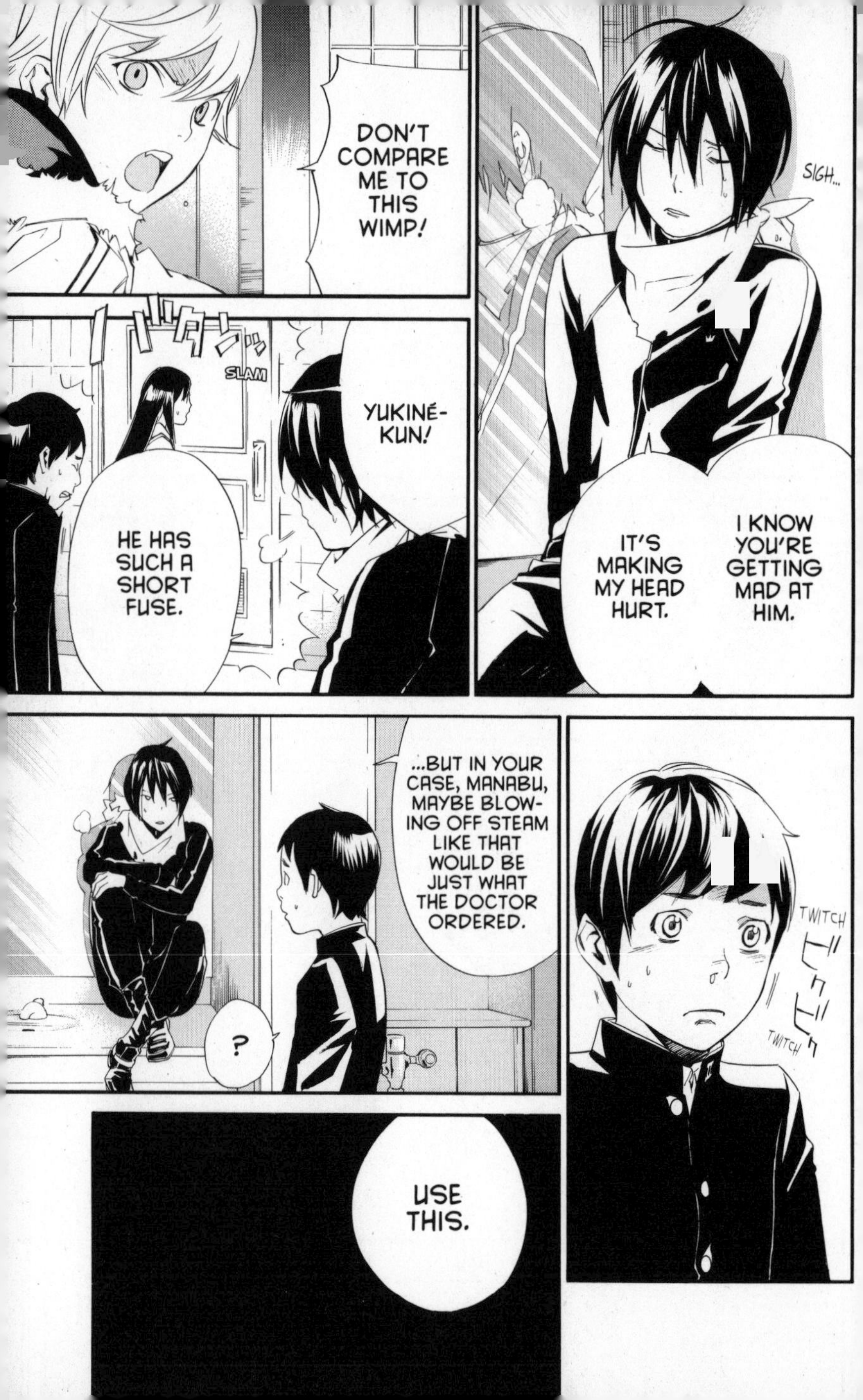
DON'T COMPARE ME TO THIS WIMP!
SLAM
YUKINÉ-KUN!
HE HAS SUCH A SHORT FUSE.
SIGH...
I KNOW YOU'RE GETTING MAD AT HIM.
IT'S MAKING MY HEAD HURT.
...BUT IN YOUR CASE, MANABU, MAYBE BLOWING OFF STEAM LIKE THAT WOULD BE JUST WHAT THE DOCTOR ORDERED.
?
TWITCH
TWITCH
USE THIS.

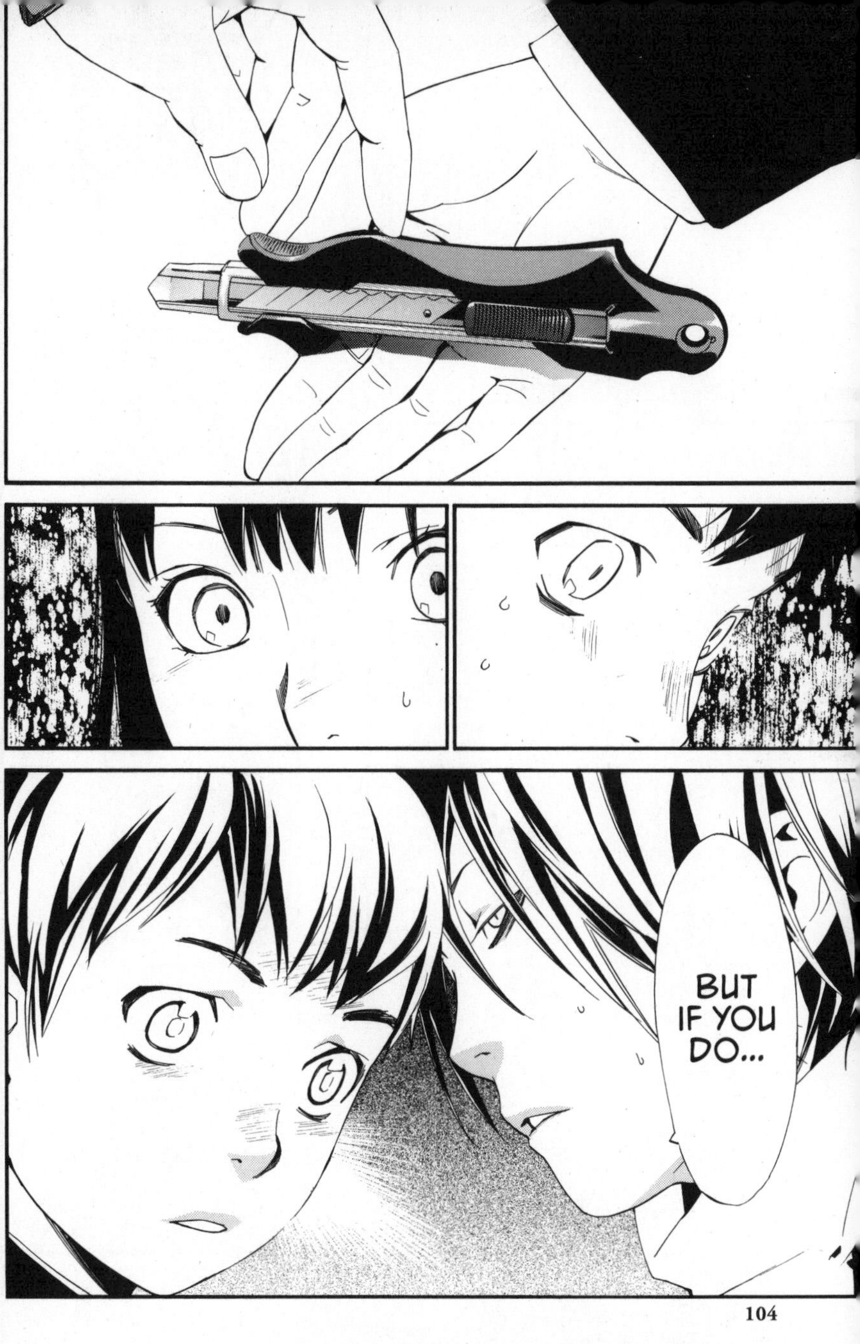
BUT IF YOU DO...

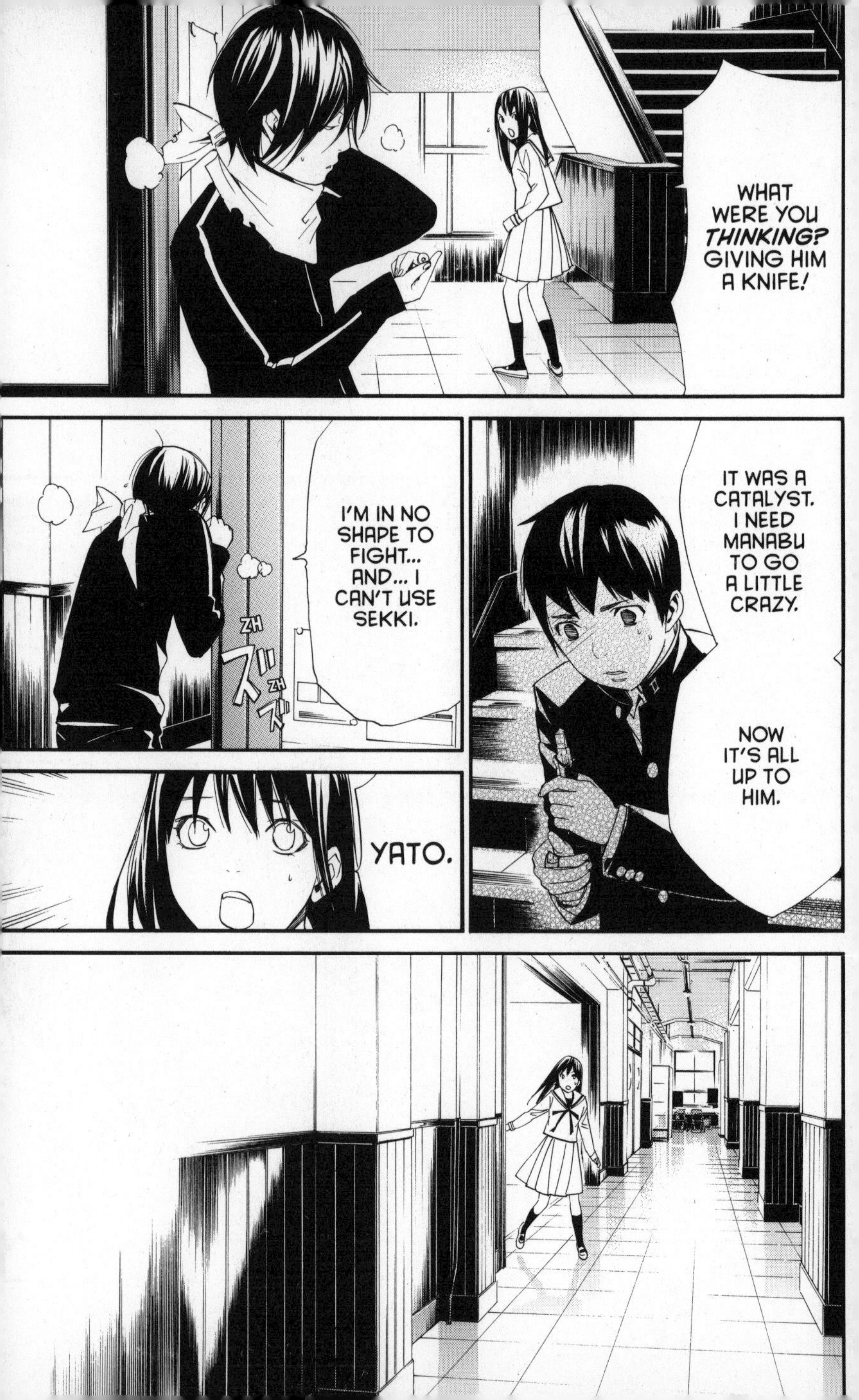
WHAT WERE YOU *THINKING?* GIVING HIM A KNIFE!
IT WAS A CATALYST. I NEED MANABU TO GO A LITTLE CRAZY.
NOW IT'S ALL UP TO HIM.
I'M IN NO SHAPE TO FIGHT... AND... I CAN'T USE SEKKI.
ZH
ZH
YATO.

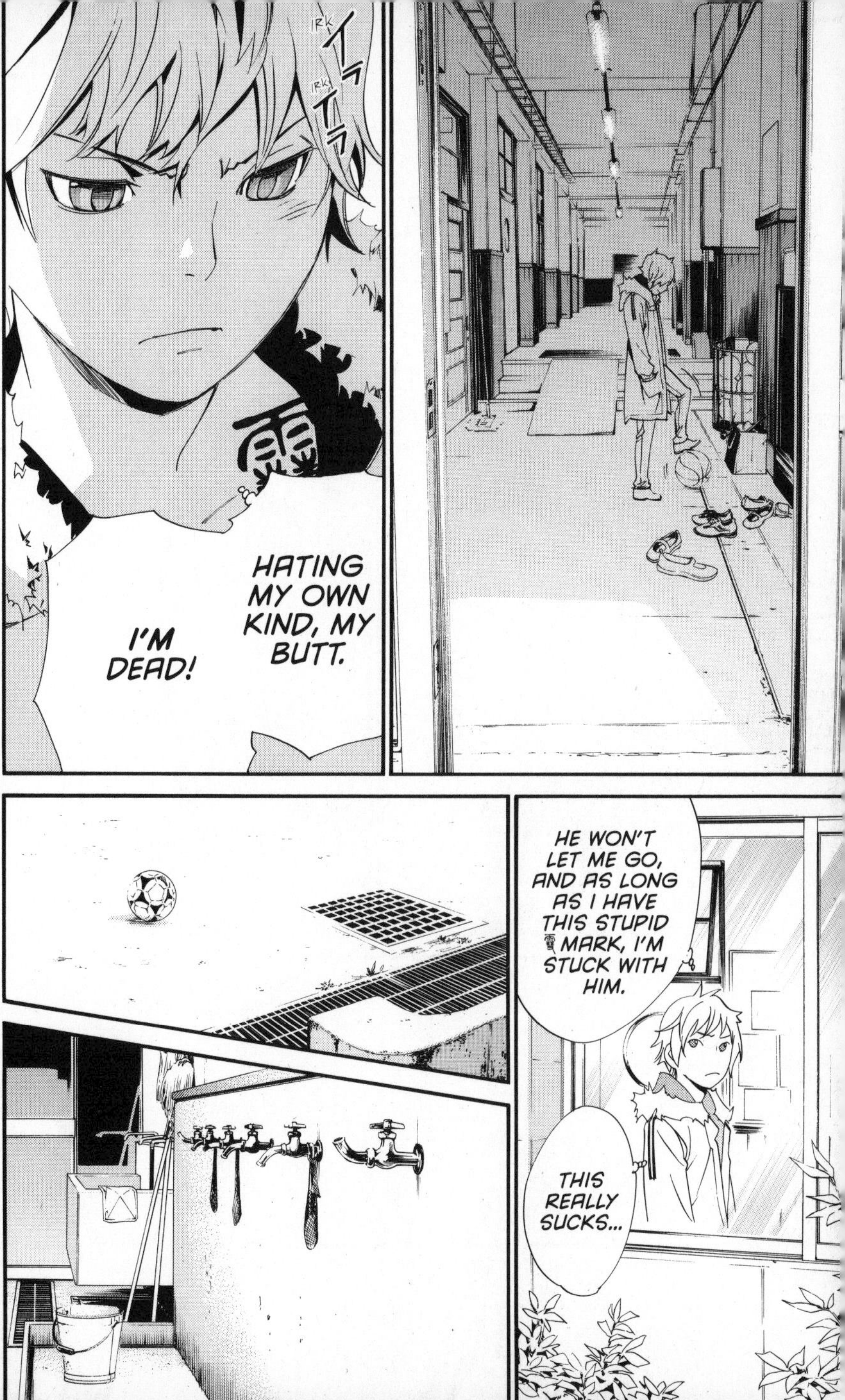
IRK
イラ
IRK
イラ
HATING MY OWN KIND, MY BUTT.
I'M DEAD!
HE WON'T LET ME GO, AND AS LONG AS I HAVE THIS STUPID 雪 MARK, I'M STUCK WITH HIM.
THIS REALLY SUCKS...

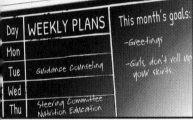

Day	WEEKLY PLANS	This month's goals:
Mon		-Greetings
Tue	Guidance Counseling	-Girls, don't roll up your skirts.
Wed		
Thu	Steering Committee Nutrition Education	

CLASS TRI.

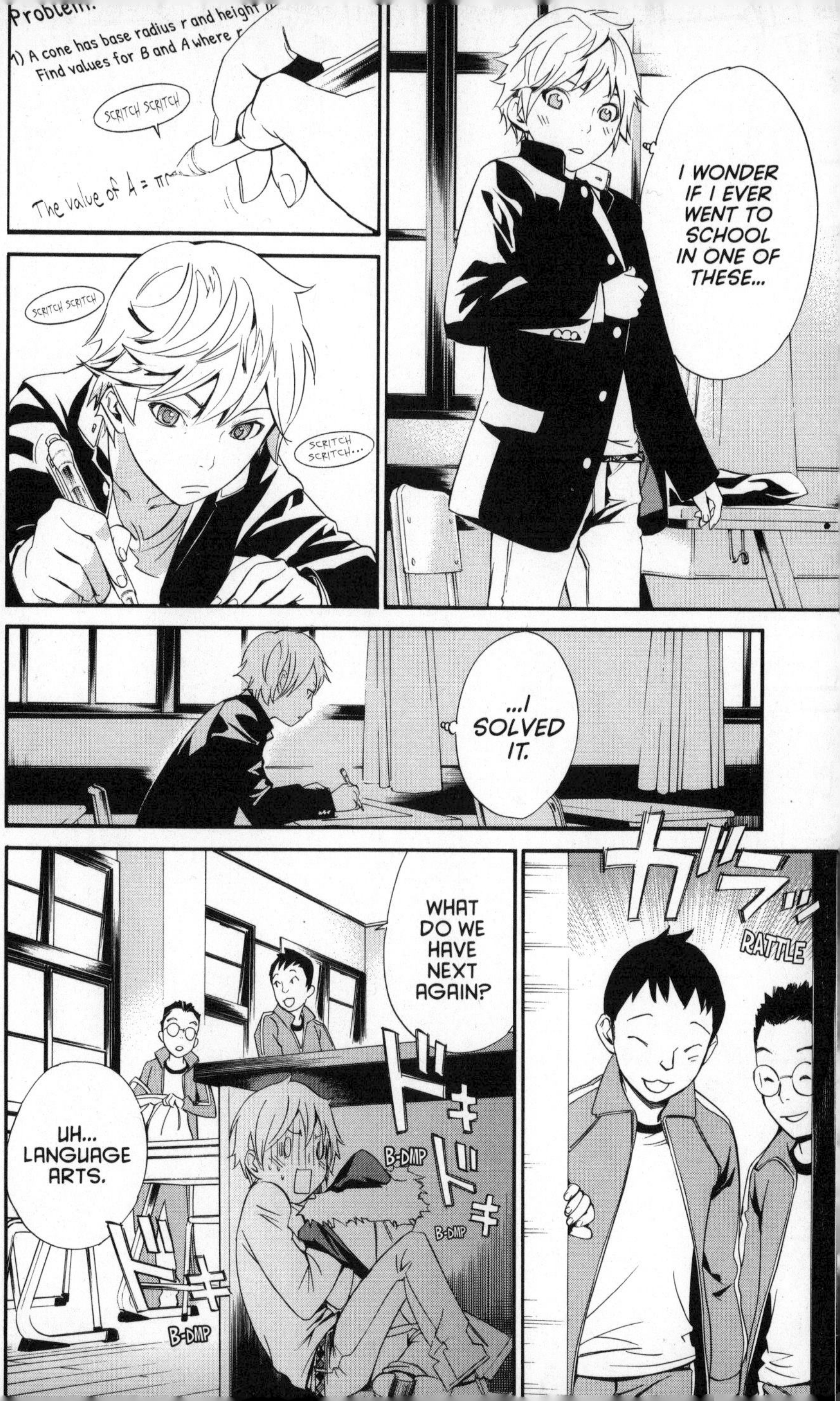
I WONDER IF I EVER WENT TO SCHOOL IN ONE OF THESE...
Problem:
1) A cone has base radius r and height
Find values for B and A where r
SCRITCH SCRITCH
The value of A = πr
SCRITCH SCRITCH
SCRITCH SCRITCH...
...I SOLVED IT.
ガラッ
RATTLE
WHAT DO WE HAVE NEXT AGAIN?
ドキ
B-DMP
ドキ
B-DMP
UH... LANGUAGE ARTS.
ドキ
B-DMP

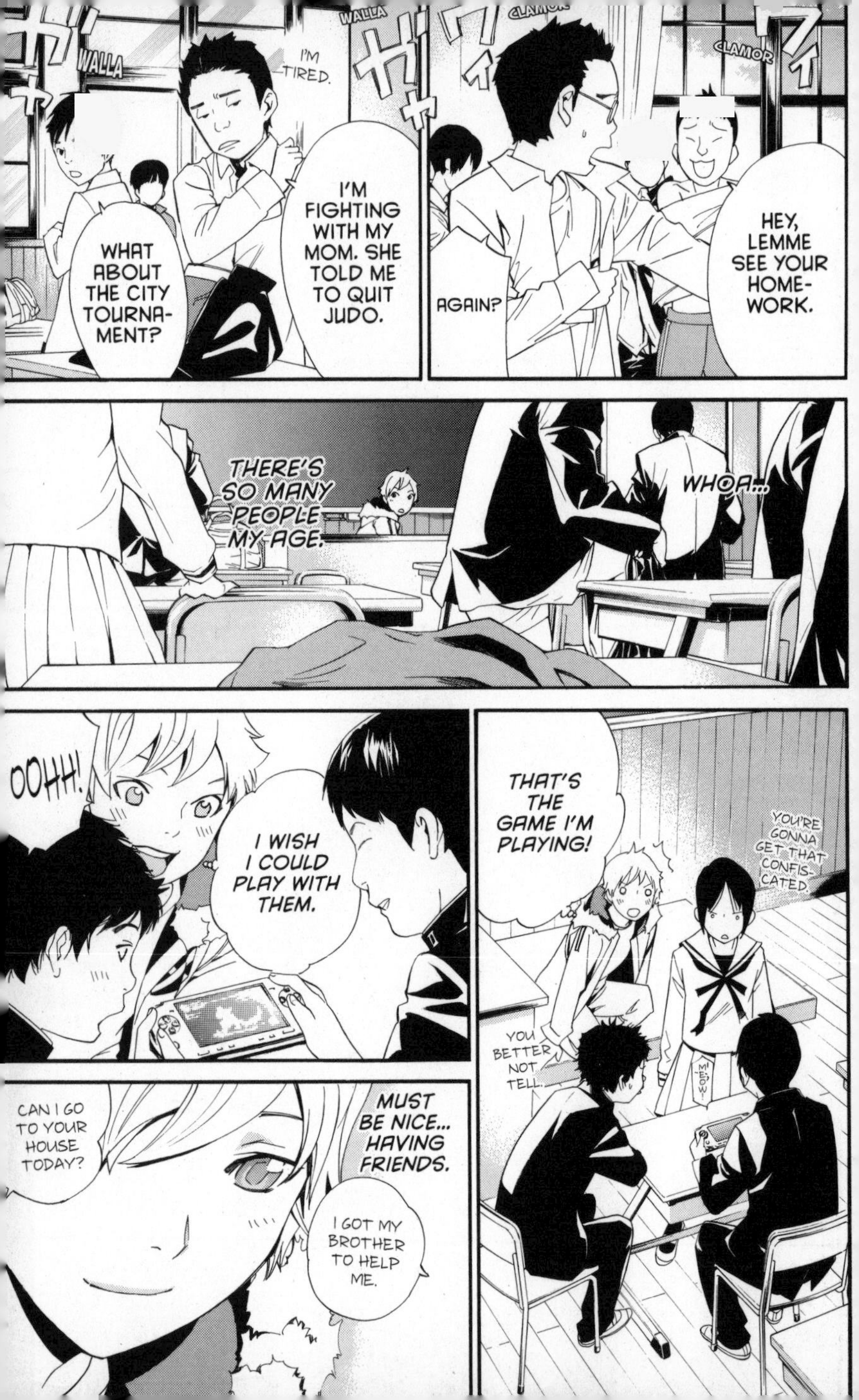
CLAMOR
CLAMOR
HEY, LEMME SEE YOUR HOMEWORK.
AGAIN?
WALLA
I'M TIRED.
I'M FIGHTING WITH MY MOM. SHE TOLD ME TO QUIT JUDO.
WALLA
WHAT ABOUT THE CITY TOURNAMENT?
WHOA...
THERE'S SO MANY PEOPLE MY AGE.
THAT'S THE GAME I'M PLAYING!
YOU'RE GONNA GET THAT CONFIS-CATED.
YOU BETTER NOT TELL.
MEOW!
OOHH!
I WISH I COULD PLAY WITH THEM.
MUST BE NICE... HAVING FRIENDS.
CAN I GO TO YOUR HOUSE TODAY?
I GOT MY BROTHER TO HELP ME.

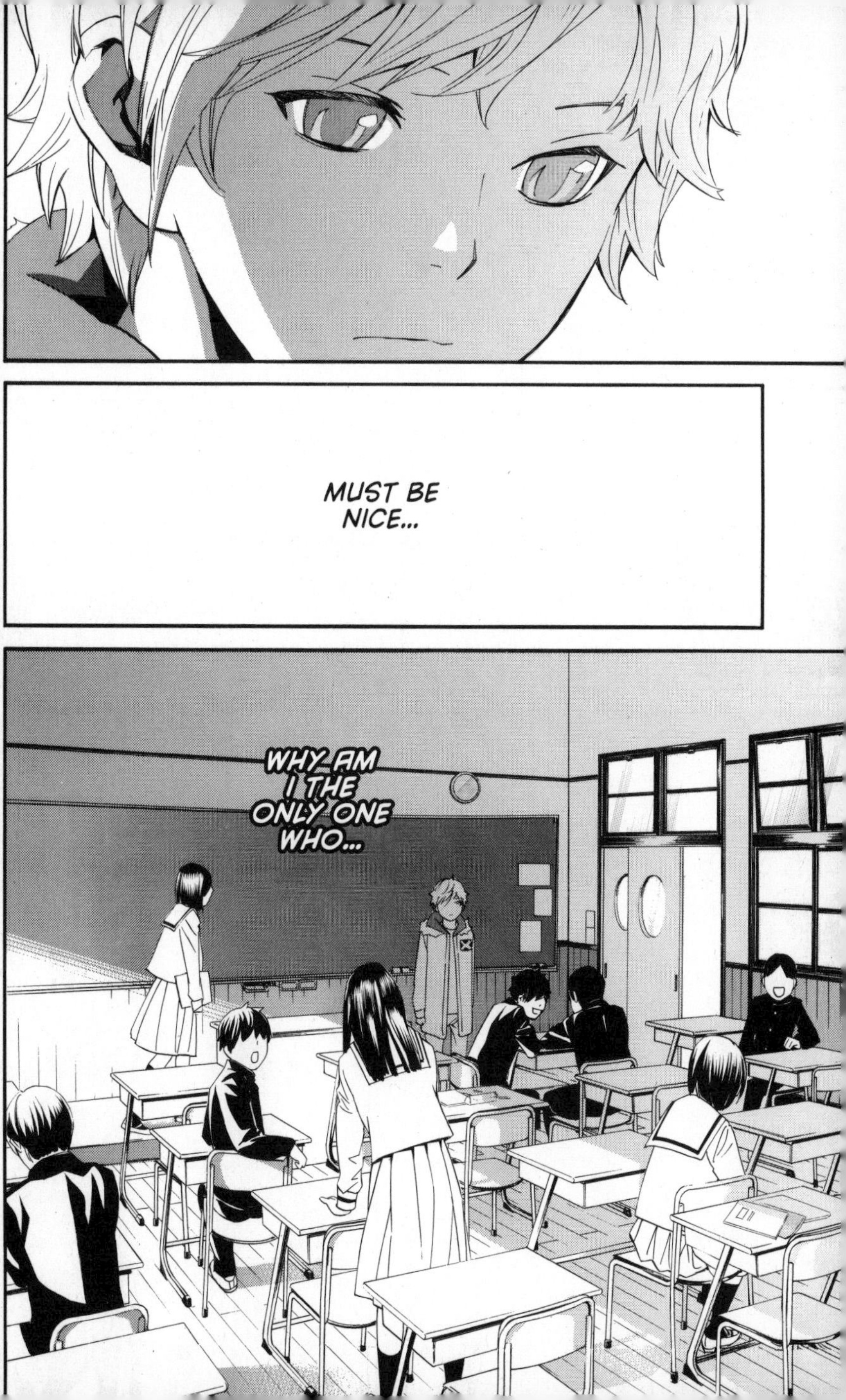
MUST BE NICE...
WHY AM I THE ONLY ONE WHO...

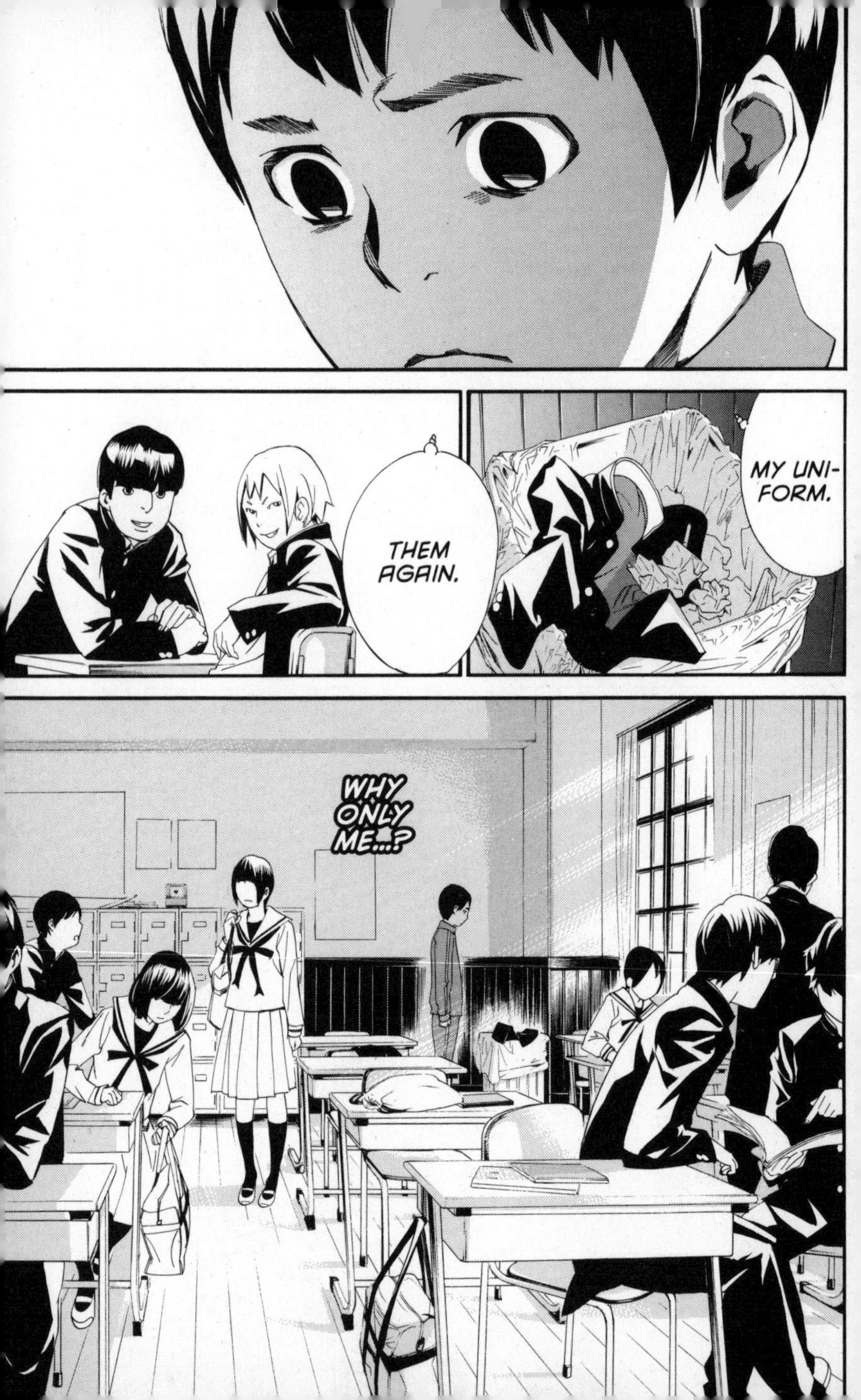
MY UNI-FORM.
THEM AGAIN.
WHY ONLY ME...?

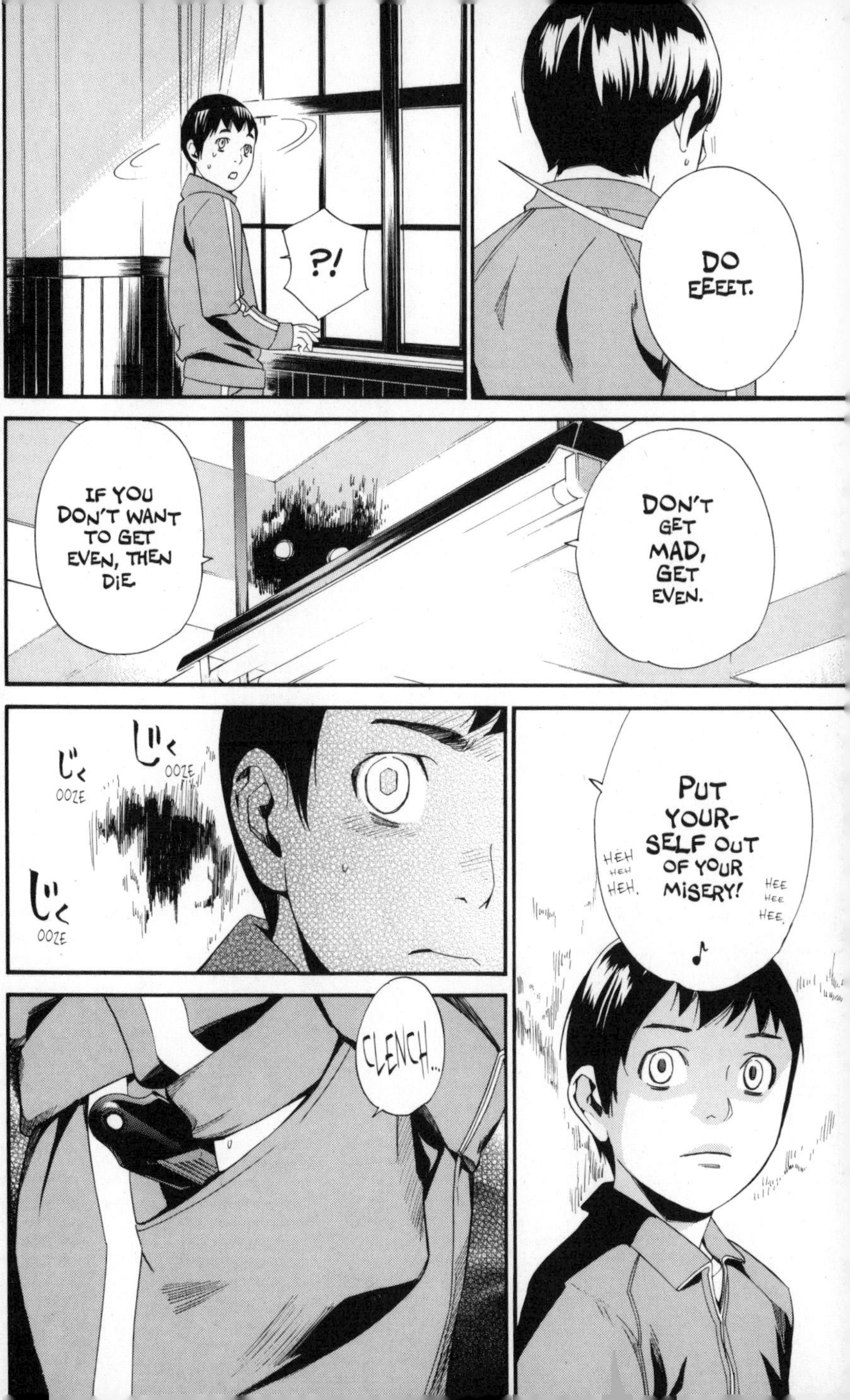
DO EEEEET.
?!
DON'T GET MAD, GET EVEN.
IF YOU DON'T WANT TO GET EVEN, THEN DIE
PUT YOURSELF OUT OF YOUR MISERY!
HEE HEE HEE.
HEH HEH HEH.
じく OOZE
じく OOZE
じく OOZE
CLENCH...

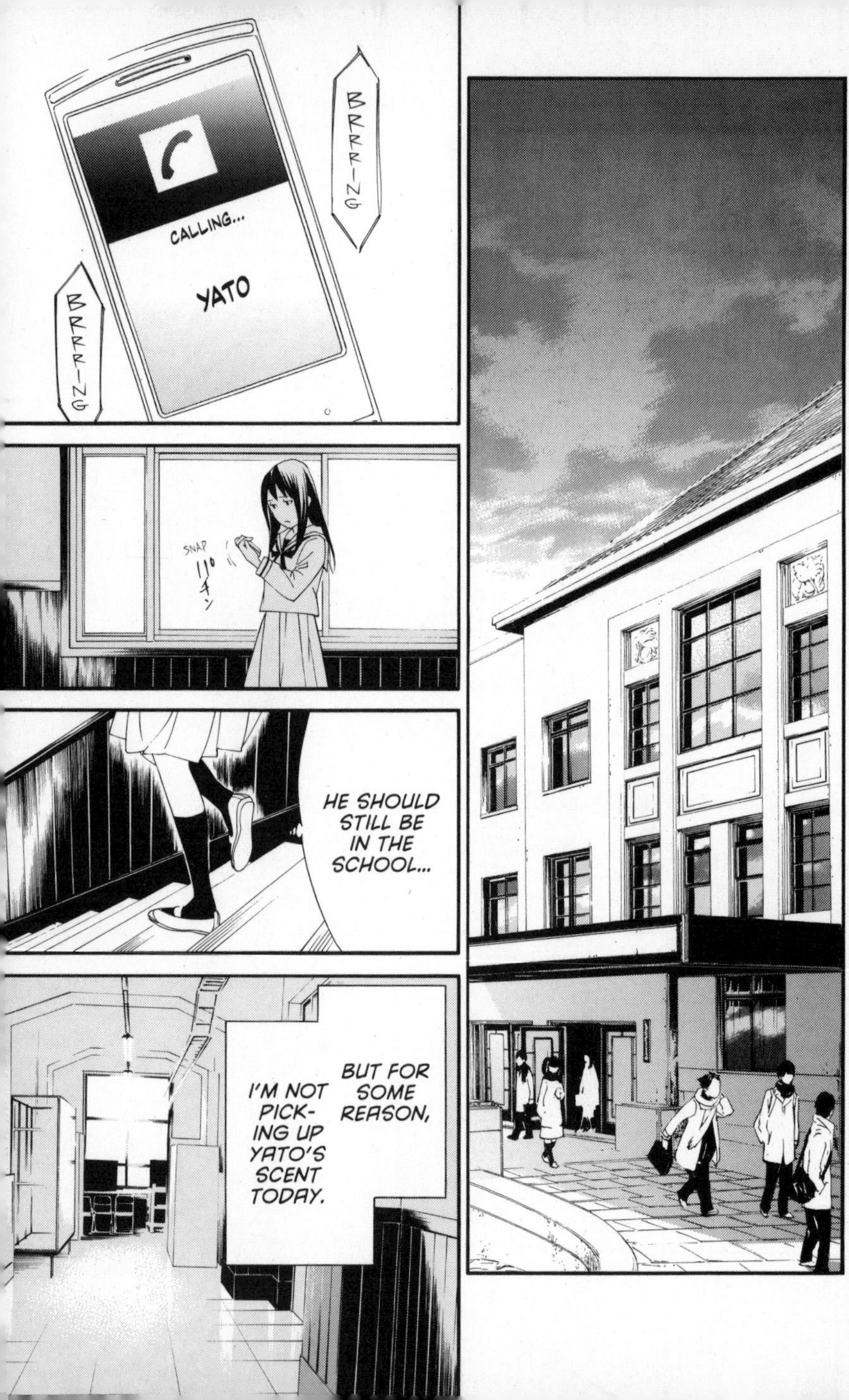
BRRRING
CALLING...
YATO
BRRRING
SNAP
パチン
HE SHOULD STILL BE IN THE SCHOOL...
BUT FOR SOME REASON,
I'M NOT PICK-ING UP YATO'S SCENT TODAY.

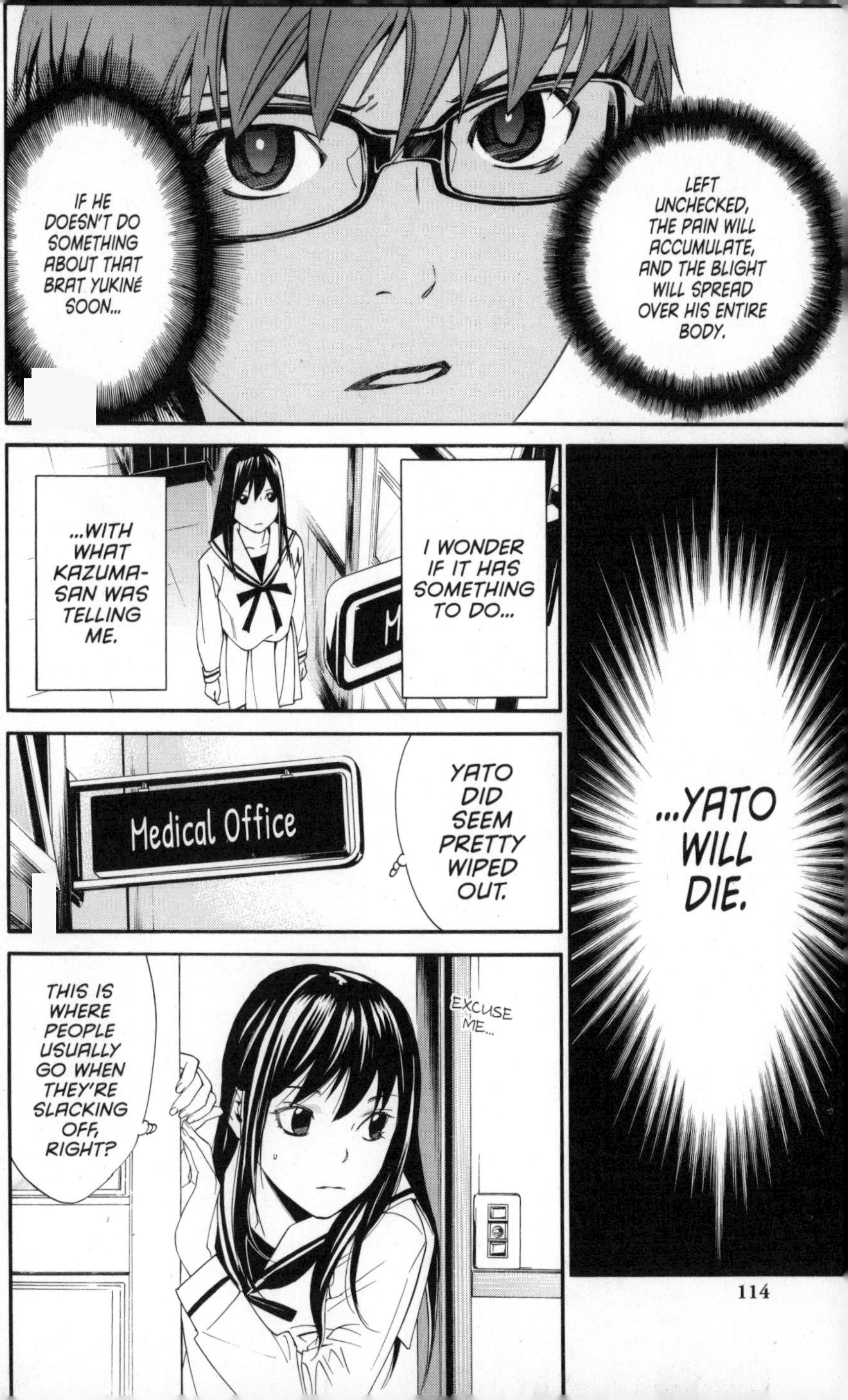
LEFT UNCHECKED, THE PAIN WILL ACCUMULATE, AND THE BLIGHT WILL SPREAD OVER HIS ENTIRE BODY.
IF HE DOESN'T DO SOMETHING ABOUT THAT BRAT YUKINÉ SOON...
...YATO WILL DIE.
I WONDER IF IT HAS SOMETHING TO DO...
...WITH WHAT KAZUMA-SAN WAS TELLING ME.
YATO DID SEEM PRETTY WIPED OUT.
Medical Office
EXCUSE ME...
THIS IS WHERE PEOPLE USUALLY GO WHEN THEY'RE SLACKING OFF, RIGHT?

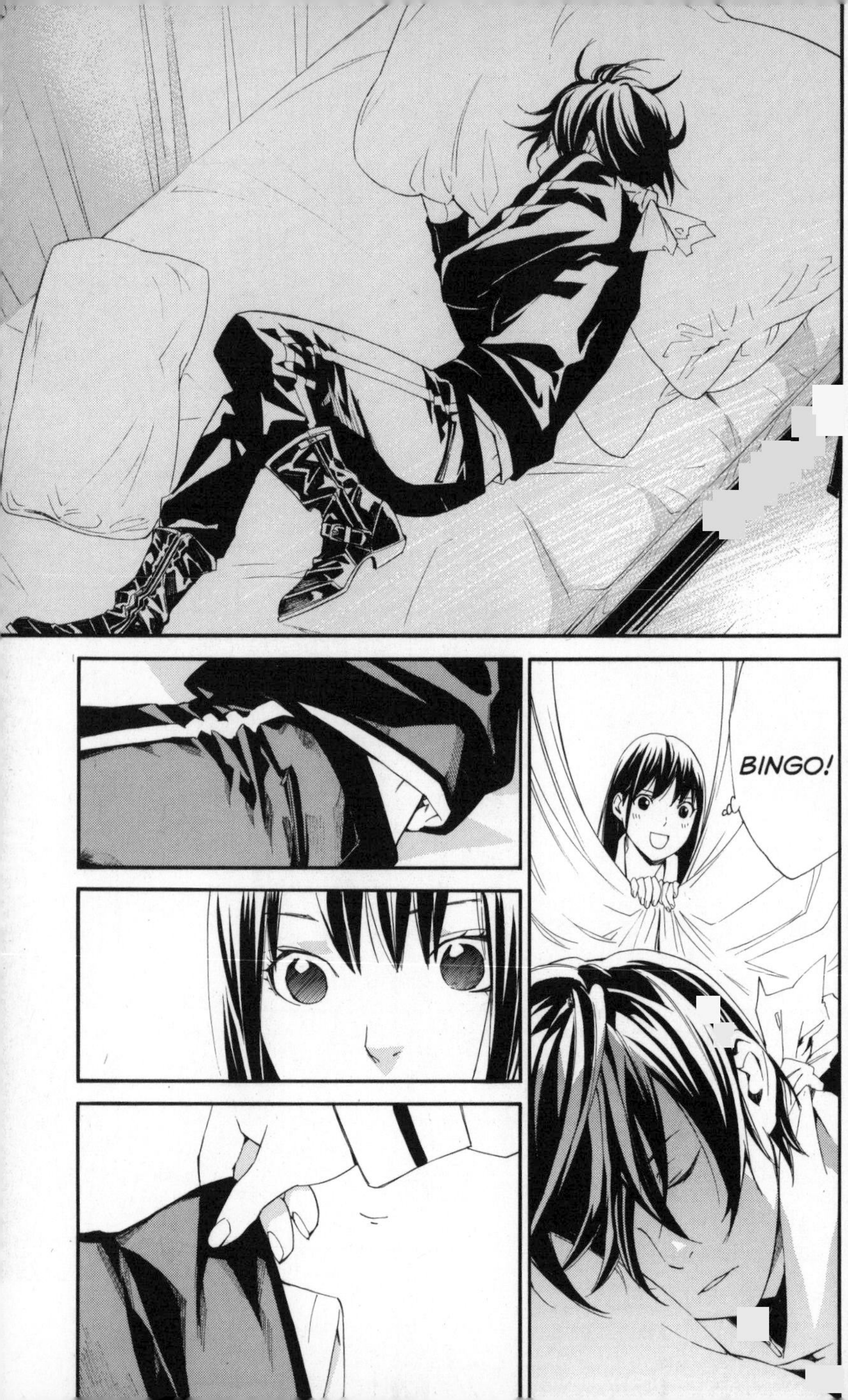
BINGO!

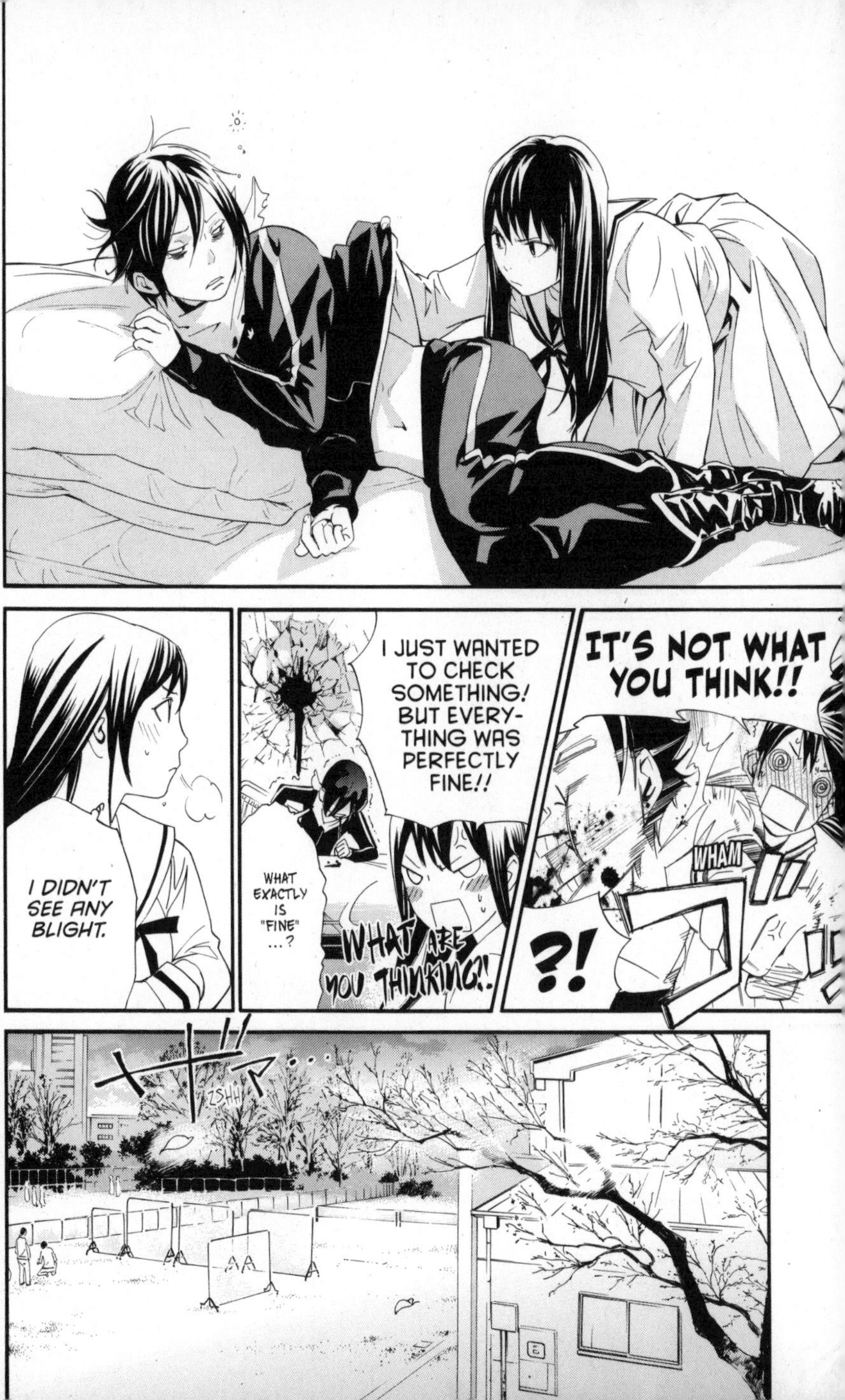
IT'S NOT WHAT YOU THINK!!
WHAM
?!
I JUST WANTED TO CHECK SOMETHING! BUT EVERY-THING WAS PERFECTLY FINE!!
WHAT ARE YOU THINKING?!
WHAT EXACTLY IS "FINE" ...?
I DIDN'T SEE ANY BLIGHT.
ZSHH
...

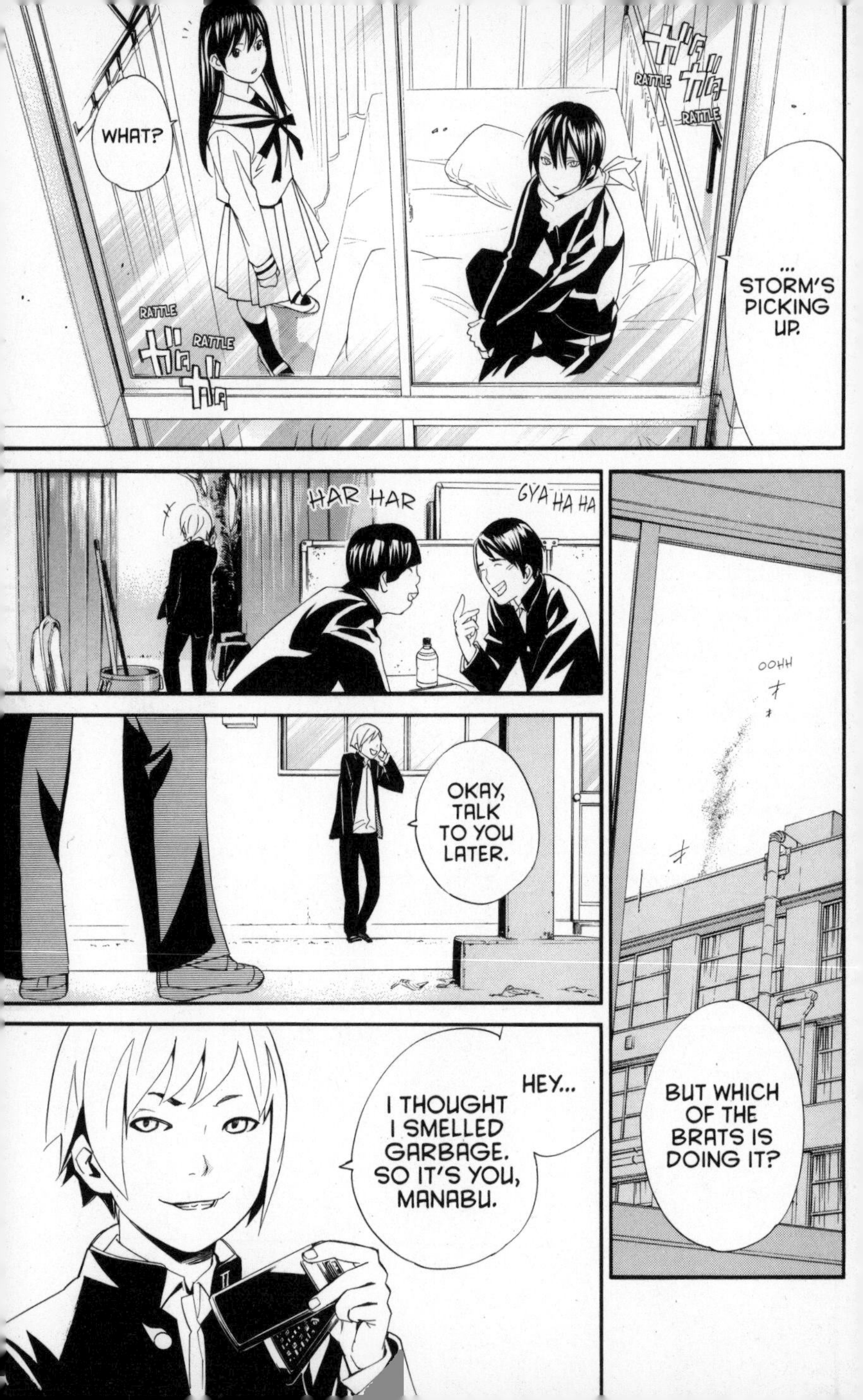
RATTLE
RATTLE
... STORM'S PICKING UP.
WHAT?
RATTLE
RATTLE
OOHH
BUT WHICH OF THE BRATS IS DOING IT?
GYA HA HA
HAR HAR
OKAY, TALK TO YOU LATER.
HEY...
I THOUGHT I SMELLED GARBAGE. SO IT'S YOU, MANABU.

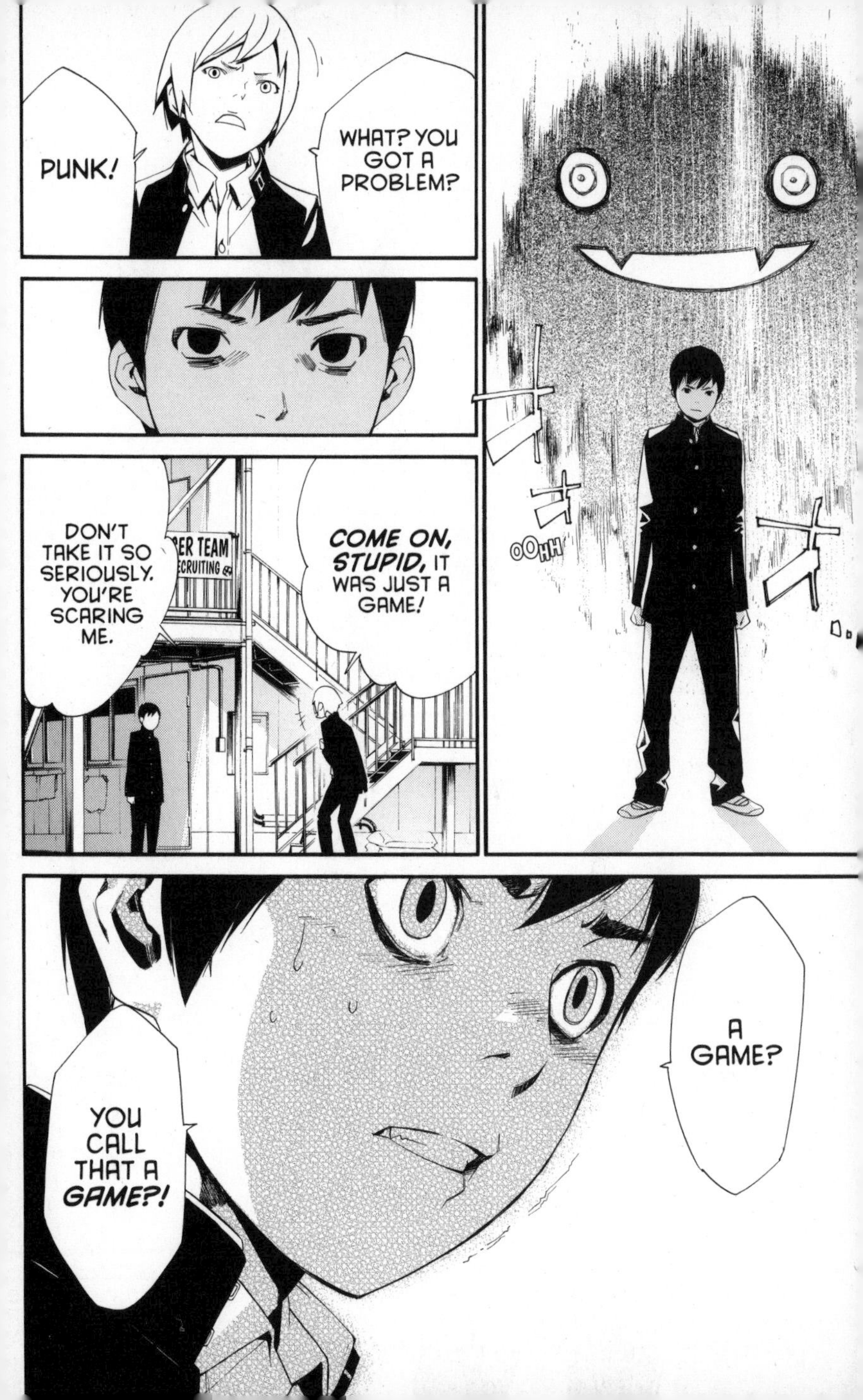

OOHH
WHAT? YOU GOT A PROBLEM?
PUNK!
COME ON, STUPID, IT WAS JUST A GAME!
DON'T TAKE IT SO SERIOUSLY. YOU'RE SCARING ME.
A GAME?
YOU CALL THAT A *GAME?!*

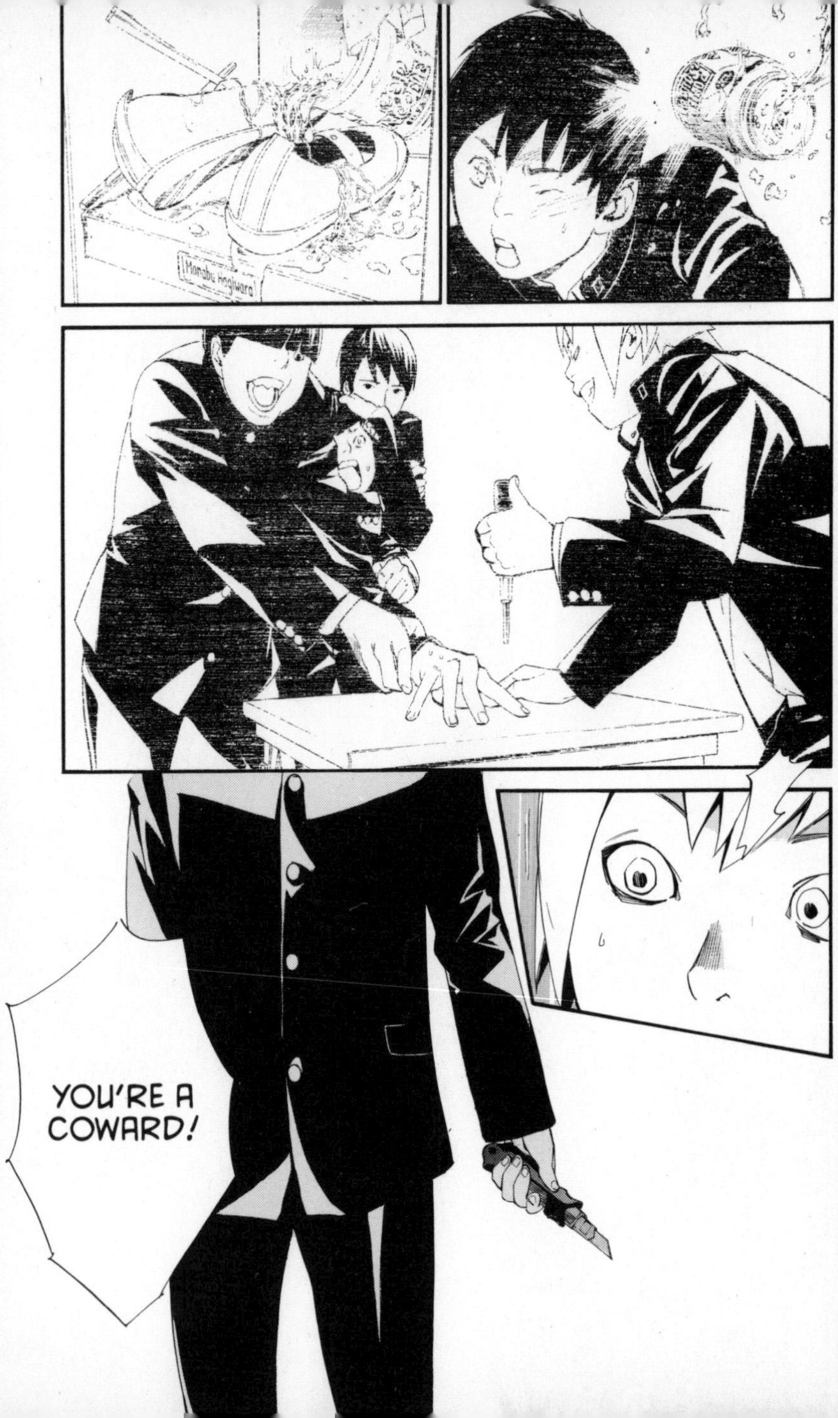
Manabu Hagiwara
YOU'RE A COWARD!

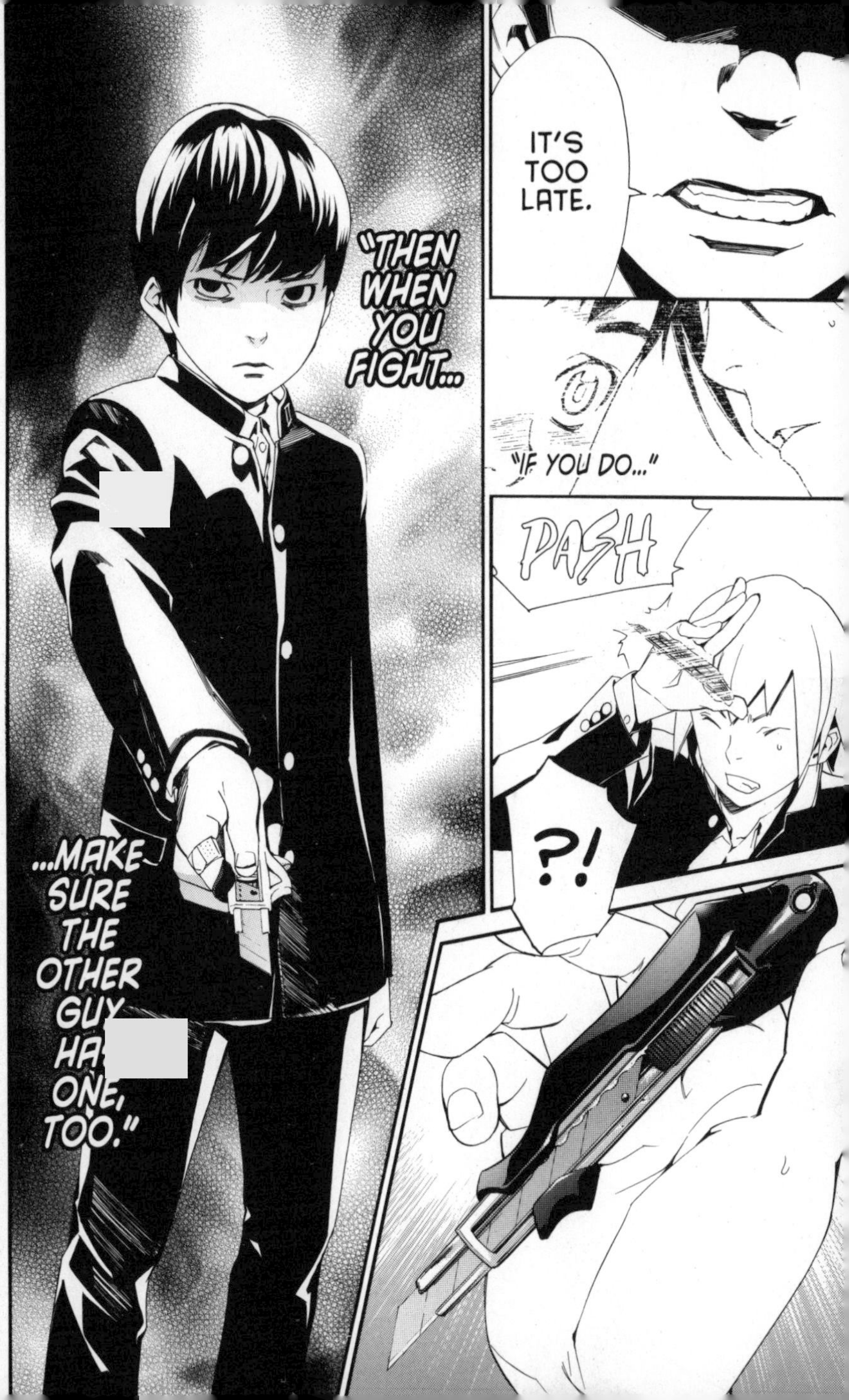
IT'S TOO LATE.
"IF YOU DO..."
PASH
?!
"THEN WHEN YOU FIGHT...
...MAKE SURE THE OTHER GUY HA ONE, TOO."

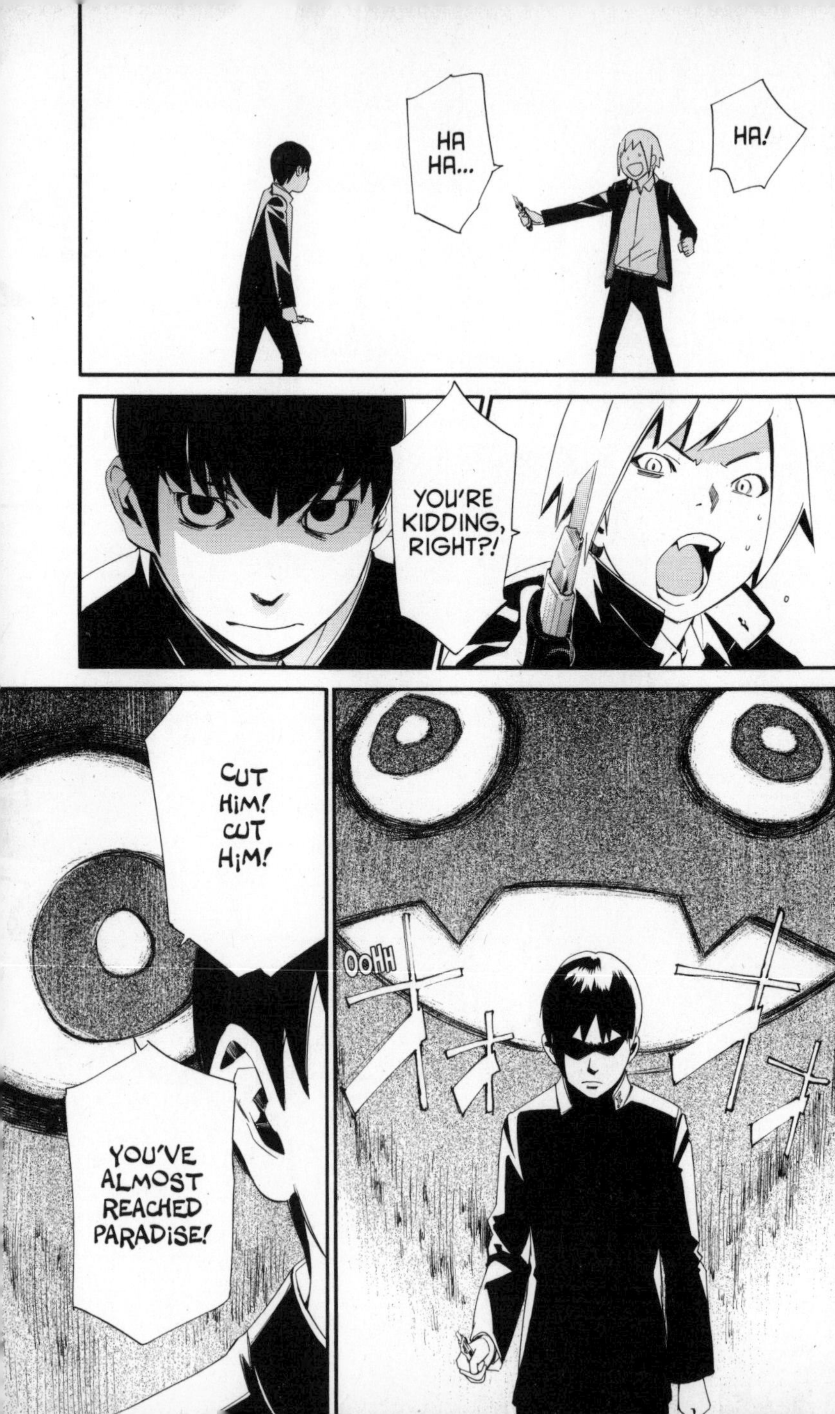
HA!
HA HA...
YOU'RE KIDDING, RIGHT?!
OOHH
CUT HIM! CUT HIM!
YOU'VE ALMOST REACHED PARADISE!

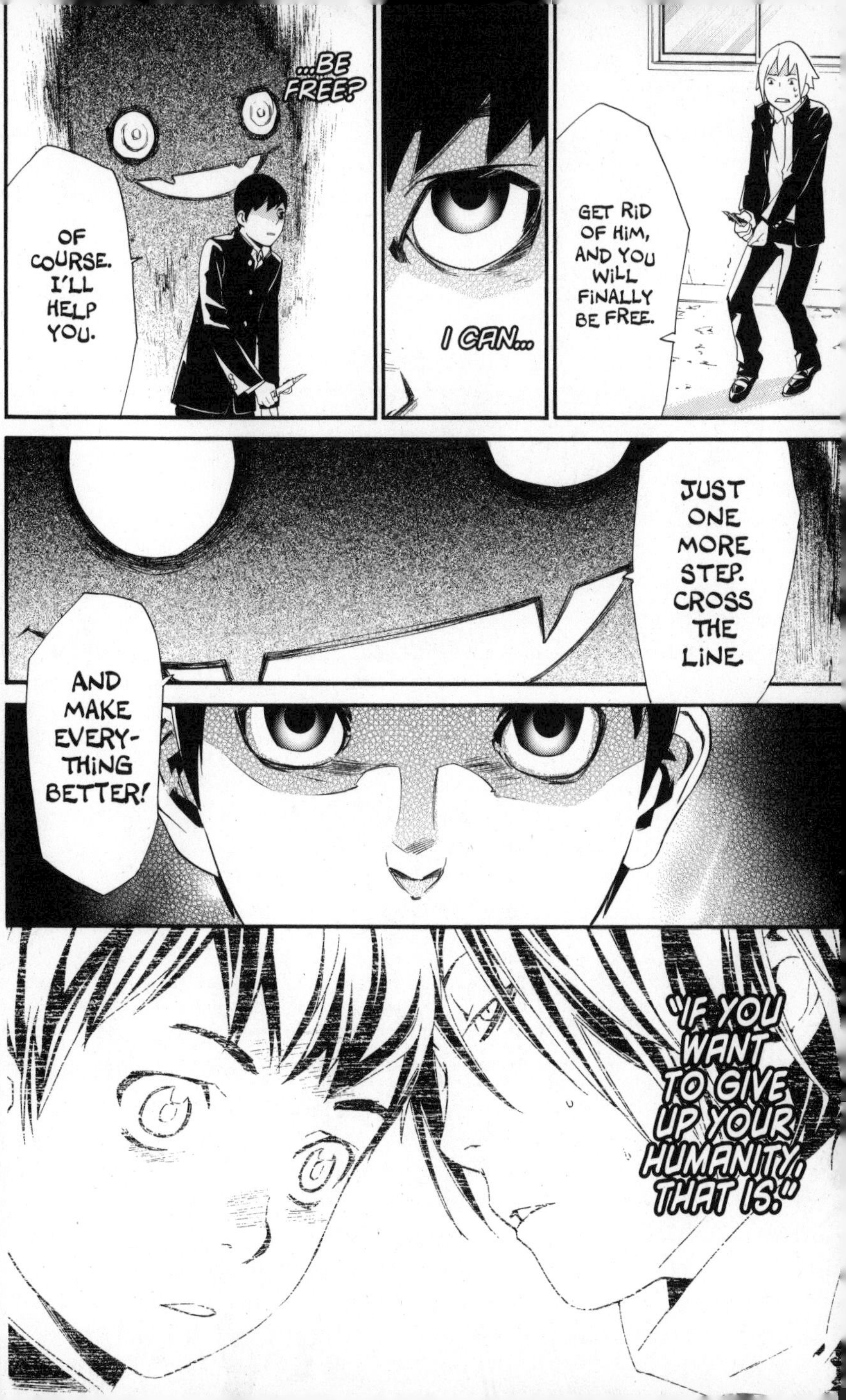
GET RID OF HIM, AND YOU WILL FINALLY BE FREE.
I CAN...
...BE FREE?
OF COURSE. I'LL HELP YOU.
JUST ONE MORE STEP. CROSS THE LINE.
AND MAKE EVERY-THING BETTER!
"IF YOU WANT TO GIVE UP YOUR HUMANITY, THAT IS."

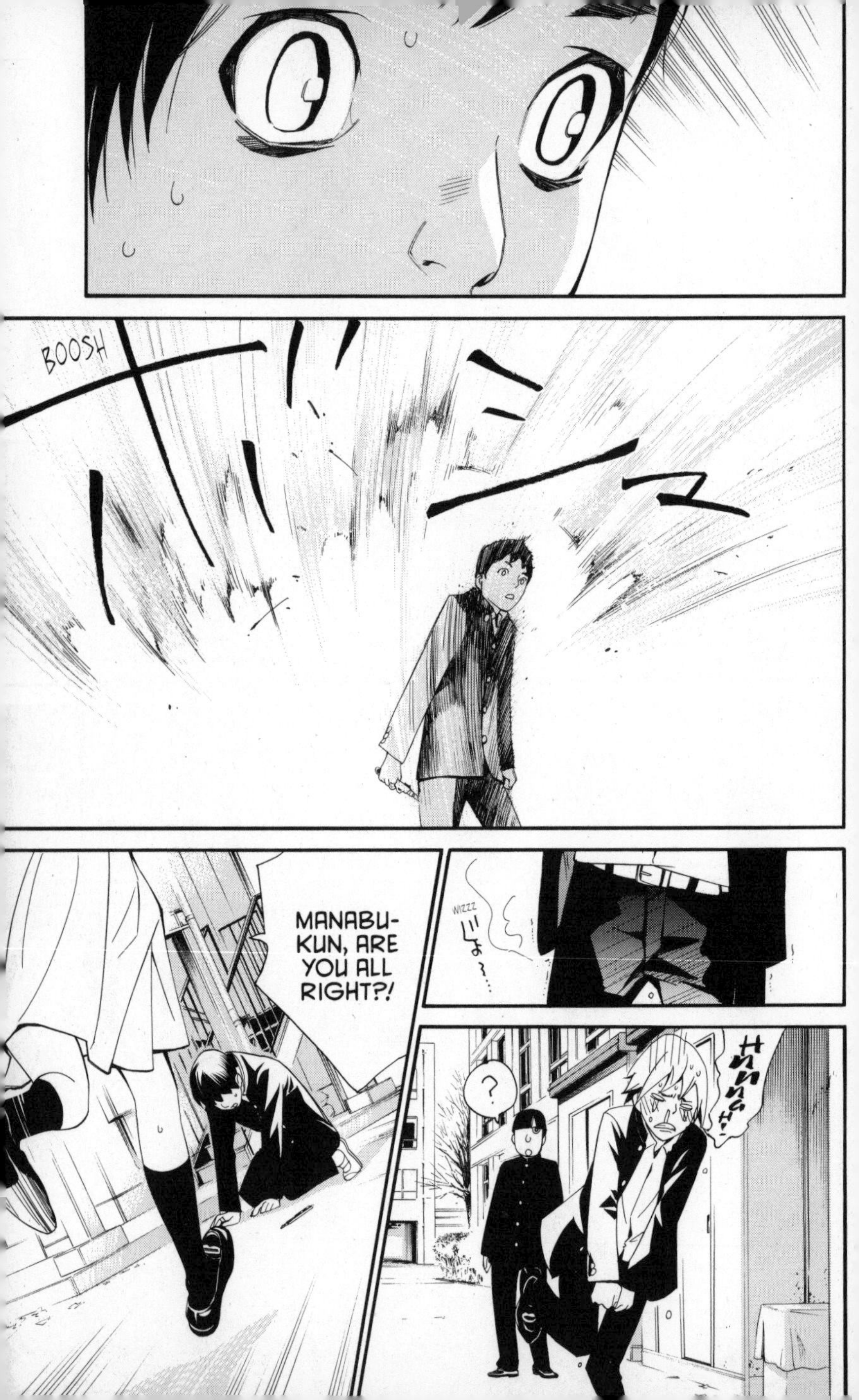
BOOSH
WIZZZ
じょ~...
?
HNNNGH!
MANABU-KUN, ARE YOU ALL RIGHT?!

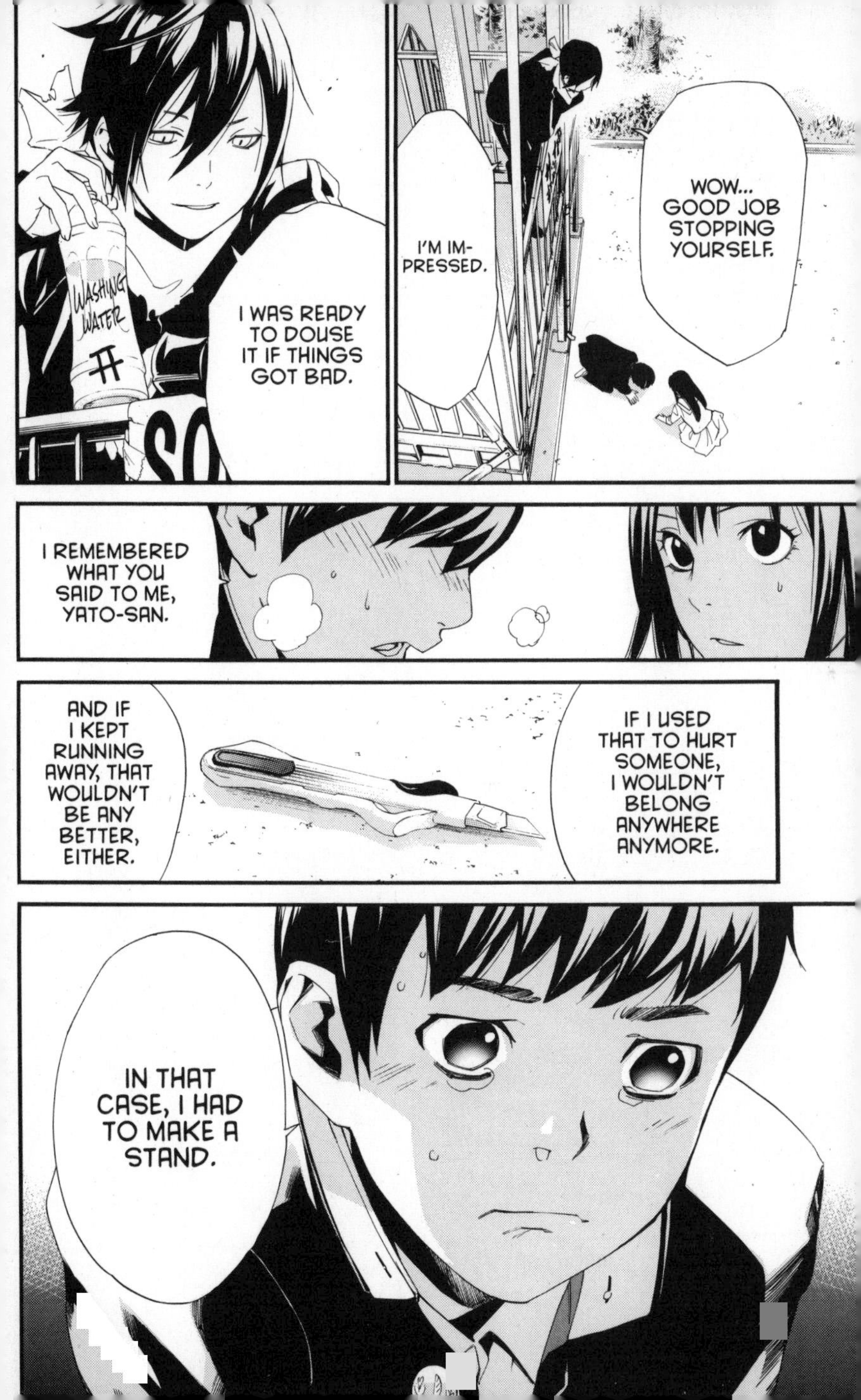
WOW... GOOD JOB STOPPING YOURSELF.
I'M IM-PRESSED.
WASHING WATER
I WAS READY TO DOUSE IT IF THINGS GOT BAD.
I REMEMBERED WHAT YOU SAID TO ME, YATO-SAN.
IF I USED THAT TO HURT SOMEONE, I WOULDN'T BELONG ANYWHERE ANYMORE.
AND IF I KEPT RUNNING AWAY, THAT WOULDN'T BE ANY BETTER, EITHER.
IN THAT CASE, I HAD TO MAKE A STAND.

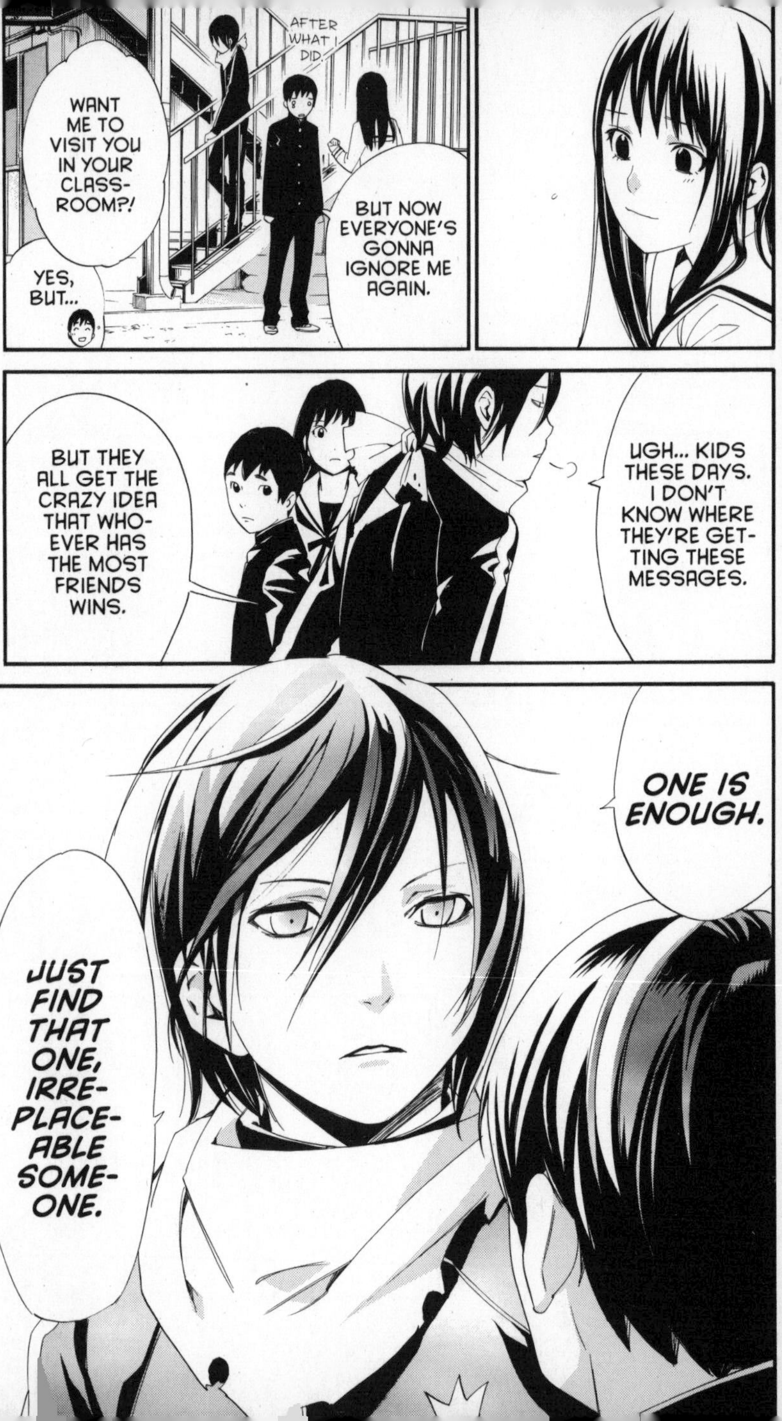
AFTER WHAT I DID.
BUT NOW EVERYONE'S GONNA IGNORE ME AGAIN.
WANT ME TO VISIT YOU IN YOUR CLASSROOM?!
YES, BUT...
UGH... KIDS THESE DAYS. I DON'T KNOW WHERE THEY'RE GETTING THESE MESSAGES.
BUT THEY ALL GET THE CRAZY IDEA THAT WHOEVER HAS THE MOST FRIENDS WINS.
ONE IS ENOUGH.
JUST FIND THAT ONE, IRREPLACEABLE SOMEONE.

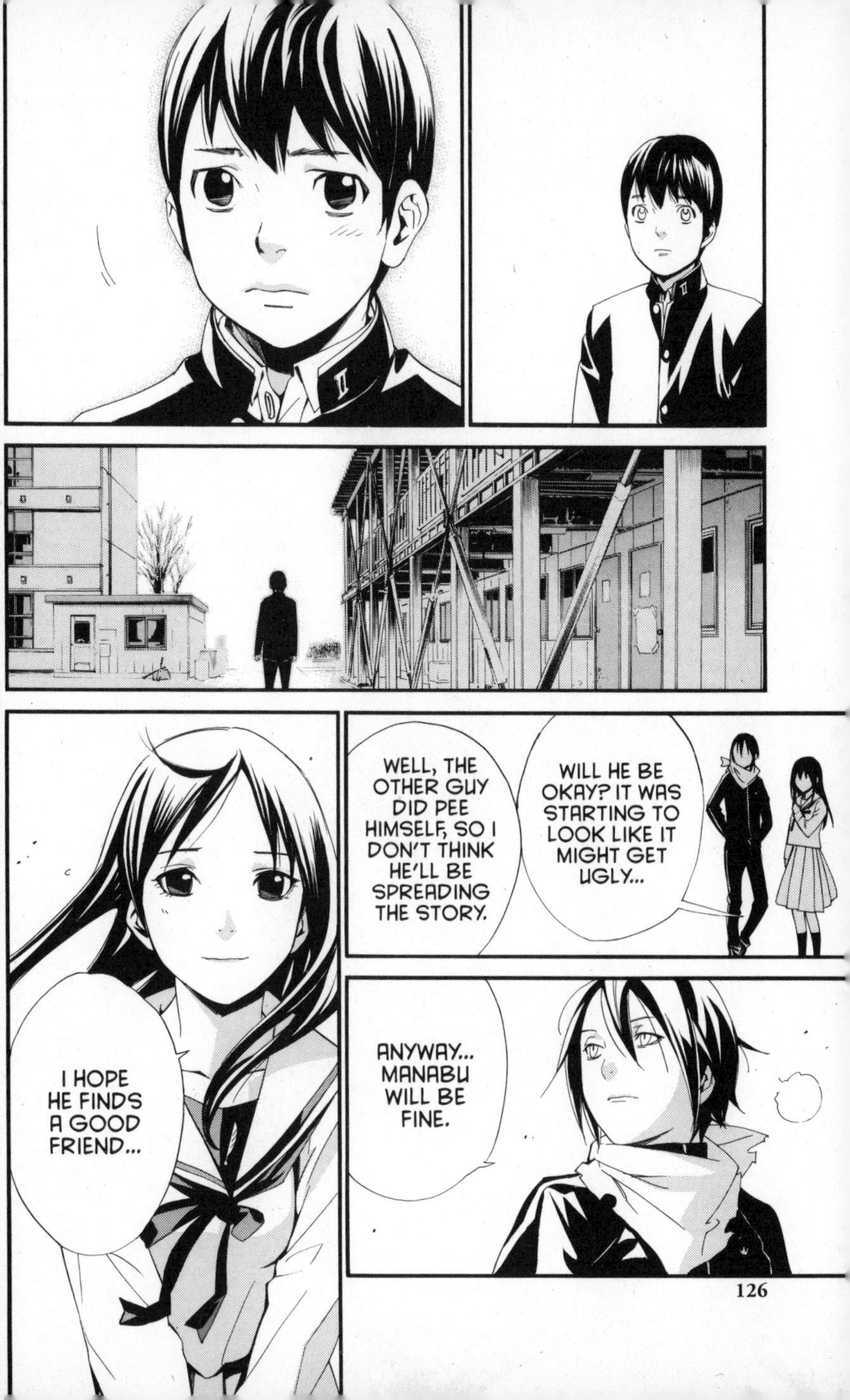
WILL HE BE OKAY? IT WAS STARTING TO LOOK LIKE IT MIGHT GET UGLY...
WELL, THE OTHER GUY DID PEE HIMSELF, SO I DON'T THINK HE'LL BE SPREADING THE STORY.
ANYWAY... MANABU WILL BE FINE.
I HOPE HE FINDS A GOOD FRIEND...

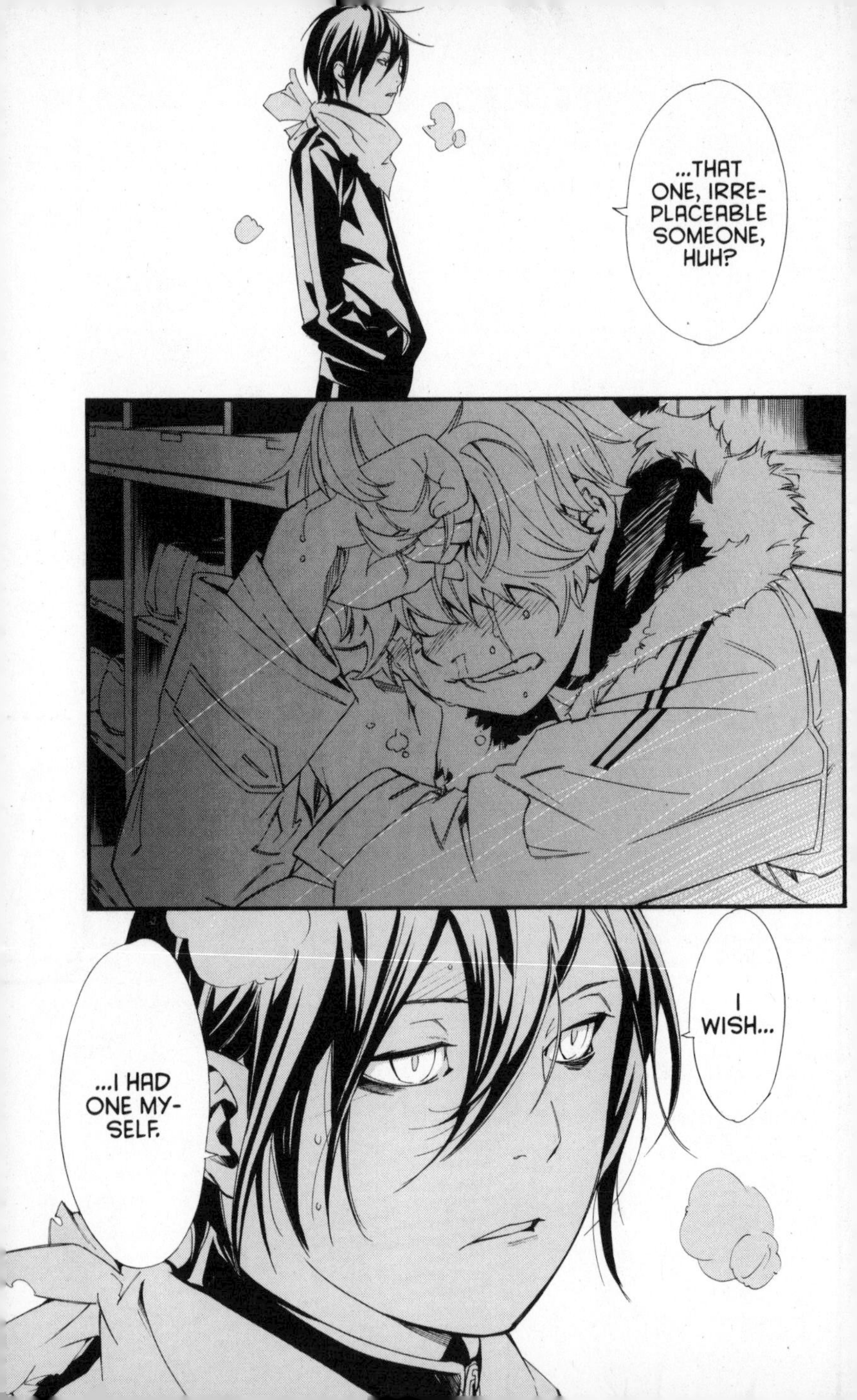
...THAT ONE, IRRE-PLACEABLE SOMEONE, HUH?
I WISH...
...I HAD ONE MY-SELF.

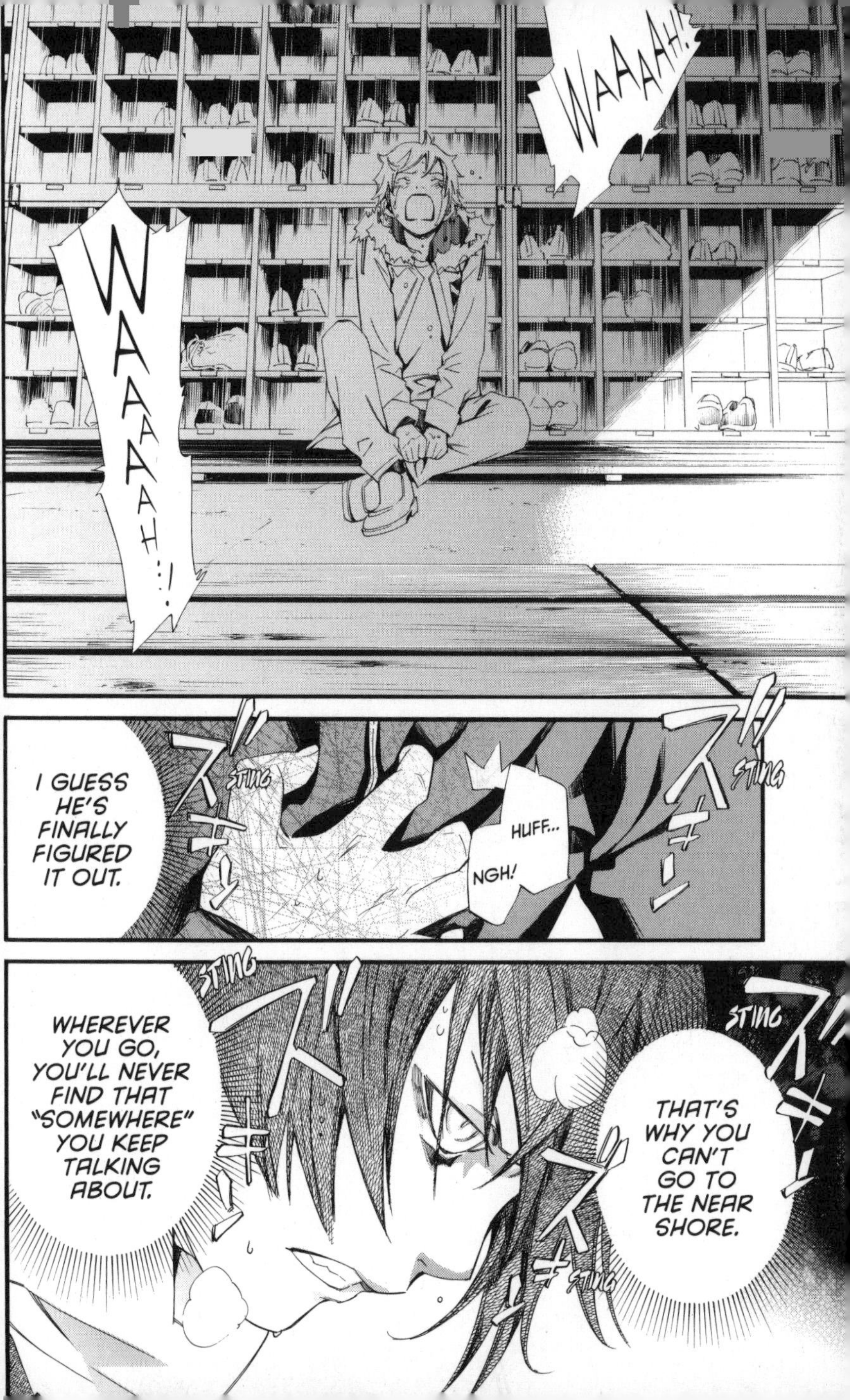
WAAAAH!
WAAAAAH...!
STING
HUFF...
NGH!
STING
I GUESS HE'S FINALLY FIGURED IT OUT.
STING
THAT'S WHY YOU CAN'T GO TO THE NEAR SHORE.
STING
WHEREVER YOU GO, YOU'LL NEVER FIND THAT "SOMEWHERE" YOU KEEP TALKING ABOUT.
STING

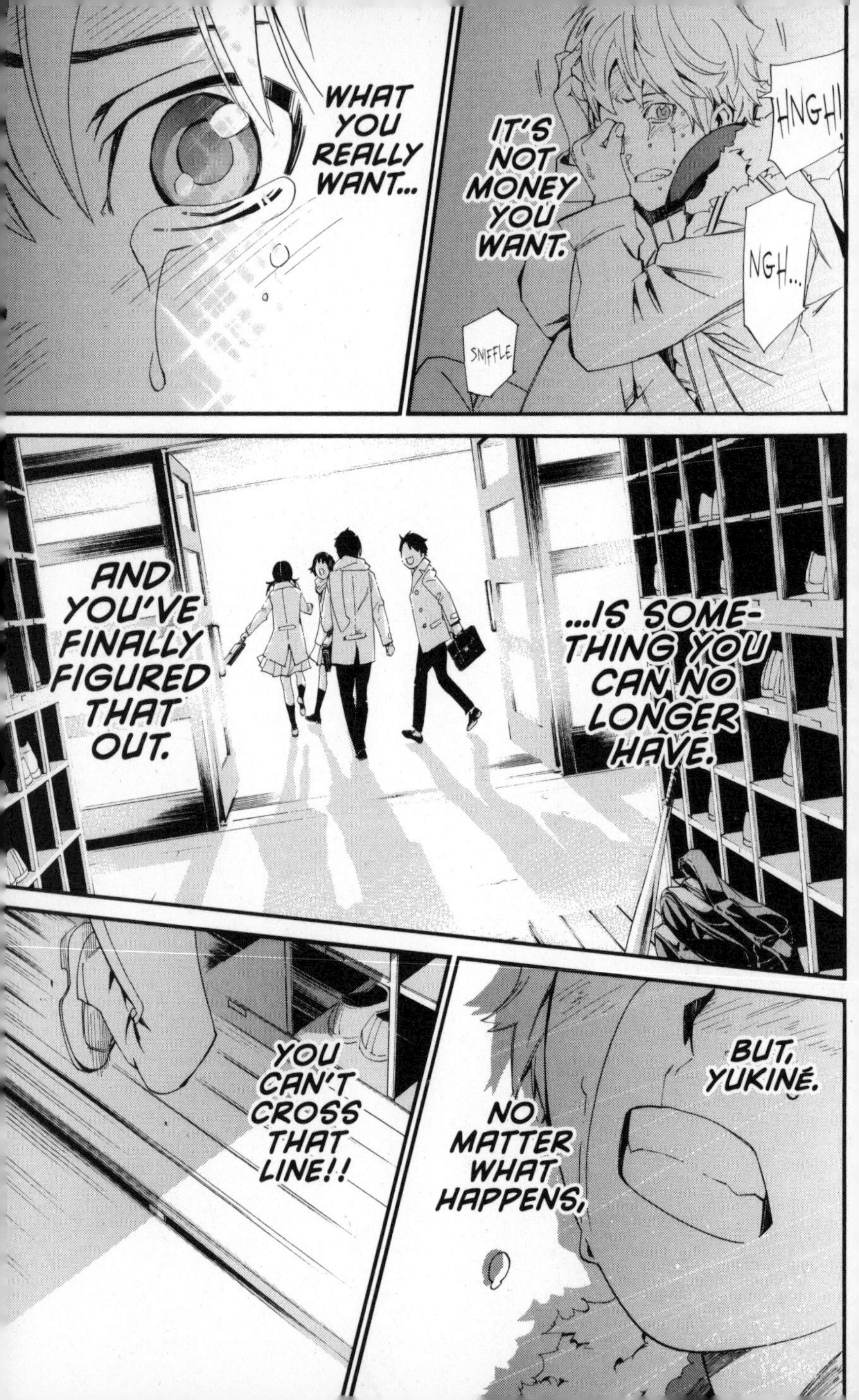

HNGH!
IT'S NOT MONEY YOU WANT.
NGH...
SNIFFLE
WHAT YOU REALLY WANT...
...IS SOME-THING YOU CAN NO LONGER HAVE.
AND YOU'VE FINALLY FIGURED THAT OUT.
BUT, YUKINE.
NO MATTER WHAT HAPPENS,
YOU CAN'T CROSS THAT LINE!!

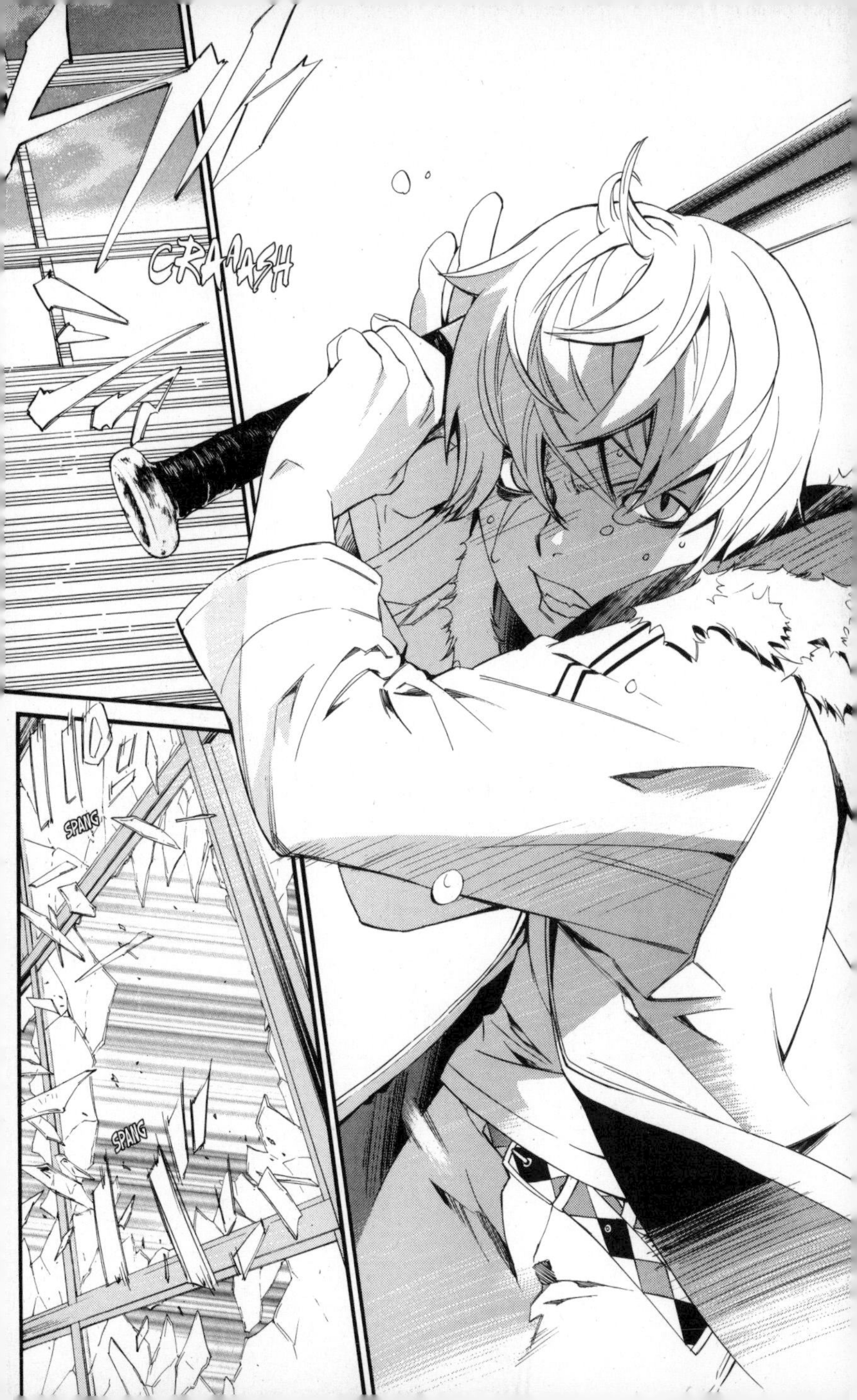
CRAAAASH
SPANG
SPANG

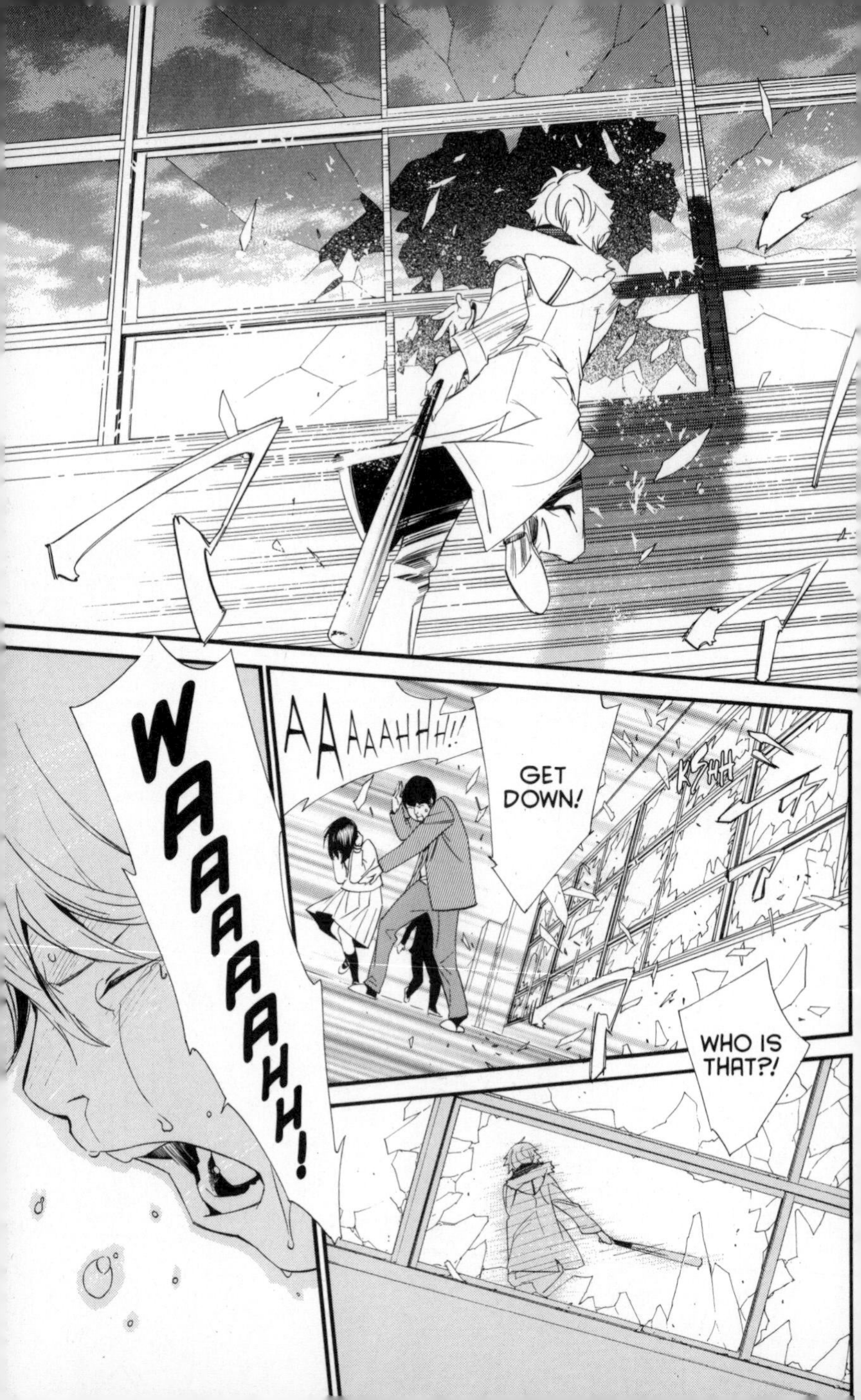
AAAAAHHH!!
GET DOWN!
KSHH
WHO IS THAT?!
WAAAAAHH!

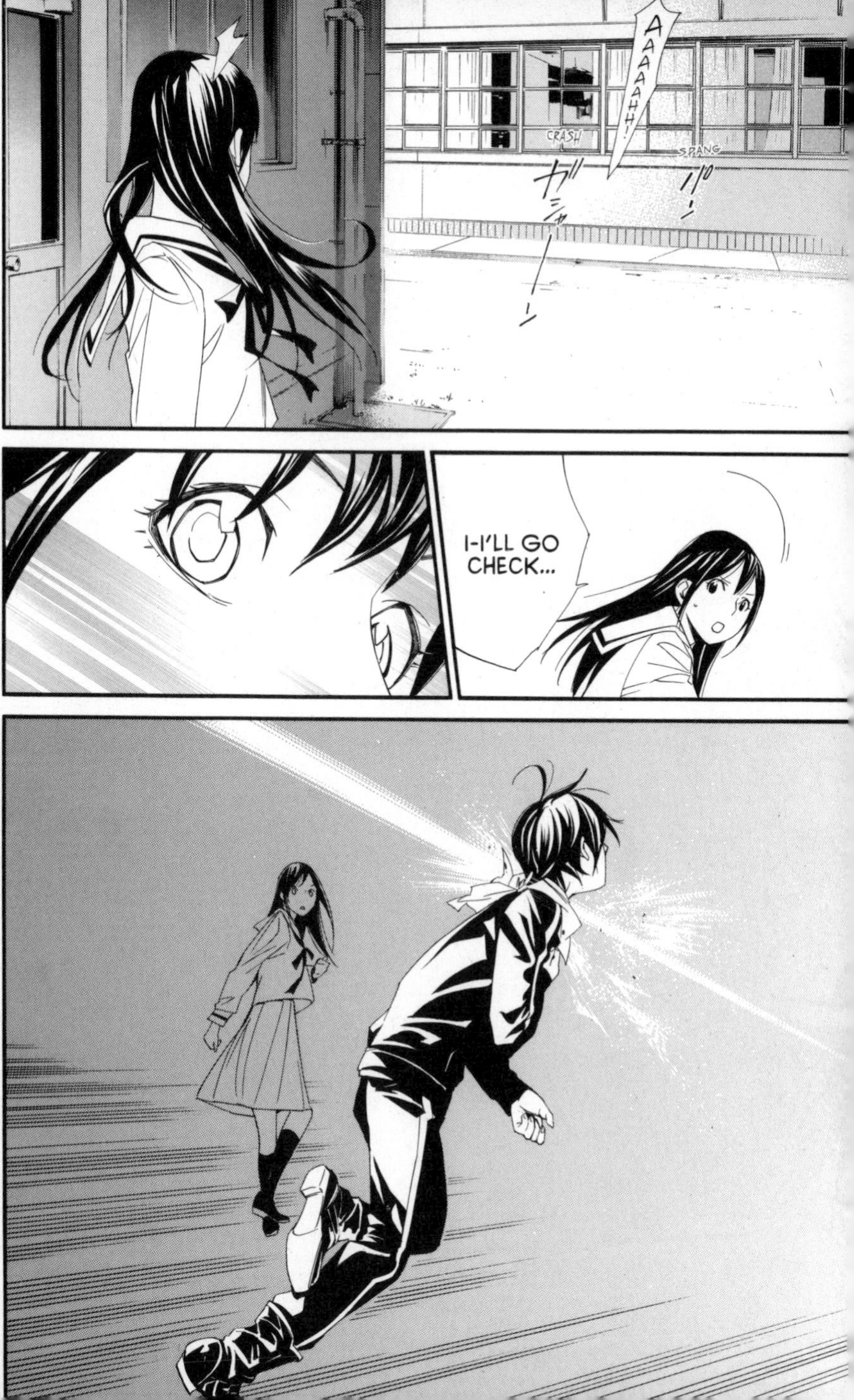
AAAAAHH!
CRASH
ガシャーン
SPANG
パリン
I-I'LL GO CHECK...

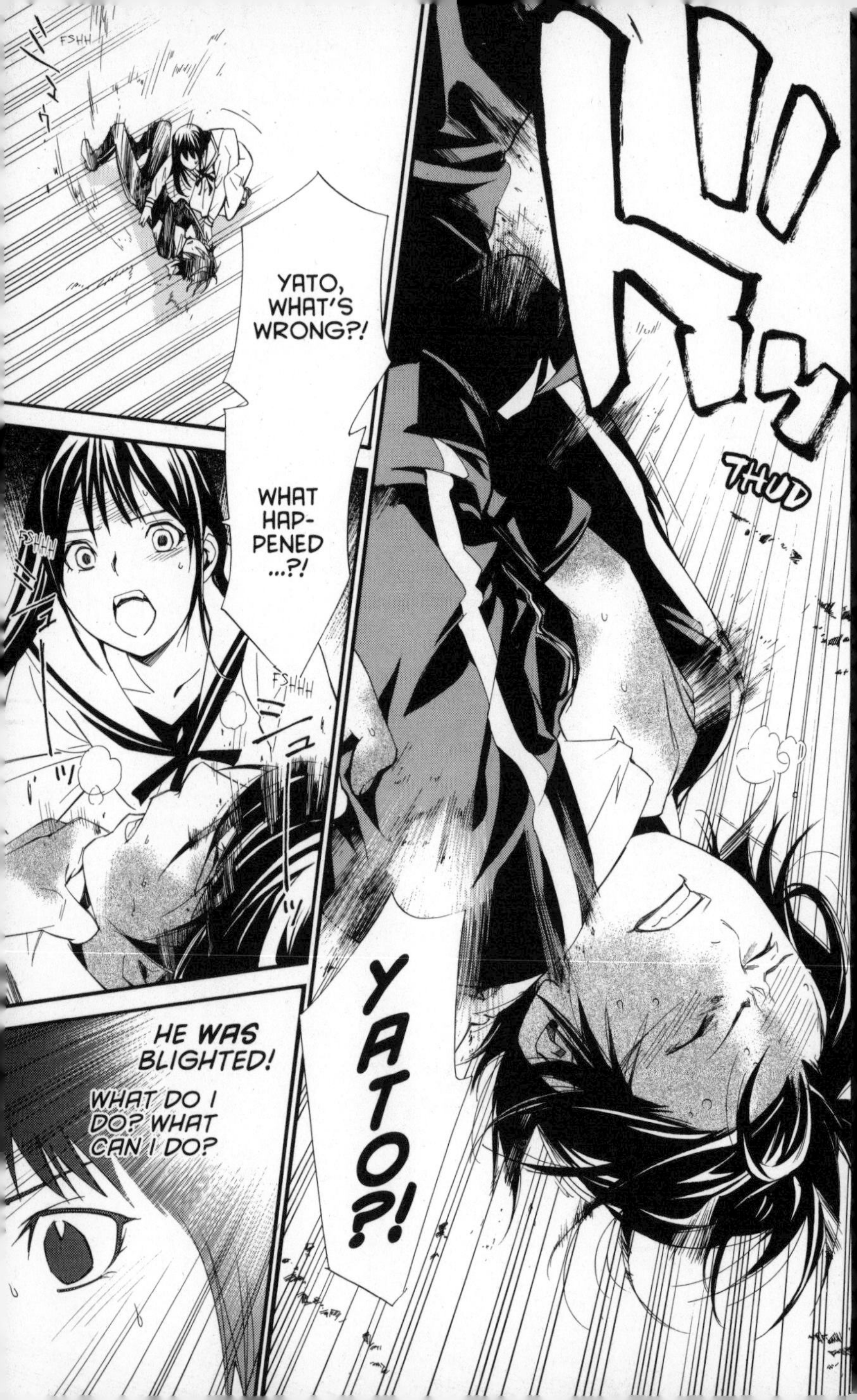
THUD
YATO?!
FSHH
YATO, WHAT'S WRONG?!
FSHHH
WHAT HAP-PENED ...?!
FSHHH
HE WAS BLIGHTED!
WHAT DO I DO? WHAT CAN I DO?

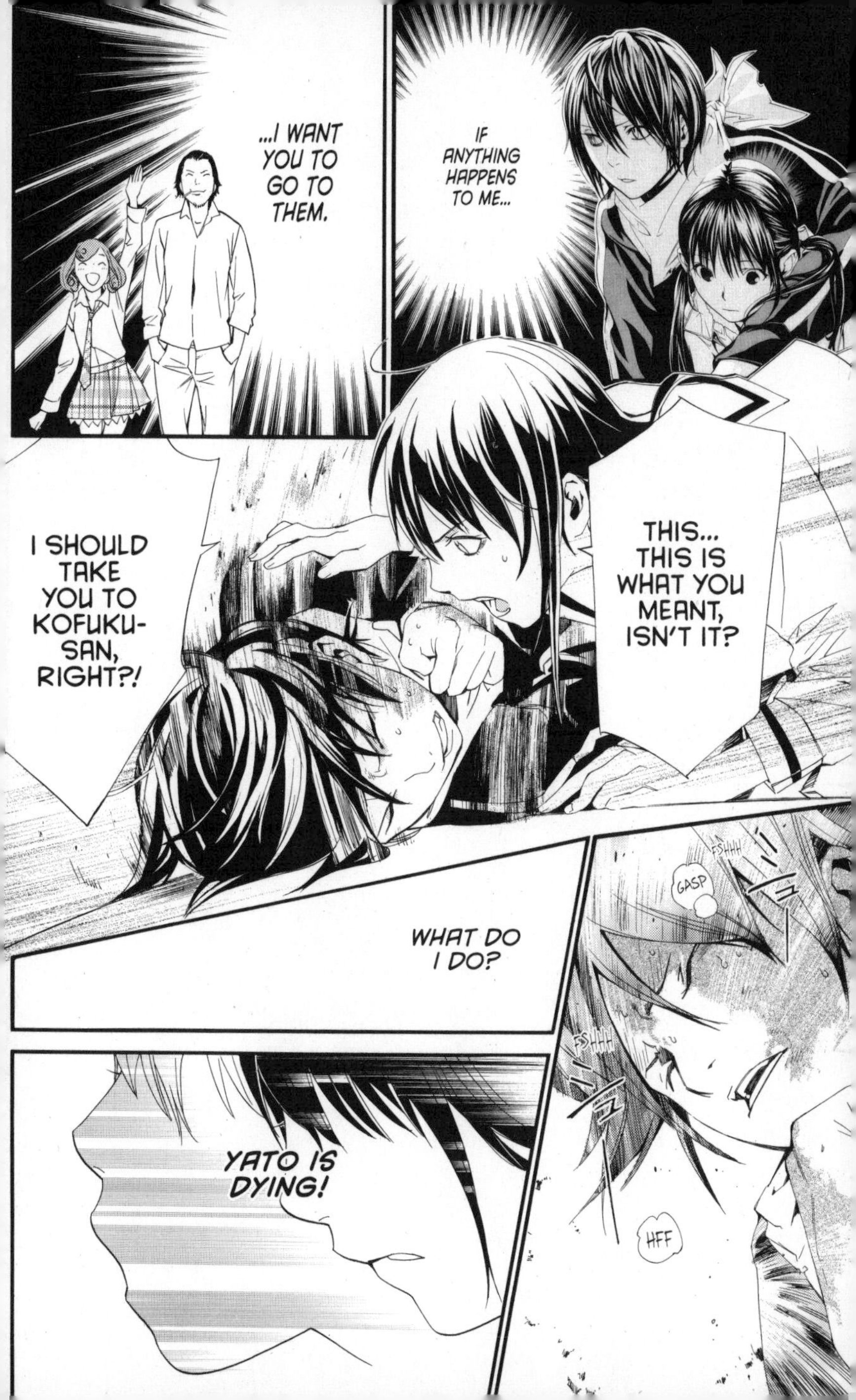

IF ANYTHING HAPPENS TO ME...
...I WANT YOU TO GO TO THEM.
THIS... THIS IS WHAT YOU MEANT, ISN'T IT?
I SHOULD TAKE YOU TO KOFUKU-SAN, RIGHT?!
FSHHH
GASP
FSHHH
HFF
WHAT DO I DO?
YATO IS DYING!

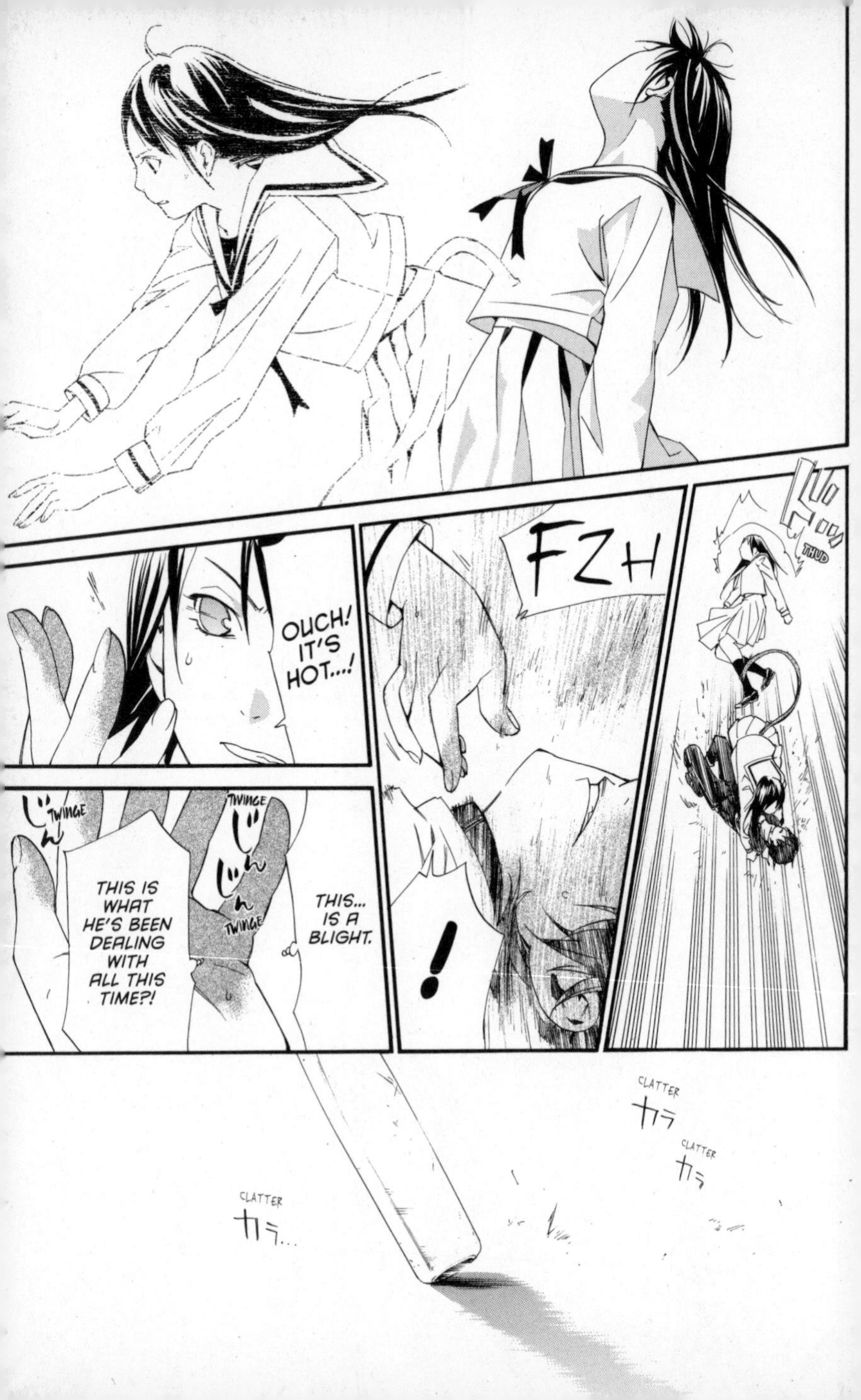

THUD
FZH
!
OUCH! IT'S HOT...!
TWINGE
TWINGE
THIS... IS A BLIGHT.
TWINGE
THIS IS WHAT HE'S BEEN DEALING WITH ALL THIS TIME?!
CLATTER
CLATTER
CLATTER

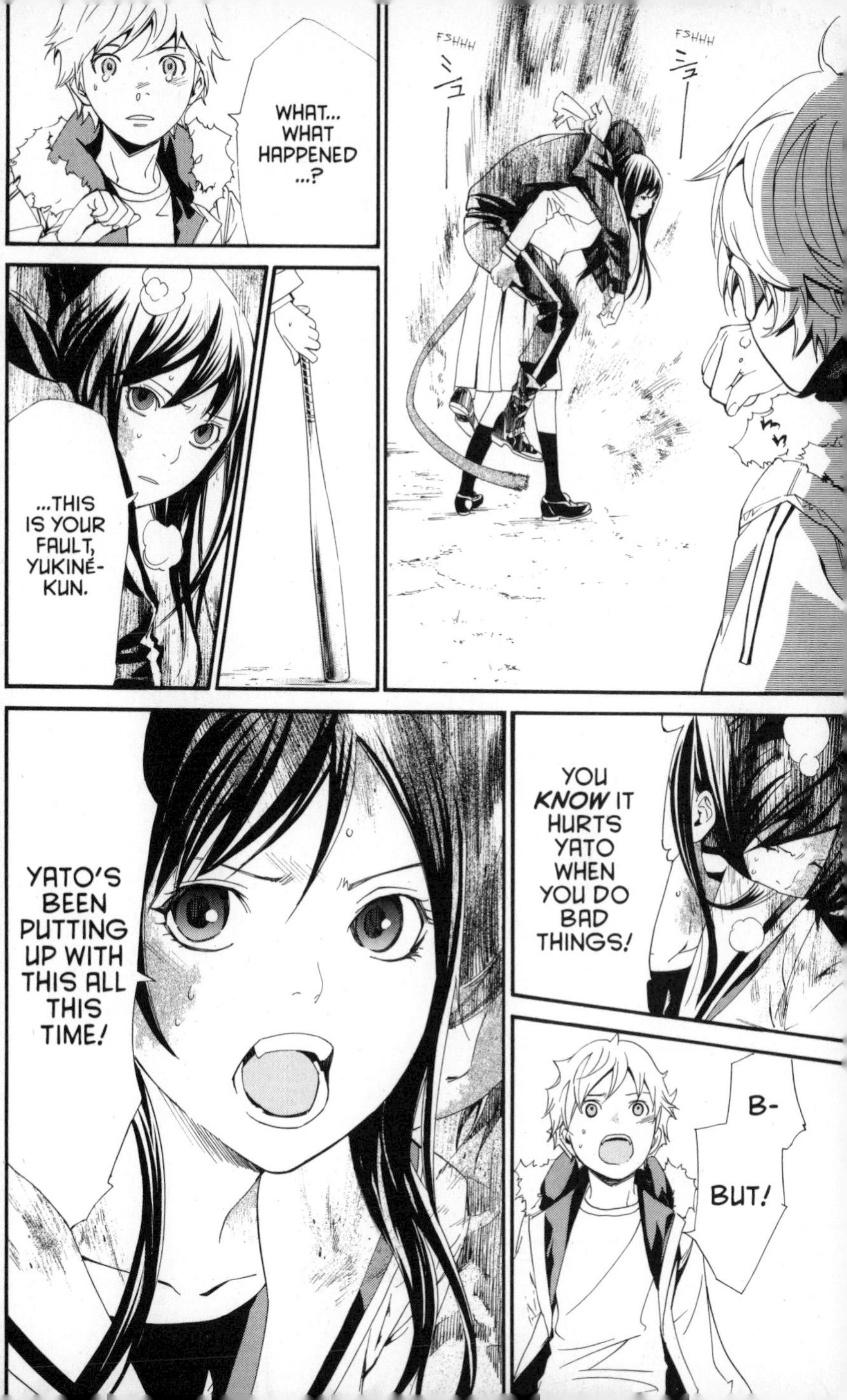
FSHHH
シュ
FSHHH
シュ
WHAT... WHAT HAPPENED ...?
...THIS IS YOUR FAULT, YUKINÉ-KUN.
YOU *KNOW* IT HURTS YATO WHEN YOU DO BAD THINGS!
B-
BUT!
YATO'S BEEN PUTTING UP WITH THIS ALL THIS TIME!

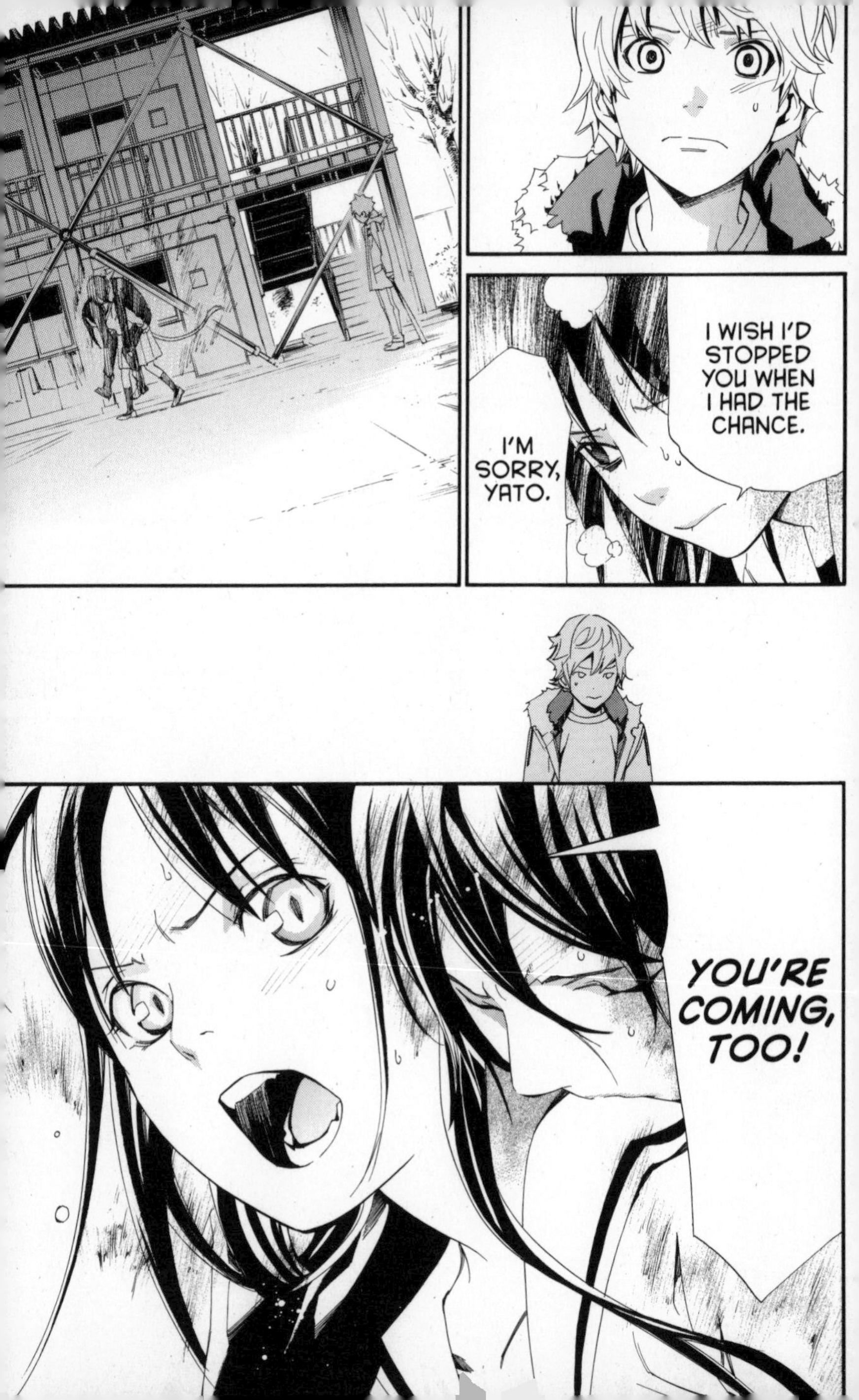
I WISH I'D STOPPED YOU WHEN I HAD THE CHANCE.
I'M SORRY, YATO.
YOU'RE COMING, TOO!

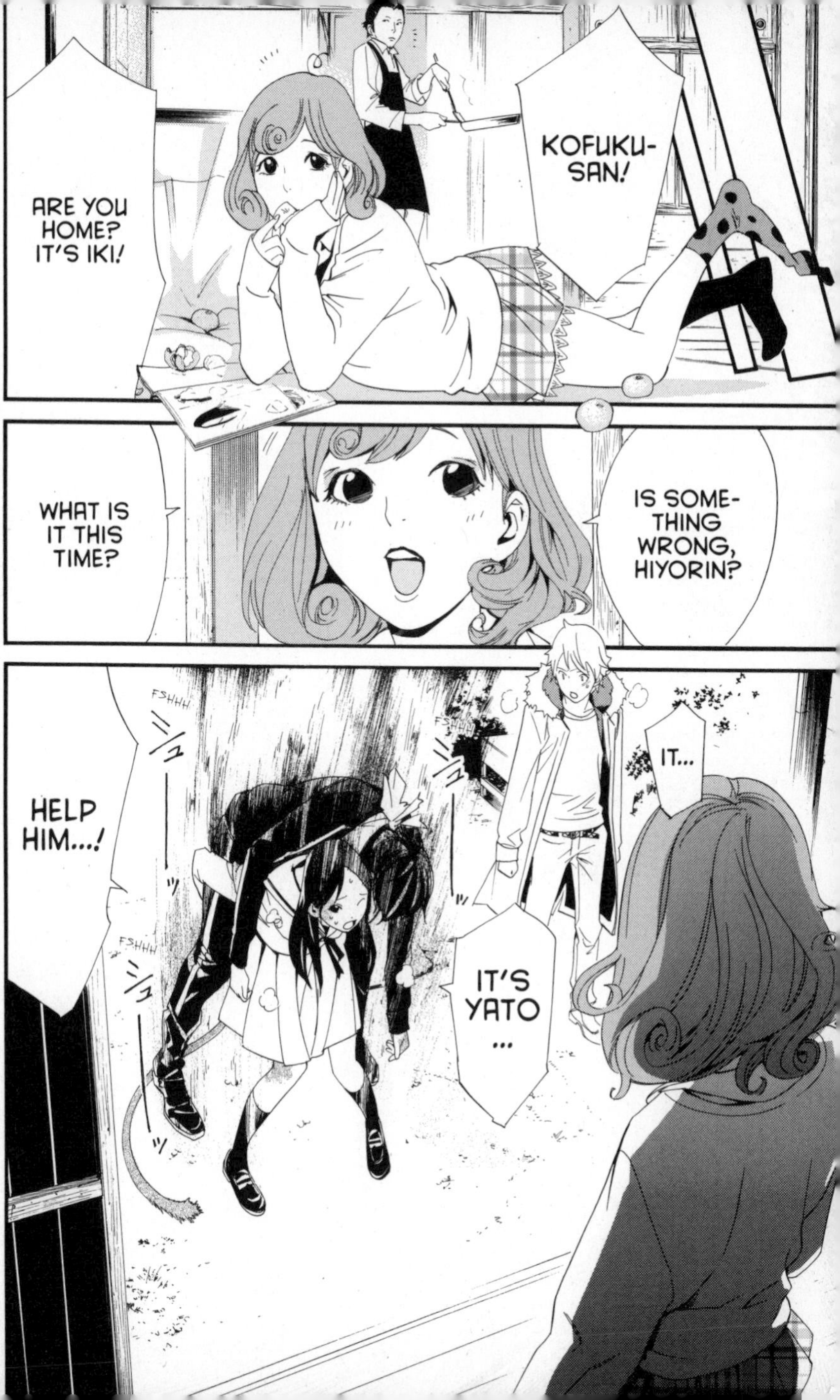
KOFUKU-SAN!
ARE YOU HOME? IT'S IKI!
IS SOME-THING WRONG, HIYORIN?
WHAT IS IT THIS TIME?
IT...
FSHHH
IT'S YATO ...
FSHHH
FSHHH
HELP HIM...!

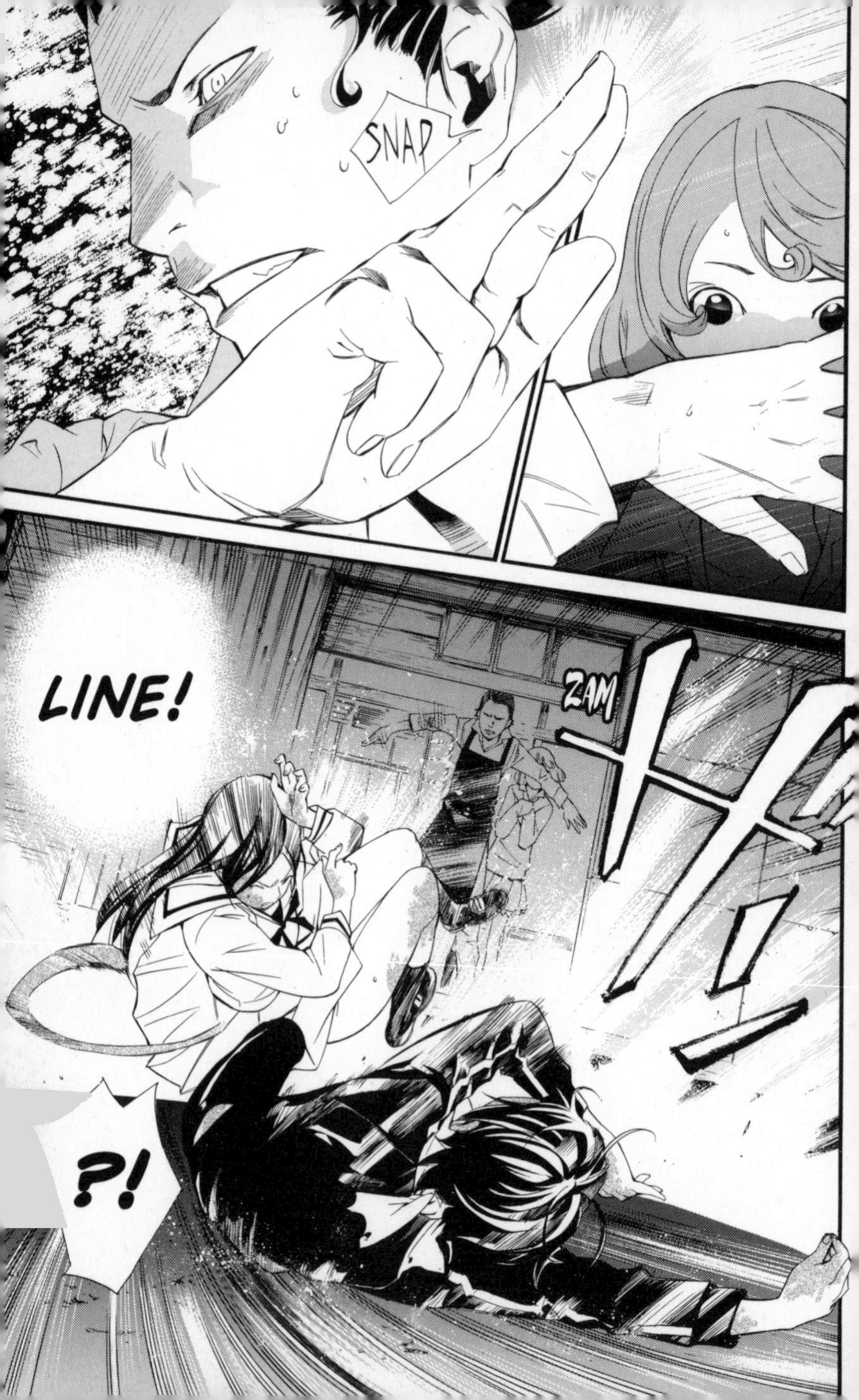
SNAP
ZAM
LINE!
?!

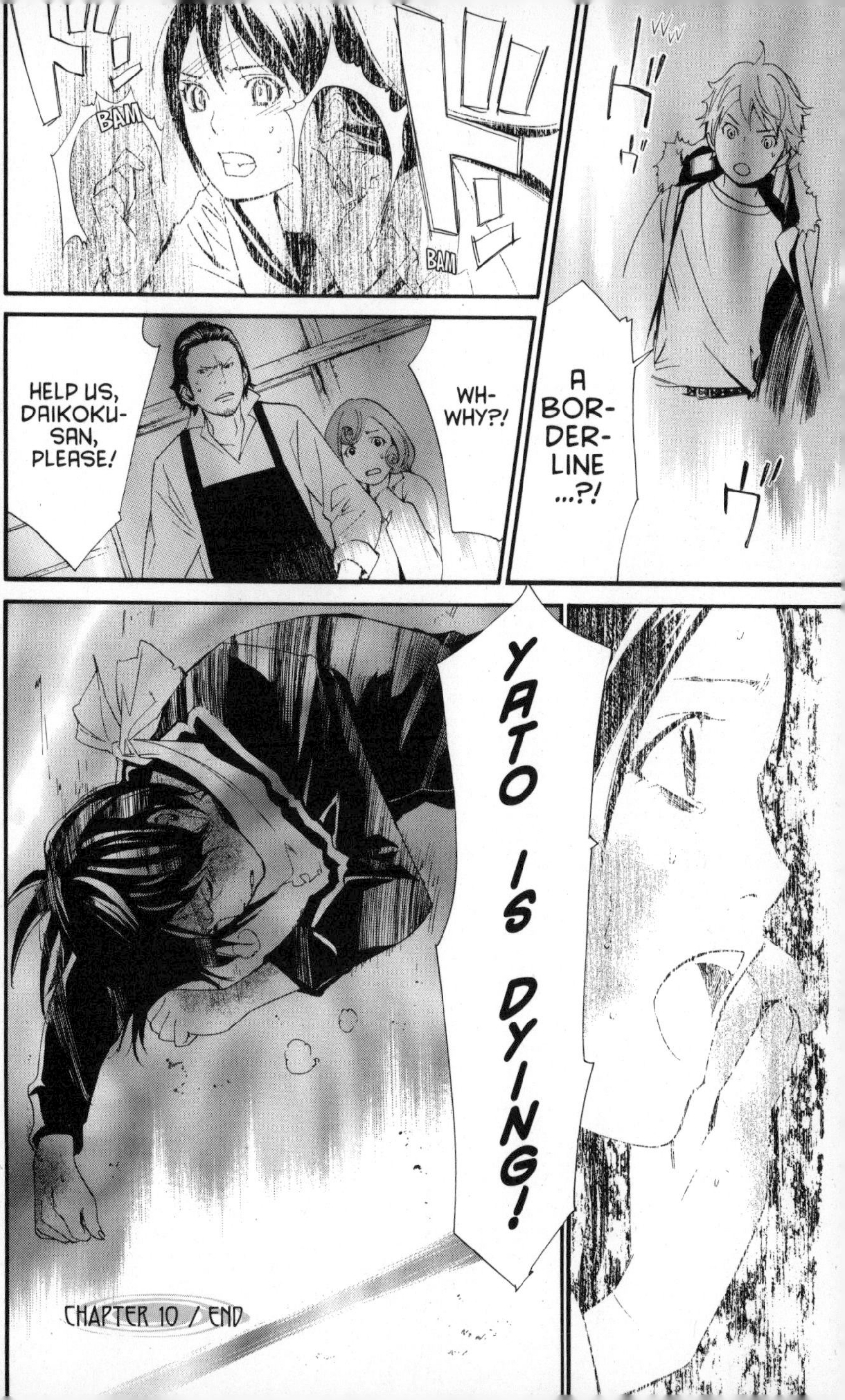
A BORDER-LINE ...?!
BAM
BAM
WH-WHY?!
HELP US, DAIKOKU-SAN, PLEASE!
YATO IS DYING!
CHAPTER 10 / END

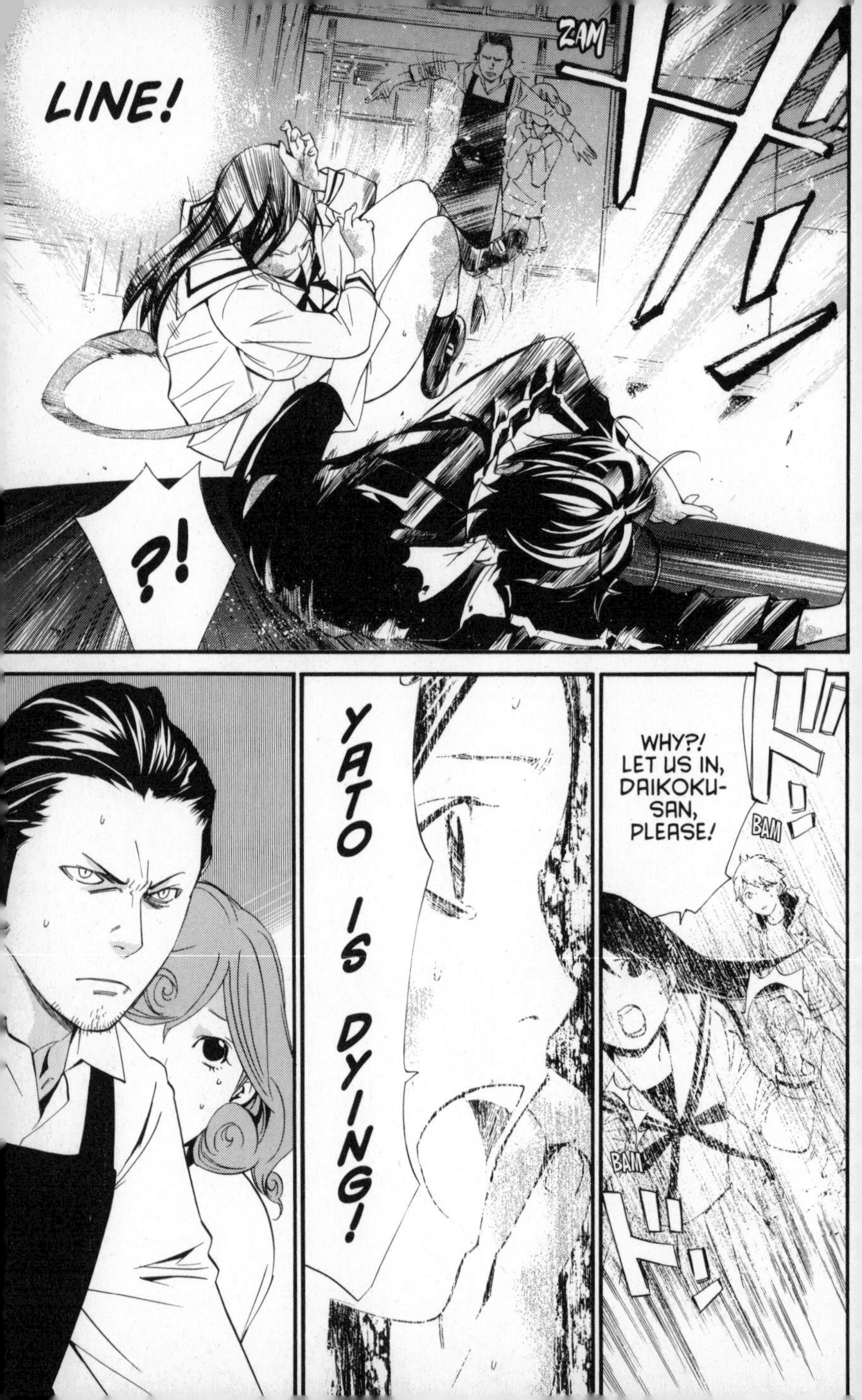
ZAM
LINE!
?!
BAM
WHY?! LET US IN, DAIKOKU-SAN, PLEASE!
BAM
YATO IS DYING!

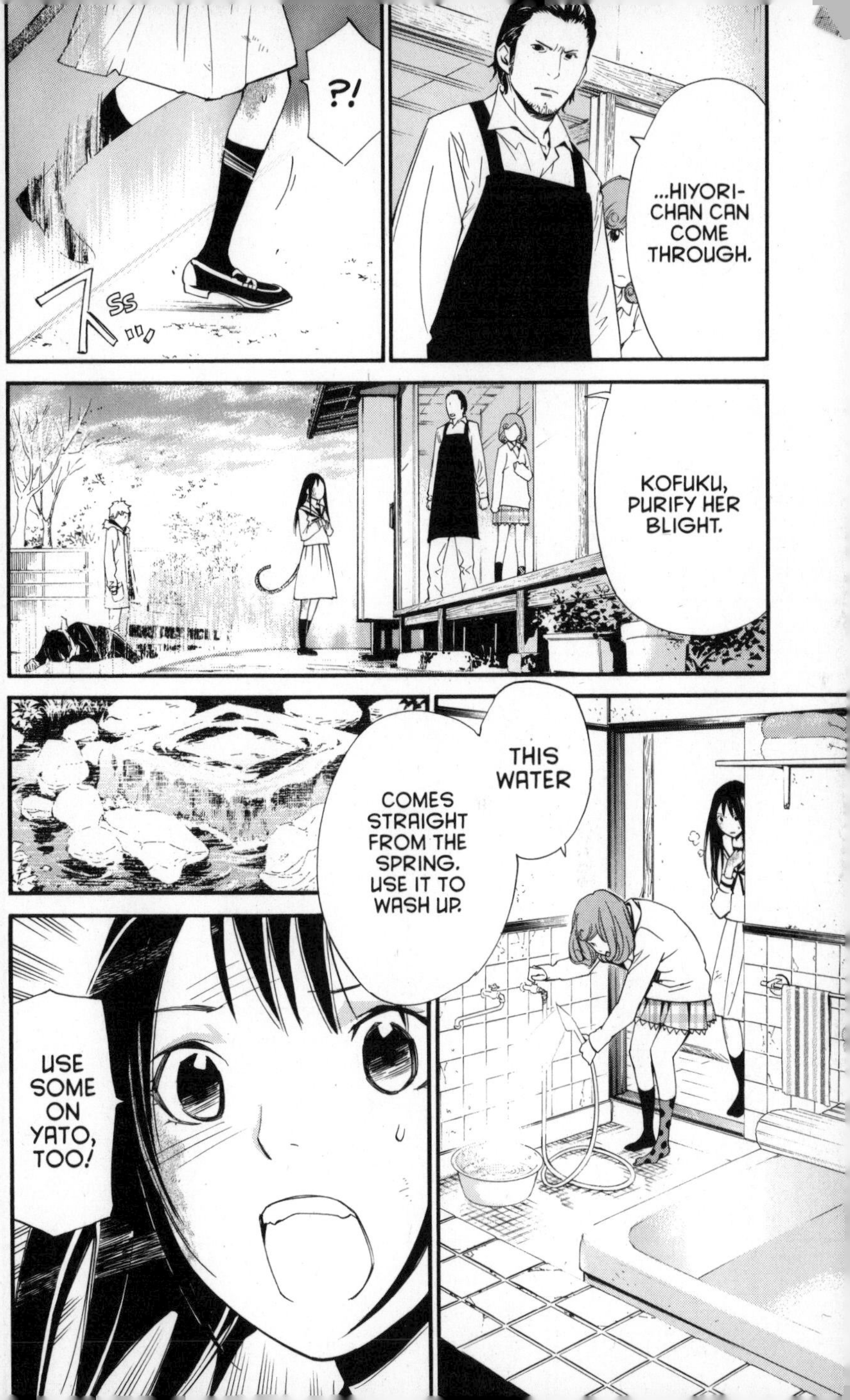
...HIYORI-CHAN CAN COME THROUGH.
?!
SS
KOFUKU, PURIFY HER BLIGHT.
THIS WATER
COMES STRAIGHT FROM THE SPRING. USE IT TO WASH UP.
USE SOME ON YATO, TOO!

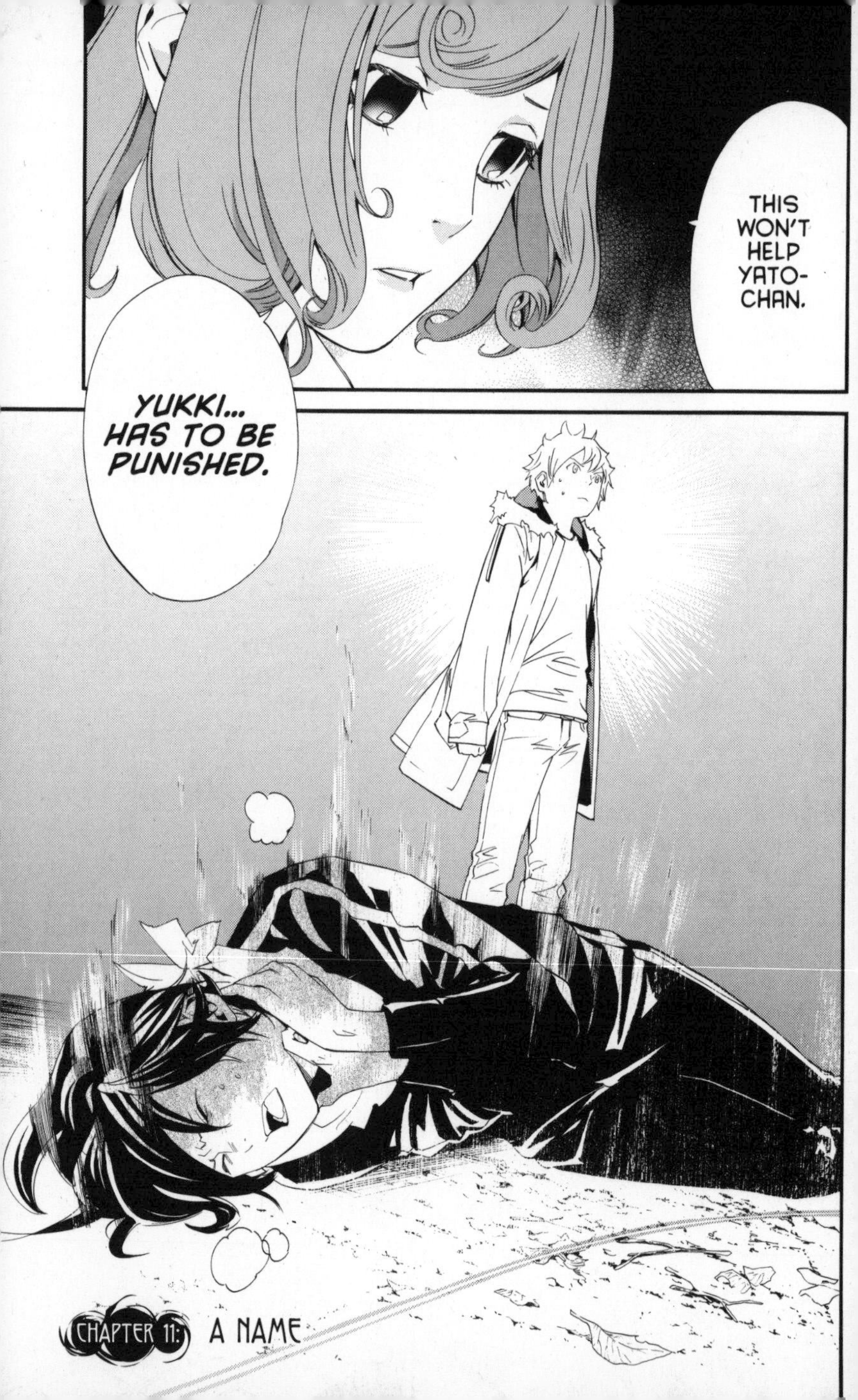
THIS WON'T HELP YATO-CHAN.
YUKKI... HAS TO BE PUNISHED.
CHAPTER 11: A NAME

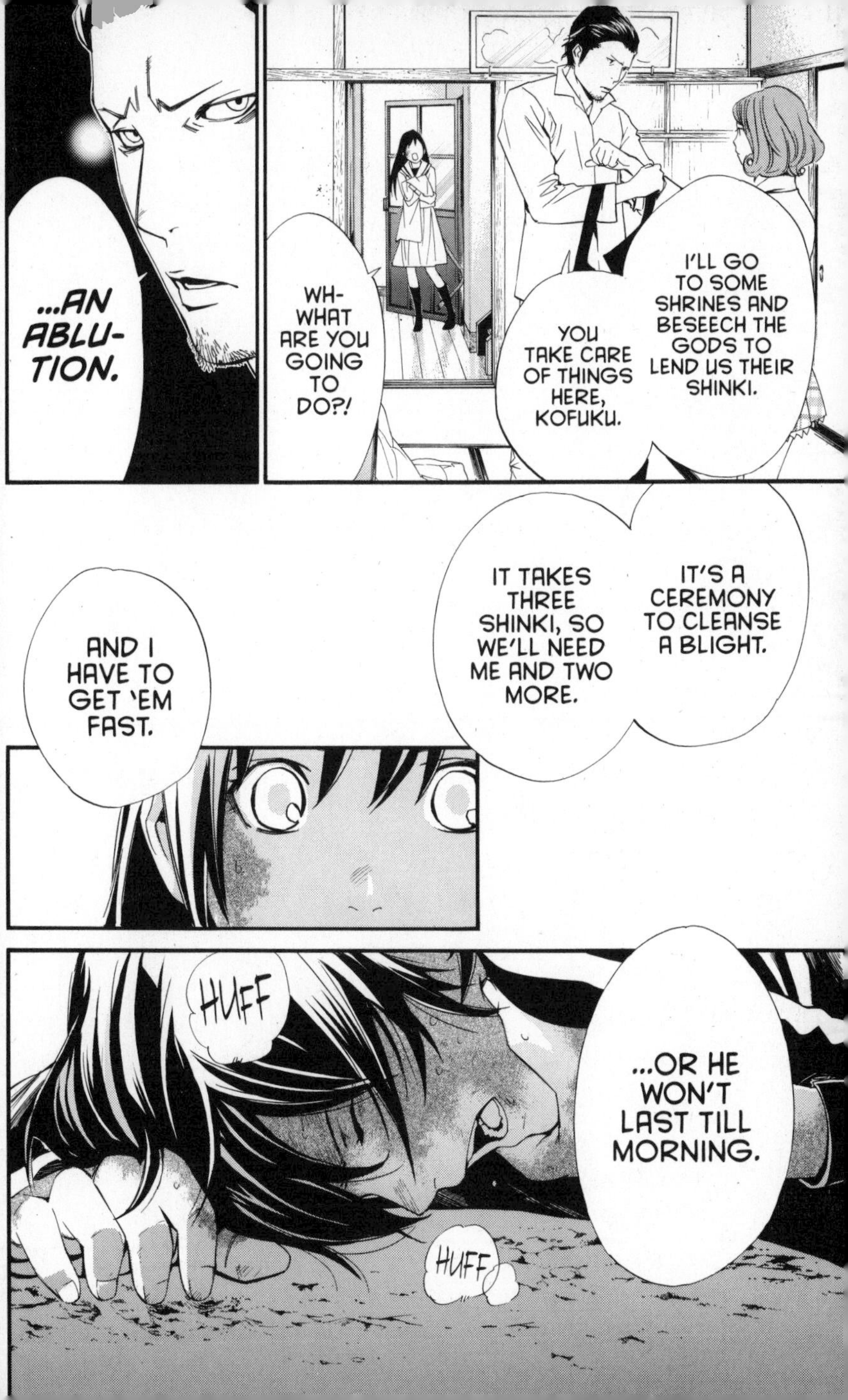
I'LL GO TO SOME SHRINES AND BESEECH THE GODS TO LEND US THEIR SHINKI.
YOU TAKE CARE OF THINGS HERE, KOFUKU.
WH-WHAT ARE YOU GOING TO DO?!
...AN ABLUTION.
IT'S A CEREMONY TO CLEANSE A BLIGHT.
IT TAKES THREE SHINKI, SO WE'LL NEED ME AND TWO MORE.
AND I HAVE TO GET 'EM FAST.
...OR HE WON'T LAST TILL MORNING.
HUFF
HUFF

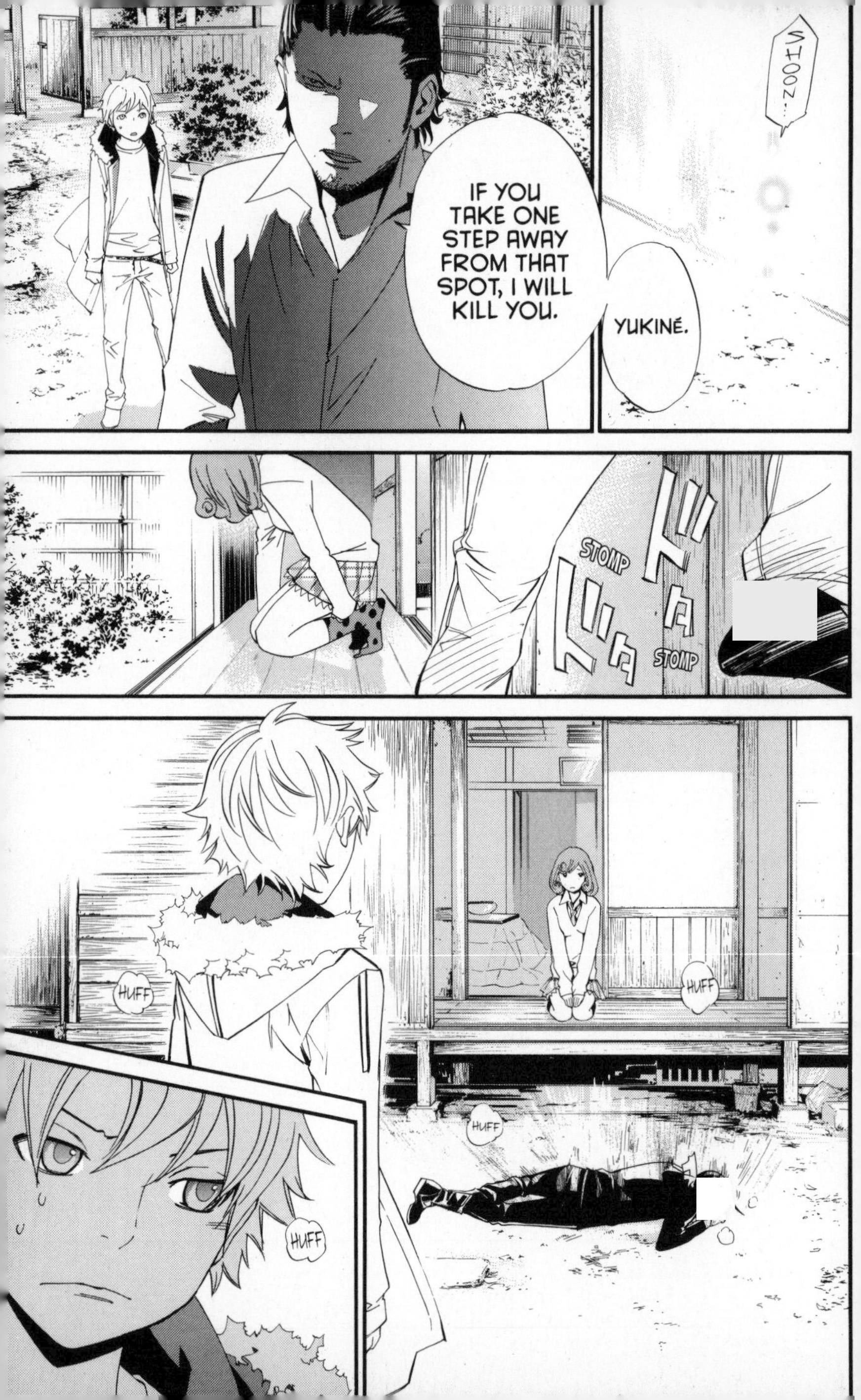
SHOON...
YUKINÉ.
IF YOU TAKE ONE STEP AWAY FROM THAT SPOT, I WILL KILL YOU.
STOMP
STOMP
HUFF
HUFF
HUFF
HUFF

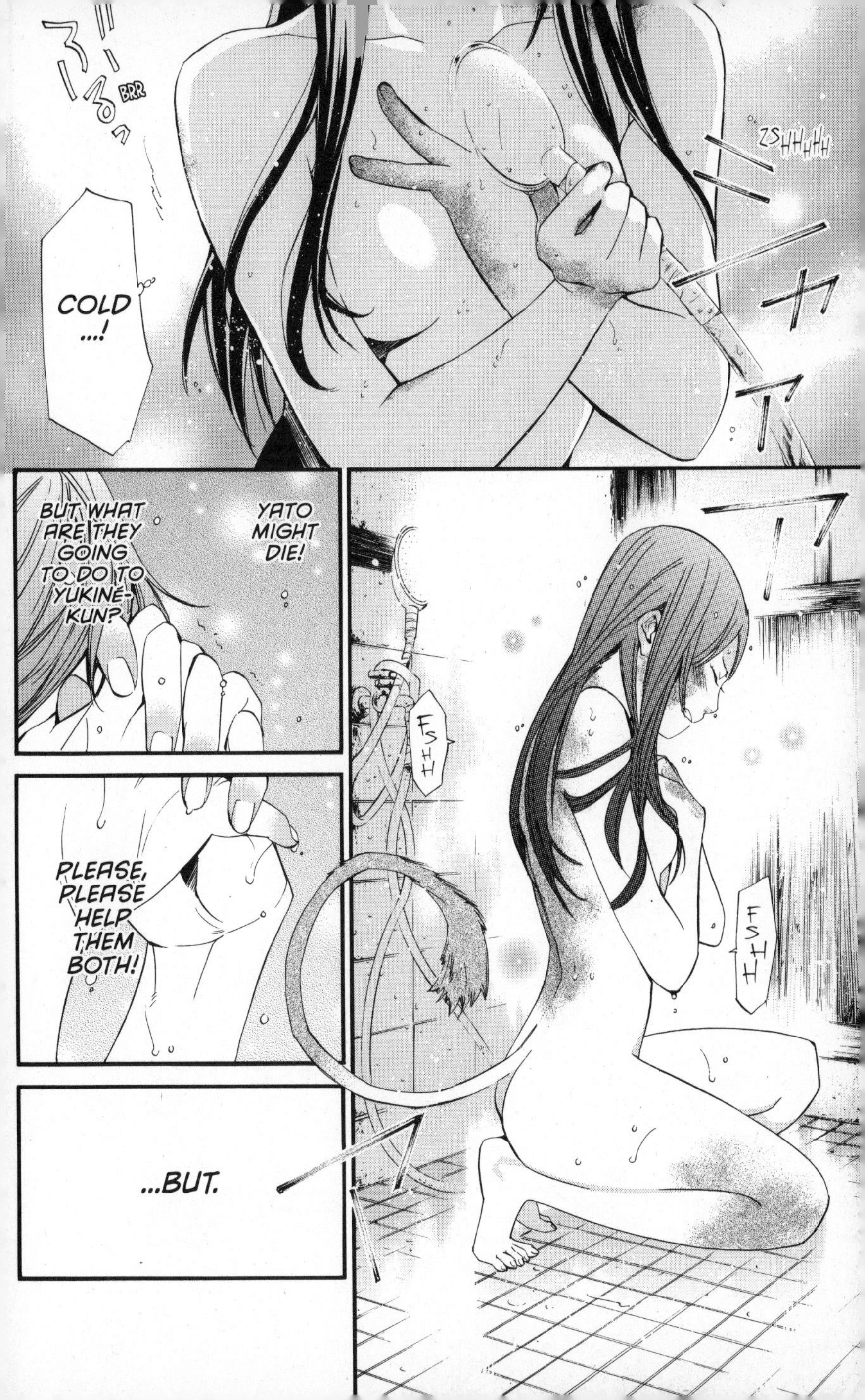
ZSHHHHH
BRR
COLD ...!
FSHH
FSHH
YATO MIGHT DIE!
BUT WHAT ARE THEY GOING TO DO TO YUKINE-KUN?
PLEASE, PLEASE HELP THEM BOTH!
...BUT.

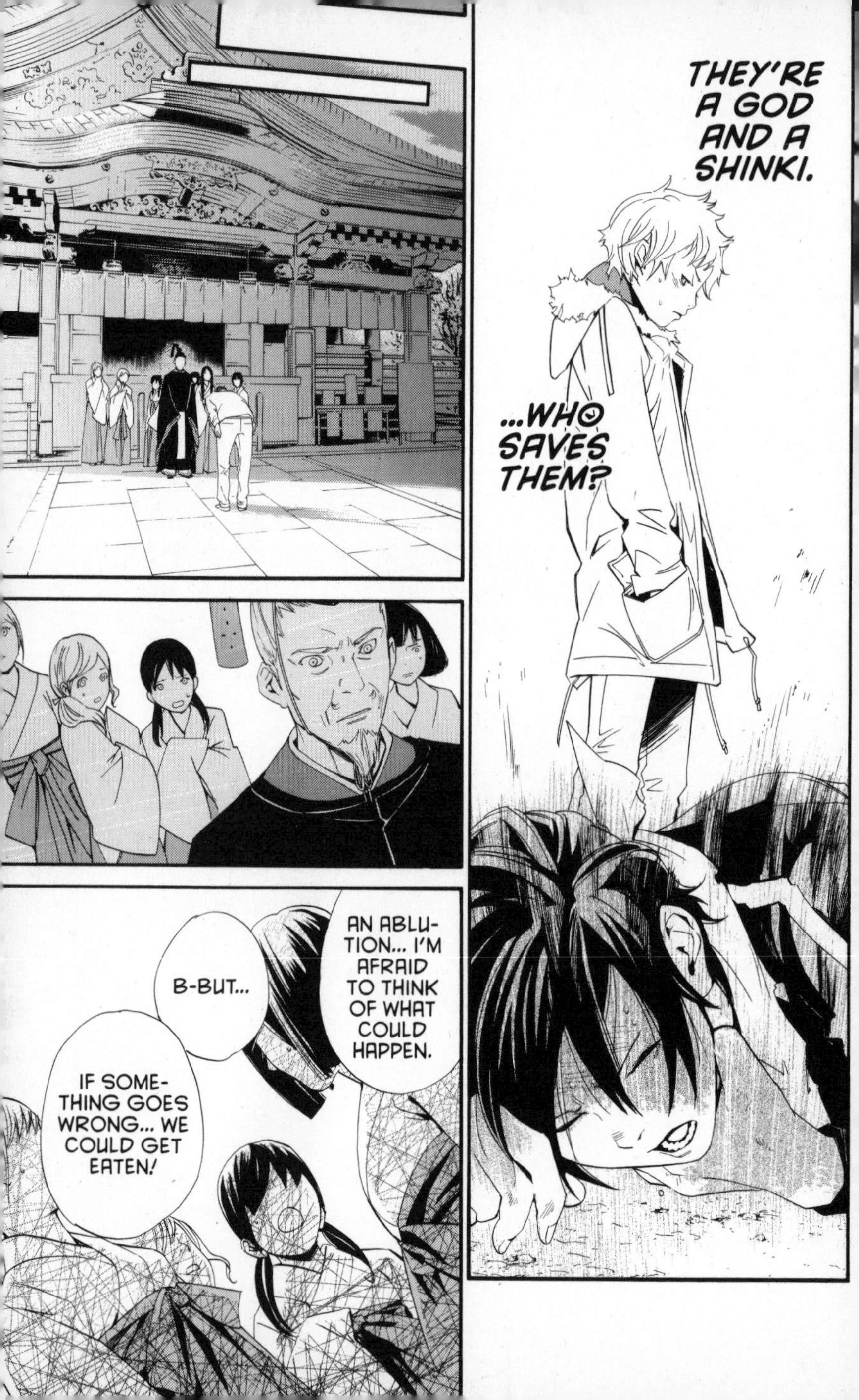
THEY'RE A GOD AND A SHINKI.
...WHO SAVES THEM?
AN ABLU-TION... I'M AFRAID TO THINK OF WHAT COULD HAPPEN.
B-BUT...
IF SOME-THING GOES WRONG... WE COULD GET EATEN!

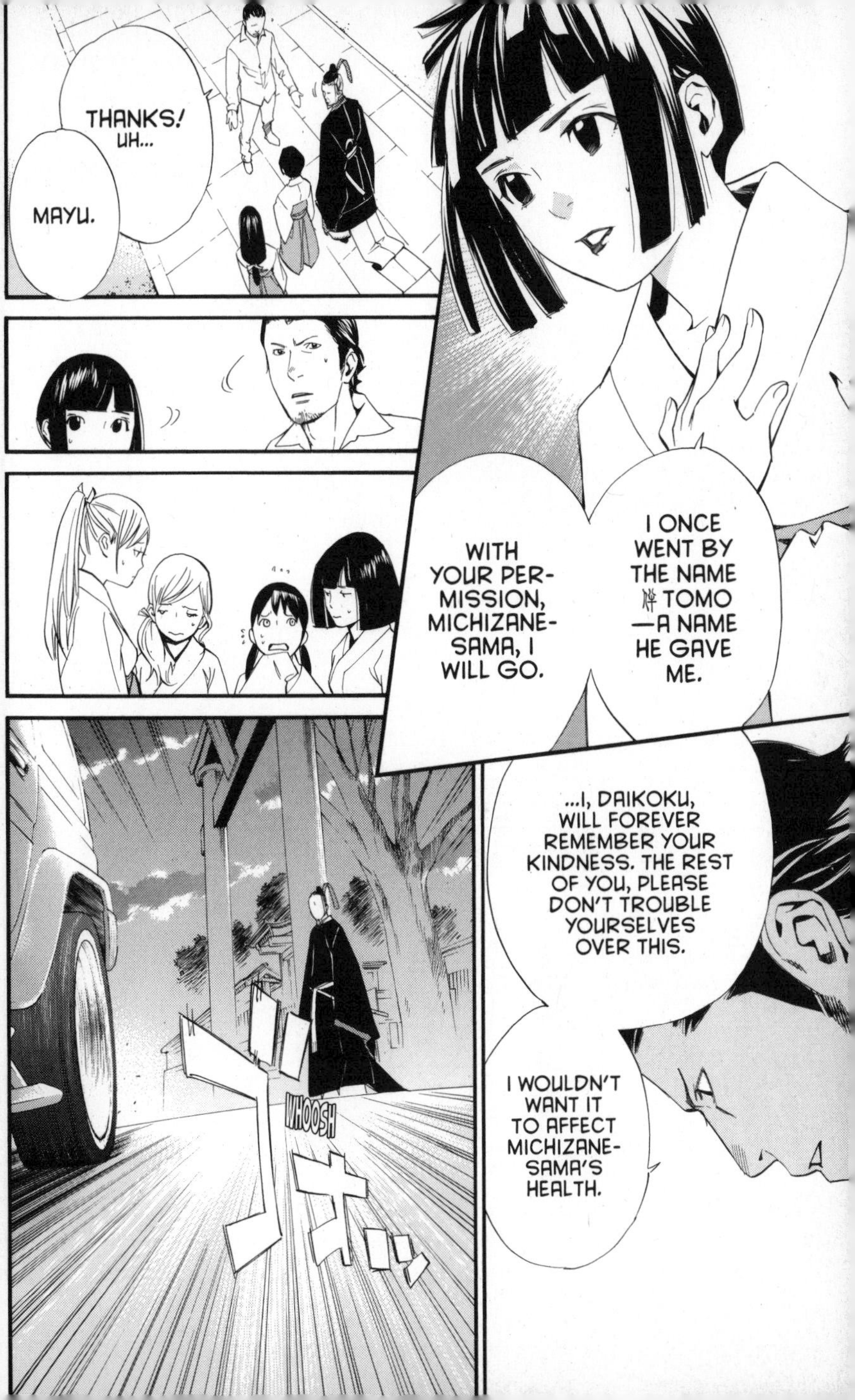

I ONCE WENT BY THE NAME 伴 TOMO—A NAME HE GAVE ME.
WITH YOUR PERMISSION, MICHIZANE-SAMA, I WILL GO.
THANKS! UH...
MAYU.
...I, DAIKOKU, WILL FOREVER REMEMBER YOUR KINDNESS. THE REST OF YOU, PLEASE DON'T TROUBLE YOURSELVES OVER THIS.
I WOULDN'T WANT IT TO AFFECT MICHIZANE-SAMA'S HEALTH.
WHOOSH

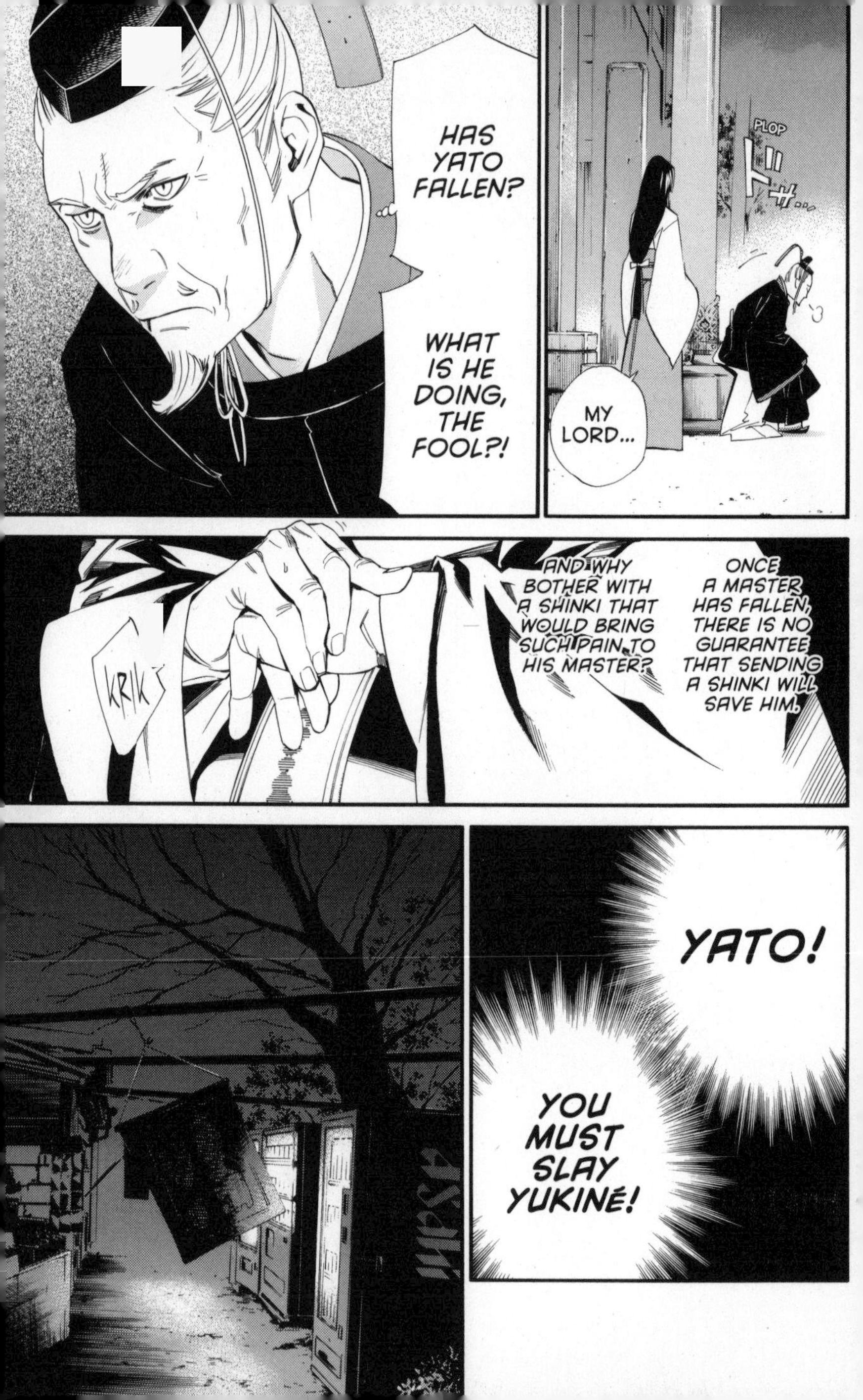
PLOP
MY LORD...
HAS YATO FALLEN?
WHAT IS HE DOING, THE FOOL?!
ONCE A MASTER HAS FALLEN, THERE IS NO GUARANTEE THAT SENDING A SHINKI WILL SAVE HIM.
AND WHY BOTHER WITH A SHINKI THAT WOULD BRING SUCH PAIN TO HIS MASTER?
KRIK
YATO!
YOU MUST SLAY YUKINÉ!

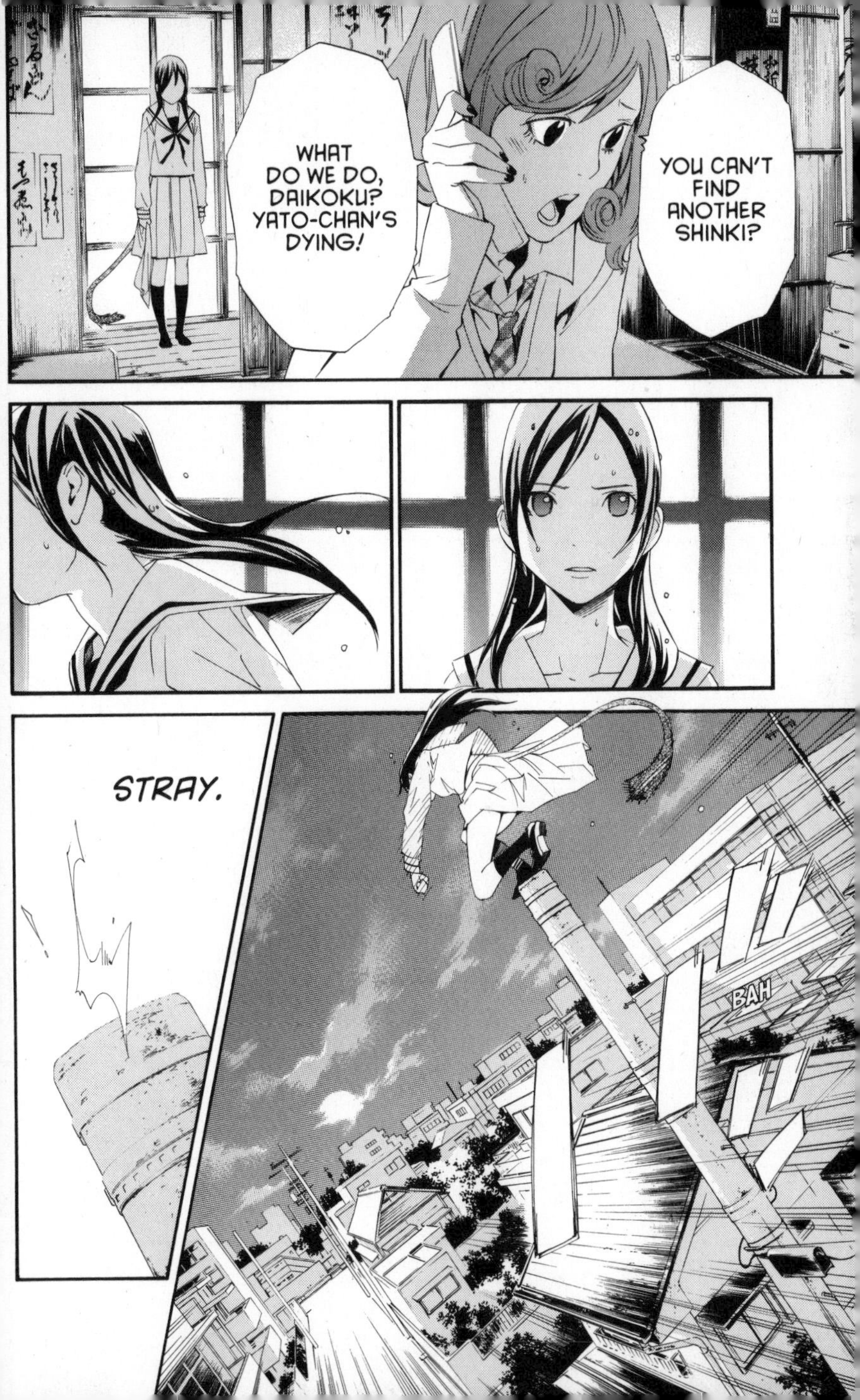
YOU CAN'T FIND ANOTHER SHINKI?
WHAT DO WE DO, DAIKOKU? YATO-CHAN'S DYING!
BAH
STRAY.

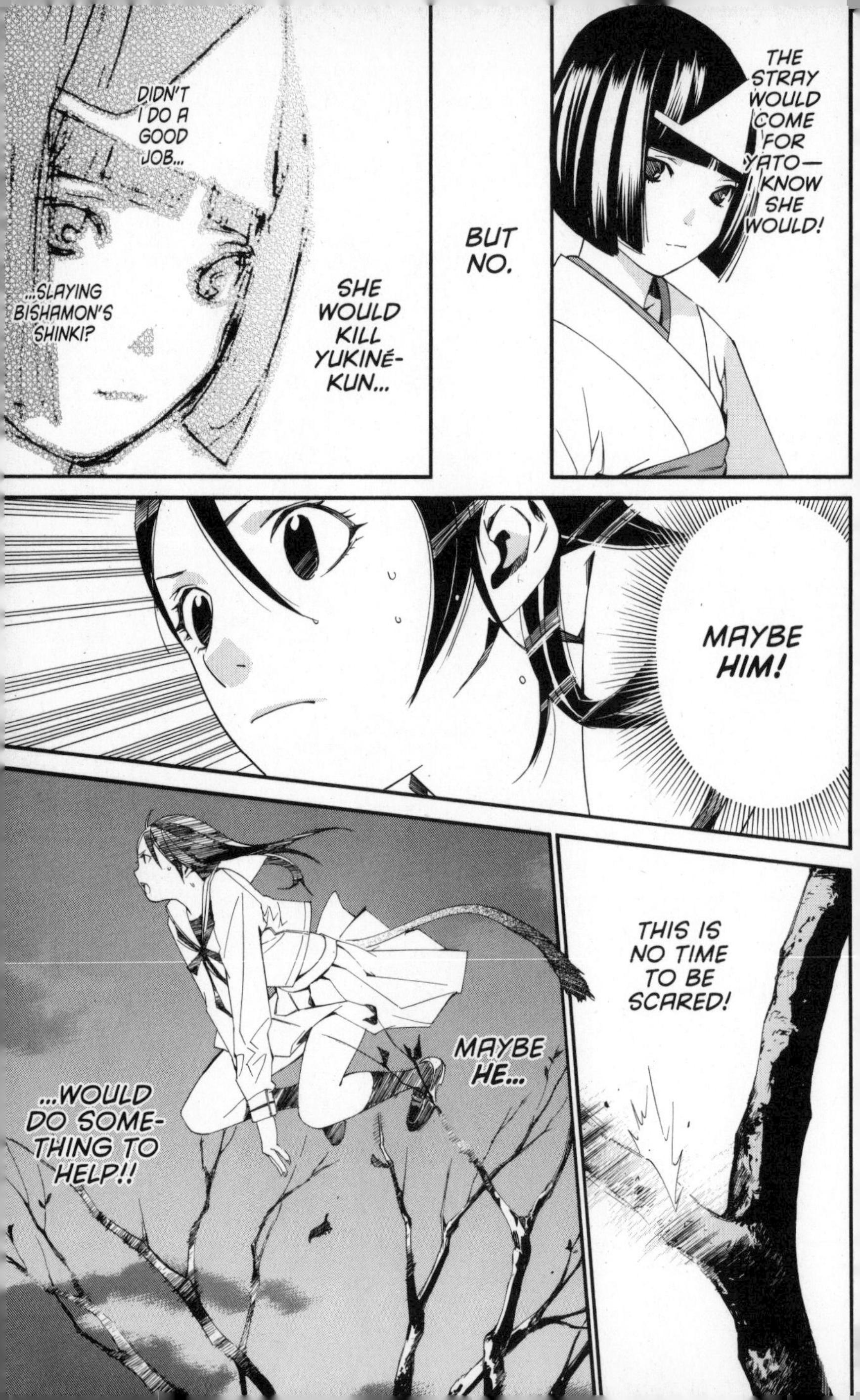
THE STRAY WOULD COME FOR YATO— I KNOW SHE WOULD!
BUT NO.
SHE WOULD KILL YUKINÉ-KUN...
DIDN'T I DO A GOOD JOB...
...SLAYING BISHAMON'S SHINKI?
MAYBE HIM!
THIS IS NO TIME TO BE SCARED!
MAYBE HE...
...WOULD DO SOME-THING TO HELP!!

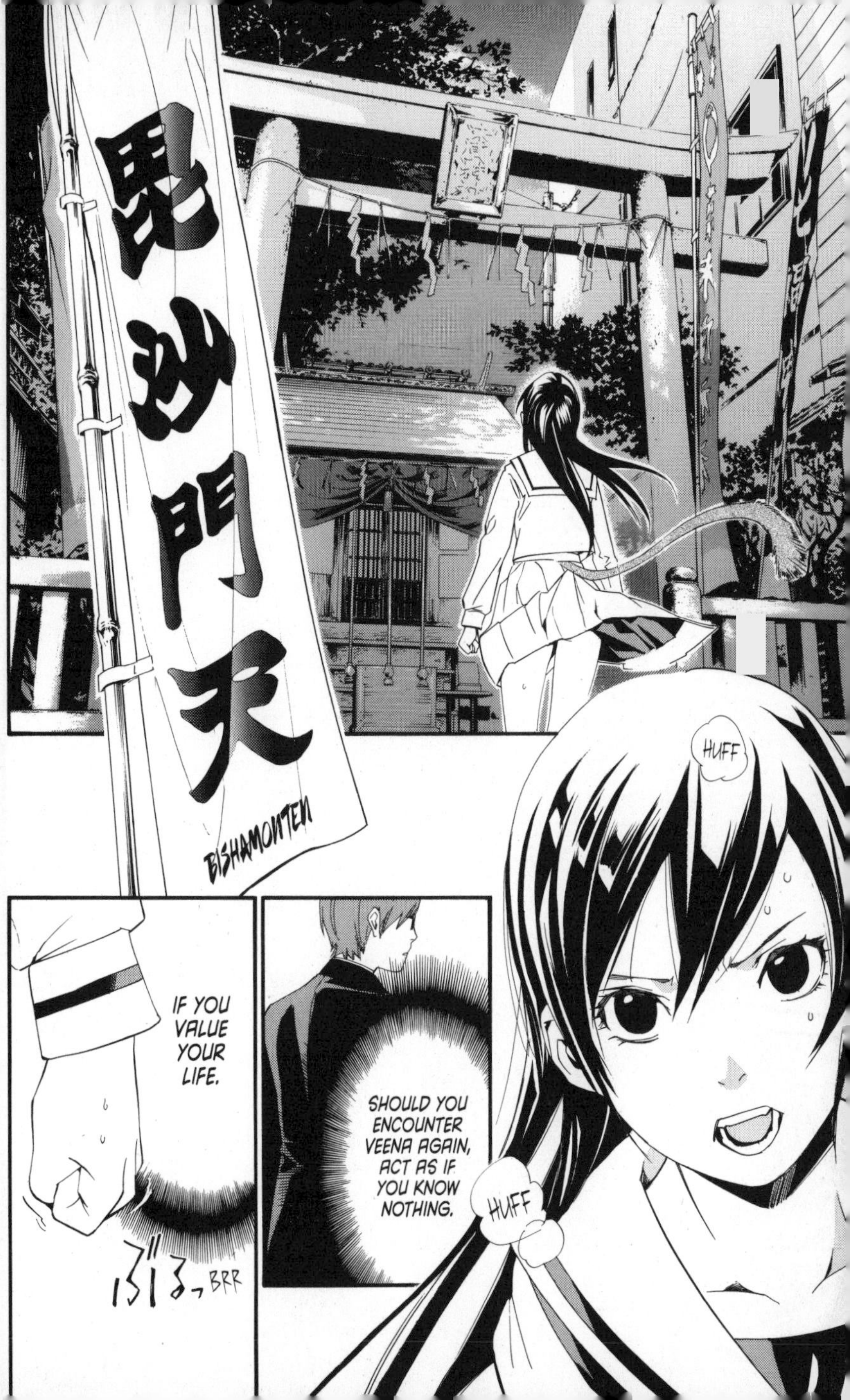
毘沙門天
BISHAMONTEN
HUFF
HUFF
SHOULD YOU ENCOUNTER VEENA AGAIN, ACT AS IF YOU KNOW NOTHING.
IF YOU VALUE YOUR LIFE.
ぶるっ BRR

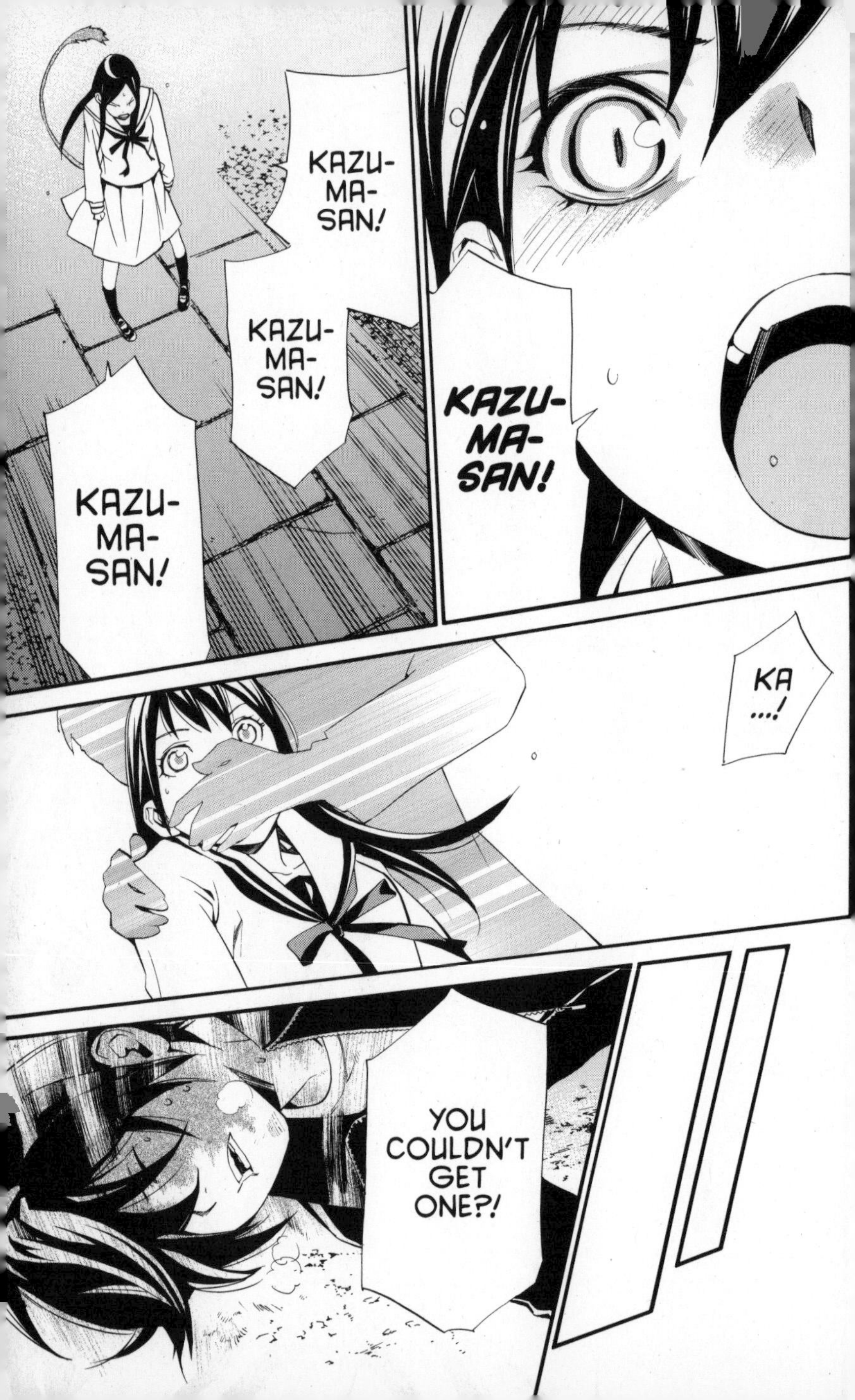
KAZUMA-SAN!
KAZUMA-SAN!
KAZUMA-SAN!
KAZUMA-SAN!
KA...!
YOU COULDN'T GET ONE?!

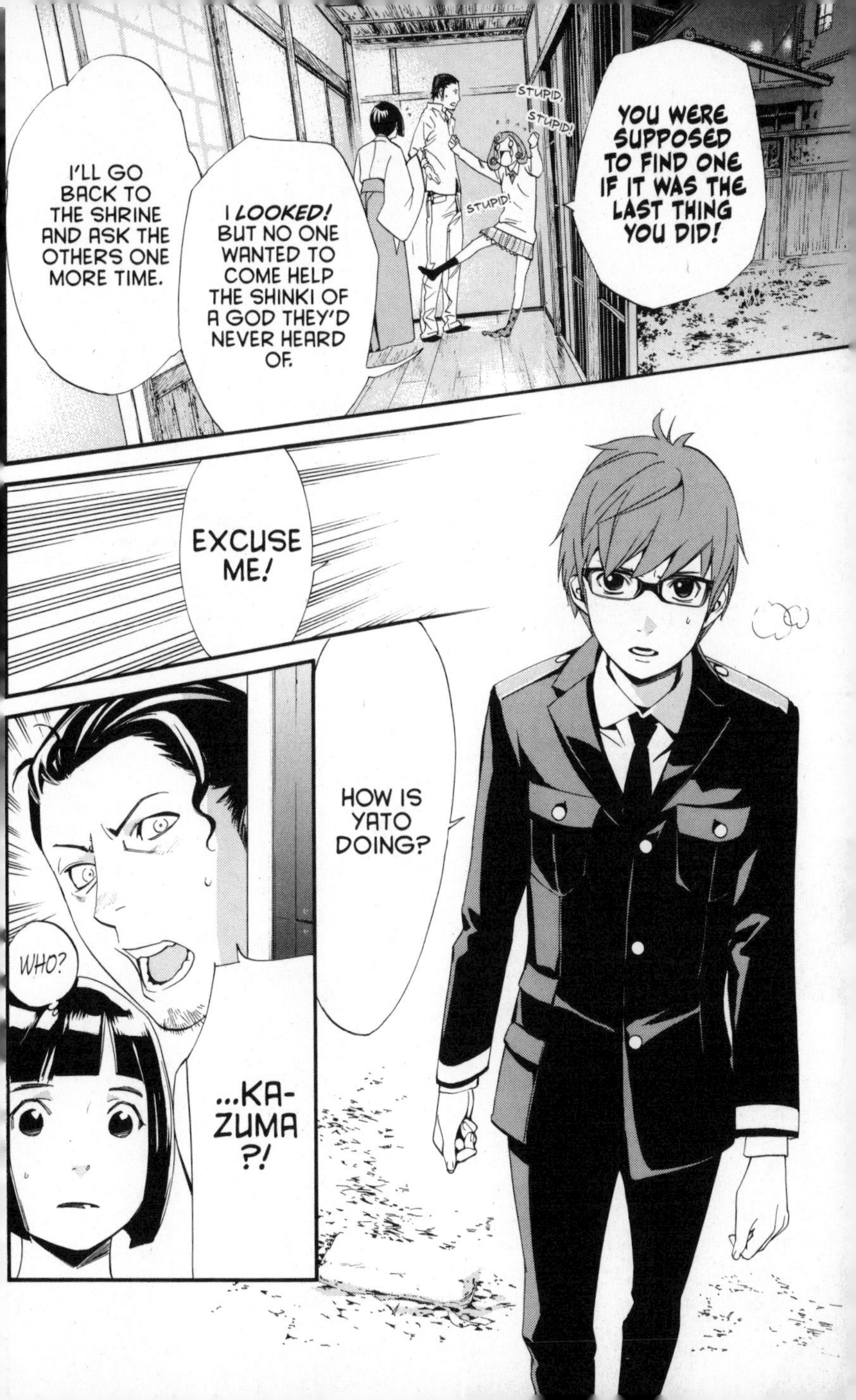
YOU WERE SUPPOSED TO FIND ONE IF IT WAS THE LAST THING YOU DID!
STUPID, STUPID!
STUPID!
I *LOOKED!* BUT NO ONE WANTED TO COME HELP THE SHINKI OF A GOD THEY'D NEVER HEARD OF.
I'LL GO BACK TO THE SHRINE AND ASK THE OTHERS ONE MORE TIME.
EXCUSE ME!
HOW IS YATO DOING?
...KA-ZUMA?!
WHO?

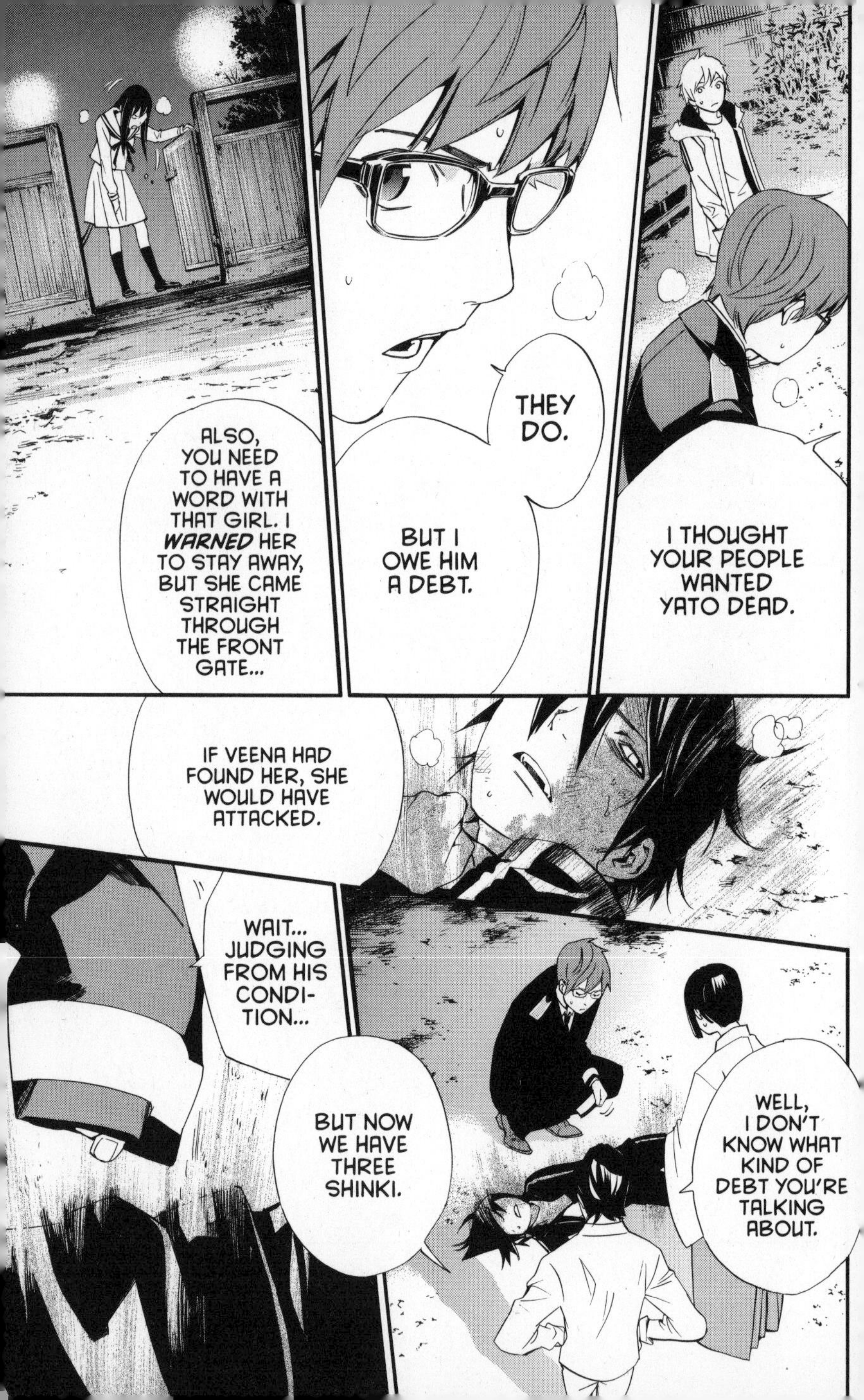
I THOUGHT YOUR PEOPLE WANTED YATO DEAD.
THEY DO.
BUT I OWE HIM A DEBT.
ALSO, YOU NEED TO HAVE A WORD WITH THAT GIRL. I *WARNED* HER TO STAY AWAY, BUT SHE CAME STRAIGHT THROUGH THE FRONT GATE...
IF VEENA HAD FOUND HER, SHE WOULD HAVE ATTACKED.
WELL, I DON'T KNOW WHAT KIND OF DEBT YOU'RE TALKING ABOUT.
BUT NOW WE HAVE THREE SHINKI.
WAIT... JUDGING FROM HIS CONDI-TION...

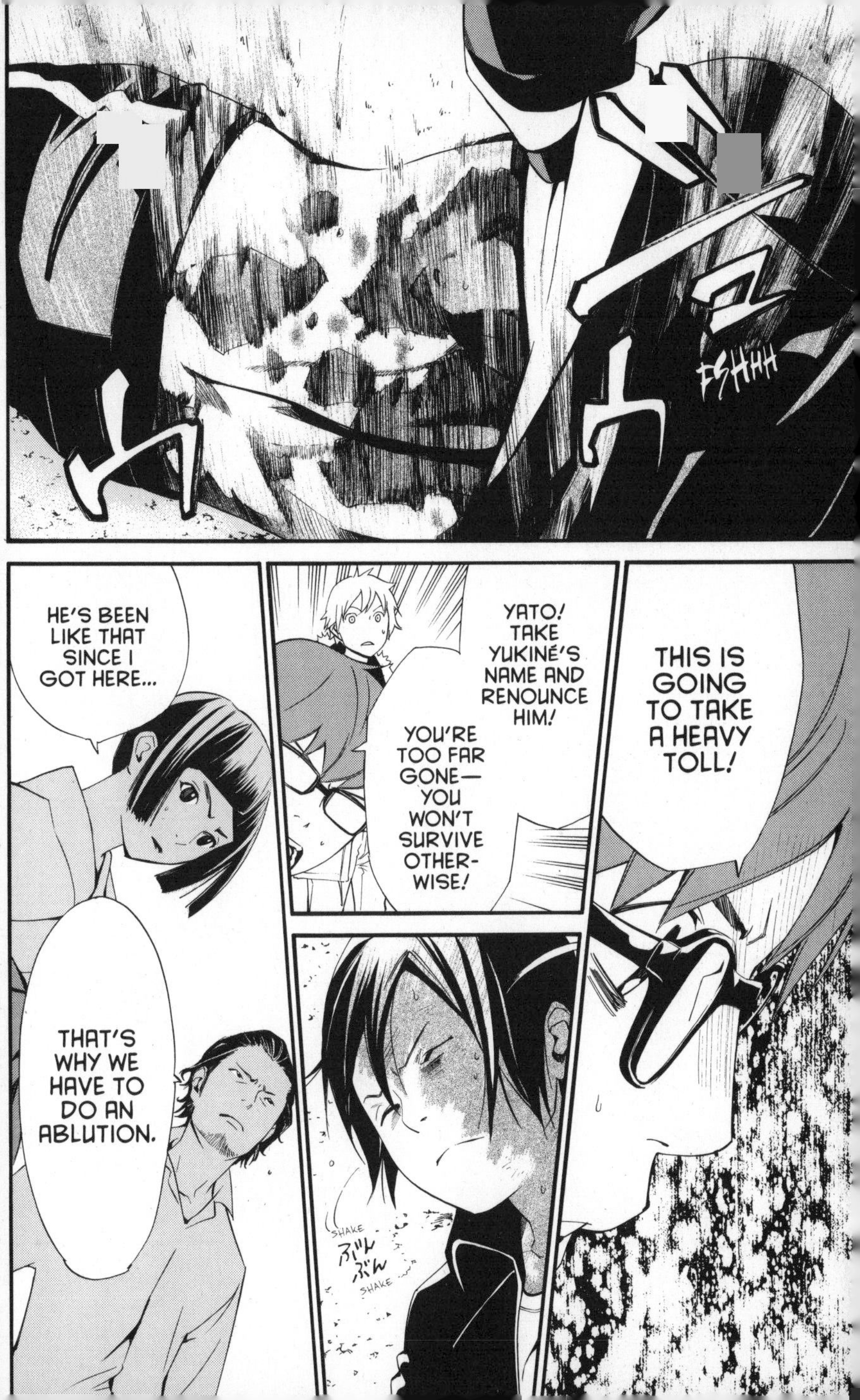
FSHHH
THIS IS GOING TO TAKE A HEAVY TOLL!
YATO! TAKE YUKINÉ'S NAME AND RENOUNCE HIM!
YOU'RE TOO FAR GONE— YOU WON'T SURVIVE OTHER-WISE!
SHAKE
ぶん ぶん
SHAKE
HE'S BEEN LIKE THAT SINCE I GOT HERE...
THAT'S WHY WE HAVE TO DO AN ABLUTION.

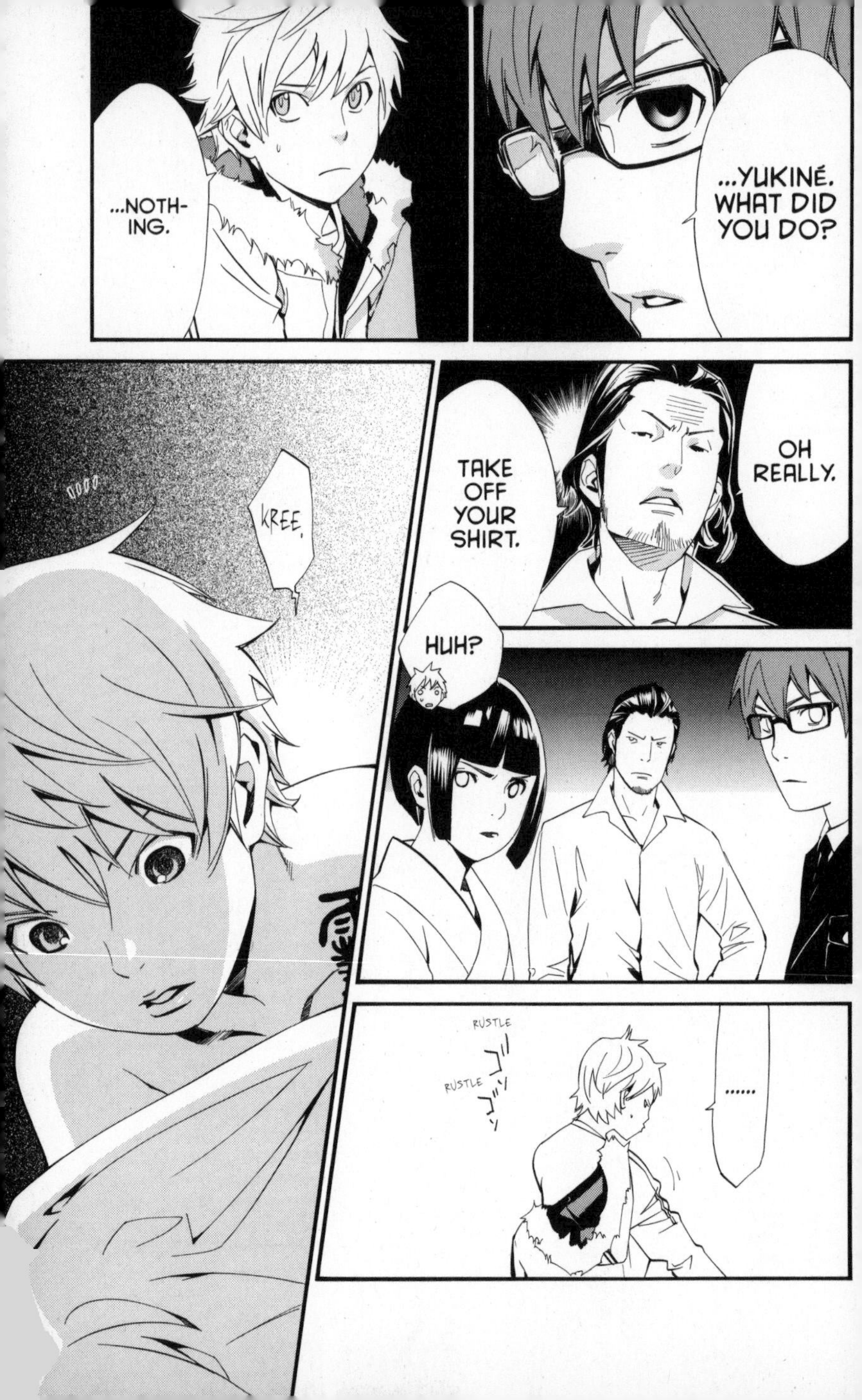
...YUKINÉ. WHAT DID YOU DO?
...NOTH-ING.
OH REALLY.
TAKE OFF YOUR SHIRT.
HUH?
......
RUSTLE
RUSTLE
KREE

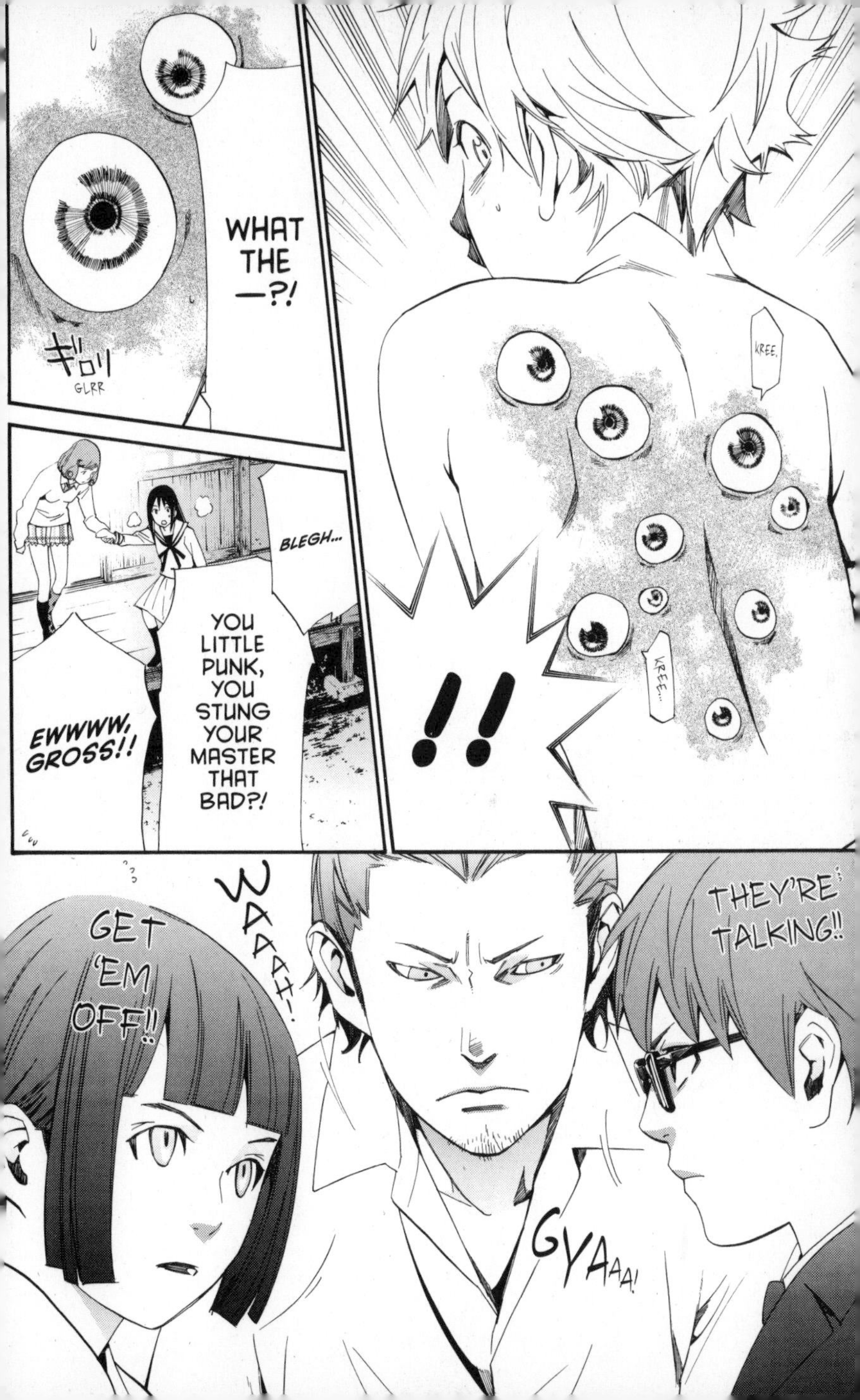
KREE.
KREE...
!!
WHAT THE—?!
ギロリ
GLRR
BLEGH...
YOU LITTLE PUNK, YOU STUNG YOUR MASTER THAT BAD?!
EWWWW, GROSS!!
THEY'RE TALKING!!
GYAAAA!
WAAAAH!
GET 'EM OFF!!

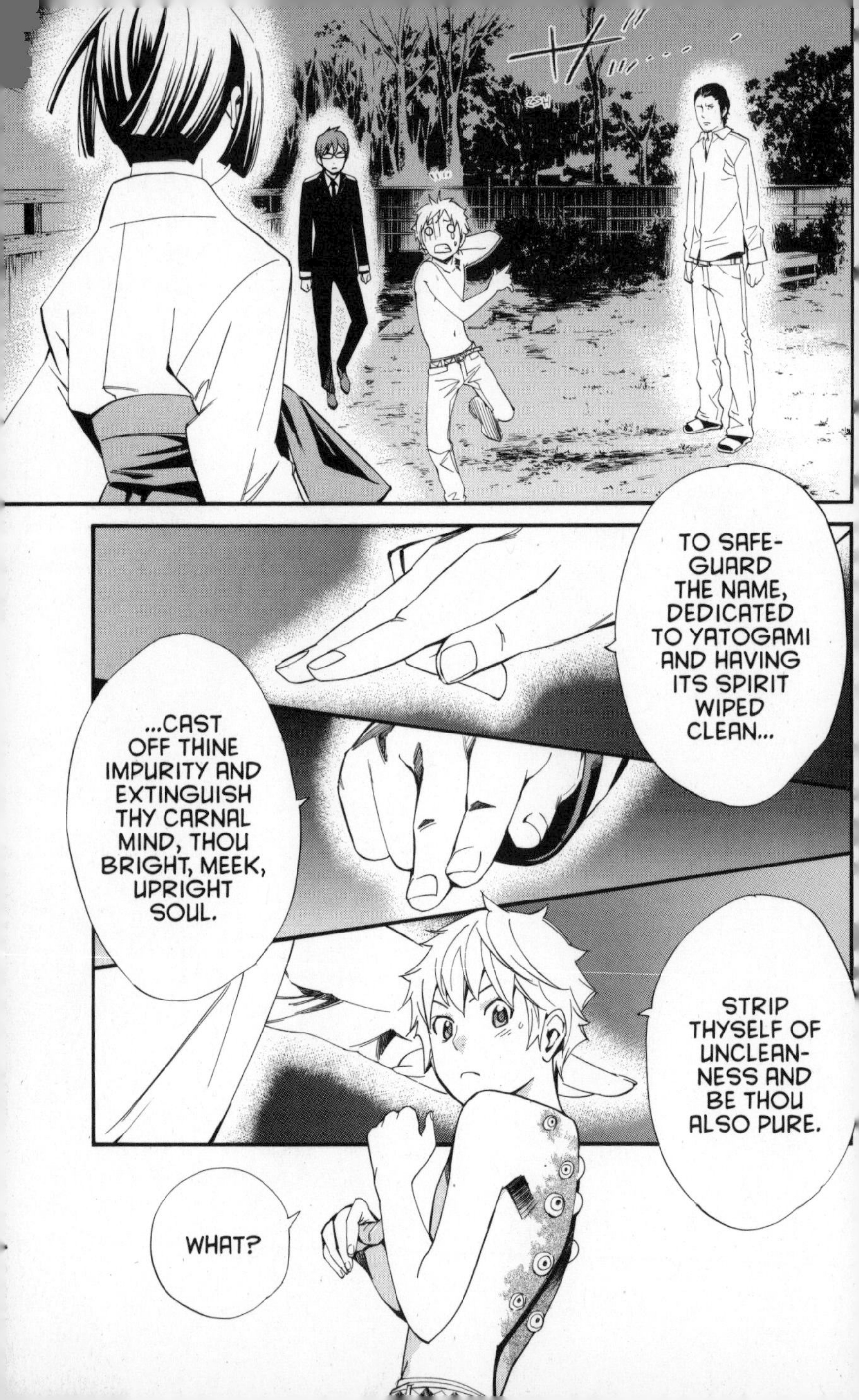
ZSH
TO SAFE-GUARD THE NAME, DEDICATED TO YATOGAMI AND HAVING ITS SPIRIT WIPED CLEAN...
...CAST OFF THINE IMPURITY AND EXTINGUISH THY CARNAL MIND, THOU BRIGHT, MEEK, UPRIGHT SOUL.
STRIP THYSELF OF UNCLEAN-NESS AND BE THOU ALSO PURE.
WHAT?

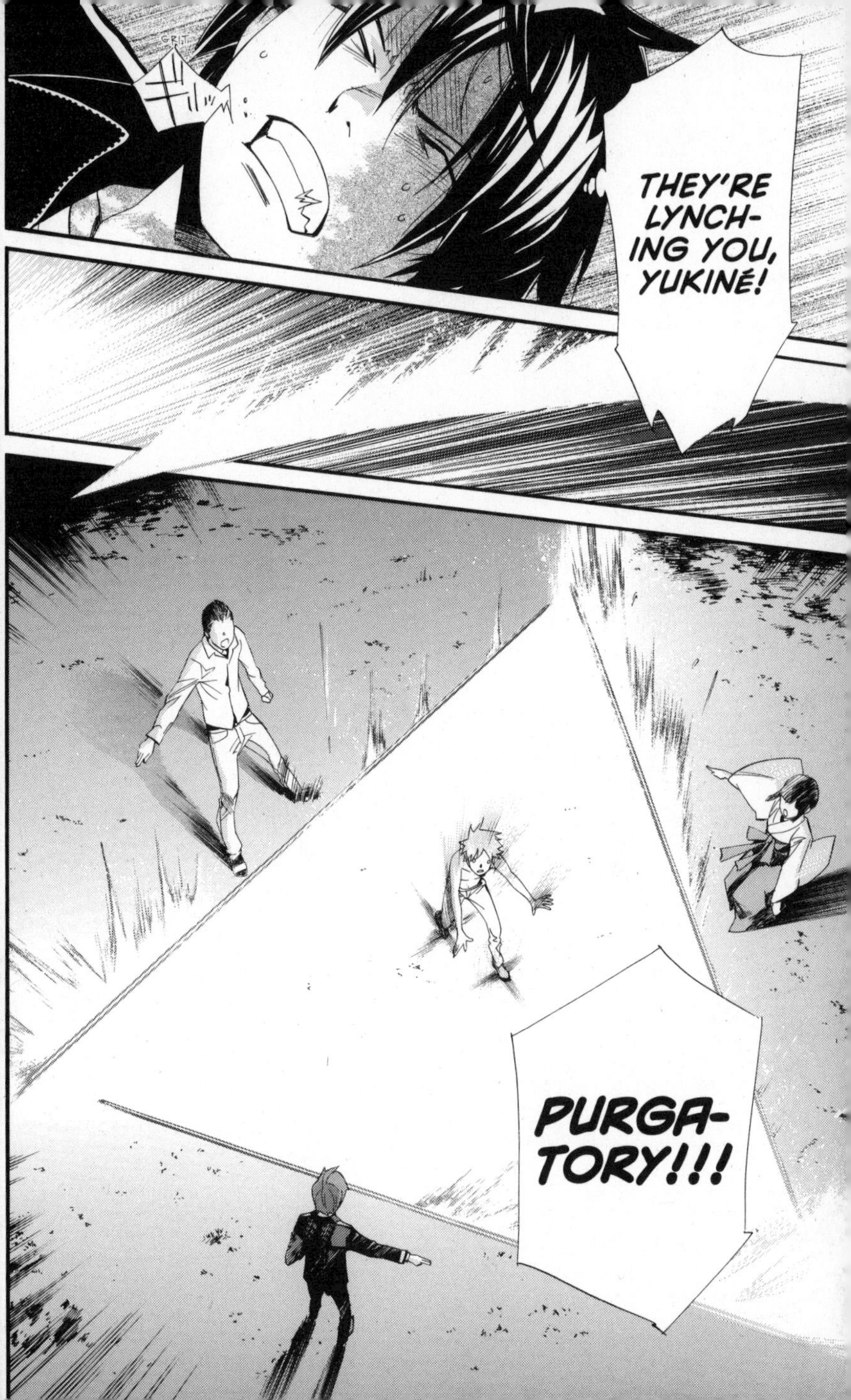
THEY'RE LYNCH-ING YOU, YUKINÉ!
GRIT
ギリッ
PURGA-TORY!!!

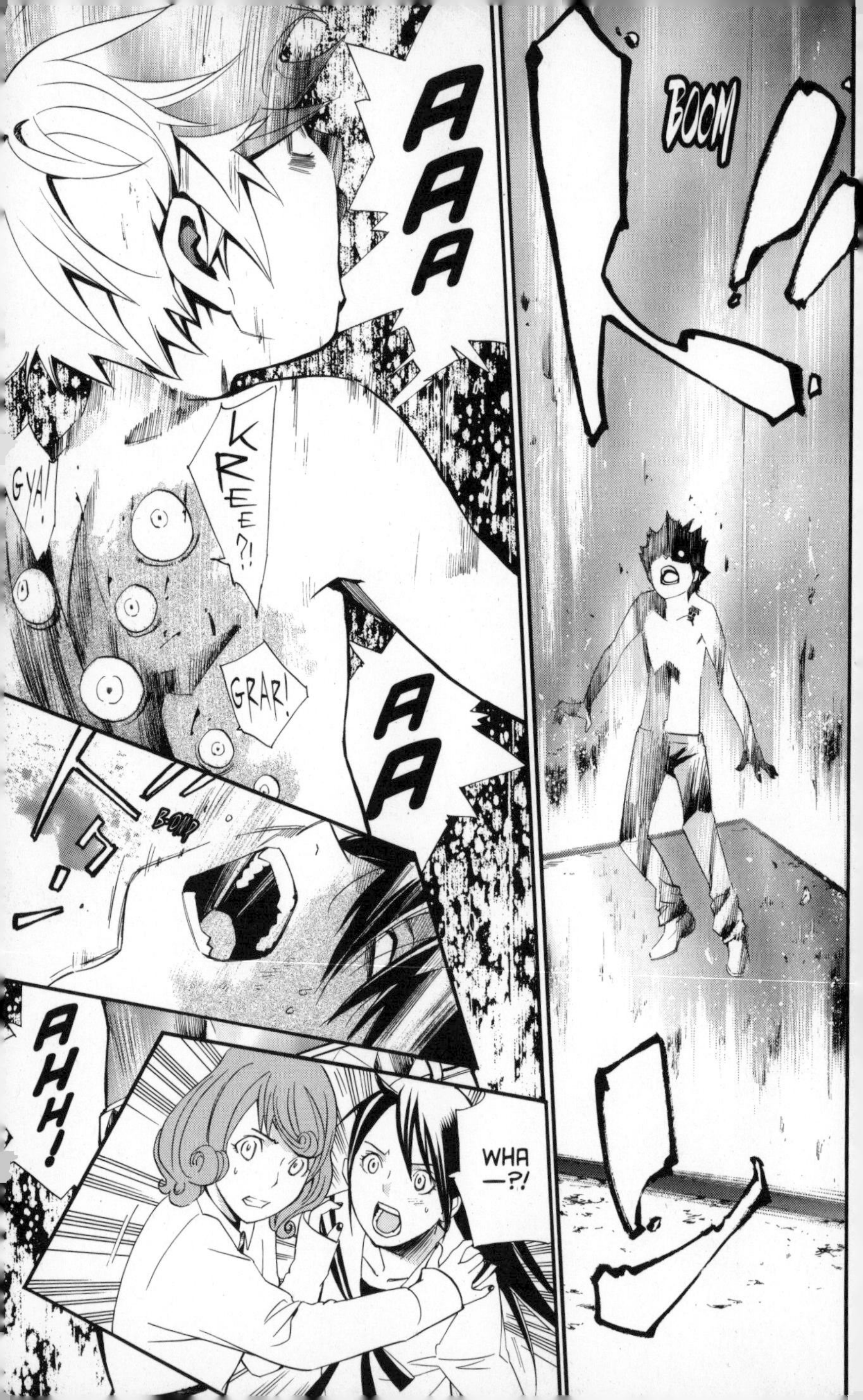
BOOM
AAAA
KREE?!
GYA!
GRAR!
AA
B-OM
WHA—?!
AHH!

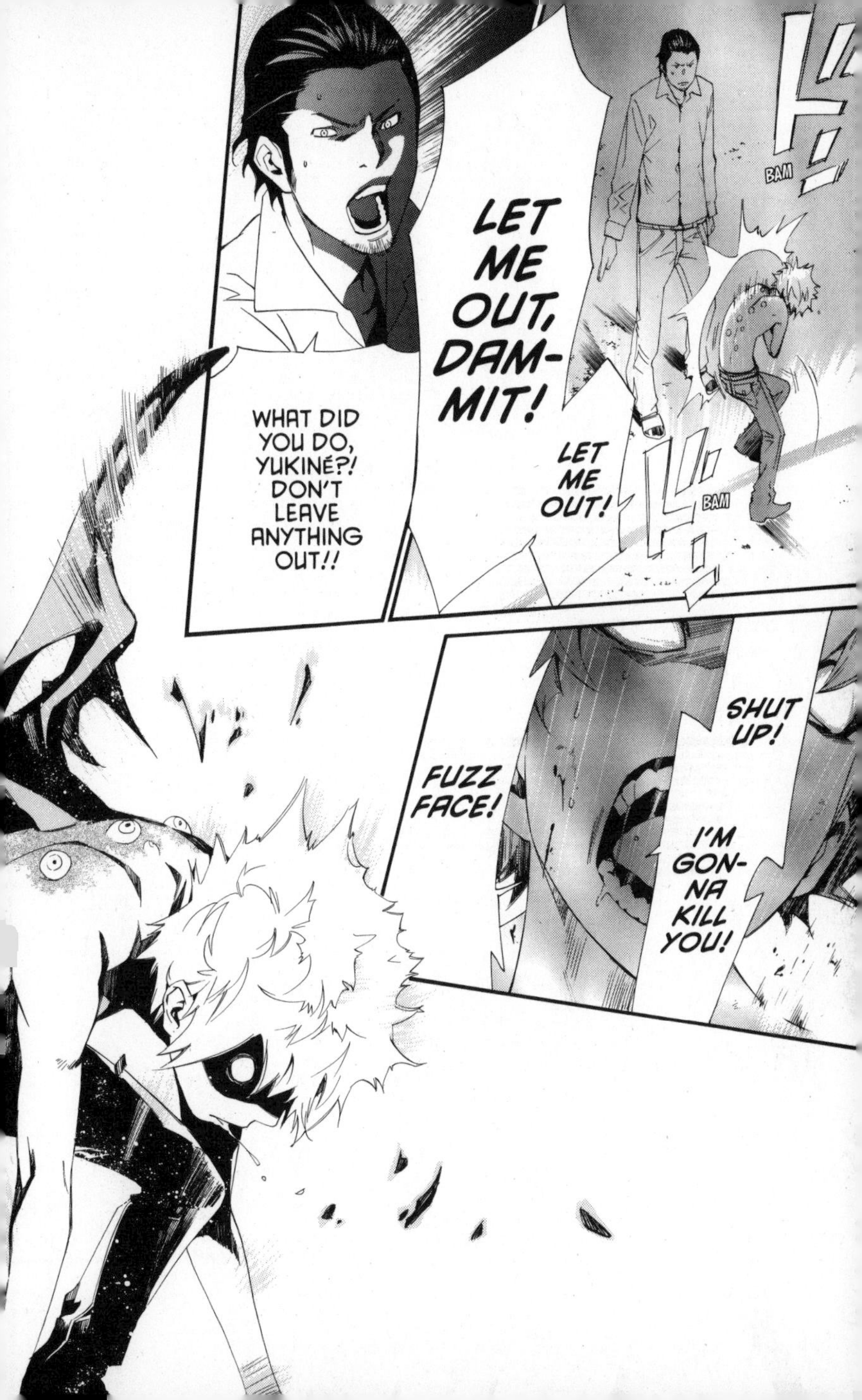
BAM
LET ME OUT, DAM-MIT!
LET ME OUT!
BAM
WHAT DID YOU DO, YUKINÉ?! DON'T LEAVE ANYTHING OUT!!
SHUT UP!
FUZZ FACE!
I'M GON-NA KILL YOU!

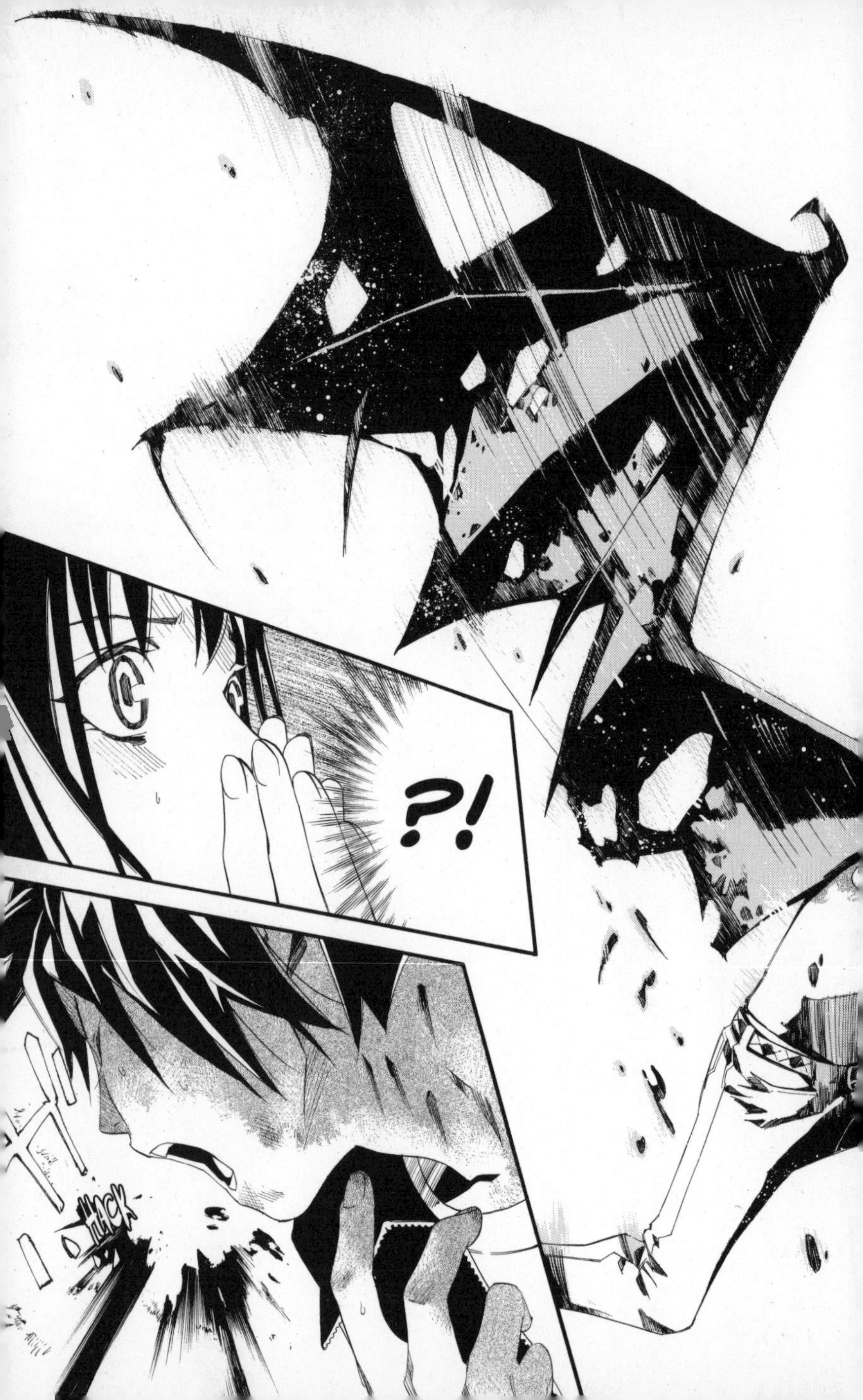
?!
HACK

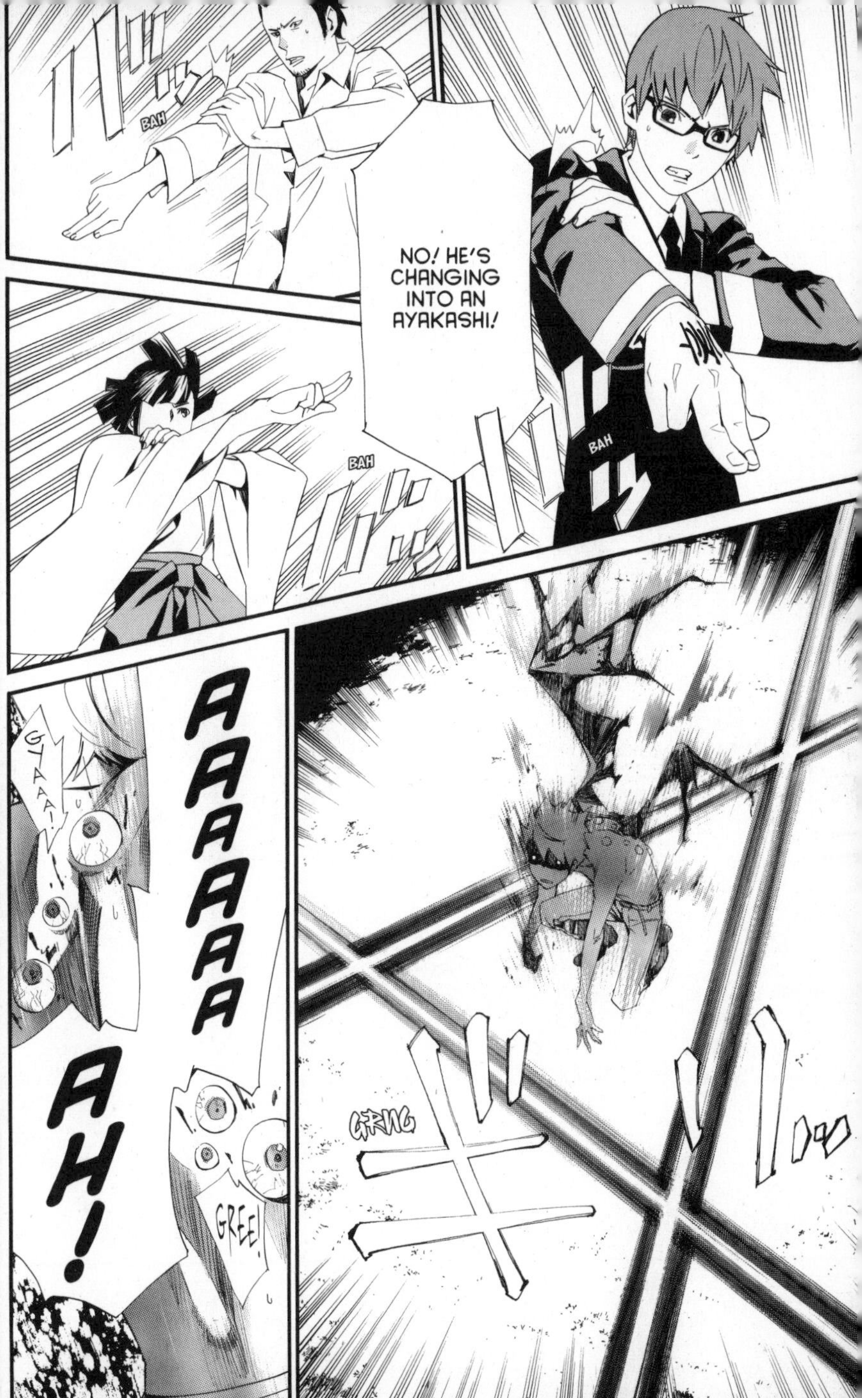
NO! HE'S CHANGING INTO AN AYAKASHI!
BAH
BAH
BAH
GRNG
GYAAA!
AAAAAAAAH!
GREE!

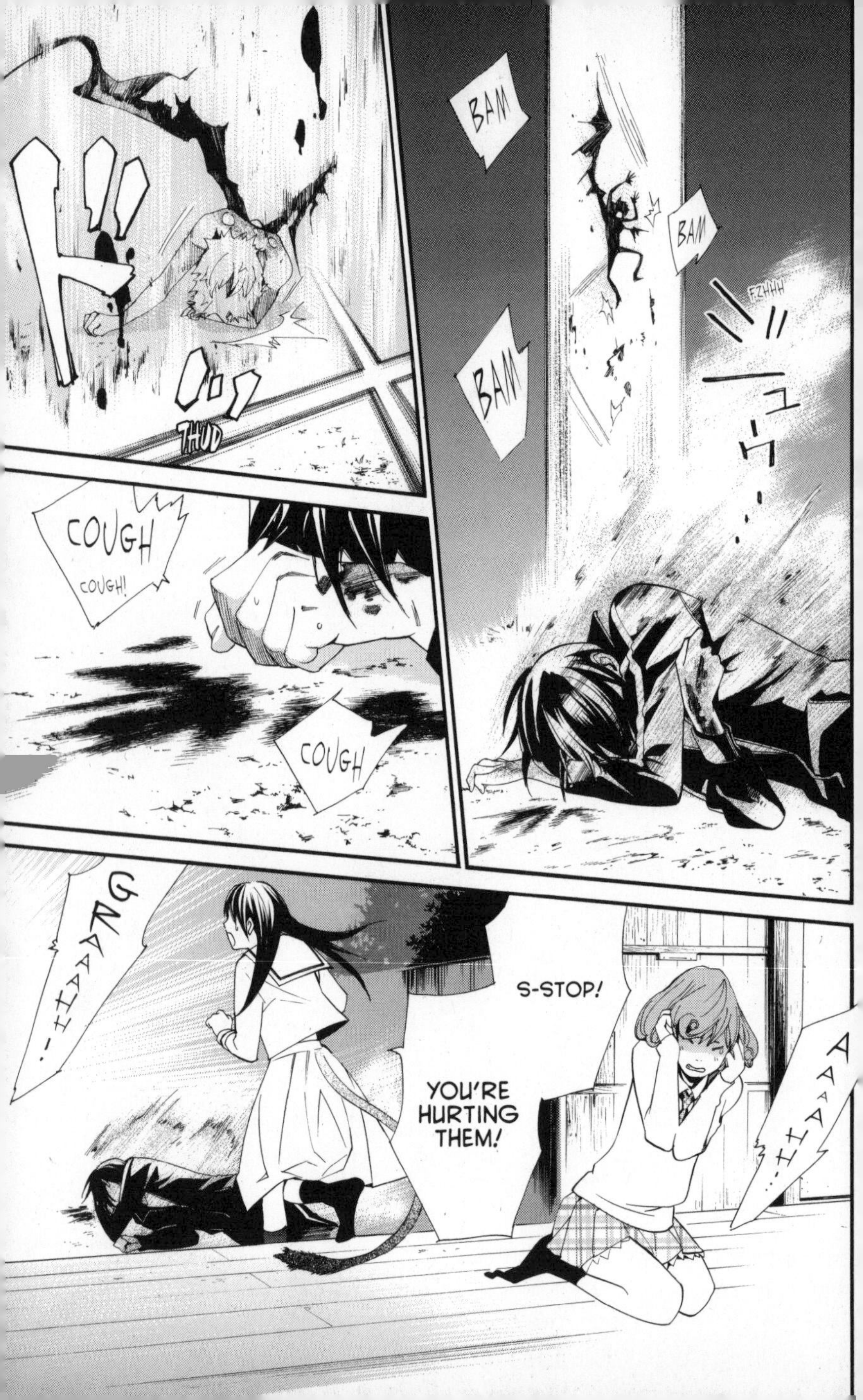
BAM
BAM
FZHHH
BAM
THUD
COUGH
COUGH!
COUGH
AAAAHH...
S-STOP!
YOU'RE HURTING THEM!
GRAAAAHH...!

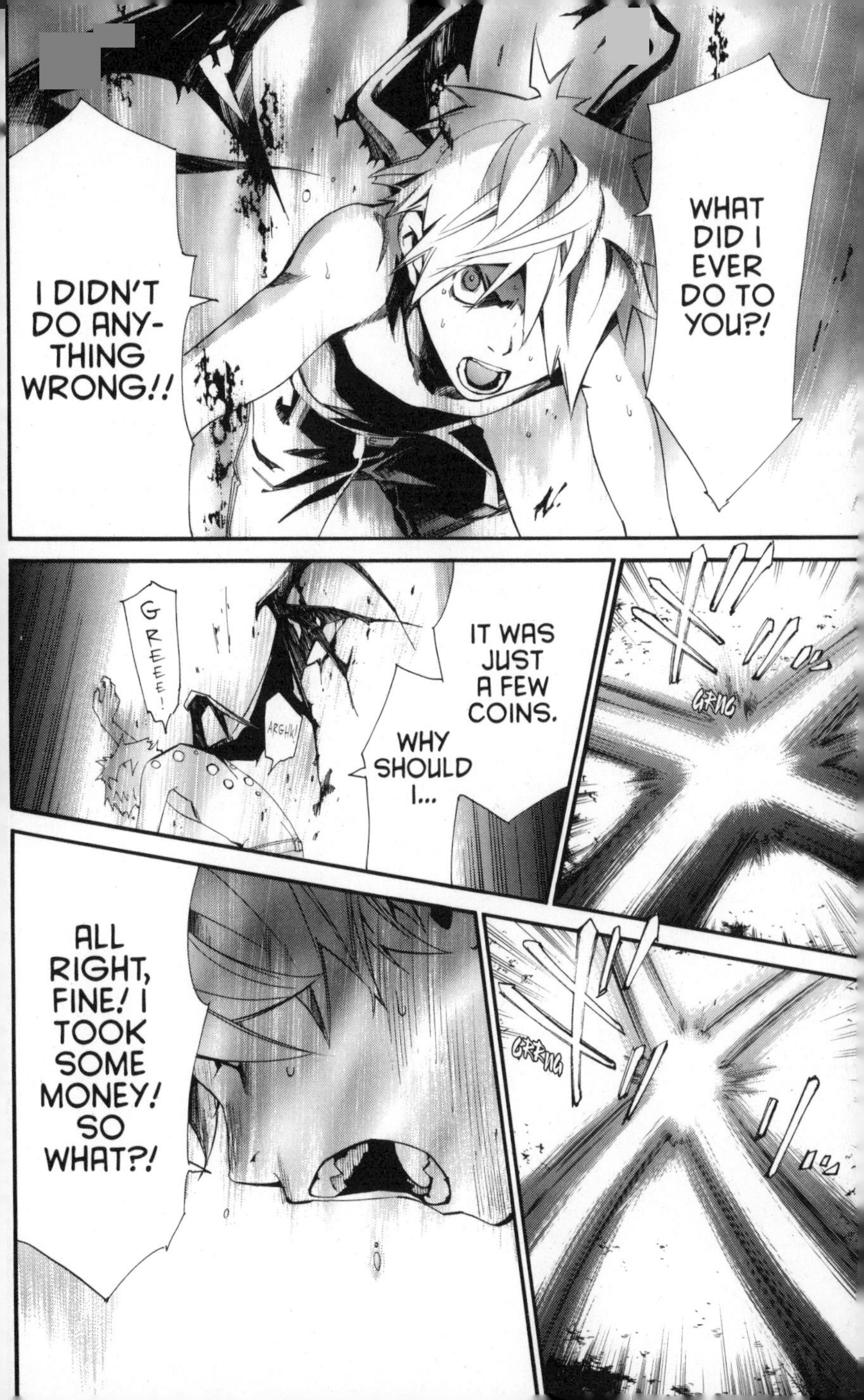
WHAT DID I EVER DO TO YOU?!
I DIDN'T DO ANY-THING WRONG!!
GRNG
IT WAS JUST A FEW COINS.
WHY SHOULD I...
ARGHH!
GREEE!
GRRNG
ALL RIGHT, FINE! I TOOK SOME MONEY! SO WHAT?!

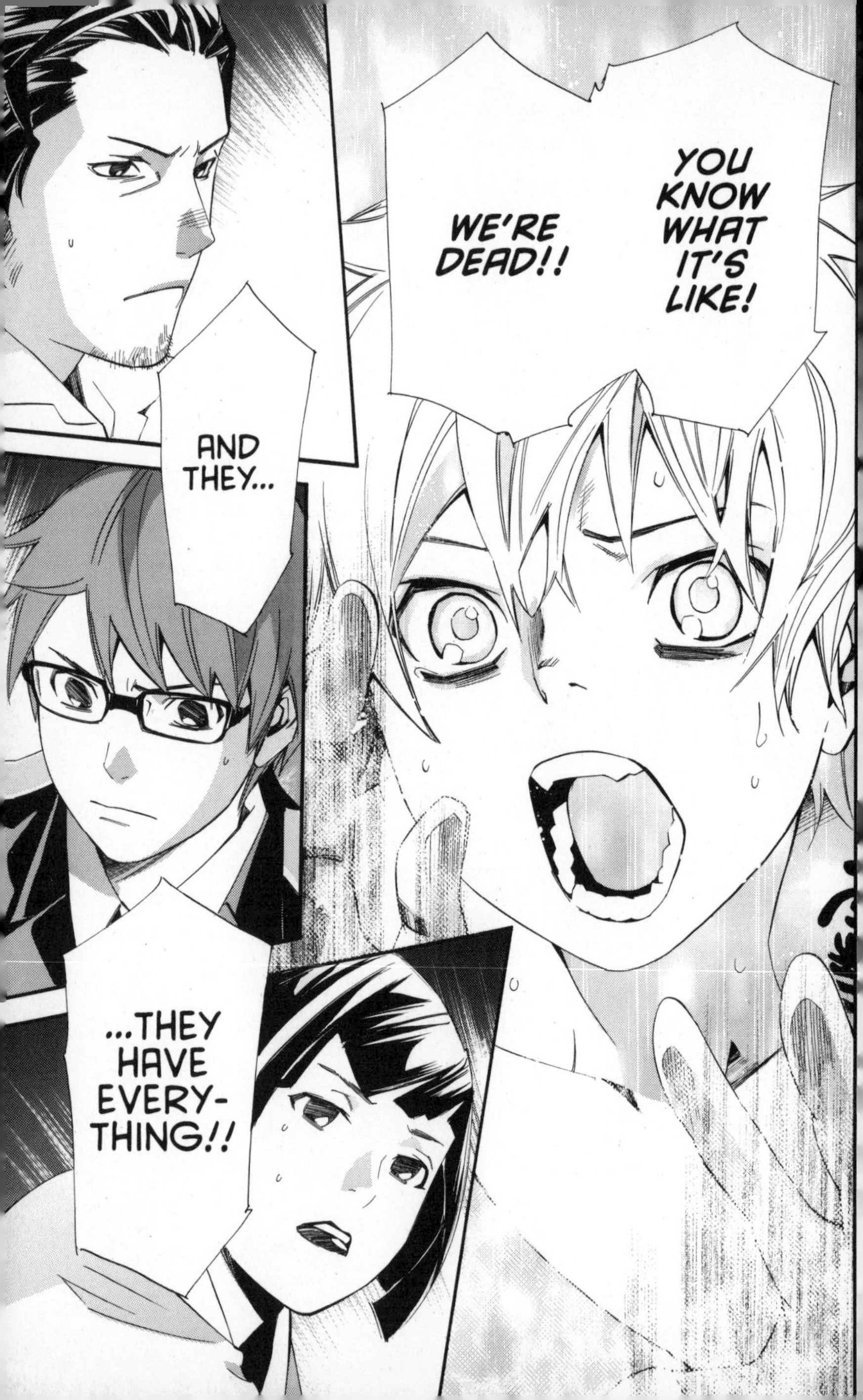
YOU KNOW WHAT IT'S LIKE! WE'RE DEAD!!
AND THEY...
...THEY HAVE EVERY-THING!!

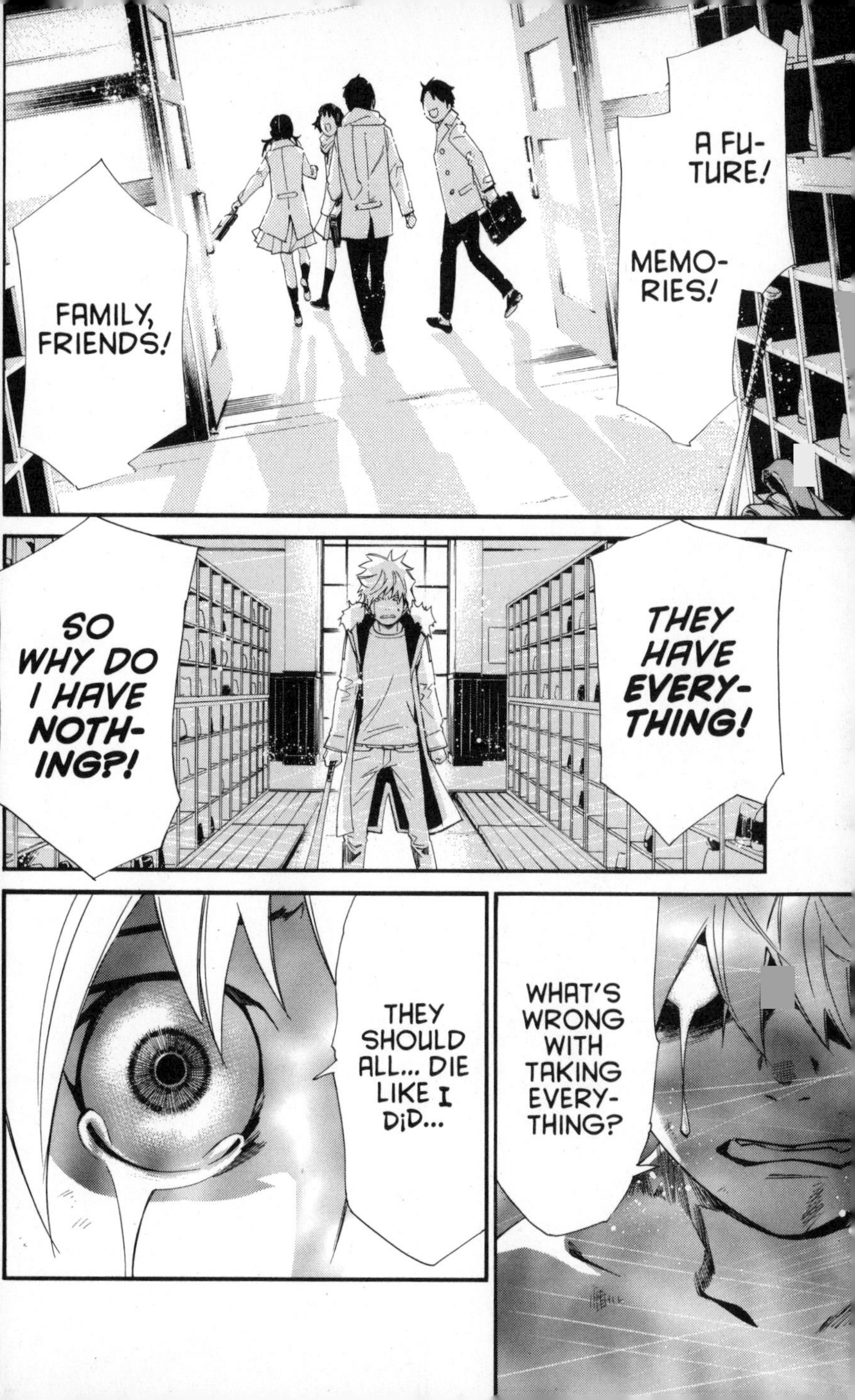
A FU-TURE!
MEMO-RIES!
FAMILY, FRIENDS!
THEY HAVE EVERY-THING!
SO WHY DO I HAVE NOTH-ING?!
WHAT'S WRONG WITH TAKING EVERY-THING?
THEY SHOULD ALL... DIE LIKE I DID...

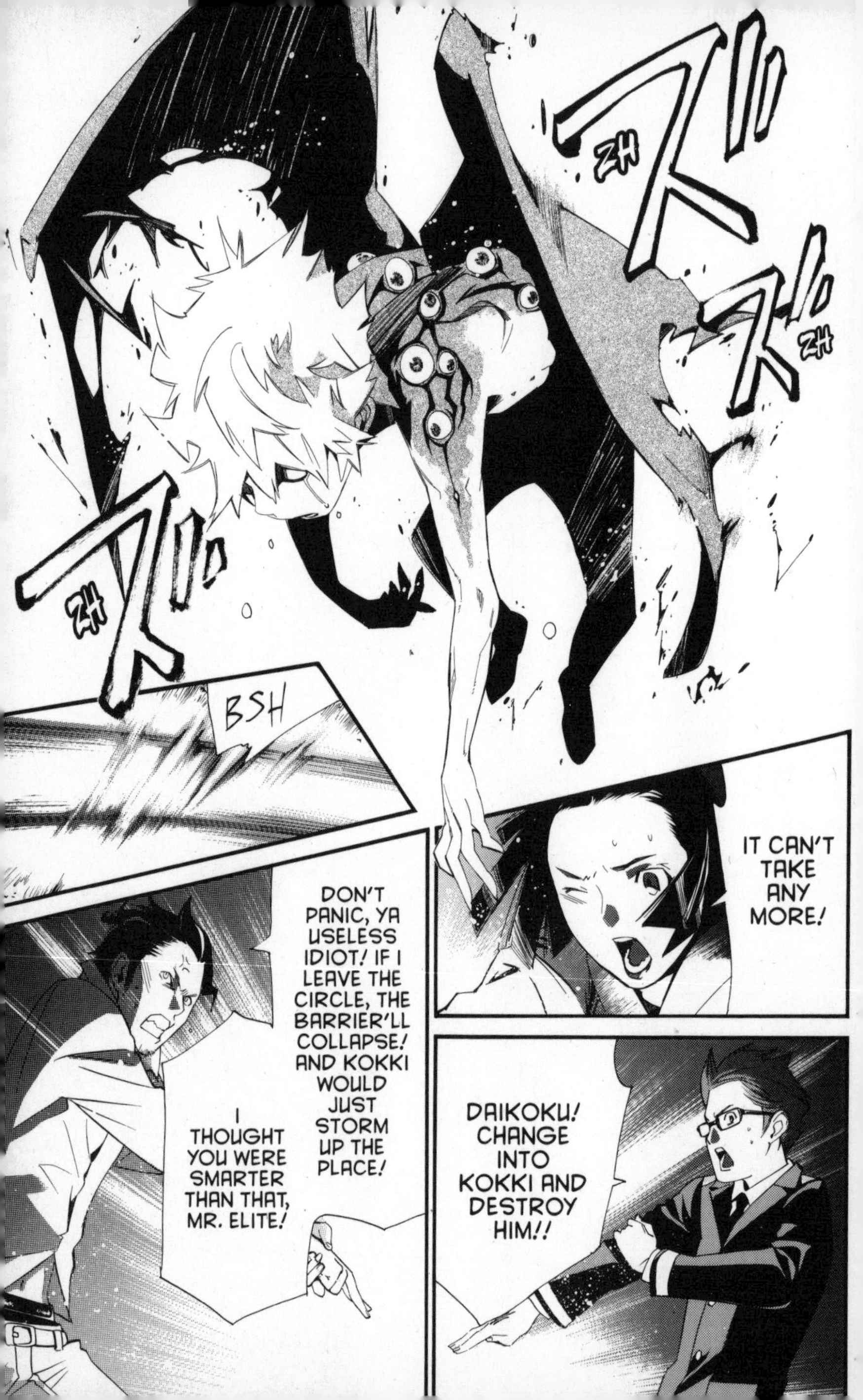
ZH
ZH
ZH
BSH
IT CAN'T TAKE ANY MORE!
DAIKOKU! CHANGE INTO KOKKI AND DESTROY HIM!!
DON'T PANIC, YA USELESS IDIOT! IF I LEAVE THE CIRCLE, THE BARRIER'LL COLLAPSE! AND KOKKI WOULD JUST STORM UP THE PLACE!
I THOUGHT YOU WERE SMARTER THAN THAT, MR. ELITE!

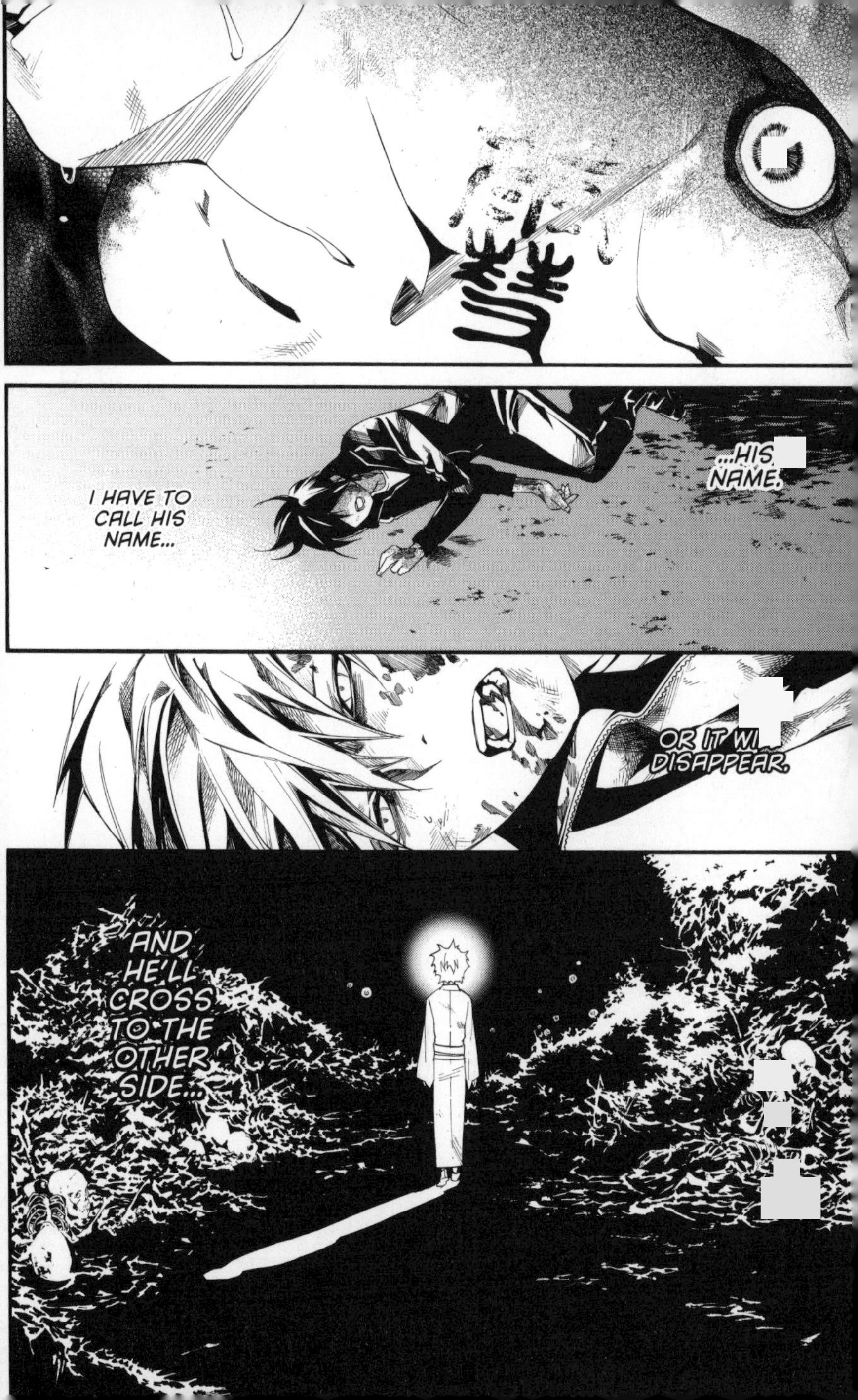
...HIS
NAME.
I HAVE TO CALL HIS NAME...
OR IT WI
DISAPPEAR.
AND HE'LL CROSS TO THE OTHER SIDE...

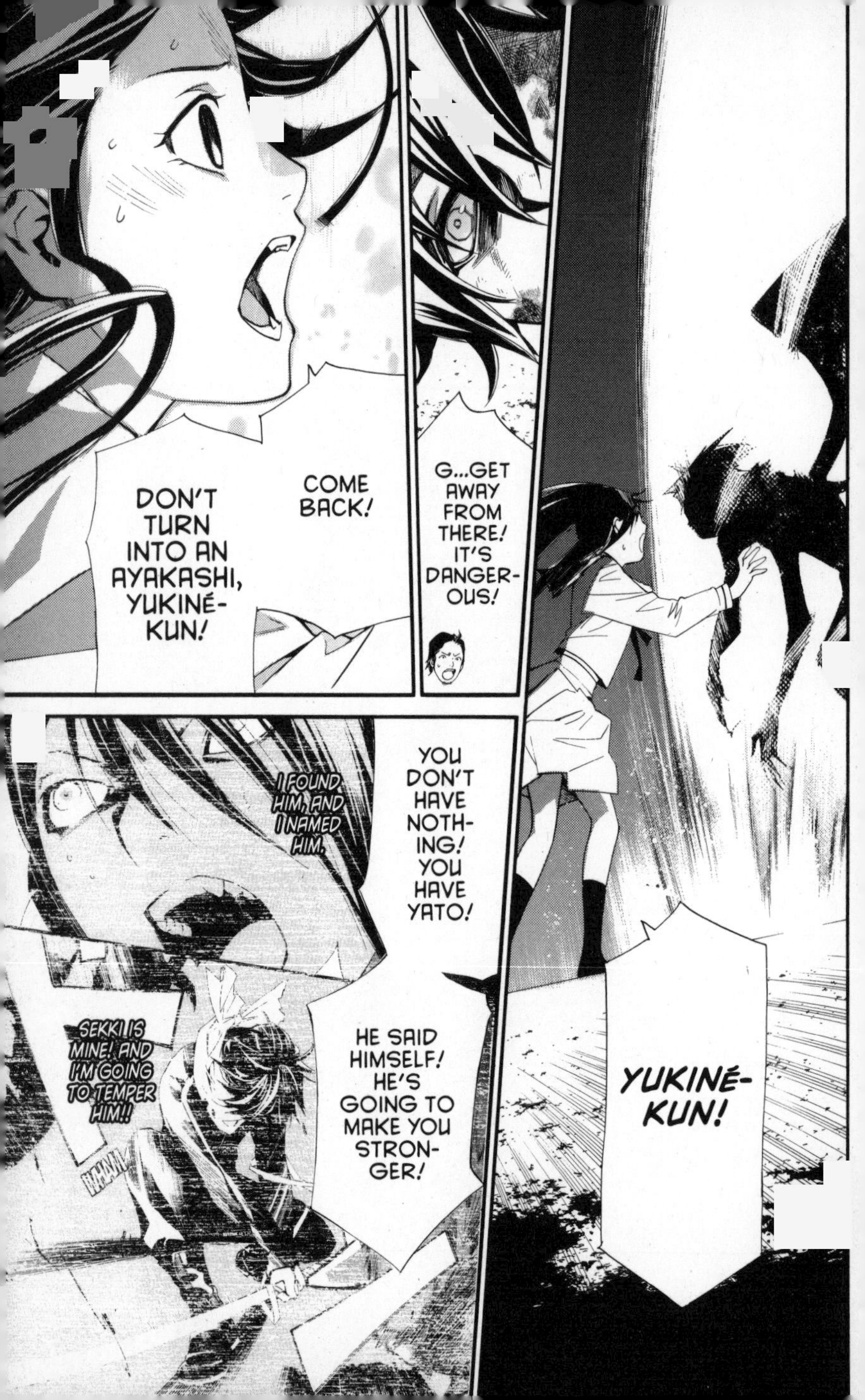
YUKINÉ-KUN!
G...GET AWAY FROM THERE! IT'S DANGEROUS!
COME BACK!
DON'T TURN INTO AN AYAKASHI, YUKINÉ-KUN!
YOU DON'T HAVE NOTHING! YOU HAVE YATO!
I FOUND HIM, AND I NAMED HIM.
HE SAID HIMSELF! HE'S GOING TO MAKE YOU STRONGER!
SEKKI IS MINE! AND I'M GOING TO TEMPER HIM!!

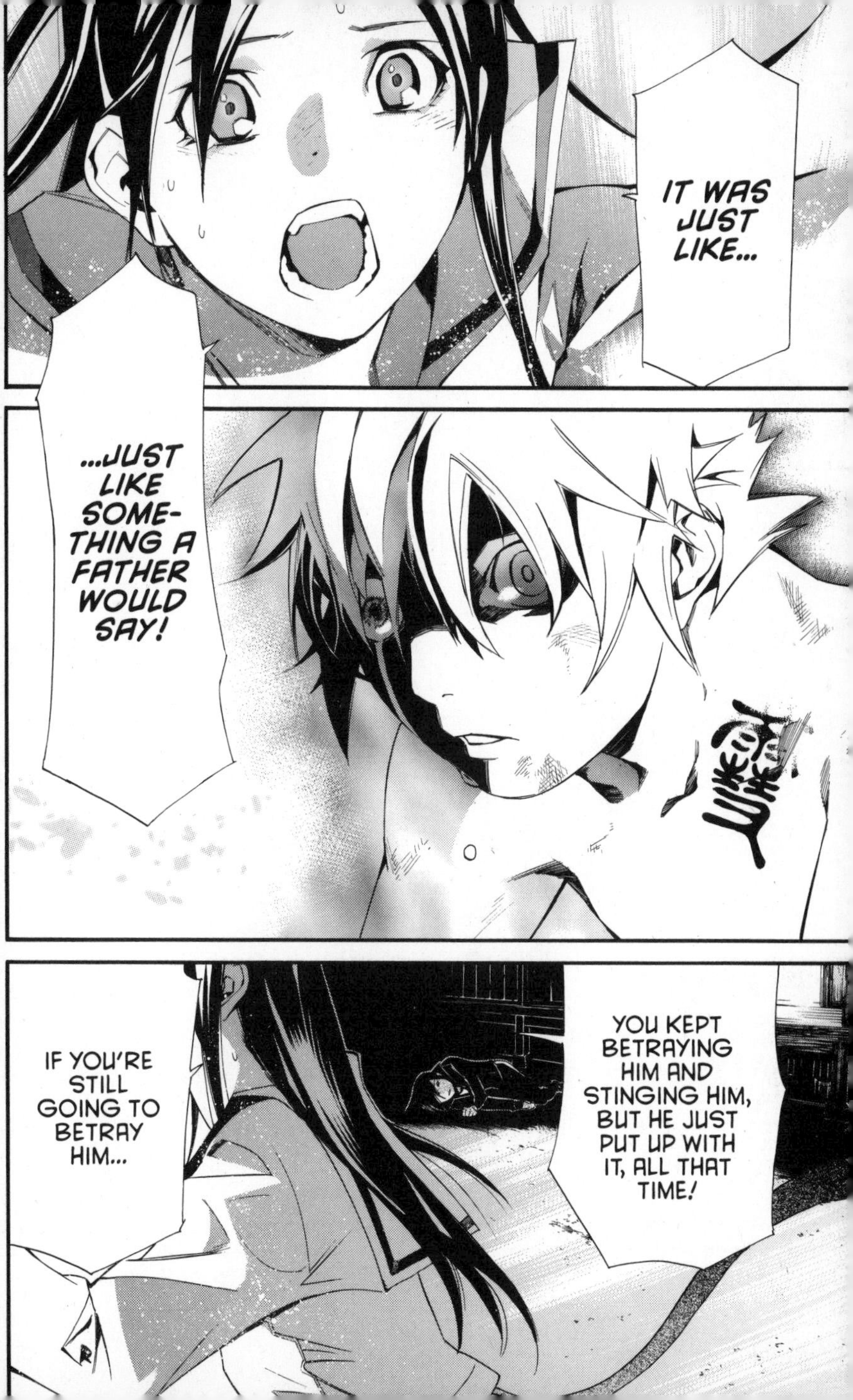
IT WAS JUST LIKE...
...JUST LIKE SOME-THING A FATHER WOULD SAY!
YOU KEPT BETRAYING HIM AND STINGING HIM, BUT HE JUST PUT UP WITH IT, ALL THAT TIME!
IF YOU'RE STILL GOING TO BETRAY HIM...

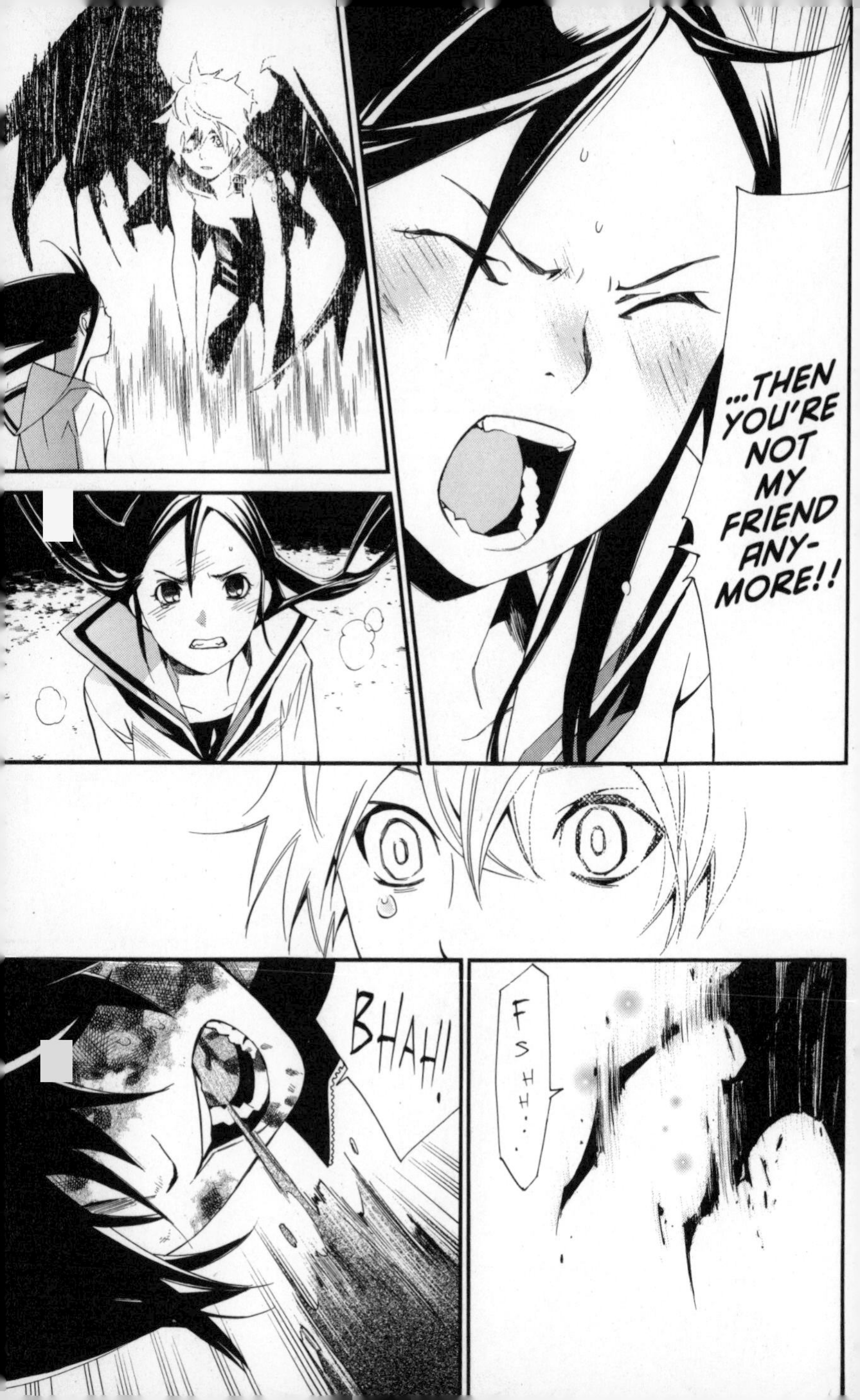
...THEN YOU'RE NOT MY FRIEND ANY-MORE!!
FSHH...
BHAH!

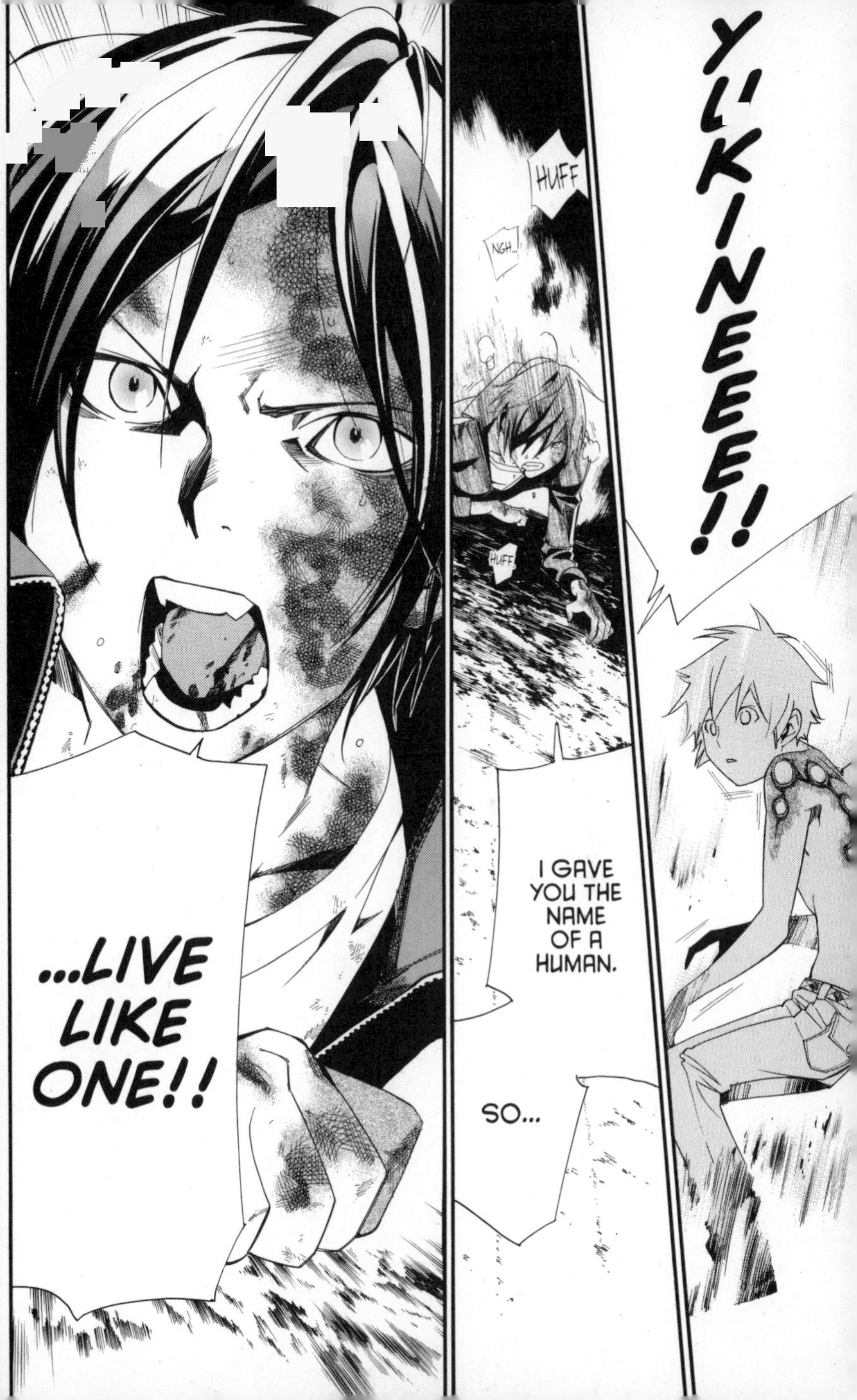
YUKINEEEE!!
HUFF
NGH..
HUFF
I GAVE YOU THE NAME OF A HUMAN.
SO...
...LIVE LIKE ONE!!

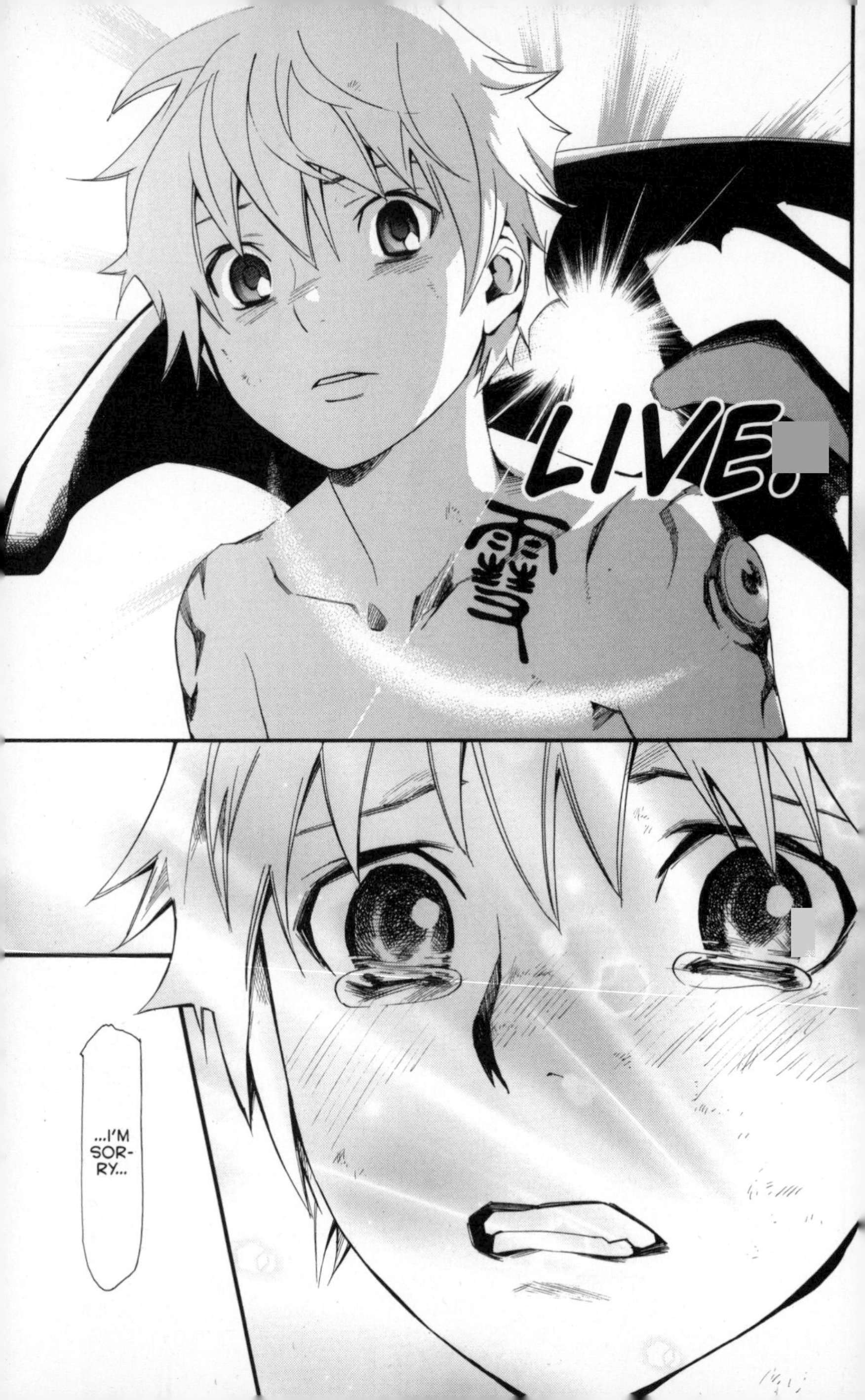
LIVE.
雪
...I'M SORRY...

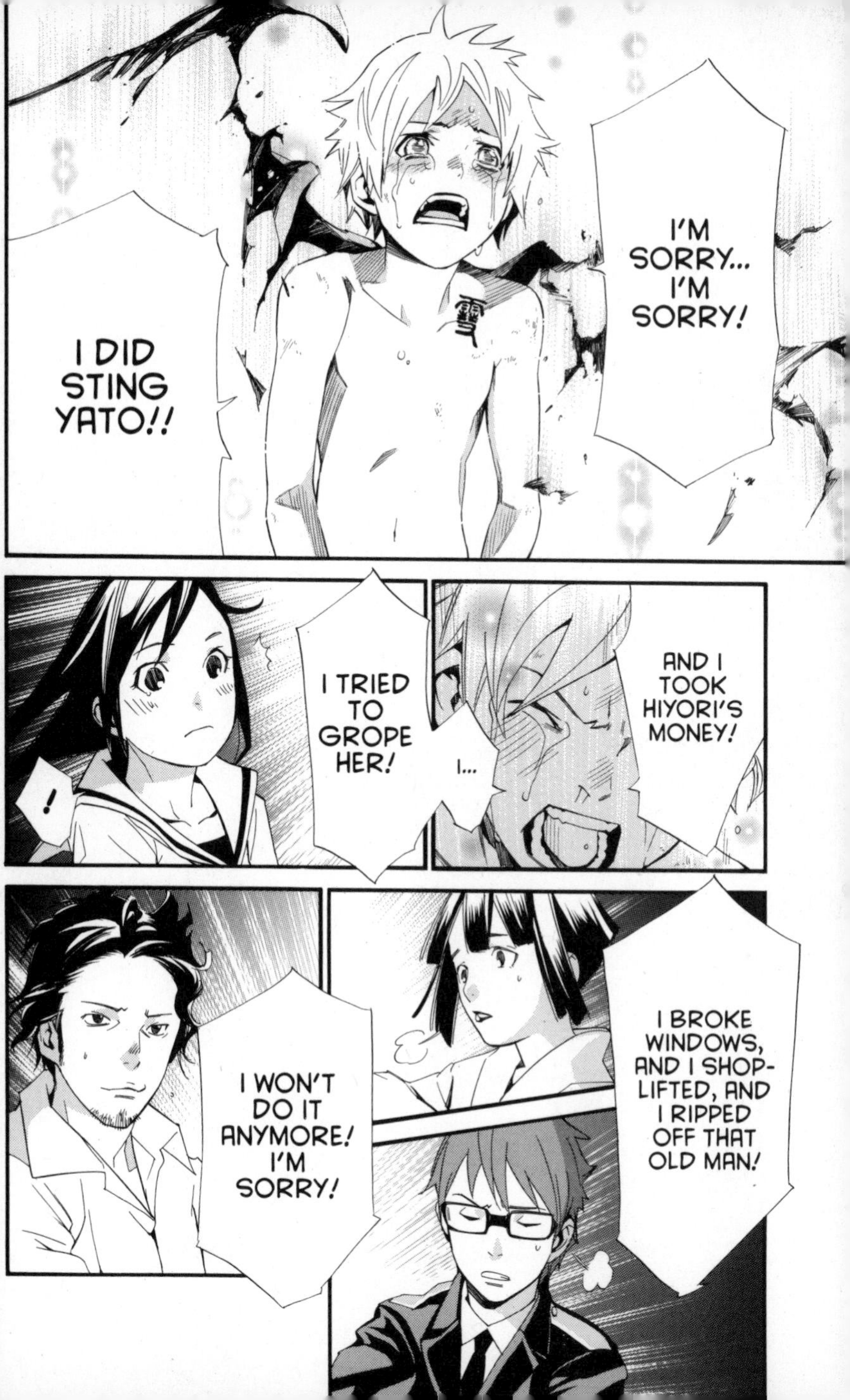
I'M SORRY... I'M SORRY!
I DID STING YATO!!
AND I TOOK HIYORI'S MONEY!
I...
I TRIED TO GROPE HER!
!
I BROKE WINDOWS, AND I SHOP-LIFTED, AND I RIPPED OFF THAT OLD MAN!
I WON'T DO IT ANYMORE! I'M SORRY!

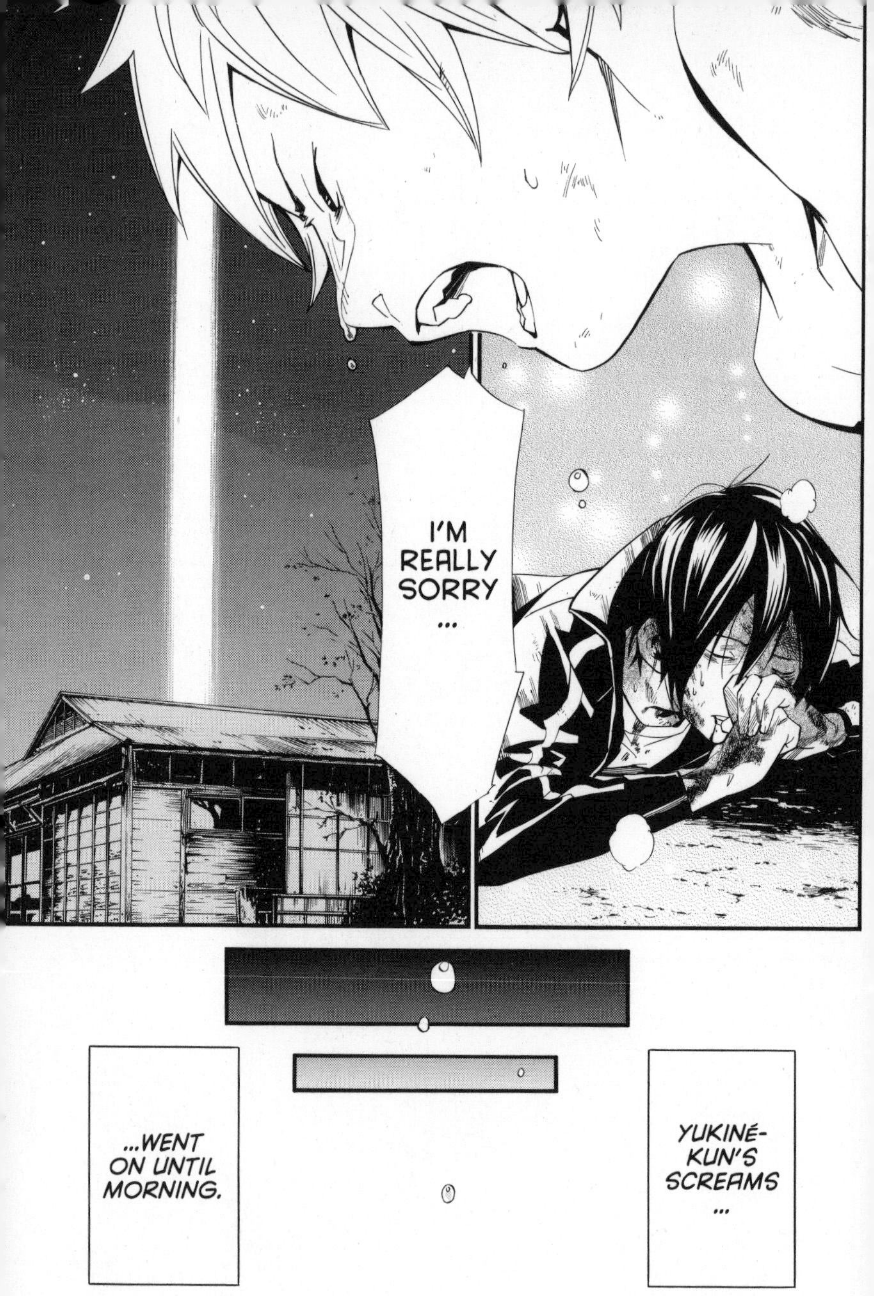
I'M REALLY SORRY ...
YUKINÉ-KUN'S SCREAMS ...
...WENT ON UNTIL MORNING.

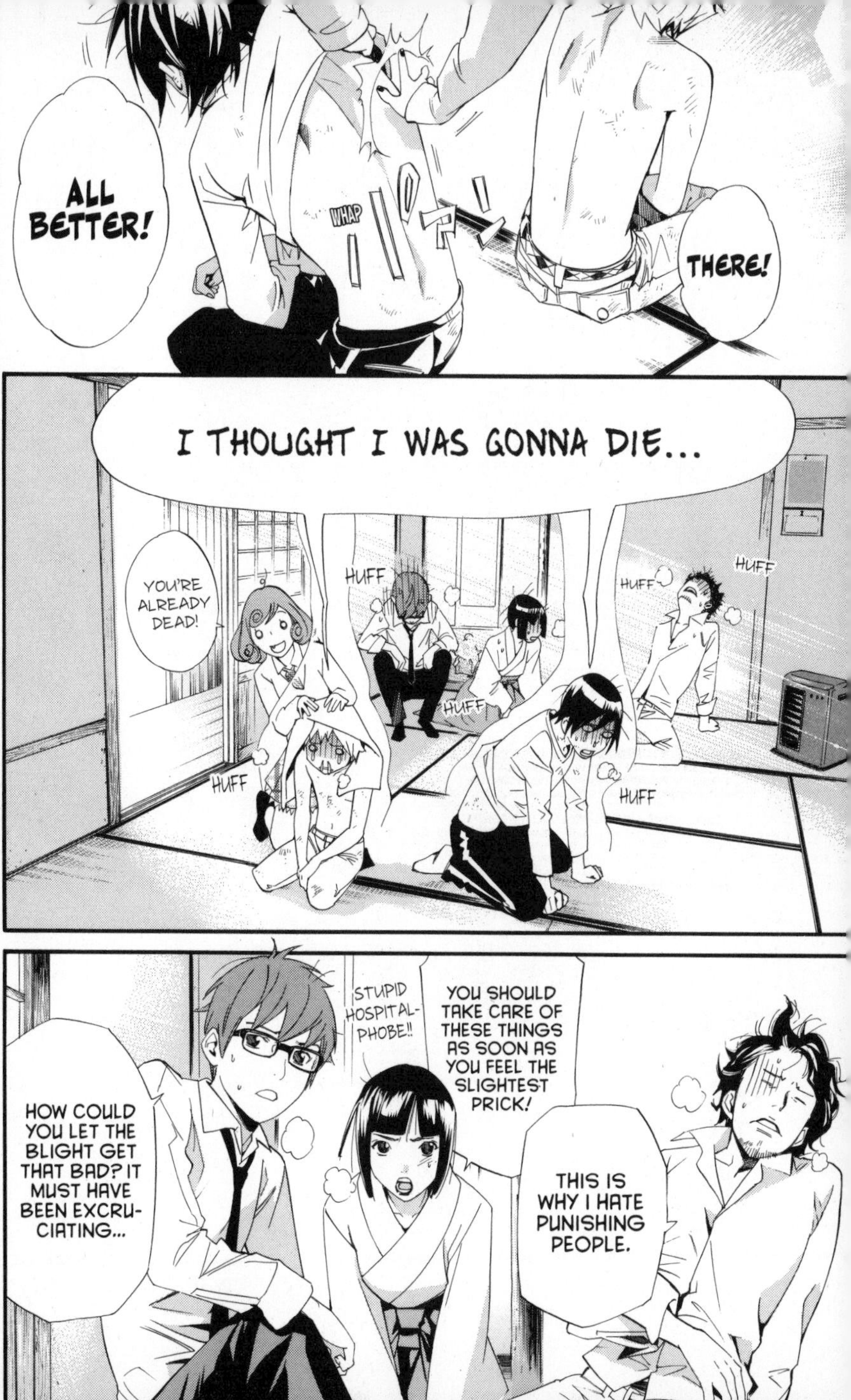
THERE!
WHAP
ALL BETTER!
I THOUGHT I WAS GONNA DIE...
HUFF
HUFF
HUFF
HUFF
HUFF
HUFF
YOU'RE ALREADY DEAD!
THIS IS WHY I HATE PUNISHING PEOPLE.
YOU SHOULD TAKE CARE OF THESE THINGS AS SOON AS YOU FEEL THE SLIGHTEST PRICK!
STUPID HOSPITAL-PHOBE!!
HOW COULD YOU LET THE BLIGHT GET THAT BAD? IT MUST HAVE BEEN EXCRU-CIATING...

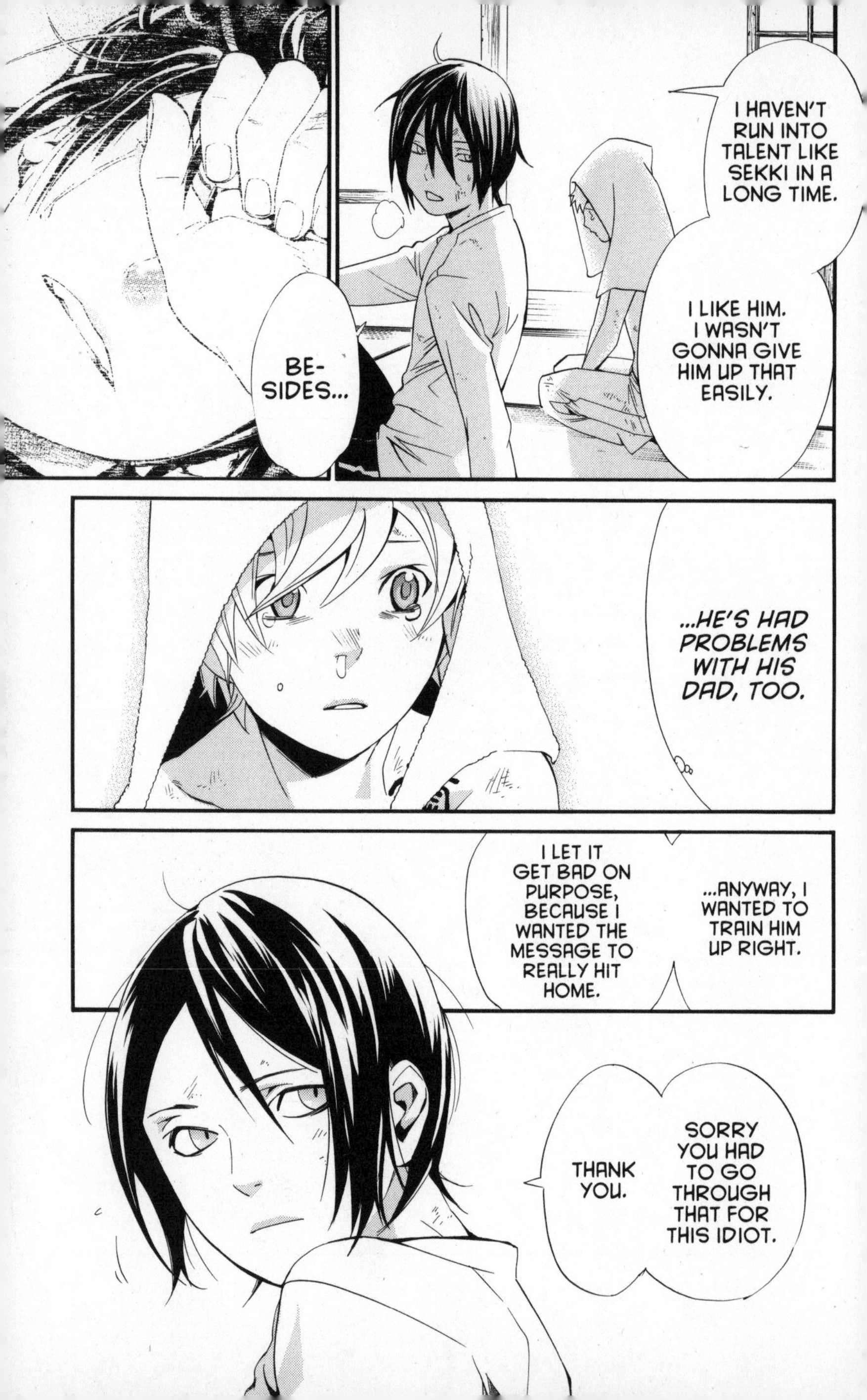
I HAVEN'T RUN INTO TALENT LIKE SEKKI IN A LONG TIME.
I LIKE HIM. I WASN'T GONNA GIVE HIM UP THAT EASILY.
BE-SIDES...
...HE'S HAD PROBLEMS WITH HIS DAD, TOO.
...ANYWAY, I WANTED TO TRAIN HIM UP RIGHT.
I LET IT GET BAD ON PURPOSE, BECAUSE I WANTED THE MESSAGE TO REALLY HIT HOME.
SORRY YOU HAD TO GO THROUGH THAT FOR THIS IDIOT.
THANK YOU.

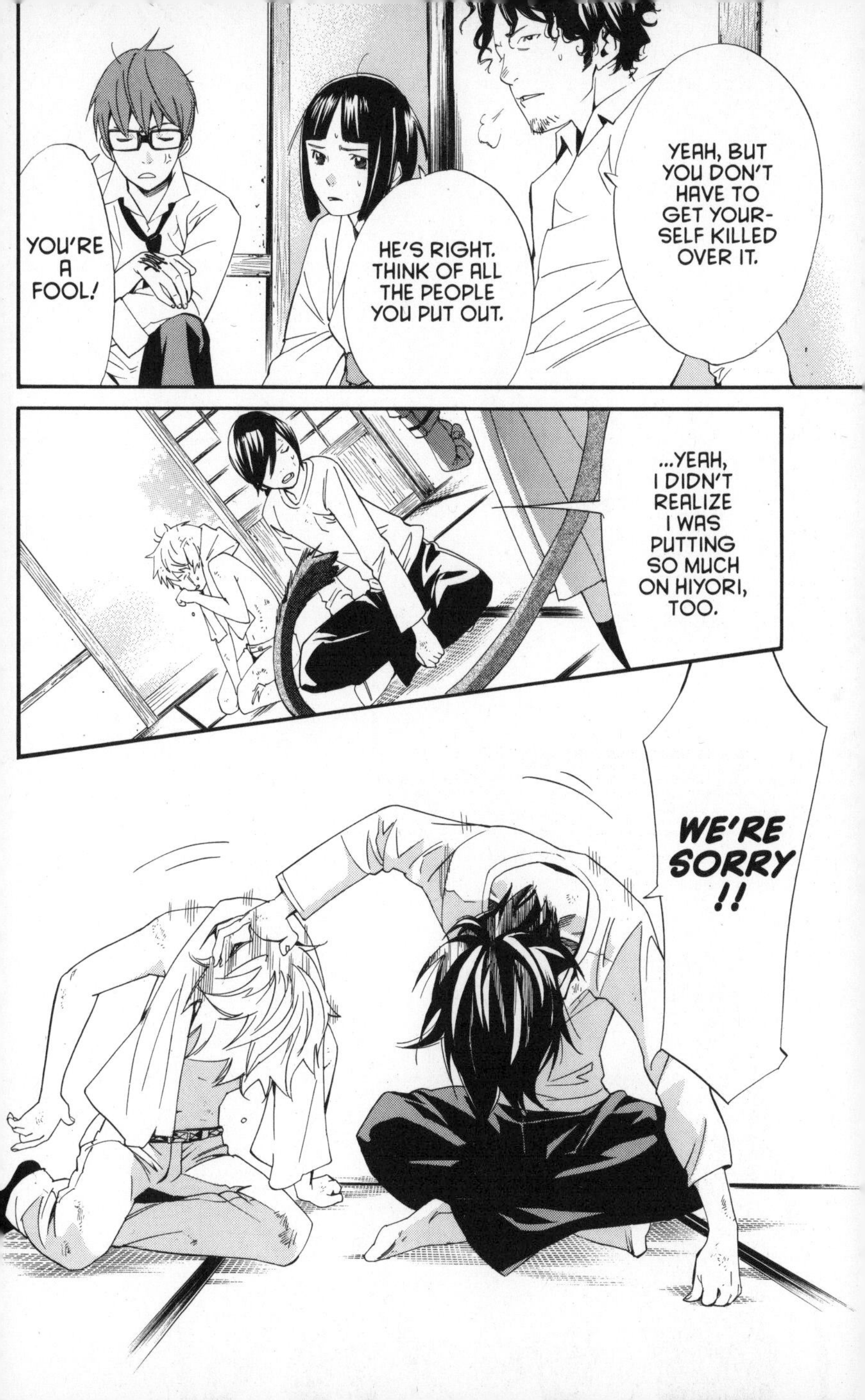
YEAH, BUT YOU DON'T HAVE TO GET YOUR-SELF KILLED OVER IT.
HE'S RIGHT. THINK OF ALL THE PEOPLE YOU PUT OUT.
YOU'RE A FOOL!
...YEAH, I DIDN'T REALIZE I WAS PUTTING SO MUCH ON HIYORI, TOO.
WE'RE SORRY!!

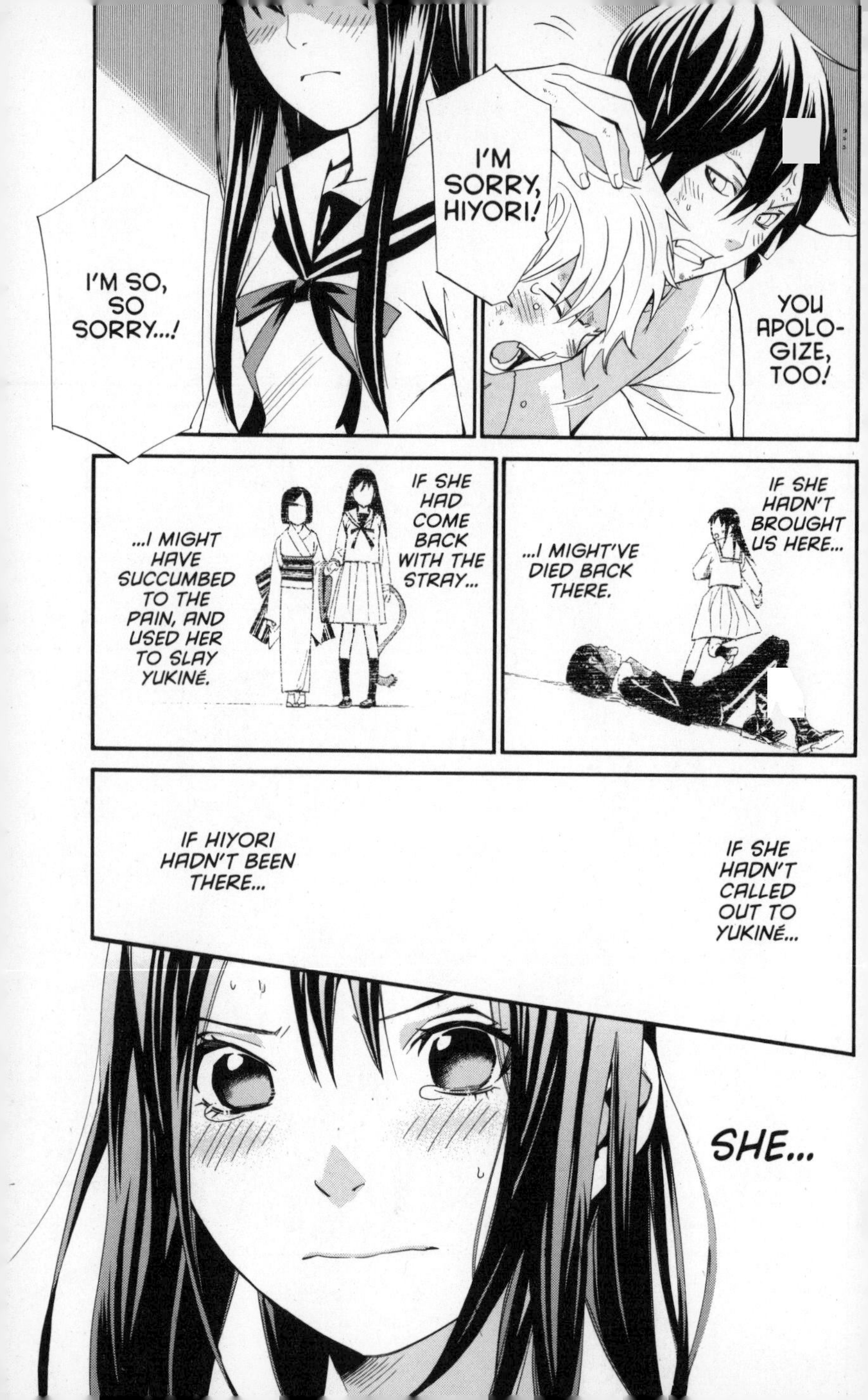
YOU APOLOGIZE, TOO!
I'M SORRY, HIYORI!
I'M SO, SO SORRY...!
IF SHE HADN'T BROUGHT US HERE...
...I MIGHT'VE DIED BACK THERE.
IF SHE HAD COME BACK WITH THE STRAY...
...I MIGHT HAVE SUCCUMBED TO THE PAIN, AND USED HER TO SLAY YUKINÉ.
IF SHE HADN'T CALLED OUT TO YUKINÉ...
IF HIYORI HADN'T BEEN THERE...
SHE...

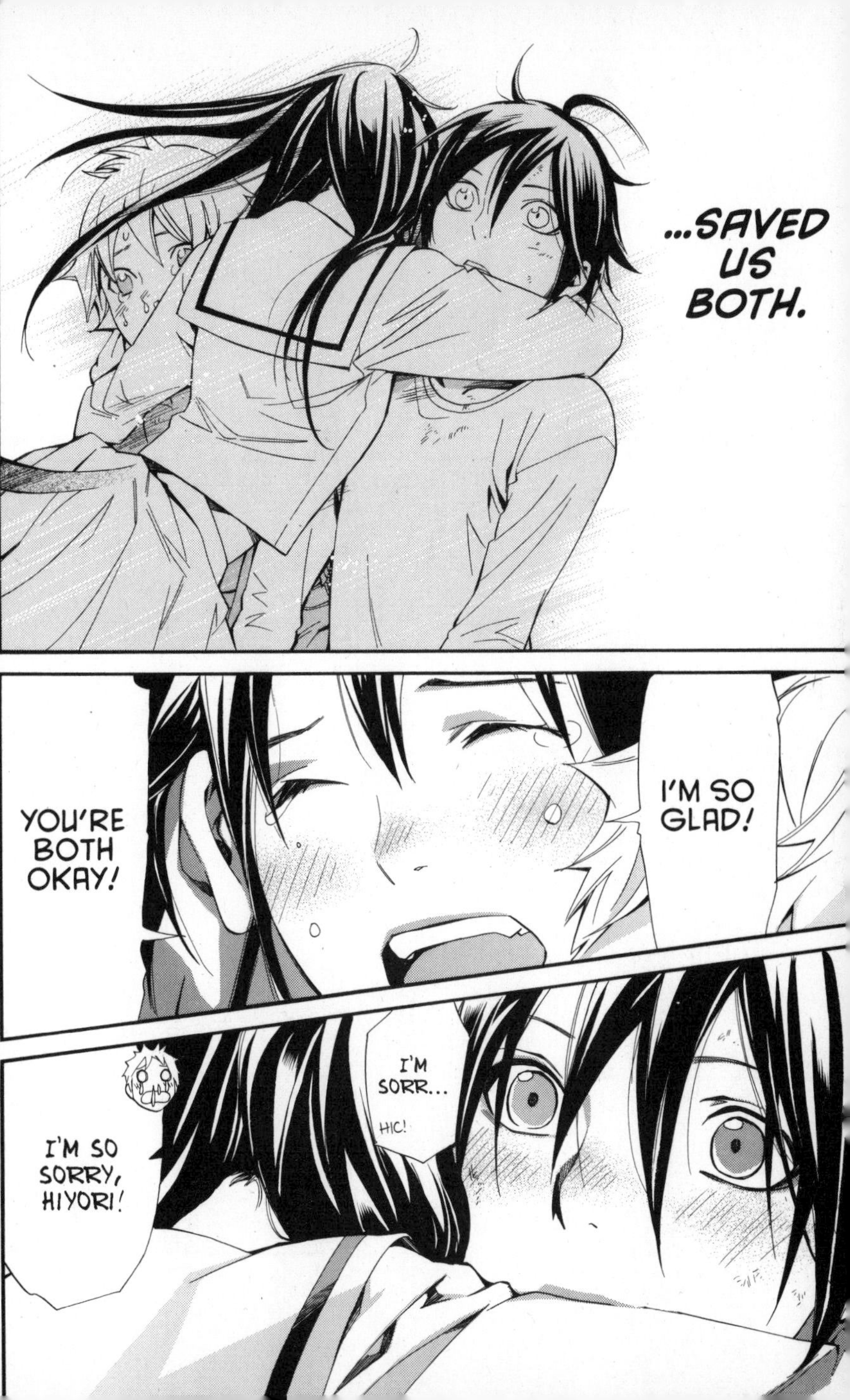
...SAVED US BOTH.
I'M SO GLAD!
YOU'RE BOTH OKAY!
I'M SORR...
HIC!
I'M SO SORRY, HIYORI!

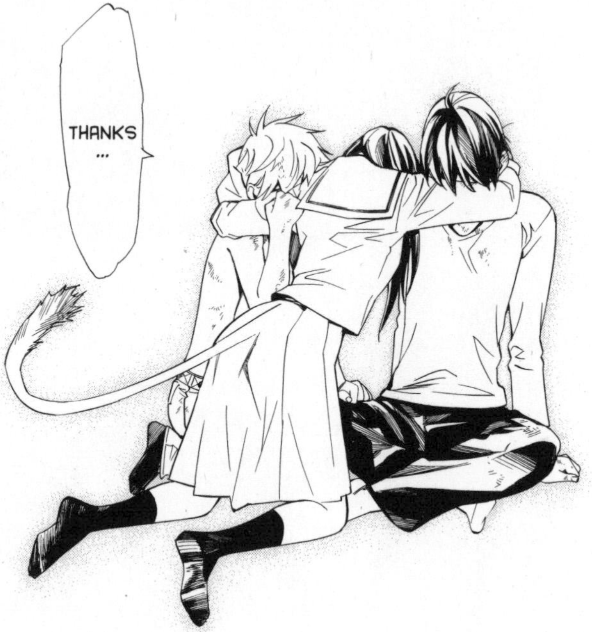
THANKS ...

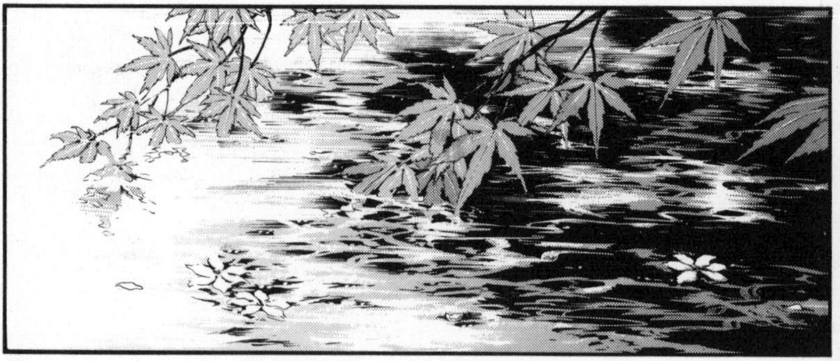

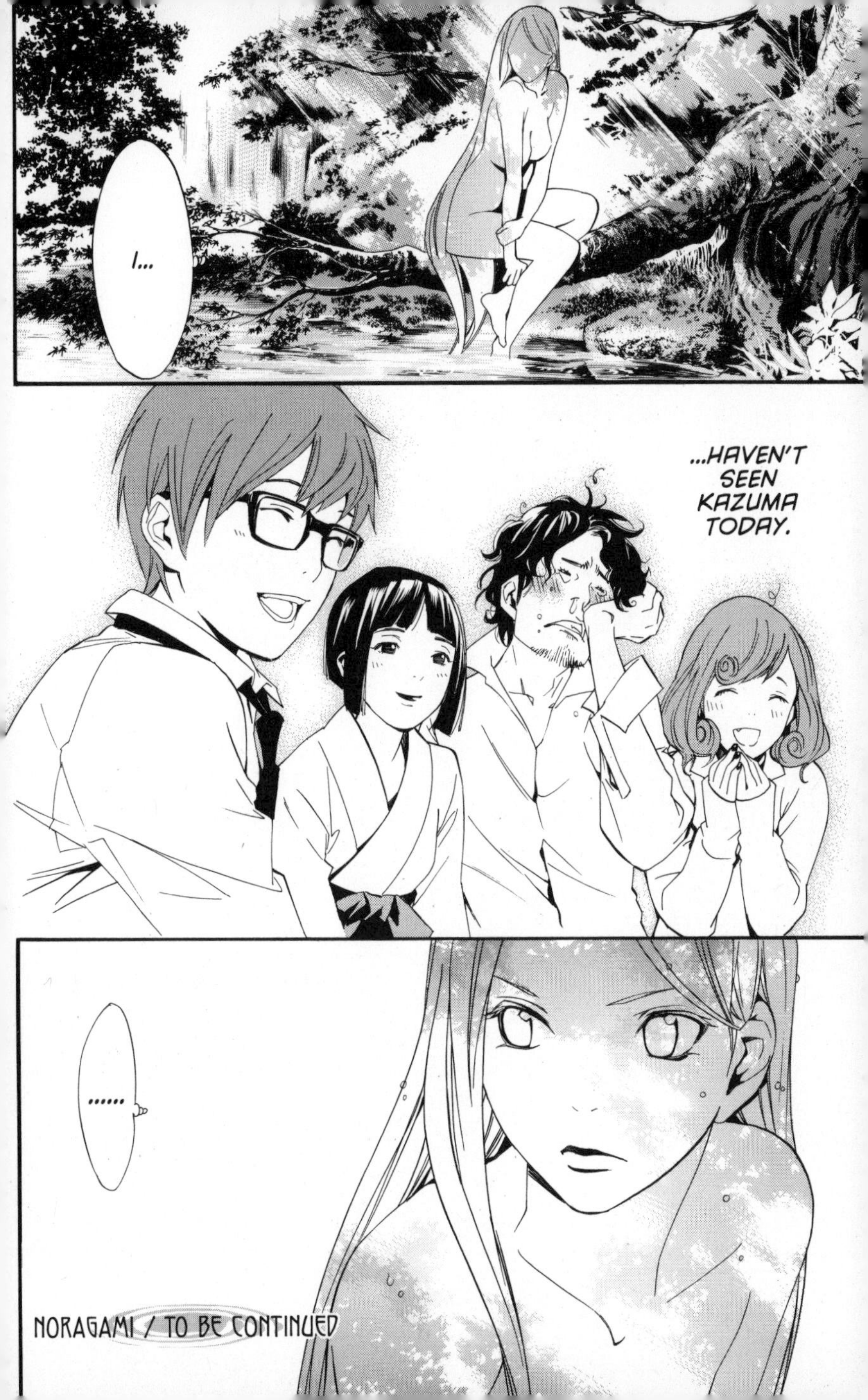
I...
...HAVEN'T SEEN KAZUMA TODAY.
......
NORAGAMI / TO BE CONTINUED

對

兑

神

ATROCIOUS MANGA

BONUS MANGA SURE IS HARD.
NO IDEAS?
POOR SING.
PSST
PSST

THEY'RE WATCHING

YOU'RE NO SON OF MINE!
I CAN'T STAND THE SIGHT OF YOU!
DARLING, HOW CAN YOU SAY THAT TO HIM!
うるっ
WHIMPER
HE SAYS SUCH TERRIBLE SINGS...
PSST
PSST
DON'T TALK BACK TO ME, WOM-AN!
WHAM
POOR SING...
I CAN'T SEE.
AAAAHH!

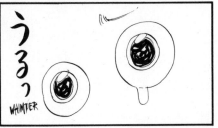

TRYING IT ON

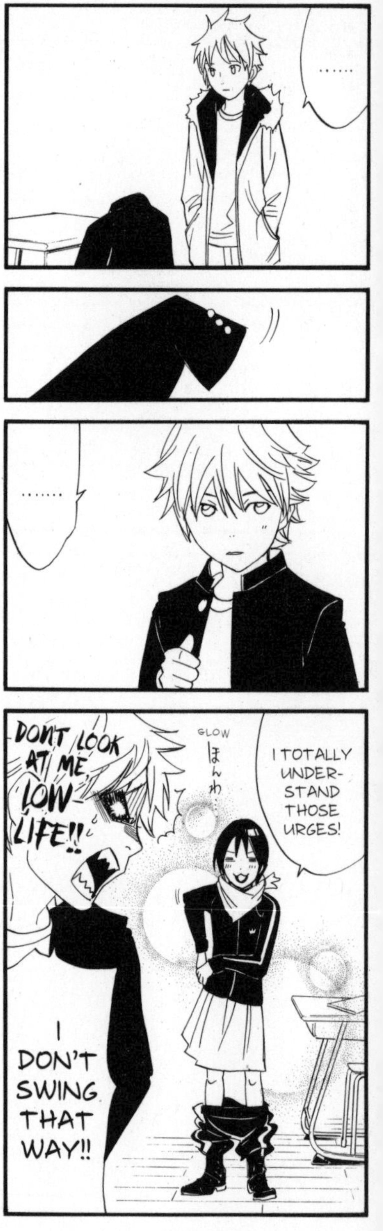
......
......
I TOTALLY UNDER-STAND THOSE URGES!
GLOW
ほんわ…
DON'T LOOK AT ME, LOW LIFE!!
I DON'T SWING THAT WAY!!

I AM A LION

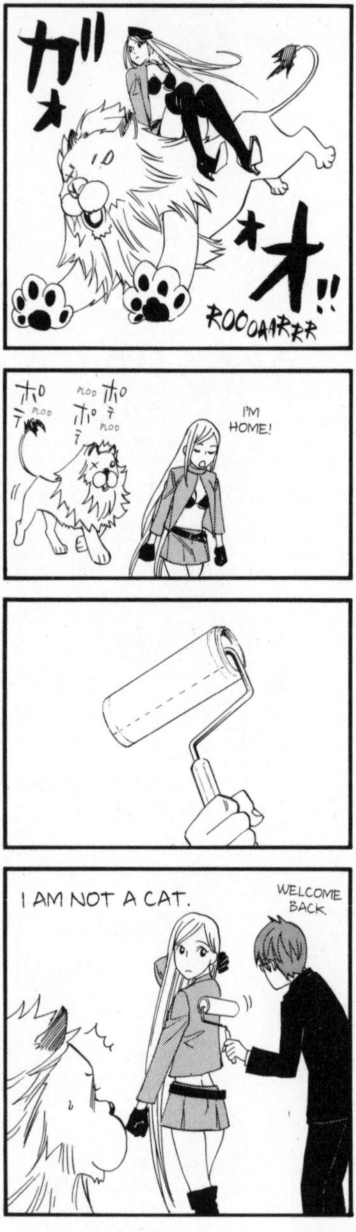
ガオオオ!!
ROOOAARRR
ポテ PLOD
ポテ PLOD
ポテ PLOD
I'M HOME!
WELCOME BACK.
I AM NOT A CAT.

BLEMISHES

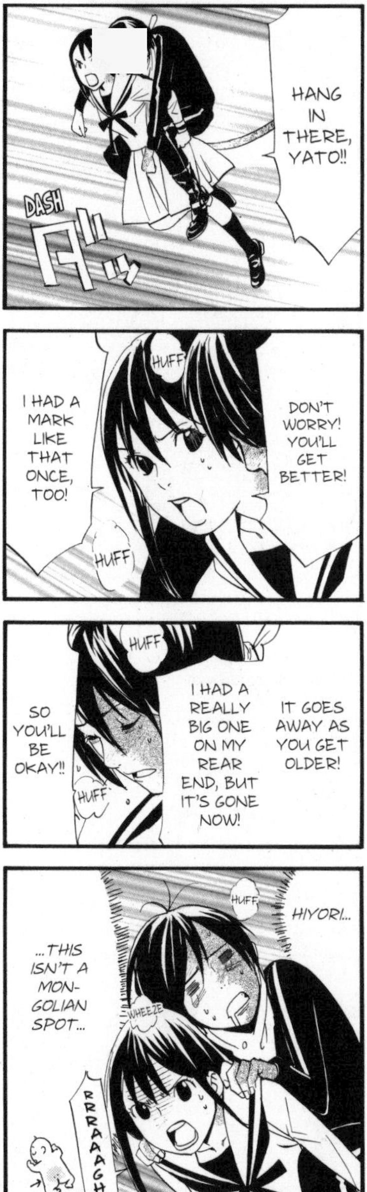
HANG IN THERE, YATO!!
DASH
HUFF
DON'T WORRY! YOU'LL GET BETTER!
I HAD A MARK LIKE THAT ONCE, TOO!
HUFF
HUFF
IT GOES AWAY AS YOU GET OLDER!
I HAD A REALLY BIG ONE ON MY REAR END, BUT IT'S GONE NOW!
SO YOU'LL BE OKAY!!
HUFF
HIYORI...
HUFF
...THIS ISN'T A MON-GOLIAN SPOT...
WHEEZE
RRRAAAGH!!

※ DAUGHTER OF A DOCTOR

MA(NSTER)YU

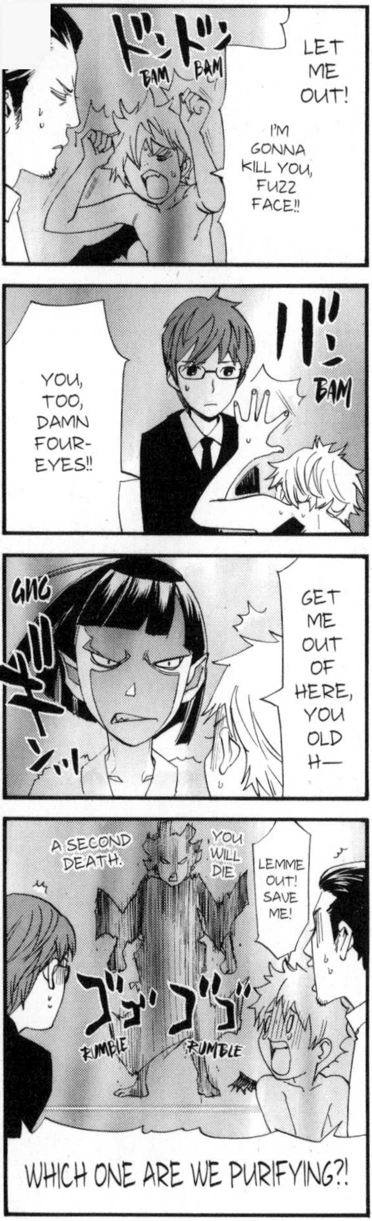
LET ME OUT!
I'M GONNA KILL YOU, FUZZ FACE!!
BAM BAM
BAM
YOU, TOO, DAMN FOUR-EYES!!
GET ME OUT OF HERE, YOU OLD H—
GNG
LEMME OUT! SAVE ME!
YOU WILL DIE
A SECOND DEATH.
RUMBLE RUMBLE
WHICH ONE ARE WE PURIFYING?!

I AM A LION

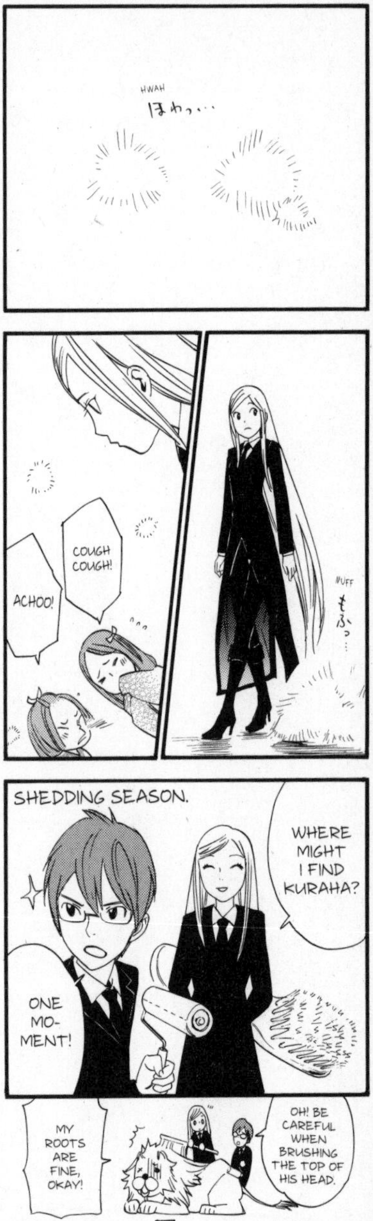
HWAH
ほわっ…
MUFF
もふっ…
COUGH COUGH!
ACHOO!
SHEDDING SEASON.
WHERE MIGHT I FIND KURAHA?
ONE MOMENT!
OH! BE CAREFUL WHEN BRUSHING THE TOP OF HIS HEAD.
MY ROOTS ARE FINE, OKAY!

MAKEOVER

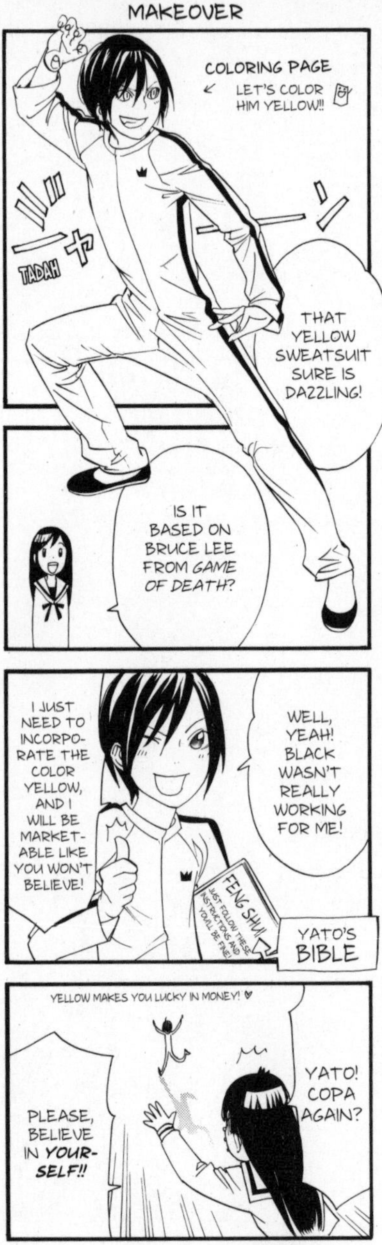
COLORING PAGE
← LET'S COLOR HIM YELLOW!!
THAT YELLOW SWEATSUIT SURE IS DAZZLING!
TADAH
IS IT BASED ON BRUCE LEE FROM GAME OF DEATH?
WELL, YEAH! BLACK WASN'T REALLY WORKING FOR ME!
I JUST NEED TO INCORPORATE THE COLOR YELLOW, AND I WILL BE MARKETABLE LIKE YOU WON'T BELIEVE!
FENG SHUI
JUST FOLLOW THESE INSTRUCTIONS AND YOU'LL BE FINE!
YATO'S BIBLE
YELLOW MAKES YOU LUCKY IN MONEY! ♥
YATO! COPA AGAIN?
PLEASE, BELIEVE IN YOURSELF!!

THANK YOU, EVERYONE WHO'S READ THIS FAR!!

TRANSLATION NOTES

Japanese is a tricky language for most Westerners, and translation is often more art than science. For your edification and reading pleasure, here are notes on some of the places where we could have gone in a different direction in our translation of the work, or where a Japanese cultural reference is used.

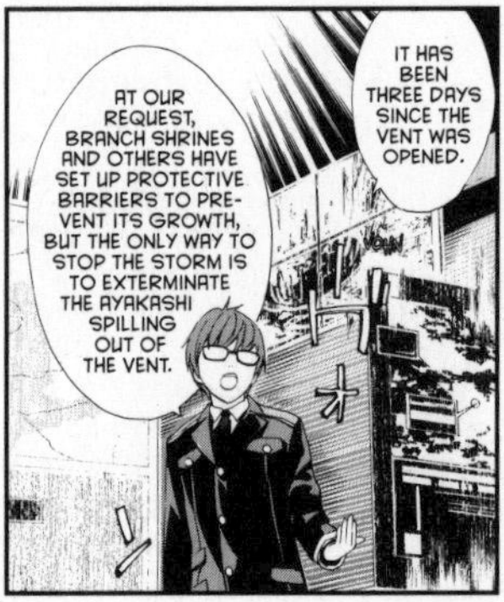
IT HAS BEEN THREE DAYS SINCE THE VENT WAS OPENED.
AT OUR REQUEST, BRANCH SHRINES AND OTHERS HAVE SET UP PROTECTIVE BARRIERS TO PRE-VENT ITS GROWTH, BUT THE ONLY WAY TO STOP THE STORM IS TO EXTERMINATE THE AYAKASHI SPILLING OUT OF THE VENT.

Branch shrines, page 9

As Bishamonten is a well-known deity across Japan, she, like Tenjin, has multiple shrines—these are the shrines to which Kazuma has applied for help. The "others" he mentioned are also shrines, likely shrines to other deities. It may be amusing to note that word for "branch shrine" can also be translated as "branch office."

Ané-sama, page 9

This is a very respectful term of address for one's older sister, or for a young woman.

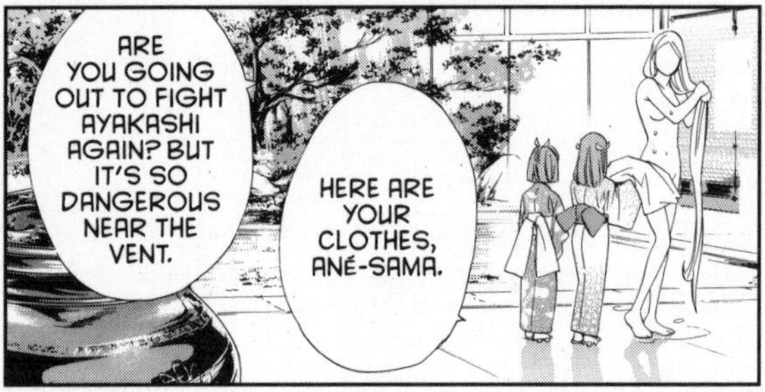
HERE ARE YOUR CLOTHES, ANÉ-SAMA.
ARE YOU GOING OUT TO FIGHT AYAKASHI AGAIN? BUT IT'S SO DANGEROUS NEAR THE VENT.

You've gotten dull, page 39

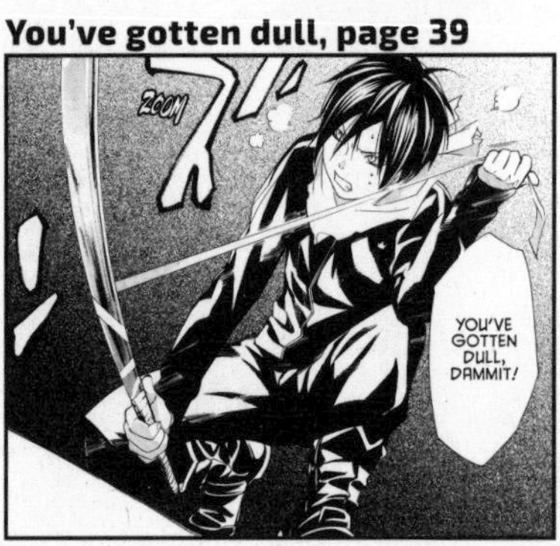
ZOOM
YOU'VE GOTTEN DULL, DAMMIT!

The word translated here as "dull" is *namakura*. Like many words used in this series, it has more than one meaning. The most obvious is "blunt" or "not sharp," as evidenced by Sekki's inability to slice up ayakashi. *Namakura* can also refer to someone who is lazy, useless, and/or cowardly. Finally, it can refer to a lack of skill or experience. All of these seem to apply to Yukiné/Sekki in his current mental state. The translators are sure Yato would also agree with the "unintelligent" definition of the English translation "dull."

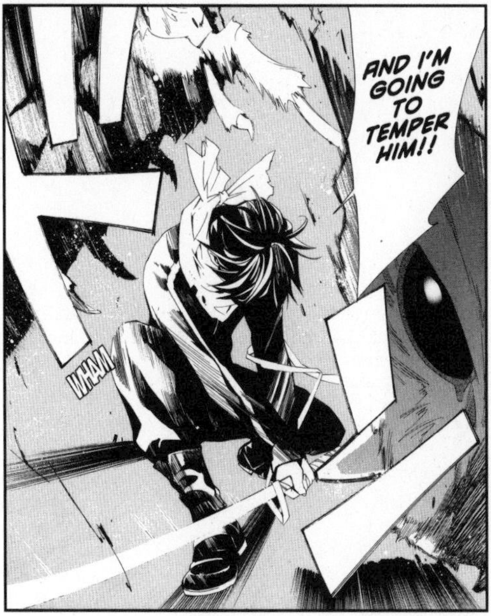
AND I'M GOING TO TEMPER HIM!!
WHAM

Tempering Sekki, page 43

In metallurgy, to "temper" a sword, for example, is to make it harder and tougher. The Japanese word *kitaeru* is used in the same way, but can also be applied metaphorically to people, i.e. they train, or are trained, to become tougher and stronger. Sekki, as a sword, obviously needs some work, first of all, because he's gotten dull. Second of all, you may remember in volume two that Sekki was too sharp, which would make him vulnerable to breakage. Finally, Yukiné could stand to get stronger as a person.

Bakufu and Inko, page 53

These incantations were left in Japanese because, as incantations, the words and sounds are probably important to the casting of the spell. *Bakufu*, or "binding cloth," is fairly self-explanatory, but *inko* (solid shade) could use some further explanation. The *in* in *inko* means "shade" or "shadow," but can also refer to a hiding place. In other words, Kazuma is solidifying a shade (like a window shade or lampshade) over Hiyori to hide her from certain eyes.

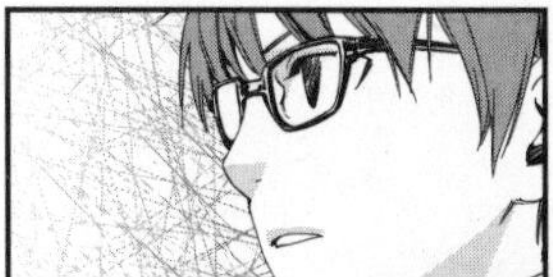
BAKUFU.
[BINDING CLOTH.]

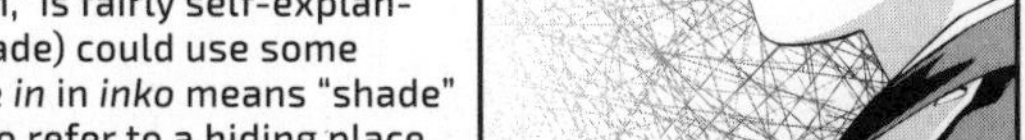
INKO.
[SOLID SHADE.]

New Year's temple visit, page 67

One of the Japanese New Year traditions is to visit a temple. Once there, one can make wishes for the new year, make offerings to the temple deities, get amulets and fortunes, etc. Some people will go all out and wear traditional Japanese clothing, namely kimonos.

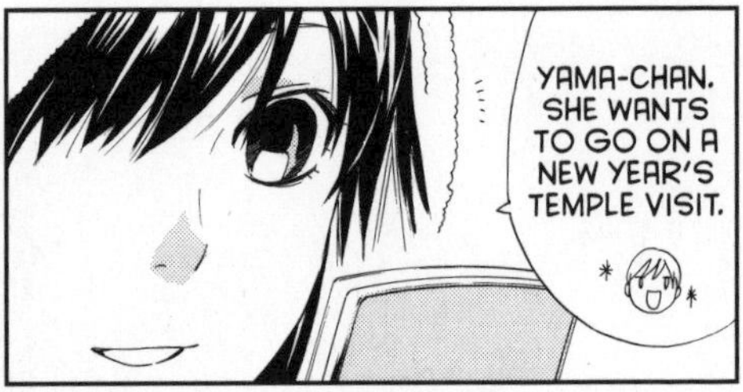
YAMA-CHAN. SHE WANTS TO GO ON A NEW YEAR'S TEMPLE VISIT.

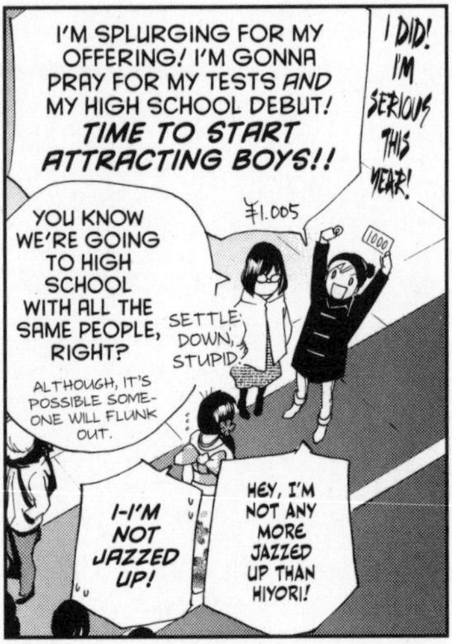
I DID! I'M SERIOUS THIS YEAR!
I'M SPLURGING FOR MY OFFERING! I'M GONNA PRAY FOR MY TESTS AND MY HIGH SCHOOL DEBUT! TIME TO START ATTRACTING BOYS!!
¥1.005
1000
SETTLE DOWN, STUPID.
YOU KNOW WE'RE GOING TO HIGH SCHOOL WITH ALL THE SAME PEOPLE, RIGHT?
ALTHOUGH, IT'S POSSIBLE SOME-ONE WILL FLUNK OUT.
HEY, I'M NOT ANY MORE JAZZED UP THAN HIYORI!
I-I'M NOT JAZZED UP!

High school debut, page 68

The change from middle school to high school in Japan can be a very big one, because, instead of just going on to the local public high school, students can choose a high school from anywhere in the country—as long as they pass the required entrance exam. This makes it a good opportunity to make a new start, by changing your look, going to a school where no one knows you, etc. This is called a high school debut.

In this case, Hiyori's friend is tired of being a nobody and is hoping that a new school setting will help her be more popular, especially if she can get the help of the local Japanese deities. Unfortunately for her, she attends an escalator school—instead of taking an entrance exam for some other high school, she and most of her class will take the promotion exam to make sure they're ready to move on to the high school division of the school that they already attend. Thus, she's going to have to work much harder to change her reputation.

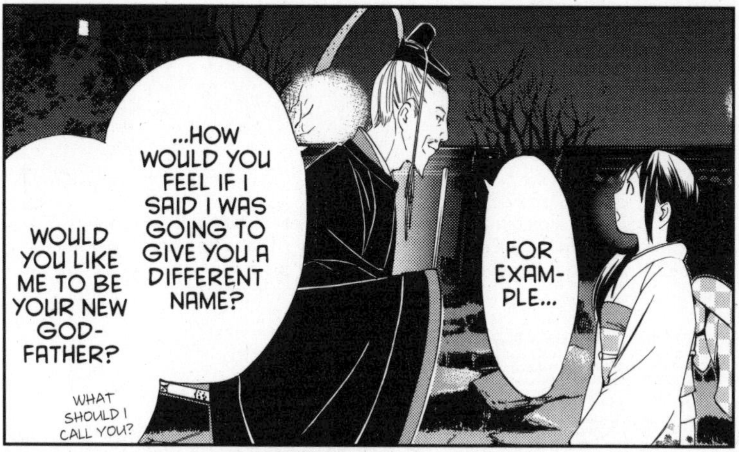
FOR EXAMPLE...
...HOW WOULD YOU FEEL IF I SAID I WAS GOING TO GIVE YOU A DIFFERENT NAME?
WOULD YOU LIKE ME TO BE YOUR NEW GODFATHER?
WHAT SHOULD I CALL YOU?

Hiyori's new godfather, page 76
Tenjin asks Hiyori if she would like him to be her new *nazuke-oya*, or new "parent who names her." Japanese to English dictionaries often give "godparent" as a translation for this, because occasionally, a godparent will be the person who names a child. In Western tradition, a godparent is someone who sponsors a child, takes an interest in them, cares for them should something happen to their parents, etc. While Tenjin may not be opposed to taking on such a role for Hiyori, it is likely he was only referring to naming her. However, since he is a god, the term is still appropriate.

The ablution ceremony, page 161
The word ablution is a translation of the Japanese *misogi*, which refers to a Shinto purification ceremony. Both an ablution and a *misogi* are washing ceremonies, symbolic of washing away sin, impurity, defilement, etc. Generally water is involved, but it would seem that when a shinki gets to this point, water isn't enough, and a deeper cleaning needs to take place.

The words used by the other shinki in the ablution ceremony refer to the Shinto belief as to the true nature of the human soul. Because humans descended from the gods, by nature they are *akaki*, *kiyoki*, *naoki*, *tadashiki* beings. All of these words are adjectives and can be synonyms with "pure" or "righteous." More specifically, *akaki* refers to a bright (cheerful, positive) attitude; *naoki* refers to being straightforward and submissive to the will of nature; and *tadashiki* means correct—upright, honest, and just. These three traits were listed in the second

line of the ceremony. The second descriptor, *kiyoki*, meaning "pure," was omitted from this part, because Yukiné's crimes have defiled him, making him anything but pure. Once he restores his purity through the ablution ceremony, he will have regained all four qualitied that a human soul is supposed to possess.

When the shinki say "strip thyself of uncleanness," the Japanese word they use is *misogi* again, but with different *kanji* characters, from *mi o sogu*, literally "to chip away at [one]self." In other words, to scrape away the layers of impurities that have accumulated over time, making that self pure again, something like scrubbing rust off of metal to make it smooth again. *Sogu* also has the connotation of sharpening, as a sword.

Finally, the words of the ceremony end with *goku*, translated here as "purgatory." As one might expect from this series, the word *goku* has two meanings. The first is "jail" or "prison," which indicates the prison created by the Daikoku, Mayu, and Kazuma to hold Yukiné during the rest of the ritual. The second meaning is "judgment," as Yukiné is now facing judgment for his sins.

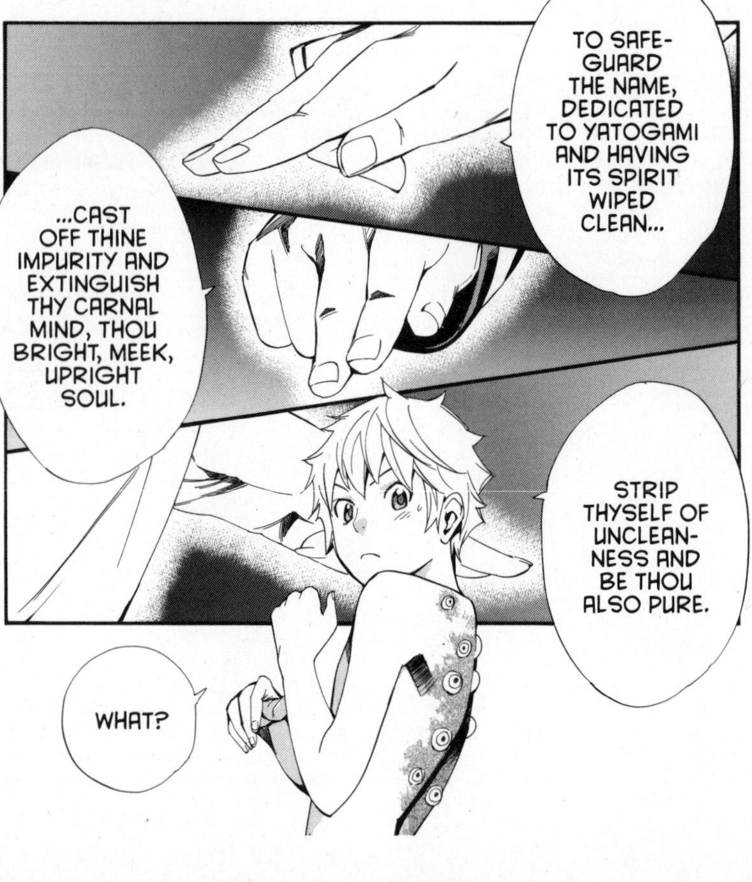
TO SAFE-GUARD THE NAME, DEDICATED TO YATOGAMI AND HAVING ITS SPIRIT WIPED CLEAN...
...CAST OFF THINE IMPURITY AND EXTINGUISH THY CARNAL MIND, THOU BRIGHT, MEEK, UPRIGHT SOUL.
STRIP THYSELF OF UNCLEAN-NESS AND BE THOU ALSO PURE.
WHAT?

HUFF
HIYORI...
THIS ISN'T A MON-GOLIAN SPOT...
WHEEZE
RRRAAAAGH!!

Hiyori's blemish, page 190
A Mongolian spot is a kind of birthmark common in Asian children. It's a bluish spot found on the lower back. It usually goes away by the time the child is old enough to attend elementary school, and almost always by puberty.

Monster Mayu, page 190
The title of this strip is a play on words, replacing Mayu's shinki character *ma* (meaning truth) to a different *ma*, which means demon or monster. The translators attempted to replicate the pun by inserting (nster) after the *ma* to make it sound kind of like "monster." Once again the success of this attempt is open for debate.

MA(NSTER)YU
GET ME OUT OF HERE, YOU OLD H—
GNG
LEMME OUT! SAVE ME!
YOU WILL DIE
A SECOND DEATH.
RUMBLE
RUMBLE

There's a super fluffy, white stray cat in my neighborhood. It's pretty old. I'm really curious to know what kinds of names people have given it..

Adachitoka

Noragami: Stray God volume 3 is a work of fiction. Names, characters, places, and incidents are the products of the author's imagination or are used fictitiously. Any resemblance to actual events, locales, or persons, living or dead, is entirely coincidental.

A Kodansha Comics Trade Paperback Original.

Noragami: Stray God volume 3 copyright © 2012 Adachitoka
English translation copyright © 2014 Adachitoka

All rights reserved.

Published in the United States by Kodansha Comics, an imprint of Kodansha USA Publishing, LLC, New York.

Publication rights for this English edition arranged through Kodansha Ltd., Tokyo.

First published in Japan in 2012 by Kodansha Ltd., Tokyo.

ISBN 978-1-61262-908-7

Printed and bound in Germany by GGP Media GmbH, Poessneck.

www.kodansha.us

9

Translator: Alethea Nibley & Athena Nibley
Lettering: Lys Blakeslee

HALF HOLLOW HILLS
COMMUNITY LIBRARY
55 Vanderbilt Parkway
Dix Hills, NY 11746